D0576276

KEYBOARDING CONNECTIONS

Projects and Applications

New York, New York
Columbus, Ohio
Chicago, Illinois
Peoria, Illinois
Woodland Hills, California

INDEX *(continued)*

ABOUT THE AUTHORS

Arlene Zimmerly is a professor at Los Angeles City College where she teaches a broad list of computer applications and office technology courses, to include keyboarding online, Web page design, and word processing. She is a co-author of the best-selling postsecondary keyboarding text in the country—*Gregg College Keyboarding & Document Processing*.

Julie Jaehne is an instructor in the College of Education at the University of Houston where she teaches a graduate course "Technology in the Classroom." She has extensive experience consulting schools in the use of technology in K–12 instruction and has written ten computer application textbooks and tutorials.

Photo Credits

Glencoe/McGraw-Hill 74; 76; 86; 128(m), 168(m); 360; 410; Garry Adams, Index Stock Imagery 128(cl); 168(cl); Banana Stock, Alamy Images 69(r); Ron Chapple, Picture Quest 1; Tim Fuller Photography 324; 358; Paul Gallaher, Index Stock Photography 128(cr); 168(cr); Spencer Grant, Photo Edit 324(inset); 358(inset); Matt Meadows 124; Michael Newman, Photo Edit 275; 323; Terry Sutherland, Sutherland Photodesign 2(c); 2(inset); 70(c); 70(inset); 82; 94; 104; 107; 129(c); 129(inset); 171(c); 171(inset); 276(c); 276(inset); 325(c); 325(inset); 361(c); 361(inset); 413(c); 413(inset); 431(c); 431(inset); A1(b); A1(bcr); A1(t); A2; A3(tl); A3(tr); A4; A5(b); A5(t); Dana White, Photo Edit 412, 428; David Young-Wolff, Alamy Images 170; 198; 223; 273; David Young-Wolff, Photo Edit 69(tl); 430.

The McGraw·Hill Companies

Glencoe Keyboarding Connections: Projects and Applications

Printed in the United States of America.

Send all inquiries to:
Glencoe/McGraw-Hill
21600 Oxnard Street, Suite 500
Woodland Hills, CA 91367

ISBN 0-07-869314-4

2 3 4 5 6 7 8 9 027 10 09 08 07 06

INDEX *(continued)*

CONTRIBUTORS

Jack E. Johnson, Ph.D.
Director of Business Education
Department of Management and Business Systems
State University of West Georgia
Carrollton, Georgia

Judith Chiri-Mulkey
Adjunct Teacher
Department of Computer Information Systems
Pikes Peak Community College
Colorado Springs, Colorado

Delores Sykes Cotton
Supervisor, Business Education
Detroit Public Schools
Detroit, Michigan

Carole G. Stanley, M.Ed.
Keyboarding and Computer Literacy Teacher, Retired
Rains Junior High School
Emory, Texas

REVIEWERS

Connie Buchanan
Roulhac Middle School
Chipley, FL

Laura de Wet
The Selwyn School
Denton, TX

Richard DiRenno
Feliz Festa Middle School
West Nyack, NY

Marc H. Doyle
Porter Middle School
Austin,TX

Beatrice Ellis
Parkman Junior High School
Woodland Hills, CA

Karen Finklestein
Pines Charter Middle School
Miramar, FL

Lee Mendenhall
Woodbrook Middle School
Lakewood, WA

Nancy Poncik
La Vernia Middle School
La Vernia, TX

Mary Reid
Mountain Shadows Middle School
Nuevo, CA

Jacque Schaffer
Clayton Middle School
Clayton, WI

Karen Sjoberg
Wauzeka-Steuben Schools
Wauzeka, WI

Jan F. Stark
Port Jervis Middle School
Port Jervis, NY

William A. Stenzel
Sierra Vista Junior High School
Canyon Country, CA

Dan Vasiloff
Stevenson Middle School
Westland, MI

Joan Wooten
Knox Middle School
Salisbury, NC

Jason Zuba
Lancaster Middle School
Akron, NY

INDEX *(continued)*

TABLE OF CONTENTS

INDEX *(continued)*

TABLE OF CONTENTS *(continued)*

UNIT 4 WORD PROCESSING

UNIT 5 DESKTOP PUBLISHING

UNIT 6 PRESENTATIONS

UNIT 7 SPREADSHEETS

UNIT 8 DATABASE

UNIT 9 CAPSTONE

INDEX *(continued)*

ABOUT YOUR BOOK

STRUCTURE

Your book is divided into 9 Units. Each unit opens with Focus on Good Keyboarding Habits to demonstrate correct posture and position at the keyboard, Warmup lines to begin each day, and a Making the Connection Feature to introduce you to the projects and applications.

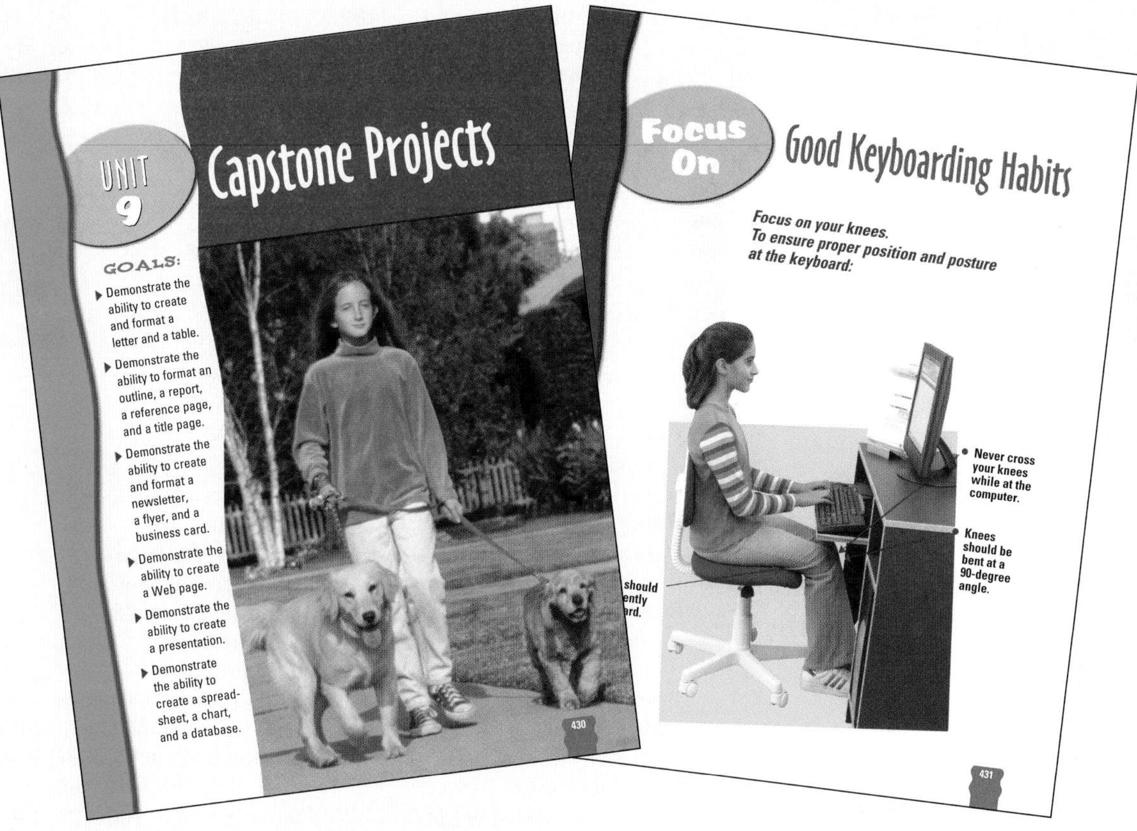

UNITS

In Units 1 and 2 you will learn keyboarding with accuracy and speed—skills you will use for many years to come. In Unit 2 you will also be introduced to the ten-key numeric keypad.

In Units 3 through 8 you will use your keyboarding skills to create documents and to format them correctly. In addition, you will learn word processing features, Internet features, desktop publishing, presentations, spreadsheets, and databases.

In Unit 9 you will use all the skills you learned throughout the book in a capstone simulation of projects called "*The Pet Sitter*." In *The Pet Sitter*, you will create and format all the documents necessary to begin and successfully run your own business!

INDEX

INDIVIDUAL KEYS

ABOUT YOUR BOOK *(continued)*

KEYBOARDING PROJECTS

Each unit is divided into several sections. Every section (except the first) begins with a Warmup that you should begin keying as soon as you are settled at your keyboard. In the early sections, new keys are introduced with practice lines for each of the new keys.

Your book emphasizes *Skillbuilding* in Units 1 and 2 that is easy to identify because of its background color. The *Skillbuilding* sections contain a variety of different activities, to include Technique Timings, Diagnostic Practice, Paced Practice, and 1- and 2-minute timings. Additionally, speed and accuracy are developed through a comprehensive back-of-the-book *Skillbuilding* section.

Many *Skillbuilding* sections include a *Pretest, Practice, Posttest* routine. This routine is designed to help you improve either speed or accuracy through step-by-step procedures. The Pretest helps you identify your speed or accuracy needs. The Practice activities contain a variety of intensive improvement drills. Finally, the Posttest measures your improvement.

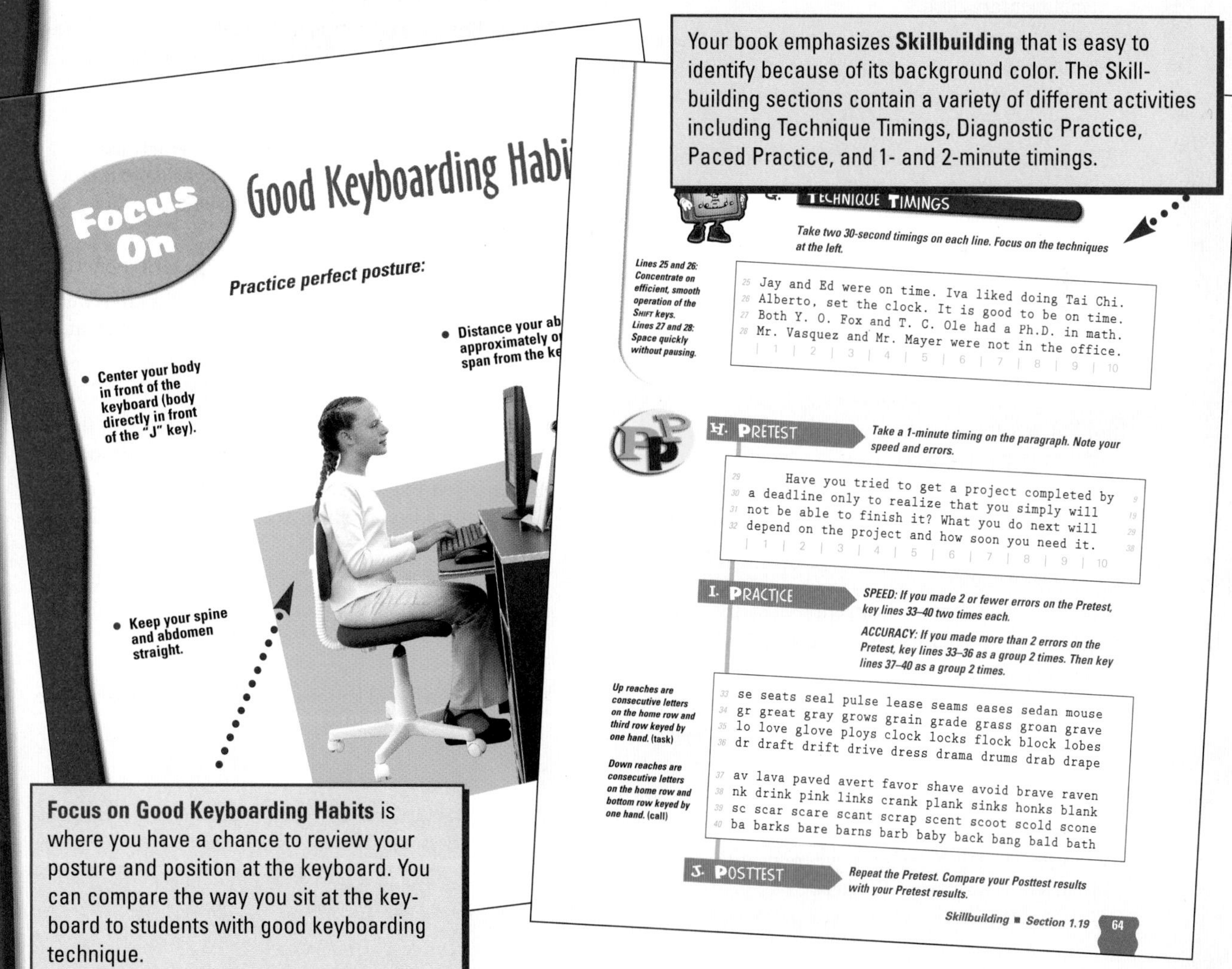

GLOSSARY *(continued)*

Shading A software feature used to add fill to cells or boxes to add visual interest.

Shortcut Key A function key or key combinations. (Section 3.1)

Side Heading The major subdivisions or major topics of a report. (Section 6.2)

Sort A software feature that enables you to rearrange data in a particular order, such as in a table, a spreadsheet, or database. (Sections 10.2, 11.2)

Spelling Check A software feature that checks the spelling of words in a document. (Sections 3.1, 3.4)

Spreadsheet A software program that enables you to perform various calculations on the data. (Section 10.1)

Spreadsheet Function A built-in formula in a spreadsheet. (Section 10.4)

Standard Punctuation Punctuation that consists of a colon after the salutation and a comma after the complimentary close.

Status Line A line displayed at the bottom of the screen that provides the page number, section number, vertical position in inches, and line number of a document as well as the horizontal position of the insertion point.

SUM Function A built-in spreadsheet formula that adds a range of cells. (Section 10.4)

Switch Screens/Windows A software feature you use to move from one open document or program to another. (Section 3.6)

T

Tab Key A key you use to move the insertion point to a preset position. (Section 2.4)

Tab Set A software feature you use to define the position of the insertion point on a line of text when you press the tab key.

Table A grid of rows and columns that intersect to form cells into which information can be keyed. (Sections 4.4, 8.2)

Template A predefined document format. (Section 7.4)

Textbox A created box that can contain text or art. (Sections 7.1, 9.1)

Thesaurus A software feature that you can use to find words that are similar to words you want to replace. (Section 4.2)

Third-Row Keys From the space bar on the keyboard, the upper alphabetic keys. (Section 1.16)

Title Bar The top of a window where the title of the document is displayed. (Section 3.1)

Title Page A page of information displaying the title of a document, the author's name and date. (Section 6.3)

Toolbar A series of selectable buttons on a word processing screen or desktop. (Section 3.1)

Transpose A mark made by a proofreader to correct letters or words that are in reverse order. (Section 3.3)

U

Undo A software command that reverses the last action taken. (Section 3.3)

URL (Uniform Resource Locator) The address of a Web site that starts with the abbreviation http://. (Sections 3.6, 8.1, 8.2)

V

View A software feature you use to look at a document in different ways or to display or hide software features on the screen. (Section 9.1)

Visual Theme Set of design elements and color schemes that can be applied to Web pages. (Section 8.1)

W

Web Page An electronic page on the Internet that is formatted to look like a page in a magazine, except it might have sound clips, video clips, and hyperlinks to other pages. (Sections 8.1, 8.2)

Web Site Two or more related Web pages. (Section 8.3)

Window A framed portion of the screen displayed while you are working in a software program or document.

Word Processing Software A program you use to create, edit, and print documents. (Section 3.1)

Word Wrap The automatic wrapping of text from the end of one line to the beginning of the next line. (Section 1.4)

Works Cited Page A page located at the end of a document with a list of sources specifically mentioned in a paper. (Section 6.4)

Worksheet A spreadsheet form that enables you to input data and formulas.

X

X-Axis A horizontal bar-chart scale that displays a range of values. (Section 10.5)

Y

Y-Axis A vertical bar-chart scale that displays a range of values. (Section 10.5)

ABOUT YOUR BOOK *(continued)*

KEYBOARDING PROJECTS

Cut and Paste Text

A quick way to change text is to use the Cut and Paste commands. When text is cut, it is stored in the **clipboard**. The **clipboard** is a temporary storage area in your software. The text on the clipboard can be placed in another location.

In order to move text, you must first select a portion of the document you want to change. An easy way to **select text** is to use the "click-Shift-click" method.

Your Turn

Symbol	Draft Copy	Final Copy
move → Move text	9. Lauren (carefully) swam	Lauren swam

1. In Sentence 9, position the insertion point before in the word "carefully."
2. Hold down the SHIFT key and move the insertion the letter "y" in "carefully." The entire word is shown in the illustration below.

Selected text is text that is highlighted by a colored or shaded box. → 9. Lauren carefully swam.

3. Choose the **Cut** command. The word "carefully
4. Position the insertion point after the letter "m" "swam."
5. Choose the **Paste** command. The word "caref again.

If you accidentally remove more text than you want to delete, be sure to use the Undo command immediately.

6. Choose the **Undo** command until the word "c in its original position.
7. Save the changes. Keep the file open for Pro

Editing Basic

Practice Projects will help you practice new features and improve your keyboarding skills.

Warmup Lines help you build speed and accuracy while getting you ready for work on the keyboard.

Color Coding helps you identify instructions. Instructions are coded in **blue**. Naming a file to be saved is coded in **green**. New skills are coded in **red**. Glossary terms are coded in **black** bold.

Making the Connection prepares you for new learning and gets you involved in the lesson at the very beginning.

SECTION 3.1

Software Basics

GOALS: Demonstrate the ability to:
- Open a new document.
- Identify menu commands, shortcut keys, and function keys.
- Use the Help feature.
- Save and close a document.

WARMUP

Select Warmup from the Skillbuilding menu. Key each Warmup line 2 times.

Speed 1 Set your goals, and then make plans to achieve those goals.
Accuracy 2 messes make some moms mad; half a dome; for his risk; mills
Speed 3 he reads ahead; his middle silo is filled; more old mirrors
Accuracy 4 jade fake held lose messes make some moms mad; half a dome;

Making the Connection

An easy way to learn software is to explore and use the features. You can learn about many software features by using the online Help feature.

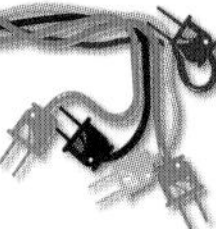

Your Turn

1. Open a new word processing document.
2. Key a list of all the software features that you find. For example, can you find the button for Bold? Do you see the word Help?
3. Keep the document open for Project 1.

LIST OF SOFTWARE FEATURES

Bold
Help

Software Basics ■ Section 3.1 130

GLOSSARY *(continued)*

P

Page Break A manually inserted page break that does not change regardless of the changes made within the document. (Section 6.2)

Page Numbering A software command that automatically numbers the pages of a document. (Section 6.2)

Page Orientation The direction (portrait or landscape) in which information is printed across the paper. (Section 7.2)

Paste To copy text or objects to a file. (Section 6.1)

Percentage Label A label that indicates what percentage is indicated. (Section 10.5)

Personal Letter A letter from an individual to another individual. (Section 5.1)

Pie Chart A graphic illustration of spreadsheet data that compares the sizes of pieces to a whole. (Section 10.5)

Point Size A reference to the size of font; 72 points equal one inch. (Section 3.4)

Portrait Orientation The printing of information across the short edge of a paper so that the page layout is tall. (Section 7.2)

Presentation A word processing software using visual aids, such as slides. (Section 9.1)

Print A software feature you use to produce hard copies of documents on paper. (Section 3.1)

Print Preview A software feature that enables you to view an entire document before it is printed. (Section 3.4)

Proofing Re-reading text. (Section 4.3)

Proofing Tools Software features, such as the spelling and grammar checks, which enable you to find errors in the text of a document. (Sections 3.4, 4.3)

Proofreaders' Marks A set of standard symbols used by an editor or proofreader to mark corrections and changes to a document. (Sections 3.3, 4.1)

Punctuation Spacing The prescribed distance on either side of a punctuation mark, such as the convention of putting one space after a period before the beginning of a new sentence. (Sections 1.6, 1.16, 1.19, 1.20)

Q

Query A database feature that enables you to locate records that meet certain criteria. (Section 11.2)

R

Raised Marker A mark on the alphabetic and numeric keys indicating where your fingers should be placed. (Section 1.1)

Range A group of spreadsheet cells. (Section 10.4)

Record A group of fields that contain the data that makes up a file. (Section 11.1)

Reference Number A raised number inserted automatically by the footnote feature in word processing software; matches the footnote number at the bottom of the page or endnote at the end of a report. (Section 6.5)

Reference Page A page at the end of a report in which the sources of information are listed, such as a bibliography or a list of citations. (Sections 6.2, 6.4)

Report A summary of information you arrange in an attractive, organized, easily understandable format. (Sections 6.1, 6.2, 6.4)

Resize A software feature you use to change the size of an object like a drawing, picture, or textbox. (Section 7.1)

Return Address The sender's address keyed in a specific location on a personal or business correspondence. (Section 5.1)

Right Justification A software feature used to align copy at the right. (Sections 7.2, 7.3)

Right Shift Key The shift key located on the right side of the keyboard used to present text in uppercase and used for some commands. (Section 1.6)

Row Information arranged horizontally in a table; in a spreadsheet, rows are identified by numbers such as 1, 2, or 3. (Section 4.4)

Row Height The distance between the top and bottom borders of a cell. (Section 4.4)

S

Salutation The greeting of a personal or business letter. (Sections 5.1, 5.2)

Save A software feature you use to store data on a hard drive, floppy disk, or CD. (Section 3.1)

Save As A software feature you use to store a file under a different name. (Section 3.2)

Saved Search A software feature you use to save the results of database search in a database file. (Section 11.2)

Scrolling The activity of moving text up and down or left and right to reveal additional copy on your screen. (Section 3.1)

Search A software feature that enables you to look for text or formats within a document.

Search Engine A software program on the Internet that looks for word matches based on keywords you key in the search window. (Section 3.5)

Select A software feature you use to highlight text in order to change it in some way. (Section 3.3)

ABOUT YOUR BOOK *(continued)*

SPECIAL FEATURES

In addition to regular keyboarding lesson content, the projects include a variety of special features. The following pages show samples of these features.

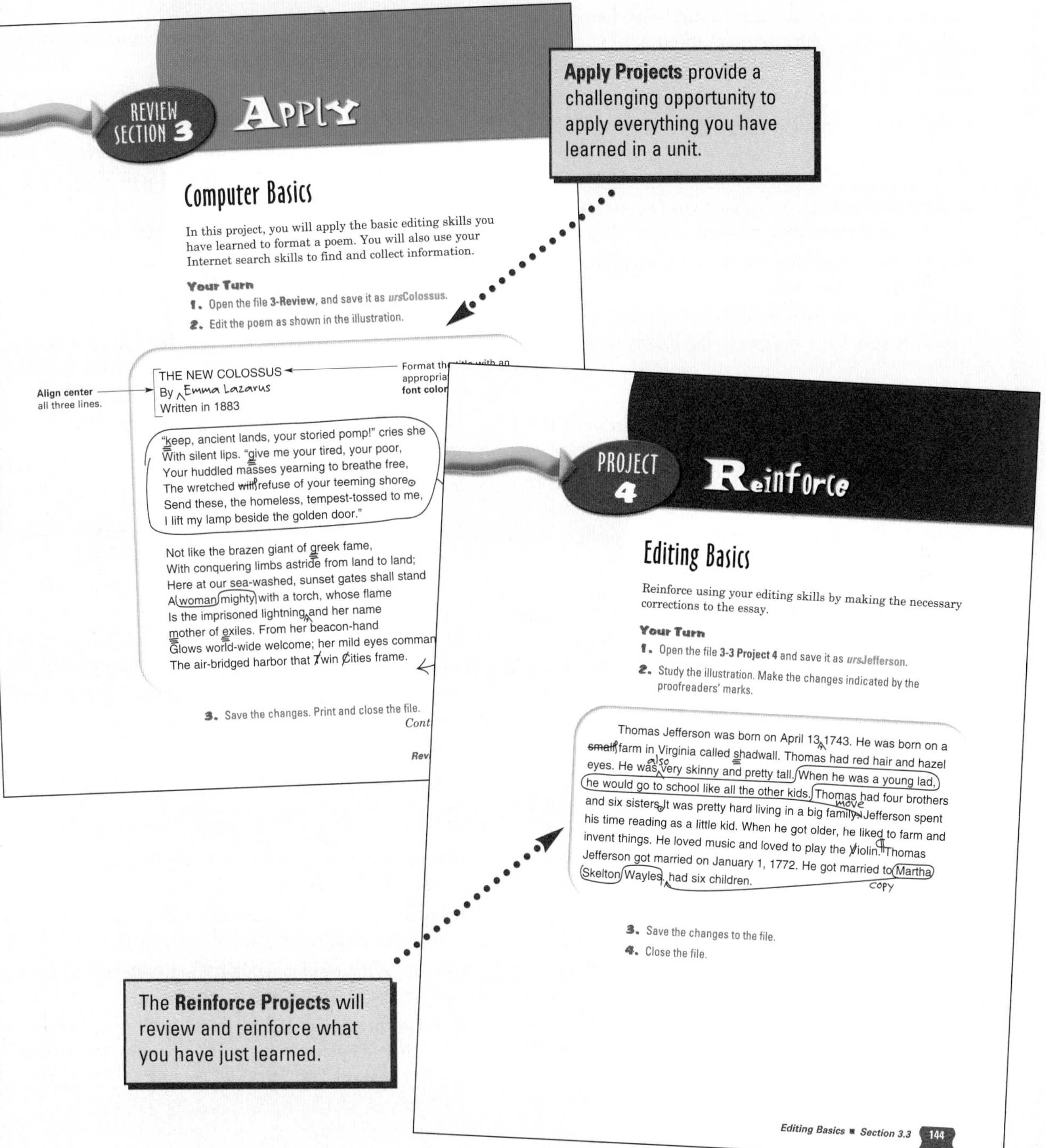

Apply Projects provide a challenging opportunity to apply everything you have learned in a unit.
REVIEW SECTION 3
APPLY
Computer Basics
In this project, you will apply the basic editing skills you have learned to format a poem. You will also use your Internet search skills to find and collect information.
Your Turn
1. Open the file 3-Review, and save it as ursColossus.
2. Edit the poem as shown in the illustration.
THE NEW COLOSSUS
By Emma Lazarus
Written in 1883
Align center all three lines.
"keep, ancient lands, your storied pomp!" cries she
With silent lips. "give me your tired, your poor,
Your huddled masses yearning to breathe free,
The wretched will refuse of your teeming shore
Send these, the homeless, tempest-tossed to me,
I lift my lamp beside the golden door."
Not like the brazen giant of greek fame,
With conquering limbs astride from land to land;
Here at our sea-washed, sunset gates shall stand
A woman mighty with a torch, whose flame
Is the imprisoned lightning and her name
mother of exiles. From her beacon-hand
Glows world-wide welcome; her mild eyes comman
The air-bridged harbor that Twin Cities frame.
3. Save the changes. Print and close the file.
PROJECT 4
Reinforce
Editing Basics
Reinforce using your editing skills by making the necessary corrections to the essay.
Your Turn
1. Open the file 3-3 Project 4 and save it as ursJefferson.
2. Study the illustration. Make the changes indicated by the proofreaders' marks.
Thomas Jefferson was born on April 13 1743. He was born on a small farm in Virginia called shadwall. Thomas had red hair and hazel eyes. He was very skinny and pretty tall. When he was a young lad, he would go to school like all the other kids. Thomas had four brothers and six sisters It was pretty hard living in a big family Jefferson spent his time reading as a little kid. When he got older, he liked to farm and invent things. He loved music and loved to play the violin. Thomas Jefferson got married on January 1, 1772. He got married to Martha Skelton Wayles had six children.
also
move
copy
3. Save the changes to the file.
4. Close the file.
Editing Basics ■ Section 3.3 144
The **Reinforce Projects** will review and reinforce what you have just learned.

GLOSSARY *(continued)*

Inside Address In a personal or business letter, the address for the recipient of the letter. (Sections 5.1, 5.2)

Internet A global network connecting millions of computers. (Section 3.5)

Internet Browser A software application used to locate and display Web pages. (Section 3.5)

Italic A special font attribute in which the characters are slanted used to emphasize text. (Section 4.2)

J

Justification The alignment of text. (Sections 7.2, 7.3)

K

Keyboard Shortcut A combination of keystrokes that enable you to perform commands. (Section 2.5)

Key Stroke Key strokes enable you to enter data into the computer. (Section 1.6)

Keyword One or more words keyed in a search box in order to search for matches on the Internet. (Section 3.5)

L

Landscape Orientation Page orientation in which the printing of information runs across the long edge of the paper so that the page layout is wide. (Section 7.2)

Launch To open. (Section 10.1)

Layer To place an object or graphic close to another object or graphic. (Section 7.2)

Leader A line or a row of characters that points to something on the page, such as the row of dots in a table of contents which leads the reader's eye to the page number, or a line drawn between part of a graphic and its defining text. (Sections 6.6, 7.3)

Left Indent A temporary left margin that is used to align text at a set position to the right of the margin. (Sections 1.14, 2.4)

Left Justification A feature that aligns text at the left margin. (Sections 7.2, 7.3)

Left Shift A key on the left side of the keyboard used to display text in capital letters and to perform commands. (Section 1.9)

Legend A guide on a chart that explains the symbols, colors, etc., used to represent categories of data. (Section 10.5)

Letterhead Stationery that has information such as the company name, address, and telephone number printed at the top. (Section 5.2)

Line Chart A chart that uses points on a grid connected by lines to represent values in a spreadsheet. (Section 10.5)

Line Draw A software feature that enables you to draw a variety of lines in a document. (Section 7.2)

Line Spacing A software command that enables you to set the amount of space between lines of text. (Section 4.1)

M

Margins The blank space at the top, bottom, left, and right sides of a document. (Section 6.1)

Masthead The title of a newsletter usually with an issue number and a date. (Section 7.3)

MAX Function A built-in formula in a spreadsheet that determines the largest or maximum number in a cell range. (Section 10.4)

Menu A list of commands or options from which you can choose. (Section 3.1)

Menu Bar Usually at the top of the active window, a list of commands or options. (Section 3.1)

MIN Function A built-in formula in a spreadsheet that determines the smallest or minimum number in a cell range. (Section 10.4)

MLA Style A format standard developed by the Modern Language Association.

N

Navigate To move around in a document electronically using arrow keys or the cursor. (Sections 2.1, 3.1)

New Document A software feature you use to create a new, blank document. (Section 3.1)

New Folder A software feature you use to create a name for a collection of files and documents. (Section 3.2)

Num Lock Key A key that switches the numeric key from number mode to cursor mode. (Section 2.8)

Numeric Keypad A set of keys that contain number 0 through 9 and a decimal. (Sections 1.2, 2.8–2.14)

O

Object A graphic representation or clip art. (Sections 7.1, 7.2)

Open A software command that enables you to retrieve a file that was previously created and saved. (Section 3.1)

Outline A listing of main topics and subtopics arranged in a hierarchy. (Section 4.5)

Outline Numbered List A list where terms of importance are treated by indenting and numbering. (Section 4.5)

Overtype Mode An input mode in which the existing text is replaced as new text is added. (Section 3.3)

ABOUT YOUR BOOK *(continued)*

SPECIAL FEATURES

Check Your Understanding

1. Open a new word processing document.
2. Describe how a business letter differs from a personal letter.
3. Explain why your return address is included at the top of a business letter.
4. Explain the purpose of an enclosure notation.
5. Save the document as *ursLetterinfo*. Print and close the file.

Check Your Understanding is where you can find out if you have learned the main ideas or if you need to go back and review.

interNET CONNECTION

In this lesson you learned to format a business letter to be mailed within the United States. What if your letter were to be mailed outside of the United States? What information would you need to include on the envelope? Would you need to format the envelope differently?

1. Open your Web browser and search for information on how to address envelopes for international addresses properly. Choose an international location.
2. Open a new word processing document and key an example of the inside address you would create for the letter. Then add any additional information that should be included on the envelope.
3. Save the document as *ursInternational Addresses*. Print and close the file.

Write On!

1. Open your journal and position the insertion point at the end of the document. Enter today's date to create a new journal e
2. Write at least one paragraph about a that you have attended or wish you c (a wedding, an awards banquet, or a in your community). Describe how y dress for the event and the proper et would be expected of you.
3. Save the changes to your journal. C

Format a Business Letter With Envelop

Write On! activities give you the chance to use the computer to write your thoughts as you are learning.

COMPLETING UNIT 3

ENRICH

Curriculum Portfolio

Use the word processing skills you have learned to help you create your curriculum portfolio project. Choose from one of the following topics.

SCIENCE:

Compose a paragraph describing fossils.

What are living fossils? Use the Internet to find at least two examples. Compose a paragraph describing the fossils. Add a title. Be sure to cite your sources at the end of the paragraph.

SOCIAL STUDIES:

Compose two paragraphs about citizenship.

Persons born in the United States are citizens. Others, through naturalization, can become citizens and enjoy the same privileges and responsibilities. Use the Internet to find facts about the steps a person must take to successfully emigrate to the United States. Be sure to answer the following questions.

1. Who is a citizen?
2. If a person is not born in the United States, how can he or she become a citizen?
3. How does a person become a citizen?
4. What are the rights and duties of a citizen?
5. How can a citizen lose his or her citizenship?

Add a title. Be sure to cite your sources at the end of the paragraphs.

Continued on next page

Curriculum Portfolio ■ Unit 3 168

Each **Internet Connection** has fun search tips, great ideas for surfing the Web and information about the Internet.

Curriculum Portfolios are projects in the curriculum areas of Math, Social Studies, Science, and Language Arts. The **Portfolios** give you the chance to demonstrate that you have mastered the concepts and skills as they apply to a computer application.

GLOSSARY *(continued)*

Field Name A name used to identify the contents of a field. (Section 11.1)

Field Type A designed space used for particular information. (Section 11.1)

File On a computer drive, a storage area that contains text or data. Files that contain text formatted using computer applications are called **documents**. Every file, or document, has a name and is organized in a folder, where it can be accessed. (Section 3.2)

Filename A unique name given to a document or file so that it can be saved and retrieved. (Section 3.2)

Fill Shading or patterns used to fill an area. In a spreadsheet, to enter common or repetitive values, or formulas, into a group of cells. (Section 10.4)

Fill Down A spreadsheet feature you use to copy cell contents to a range of cells below the active cell. (Section 10.4)

Fill Right A spreadsheet feature you use to copy cell contents to a range of cells to the right of the active cell. (Section 10.4)

Fill Handle The small box in the lower right corner of an active spreadsheet cell that can be dragged to create the desired fill. (Section 10.4)

Find and Replace A software command that enables you to search for and replace specific text, formatting commands, or special attributes. (Section 6.1)

Find File A software feature used to locate a file using the name of the document. (Section 3.2)

Flush Right Alignment of text at the right margin. (Section 4.2)

Folder On a computer drive, a collection of files and documents linked by a common name. Folders are arranged in a hierarchy. (Section 3.2)

Font A set of type characters of a particular design and size. Also, a software feature you use to change the style of the text in a document. (Sections 3.4, 4.2)

Footers Repetitive information or text that is repeated at the bottom of a page throughout a section of a document. See also headers. (Section 6.4)

Footnote At the bottom of a page, a note that identifies the source of information in a report. (Section 6.5)

Format The appearance of information such as bold or italics on a page or in a computer document; in a spreadsheet displaying commas, dollar signs, percent signs, or decimal places. (Section 4.2)

Formula A mathematical expression entered into a cell of a spreadsheet that solves a problem (for example, adding, subtracting, multiplying, dividing, or averaging) using data from other cells. (Section 10.3)

Full Justification An alignment feature that aligns text at the left and right margins by adding space between characters. (Section 7.3)

Function Keys Special keys located at the top of the keyboard (F1, F2, F3, etc.) that are used alone or with the Ctrl, Alt, and Shift keys to execute software commands. (Sections 1.2, 1.7, 2.4)

G

Grammar Check A software feature that locates grammar inconsistencies. (Sections 3.1, 3.4, 4.3)

Graphics Pictures, clip art, bar graphs, pie charts, or other images available on or created on a computer. (Sections 7.4, 8.1)

Gridlines The lines appearing around the cells in a table. (Section 4.4)

H

Hanging Indent A temporary left margin that indents all lines but the first line of the text. (Section 6.2)

Header Repetitive information or text that is repeated at the top of each page of a section or a document. (Section 6.4)

Help On-screen information about how to use a program and its features. (Section 3.1)

Home Keys On the alphabetic keyboard, the row where the a s d f j k l ; keys are located. (Section 1.1)

Home-Key Position (Keyboard) The row where fingers are to be placed. (Section 1.1)

Home-Key Position (Keypad) The row where fingers are to be placed on the numeric keypad. (Section 2.8)

Hyperlink Text or a graphic on a Web page that you can click on to jump or go to information on another Web page, a location on the same Web page, or a file. (Sections 3.5, 8.3)

I

Indent A temporary left margin that is used to align text at a set position to the right of the margin. (Sections 1.14, 2.4)

Insert A software command that enables you to add text, page and column breaks, graphics, tables, charts, cells, rows, columns, formulas, dates, time, fields, and so on, to a document. (Sections 4.1, 10.2)

Insertion Mode An input mode in which the existing text moves to the right as new text is added. (Sections 1.1, 2.1, 3.1)

Insertion Point A vertical blinking bar on the computer screen that indicates where an action will begin. (Section 1.1)

ABOUT YOUR BOOK *(continued)*

SPECIAL FEATURES

F. PRETEST *Take a 1-minute timing on the paragraph. Note your speed and errors.*

```
20      The blind slats are broken. Can you fix the        9
21 broken ones? My WILY dog jumped out of the window      19
22 which is how this happened. There should be some       29
23 way to stop him. For a young dog, he is AMAZING.       39
   | 1 | 2 | 3 | 4 | 5 | 6 | 7 | 8 | 9 | 10
```

G. PRACTICE *Key each line 2 times.*

```
24 slat slit skit suit quit quid quip quiz whiz fizz
25 LASS bass BASE bake CAKE cage PAGE sage SAGA sags
26 maze mare more move wove cove core cure pure pore
27 mix; fix; fin; kin; kind wind wild wily will well

28 cape cane vane sane same sale pale pals pats bats
29 jump pump bump lump limp limb lamb jamb jams hams
30 slow BLOW blot SLOT plot PLOP flop FLIP blip BLOB
31 mite more wire tire hire hide hive jive give five
```

H. POSTTEST *Repeat the Pretest. Compare your Posttest results with your Pretest results.*

I. COMPOSING AT THE KEYBOARD

Answer each question with a single word. Press ENTER a each answer.

Keep your eyes on the screen as you key.

32 What day of the week is t
33 What is your favorite ani
34 What is your favorite foo
35 What is your favorite ice
36 What month is your birt

New Keys: ? CAPS LOCK

Language Links are activities that help you practice correct grammar and punctuation.

Student Guides have been developed for use with *Glencoe Keyboarding Connections: Projects and Applications.* Currently there are two versions: Microsoft® Office 2000 and Microsoft® Office XP. Each Student Guide provides step-by-step instructions for using each new software feature introduced.

ANCHOR

A home key that helps you return each finger to its home-key position after "reaching" to another key.

Anchor means to hold steady. Hold (anchor) your finger on the J key while reaching for the O key.

CAPS LOCK KEY

The CAPS LOCK is used to key letters or words in all capital letters without having to press SHIFT.

CURSOR OR INSERTION POINT

A blinking line on the computer screen that shows the position of the next character.

ENTER KEY

The ENTER key moves the cursor, or insertion point, to the beginning of the next line. Use the SEM finger to press the ENTER key.

FINGERING

Keep your fingers slightly curved in a scratch-like position over the home keys. Your wrists should be relaxed, straight, and up, not touching the keyboard. Press each key lightly but steadily. Control hand bounce. Be sure to hold the anchor keys when shifting or reaching from the home keys.

Line Number—The small number at the left of each keyboarding line used to identify which lines of text are to be keyed.

Keyboarding ■ Unit 1  5

GLOSSARY *(continued)*

Close File A software command that enables you to exit the current document without exiting from the program. (Section 3.1)

Closing An ending to a letter such as *Sincerely, Yours truly*, etc. before the signature line of a business or personal letter. (Sections 5.1, 5.2)

Colon Used to indicate a range of data to be included in a formula. (Section 10.4)

Column Information arranged vertically. (Section 4.4)

Column Bar Chart A display of data represented in a graphic illustration. (Section 10.5)

Column Heading A vertical row of cells usually with enhanced formatting. (Section 4.4)

Computer Hardware The physical parts of a computer system such as the monitor, the keyboard, and the hard drive.

Computer Software Programs that tell the computer what to do. (Section 3.1)

Copy To duplicate text or data from one location to another. (Sections 3.3, 6.1)

Cursor See Insertion point. (Sections 1.2, 3.1)

Cut/Copy/Paste Computer software features that enable you to move or copy text from one place to another. (Sections 3.3, 6.1)

D

Data Label A label that provides information from the spreadsheet. (Section 10.5)

Database A software program used to organize, find, and display information. (Section 11.1)

Database Search A software feature that enables you to look for text or numbers in database fields according to certain criteria. (Section 11.2)

Database Table A collection of records organized into a table format containing fields. (Section 11.1)

Decimal (.) Used with the numeric keypad refers to a number in a base of 10. (Section 2.12)

Delete (File) To remove or erase a file from storage on the computer. (Section 3.2)

Delete Key A key which deletes one character at a time to the right of the insertion point. (Section 3.3)

Descending Order A sort of data in descending alphabetical (Z–A) or numerical (9–0) order. (Section 10.2)

Design Template A pre-formatted set of fonts and margins stored in a document. (Section 9.1)

Desktop Publishing Special software or software features that enable you to design and create documents such as newsletters, flyers, and brochures. (Sections 7.1–7.4)

Document A file created in a word processor which may contain text or graphics. (Section 3.2)

Dot Leader The same as a line of periods used to separate titles from page numbers. (Section 6.6)

Double Space An electronic method to add an additional space between lines of text. (Section 4.1)

Drawing Tool A software feature you use to draw objects like lines and shapes in a document. (Section 7.2)

E

Edit Using proofreaders' marks to indicate changes to a document, such as deleting, moving, or adding characters. (Sections 3.3, 4.1)

E-Mail An electronic message that usually includes the e-mail address, subject line, and body of the message. (Section 5.3)

E-Mail Address An electronic address that has two parts (user name and domain name) separated by the @ (at) symbol. (Section 5.3)

Emoticon An acronym for **emot**ion **icon**, a small icon composed of punctuation characters that indicate how an e-mail message should be interpreted (that is, the writer's mood). For example, a :-) emoticon indicates that the message is meant to be humorous and shouldn't be taken seriously. (Section 5.3)

Enclosure Notation A special notation at the end of a letter (usually the word Enclosure); indicates that an item(s) is included with the letter. (Section 5.2)

Endnote A software feature you use to create endnotes; notes at the end of a report that identify the source of information in a report. (Section 6.5)

Enter Key (Keyboard) A key that moves the insertion point to the beginning of the next line or moves the insertion point to the next field. (Sections 1.1, 1.4)

Enter Key (Numeric Keypad) A key that moves the insertion point to the beginning of the next line or moves the insertion point to the next field. (Section 2.8)

Envelope Format A format for an envelope address in which all lines are keyed in all capital letters with no punctuation.

Error A mis-stroked key. (Section 1.7)

Esc (Escape) Key A key that can undo a previous keystroke. (Section 1.2)

F

Favorite An Internet software feature used in *Internet Explorer* that allows you to save a Web site or Web page for future use. (Section 3.5)

Field A category of information in a database. (Section 11.1)

REFERENCE SECTION *Table of Contents*

PROJECT SAMPLES

GLOSSARY

A

Adjust Column Width A column is a vertical line extending from the top to the bottom of the screen. The size can be adjusted manually by hesitating the insertion point over the line and dragging the line to a new location. (Section 4.4)

Alignment A software feature you use to change the horizontal or vertical position of text such as left, right, or center. (Sections 3.4, 4.2, 6.3)

Alphanumeric Keys Alphanumeric keys are the combined set of all letters in the alphabet and the numbers 0 through 9. (Sections 1.2, 2.1)

Anchor A home-key position of another finger that helps bring a reaching finger back to its home-key position. (Section 1.1)

Animation A simulation of movement created by displaying a series of pictures. (Section 9.4)

APA Style A formatting style standardized by the American Psychological Association.

Ascending Order A sort of data in alphabetical (A–Z) order or numerical (0–9) order. (Section 10.4)

Attachment A file attached to an e-mail message. (Section 5.3)

AVERAGE Function A built-in spreadsheet formula that adds and divides numbers. (Section 10.4)

B

Backspace Key A key that moves the insertion point backward one space at a time. The backspace key deletes text to the left of the insertion point one space at a time. (Sections 1.6, 1.7, 3.3)

Bar Chart A graphic illustration of spreadsheet data, in which vertical and horizontal bars, lines, or charts represent data values. (Section 10.5)

Bibliography An alphabetical listing of all the books, online sources, and articles consulted by the author of a report. (Section 6.2)

Block Style A letter style that has all lines, keyed at the left margin. (Sections 5.1, 5.2)

Body The main text of personal letter, business letter, or report. (Sections 5.1, 5.2)

Bold A print enhancement used to make characters appear darker than other text to add emphasis. (Section 4.2)

Bookmark An Internet software feature used in *Netscape Navigator* that allows you to place an electronic bookmark on a page so you can easily revisit the page. (Section 3.5)

Boolean operators The five Boolean operators refine and limit searches conducted on the Internet. (Section 3.5)

Borders A software feature (usually a line) you use to add an outline around a page, an object, or spreadsheet cells. (Section 4.4)

Bound Report A report with extra space added at the left margin to allow for pages to be placed in a notebook. (Section 6.2)

Bullets and Numbering A software feature you use to create a list in which each item begins with a number or a bullet—such as a circle, diamond, square, or triangle. (Sections 4.5, 9.1)

Business Card Personal or professional information including name and contact information formatted onto a card. (Section 7.4)

Business Letter A letter to a company or organization. (Section 5.2)

Byline The name of the author of a report keyed below the title. (Section 6.1)

C

Callout A textbox with a leader that points to something on the page. (Section 7.2)

Capitalization Uppercase treatment of alphabetic keys. (Section 2.8)

Caps Lock Key A key you use to input all characters in uppercase. (Section 1.17)

Caption The words or phrases that draw attention or emphasize a photo or graphic. (Section 8.2)

Caret A symbol used in some programming languages. (Section 2.6)

Cell The box formed at the intersection of a row and a column, either in a table or a spreadsheet. (Section 10.1)

Cell Reference The location (column letter and row number) of the active cell in a spreadsheet. (Section 10.4)

Center Alignment An alignment feature that centers text between margins. (Section 3.4)

Citation Usually the author's last name and page number in a report; used to give credit to the source of information. (Sections 3.6, 6.4)

Clip Art A gallery or collection of graphic images or pictures that you can add to documents. (Sections 7.1, 9.3)

Clipboard A special file or memory area where data is stored temporarily before being copied to another location. (Section 3.3)

REFERENCE SECTION *(continued)*

PERSONAL LETTER

1719 Lakeview Drive
Fontana, WI 53125
March 21, 20--
↓ 4x

Ms. Susan Yu, Director
Turtle Creek Animal Shelter
2023 North Lake Shore Drive
Fontana, WI 53125
↓ 2x
Dear Ms. Yu:
↓ 2x
I am interested in volunteering at your animal shelter. I love animals, and I have pets of my own, including a dog and a cat. I can help you feed, groom, and exercise the animals in your shelter.
↓ 2x
I am available to help you on weekdays after school and on weekends. I would be willing to work up to six hours a week. I can start working next week.
↓ 2x
Please call me at 555-6978 and let me know how I can help.
↓ 2x
Sincerely,
↓ 4x

Your Name

BUSINESS LETTER

LINCOLN MIDDLE SCHOOL
8021 Brobeck Street • Flint, MI 48532
Phone: 810-555-9001 • Fax: 810-555-9004

Today's Date
↓ 4x

Mr. Anthony Martinez
Cyber Foundation
4092 Barnes Avenue
Burton, MI 48529
↓ 2x
Dear Mr. Martinez:
↓ 2x
My friends and I at Lincoln School want to help your organization.
↓ 2x
Our district is replacing our computers with new ones. Our computer technology teacher Mrs. Jones explained that your organization recycles computers to help developing countries keep up with technology. We want our school district to consider donating our computers.
↓ 2x
I am enclosing a copy of the specs for the computers in my classroom at our school. These computers are going to be replaced in the next six months. Can you please let me know if your organization would be interested in recycling these computers? If they can be recycled, my teacher will give the information to the administrators in our school district.
↓ 2x
Sincerely,
↓ 4x

Steve Rach
↓ 2x
Enclosure

PERSONAL BUSINESS LETTER

5419 Mirra Loma Drive
Reno, NV 89502
Today's Date
↓ 4x

Mainstream Music, Inc.
270 Clara Street
San Francisco, CA 94107
↓ 2x
Ladies and Gentlemen:
↓ 2x
About four weeks ago, I mailed you an order for a DVD movie package. I purchased DVD package #41-809 from page 5 of your catalog. The total cost of the order was $47.35.
↓ 2x
Today I saw a package at my door. I was so excited that my order had finally arrived. But I was really disappointed when I opened it and saw that you sent me the wrong DVDs.
↓ 2x
I am returning the DVD package with this letter and I am enclosing the order return form. I am asking for a full refund of $47.35. And I also want to be reimbursed for the $5.00 it cost me to ship the DVD package back to you. Please send the refund to me at the above address.
↓ 2x
Sincerely,
↓ 4x

Martine Pico
↓ 2x
Enclosure

OUTLINE

↓ 1 inch

OCEAN WATER AND LIFE

I. WAVES AND TIDES
- ***A. Waves***
  - **1. How waves move**
  - **2. How waves form**
- ***B. Tides***
  - **1. The gravitational pull of the moon**
  - **2. Spring and neap tides**
- ***C. Life in the intertidal zone***

II. OCEAN CURRENTS
- ***A. Definition of currents***
- ***B. Surface currents***
- ***C. Density currents***
- ***D. Upwellings***

APPENDIX *(continued)*

From page 53

CARE AND OPERATION OF EQUIPMENT

Why should you protect your computer from computer viruses?

Answer: It is time-consuming and expensive to repair the damage done by a virus. You should protect your computer against computer viruses as insurance against damage to hardware, software, and data.

From page 68

CARE AND OPERATION OF EQUIPMENT

Describe how computer viruses can infect your computer and what precautions you can take to prevent infections. Demonstrate how to protect a disk from computer viruses.

Answer: Some computer viruses infect your computer as soon as you use an infected file. Others are programmed to activate on a certain date. If your hard drive is infected, the virus will activate when you turn on your computer on the target date. Make sure you know how to scan disks you have used at home before you use them in the computers at school.

CARE AND OPERATION OF EQUIPMENT

Describe a problem that could occur because of a computer virus.

Answer: A virus might damage computer hardware, software or data.

REFERENCE SECTION *(continued)*

ONE-PAGE REPORT

↓ 1 inch

ALL THE CHOCOLATE YOU CAN EAT!

By Rachelle Cantin

I read the book *Charlie and the Chocolate Factory*. The author of the book is Roald Dahl. The book is 155 pages long, and it was published by Puffin.

Charlie Bucket is a poor boy who lives in a tiny house with his parents. Both sets of grandparents also live with Charlie in that tiny house. Charlie didn't have any money, but he found a dollar bill in the street. He used the money to buy a Wonka candy bar. The Willy Wonka Chocolate Company held a contest. When Charlie opened the candy bar, he found a golden ticket. He was one of five winners.

The other four winners were Augustus Gloop, Violet Beauregarde, Veruca Salt, and Mike Teavee. Charlie went on the tour of the chocolate factory with his Grandpa Joe. The other four winners were there with their parents. They saw lots of amazing things, and they met the Oompa-Loompas. The Oompa-Loompas were the tiny people who lived and worked in the factory.

The other four kids behaved very badly on the tour. When they didn't follow directions, Mr. Wonka punished them. Funny things happened to them that made them disappear. Charlie was kind and polite. Mr. Wonka liked Charlie, and he knew he could trust Charlie. At the end of the tour, Charlie was the only kid left, and Mr. Wonka gave him the chocolate factory. Charlie and his family could live at the factory, and they could have all the chocolate they could eat!

My favorite part about this book was when the other four kids didn't follow directions and Mr. Wonka punished them. Charlie followed directions, and Mr. Wonka rewarded him for that.

MULTIPAGE REPORT

(MLA Style)

↓ 1 inch

Last Name 1

Your First and Last Name

↓ 1x

Your Teacher's Name

↓ 1x

Class

↓ 1x

Current Date

↓ 1x

King of the Wild Frontier

↓ 1x

ds

1 inch | 1 inch

"Be always sure you are right, then go ahead" (Lofaro 1148d). You're probably wondering what that means. Well, a guy named Davy Crockett used to say that. It is one of his best known quotes. Read on to find out more about this legendary person.

Actually, his name was David Crockett. He was born in a small cabin in Tennessee on August 17, 1786. (*Davy Crockett*). His family lived in a cabin on the banks of the Nolichucky River. Davy had eight brothers and sisters. Four were older and four were younger.

Davy lived with his family in Tennessee until he was 13. He went to school, but he didn't like it. He skipped school a lot. He ran away from home because he knew his dad was going to punish him for playing hooky. He joined a cattle drive to make money. He drove the cattle to Virginia almost 300 miles away. He stayed in Virginia and worked a lot of jobs for over two years. He returned to his family in Tennessee when he was 16 (*Davy Crockett Biography*).

When Davy returned home his dad was in debt. Now Davy was 6 feet tall and he could do a man's work. Davy went to work for Daniel Kennedy. Davy's dad owed Daniel 76 dollars and Davy worked for one year to pay the debt (The Texas State Historical Association).

In 1806 Davy married Polly Finley. They had two sons, John Wesley and William. Then Davy went to fight for the Tennessee Volunteer Militia under Andrew Jackson in the Creek Indian War. When he returned home from the war, he found his wife very ill. She died in 1815 (Davy Crockett Birthplace Association).

MULTIPAGE REPORT CONTINUED

(MLA Style)

↓ 1 inch

Last Name 2

Davy then married Elizabeth Patton in 1817. She was a widow and she had two children of her own, George and Margaret Ann (The Texas State Historical Association).

Davy was well known in Tennessee as a frontiersman. He was a sharpshooter, a famous Indian fighter, and a bear hunter. In 1821, he started his career in politics as a Tennessee legislator. People liked Davy because he had a good humor and they thought he was one of their own. He was re-elected to the Legislature in 1823, but he lost the election in 1825.

In 1827 Davy was elected to Congress. He fought for the land bill. The land bill allowed those who settled the land to buy it at a very low cost. He was re-elected to Congress in 1829 and again in 1833, but he lost in 1836 (Lofaro, 1148d).

1 inch | 1 inch

Many Americans had gone to Texas to settle. In 1835, Davy left his kids, his wife, his brothers, and his sisters to go to Texas. He loved Texas. When the Texans were fighting for their independence from Mexico, Davy joined the fight. He was fighting with a group of Tennessee volunteers defending the Alamo in San Antonio on March 6, 1836 (The Texas State Historical Association). He was 49 years old.

WORKS CITED

↓ 1 inch

Last Name 3

Works Cited

ds

Author Unknown. "Davy Crockett Biography." 6 April 2002. <http://www.infoporium.com/heritage/crockbio.shtml>.

"Davy Crockett." *Microsoft Encarta Online Encyclopedia 2002*. <http://encarta.msn.com>.

Davy Crockett Birthplace Association. "American West-Davy Crockett." 6 April 2002. <http://www.americanwest.com/pages/davycroc.htm>.

Lofaro, Michael A. "Davy Crockett." *The World Book Encyclopedia 2002*. Chicago: World Book, Inc., Vol. 14, pp. 1148d-1149.

The Texas State Historical Association. *The New Handbook of Texas-Online*. "Davy Crockett (1786-1836)-Biography." 6 April 2002. <http://www.alamo-de-parras.welkin.org/history/bios/crockett/crockett.html>.

APPENDIX *(continued)*

From page 47

CARE AND OPERATION OF EQUIPMENT

Demonstrate the proper way to insert and eject a disk from your computer.

Gently insert a disk into the drive. Disks are encased in a plastic or vinyl cover to protect them from fingerprints and dust. Once information has been saved on the disk, it can be removed from the computer disk drive and stored for later use.

Gently insert a CD into the drive. When handling a CD, carefully avoid scratching the surface.

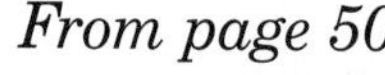

From page 50

CARE AND OPERATION OF EQUIPMENT

Describe the proper care of a disk.

Answer: Treat a disk with care to avoid losing the information stored there. Keep the disk in a cool, dry place when not in use. Protect the disk from moisture, magnetic fields, and extreme heat or cold. Do not bend the disk or remove it from its hard plastic covering.

REFERENCE SECTION *(continued)*

TITLE PAGE

↓ center vertically

THE STAR-SPANGLED BANNER
↓ 13x

Prepared by
↓ 2x
Hallie Thompson
La Mesa Valley School
↓ 13x

Prepared for
↓ 2x
Ms. Gibson
Social Studies--5th Hour
↓ 2x
Today's Date

MULTIPAGE REPORT

(with side headings)

↓ 1 inch

THE STAR-SPANGLED BANNER

By Hallie Thompson

The Story Behind the Flag

During the War of 1812, Americans knew that the British would likely attack the city of Baltimore. In the summer of 1813, Major George Armistead was the commander at Fort McHenry at the Baltimore harbor. He asked Mary Young Pickersgill to make a flag for the fort. Armistead wanted the flag to be so big that the British would be sure to see it from a distance.

Mary's 13-year-old daughter Caroline helped her make the flag. They cut 15 stars. Each star was two feet long from point to point. They also cut eight red stripes and seven white stripes. Each stripe was two feet wide. It took them several weeks to make the flag. When they sewed everything together, the flag measured 30 feet by 42 feet. The flag weighed 200 pounds.

Francis Scott Key's Point of View

Francis Scott Key was 35 years old and he was a well-known and successful lawyer in Georgetown, Maryland. He opposed the War of 1812, but in 1814 he had to get involved. His long-time friend Dr. William Beanes was being held prisoner on a British warship.

On September 3, 1814, Key and a government agent named John S. Skinner boarded a ship that flew a flag of truce. They went to the British warship and negotiated the release of Beanes. On September 7, the British agreed to let Beanes go, but by then Key, Skinner, and Beanes knew too much about the planned attack on the city of

1

MULTIPAGE REPORT CONTINUED

(with side headings)

↓ 1 inch

Baltimore. So the British held all three Americans as prisoners on the warship while they attacked Baltimore.

On September 13, the three American prisoners watched from the warship as the British battleships fired upon Fort McHenry. They knew it would be difficult for the American soldiers to fight off the British. The battle continued through the night, and they feared the American soldiers would surrender.

The Story Behind the Song

When the sun rose the next morning, they saw a big American flag flying over the fort. It was the flag Pickersgill had made. The Americans had survived the battle.

Oh! Say, can you see, by the dawn's early light,
What so proudly we hailed at the twilight's last gleaming?
Whose broad stripes and bright stars, through the perilous fight.
O'er the ramparts we watched were so gallantly streaming?
And the rocket's red glare, the bombs bursting in air,
Gave proof through the night that our flag was still there.
Oh! Say, does that Star-Spangled Banner yet wave
O'er the land of the free and the home of the brave.

2

BIBLIOGRAPHY

↓ 1 inch

BIBLIOGRAPHY

Armed Forces Collections. "Star-Spangled Banner and the War of 1812." 10 May 2002. <http://www.si.edu/resource.faq/nmah/starflag.htm>.
↓ 2x

Author Unknown. "Francis Scott Key." 10 May 2002. <http://www.usflag.org.francis.scott.key.html>.
↓ 2x

Goertzen, Valerie Woodring. "Star-Spangled Banner." *The World Book Encyclopedia 2002*. Chicago: World Book, Inc., Vol. 18, pp. 853-854.
↓ 2x

"Star-Spangled Banner." *Microsoft Encarta Online Encyclopedia 2002*. <http://encarta.msn.com/encnet/refpages/refarticle.aspx?refid=761575047>.

APPENDIX *(continued)*

From page 22

CARE AND OPERATION OF EQUIPMENT

Discuss why you should keep food and drinks away from your computer.

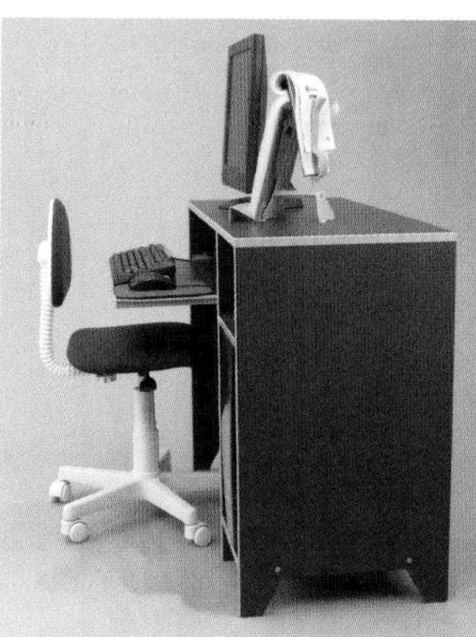

Answer: Food and drinks can ruin computer parts. Spilled drinks can cause electrical parts to short out. Food can get stuck in the keyboard and cause the keys and mouse to be sticky.

Remember to keep your work area neat and free of clutter.

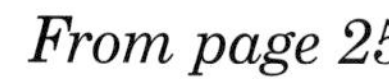

From page 25

THE FUNCTION KEYS

Where are the Function keys located on the computer keyboard?

Answer: The Function keys (F1, F2, and so on) are usually arranged in a row along the top of the keyboard. They allow you to quickly perform specific software tasks.

From page 32

THE FUNCTION KEYS

Where is the purpose of the Function keys?

Answer: The purpose of each function key depends on the program you are using. For example, in some computers, the F1 key displays the help information.

REFERENCE SECTION *(continued)*

FORMAT FOR ENVELOPES

A standard large (No. 10) envelope is 9½ by 4⅛ inches. A standard small (No. 6¾) envelope is 6½ by 3⅝ inches. The format shown is recommended by the U.S. Postal Service for mail that will be sorted by an electronic scanning device.

Your Name
4112 Bay View Drive
San Jose, CA 95192

Mrs. Maria Chavez
1021 West Palm Blvd.
San Jose, CA 95192

LINCOLN
MIDDLE SCHOOL
6021 Brobeck Street • Flint, MI 48532

Mr. Anthony Martinez
Cyber Foundation
4092 Barnes Avenue
Burton, MI 48529

HOW TO FOLD LETTERS

To fold a letter for a small envelope:

1. Place the letter *face up* and fold up the bottom half to 0.5 inch from the top edge of the paper.
2. Fold the right third over to the left.
3. Fold the left third over to 0.5 inch from the right edge of the paper.
4. Insert the last crease into the envelope first, with the flap facing up.

To fold a letter for a large envelope:

1. Place the letter *face up* and fold up the bottom third.
2. Fold the top third down to 0.5 inch from the bottom edge of the paper.
3. Insert the last crease into the envelope first, with the flap facing up.

APPENDIX *(continued)*

From page 18

CARE AND OPERATION OF EQUIPMENT

Computers would be useless without devices to help you input information. The most common input devices are the keyboard and the mouse. Demonstrate the proper use of the mouse and the keyboard.

Answers:

Resting your hand on the mouse, use your thumb and two fingers to move the mouse on the desk. Use your two remaining fingers to press the mouse buttons.

- A click often selects an item on the screen. To click, press and release the left mouse button.
- A double-click often opens a document or starts a program. To double-click, quickly press and release the left mouse button twice.
- A right-click often displays a list of commands on the screen. To right-click, press and release the right mouse button.

REFERENCE SECTION *(continued)*

BOXED TABLE

Bills Passed for E-Waste or E-Cycling	
State	**Bill**
Arkansas	SB807, Enacted 4/9/01
California	SP1523, Introduced 2/20/02 SB1619, Introduced 2/21/02
Florida	SB1922, Introduced 2/6/02
Georgia	HB2, Passed the House, in the Senate 2/5/2002
Hawaii	HB1638, Carried over to 2002 Session
Idaho	S1416, Sent to Committee 2/12/2002
Illinois	HB4464, Passed the House, in the Senate 4/10/01
Maryland	HB111, Unfavorable Environmental Committee Report

CONTENTS

CONTENTS

PROOFREADERS' MARKS

Proofreaders' Marks	Draft	Final Copy
⁀ Omit space	data base	database
∨ or ∧ Insert	if hes going (not)	if he's not going,
≡ Capitalize	Maple street	Maple Street
Delete	a ~~final~~ draft	a draft
# Insert space	allready to	all ready to
when / ~~if~~ Change word	and ~~if~~ you (when)	and when you
/ Use lowercase letter	our President	our president
¶ Paragraph	¶ Most of the	Most of the
••• Don't delete	a ~~true~~ story	a true story
○ Spell out	the only (1)	the only one
∽ Transpose	they all see	they see all
ss Single-space	ss [first line second line	first line second line
ds Double-space	ds [first line second line	first line second line
Move right	Please send	Please send
Move left	May I	May I
∿∿ Bold	Column Heading	**Column Heading**
ital Italic	*ital* Time magazine	*Time* magazine
u/l Underline	u/l Time magazine	Time magazine
Move as shown	readers will see	will see readers

DEMONSTRATE CORRECT POSTURE

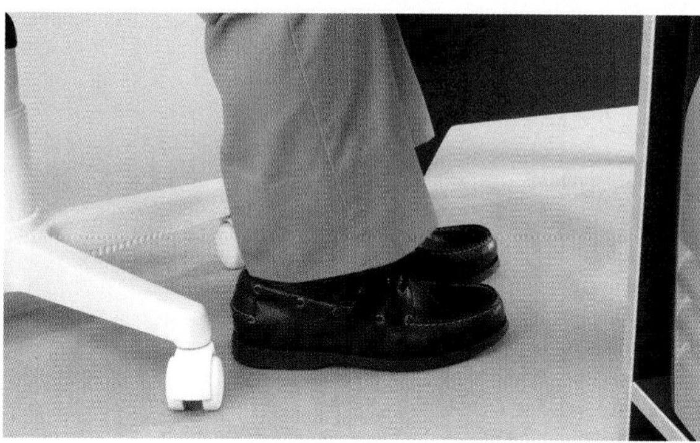

Remember to keep your feet flat on the floor.

From page 12

CARE AND OPERATION OF EQUIPMENT

What is the proper way to turn on the computer? Demonstrate to your teacher.

Answer: Before turning on the computer, make sure that there are no diskettes in the computer's diskette drive. Some computers take a minute or two to start. During the start-up process, your computer may display messages. Messages may prompt you to perform an action such as providing a user ID or password. After the computer has started, the desktop will appear on your screen.

From page 16

CARE AND OPERATION OF EQUIPMENT

What is the proper way to turn off the computer? Demonstrate to your teacher.

Answer: Before turning off the computer, make sure you have removed any disks from the diskette and CD-ROM drive. Make sure that all data is saved and all running programs are closed. Then proceed with the proper shut down step for your computer system.

REFERENCE SECTION *(continued)*

PUNCTUATION AND USAGE

ALWAYS SPACE ONCE . . .

- After a comma.
  We ordered two printers, one computer, and three monitors.
- After a semicolon.
  They flew to Dallas, Texas; Reno, Nevada; and Rome, New York.
- After a period following someone's initials.
  Mr. A. Henson, Ms. C. Hovey, and Mr. M. Salisbury will attend the meeting.
- After a period following the abbreviation of a single word.
  We will send the package by 7 p.m. next week. [Note: space once after the final period in the "p.m." abbreviation, but do not space after the first period between the two letters.]
- Before a ZIP code.
  Send the package to 892 Maple Street, Grand Forks, ND 58201.
- Before and after an ampersand.
  We were represented by the law firm of Bassett & Johnson; they were represented by the law firm of Crandall & Magnuson.
- After a period at the end of a sentence.
  Don't forget to vote. Vote for the candidate of your choice.
- After a question mark.
  When will you vote? Did you vote last year?
- After an exclamation point.
  Wow! What a performance! It was fantastic!
- After a colon.
  We will attend on the following days: Monday, Wednesday, and Friday.

PUNCTUATION

COMMAS:

1. Use a comma between independent clauses joined by a conjunction. (An independent clause is one that can stand alone as a complete sentence.)
   We requested Brown Industries to change the date, and they did so within five days.
2. Use a comma after an introductory expression (unless it is a short prepositional phrase).
   Before we can make a decision, we must have all the facts.
   In 1992 our nation elected a president.

APPENDIX

DEMONSTRATE CORRECT POSTURE

Keep your hands slightly curved in a scratch like position over the home keys. Your wrists should be relaxed, straight, and level, not touching the keyboard.

Press each key lightly but steadily. Control hand bounce.

DEMONSTRATE CORRECT POSTURE

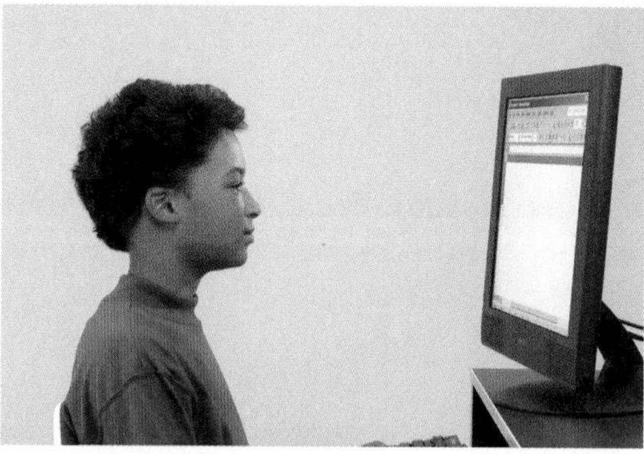

Position the monitor so that it is about 20 to 26 inches from your eyes. Remember to keep eyes on the copy.

REFERENCE SECTION *(continued)*

PUNCTUATION

3. Use a comma before and after the year in a complete date.
   We will arrive at the plant on June 2, 2003, for the conference.

4. Use a comma before and after a state or country that follows a city (but not before a ZIP Code).
   Joan moved to Vancouver, British Columbia, in September.
   Send the package to Douglasville, GA 30135, by express mail.

5. Use a comma between each item in a series of three or more.
   There are lions, tigers, bears, and zebras at the zoo.

6. Use a comma before and after a transitional expression (such as therefore and however).
   It is critical, therefore, that we finish the project on time.

7. Use a comma before and after a direct quotation.
   When we left, James said, "Let us return to the same location next year."

8. Use a comma before and after a nonessential expression. (A nonessential expression is a word or group of words that may be omitted without changing the basic meaning of the sentence.)
   Let me say, to begin with, that the report has already been finalized.

9. Use a comma between two adjacent adjectives that modify the same noun.
   We need an intelligent, enthusiastic individual for this project.

SEMICOLONS:

1. Use a semicolon to join two closely related independent clauses that are not connected by a conjunction (such as and, but, or nor).
   Students favored the music; teachers did not.

2. Use a semicolon to separate three or more items in a series if any of the items already contain commas.
   Region 1 sent their reports in March, April, and May; and Region 2 sent their reports in September, October, and November.
   The Home room class sent their reports in 1st, 2nd, 3rd, and 4th hour;
   the history class sent their reports in 4th, 5th, 6th, and 7th hour.

HYPHENS:

1. Hyphenate compound adjectives that come before a noun (unless the first word is an adverb ending in *-ly*).
   We reviewed an up-to-date report on Wednesday.
   We attended a highly rated session on multimedia software.

SKILLBUILDING *(continued)*

TIMING 19

Some specialists who work in memory training tell us 11
to think of memory as something we can control through the 23
use of strategies and organization. If you are trying to 34
remember a new name, spend a few seconds creating a mental 46
image to go along with the name. For example, to remember 57
the name Morehouse, you could make a quick mental image of 69
a person standing by a growing house. If you often misplace 81
your keys or your glasses, you could keep these objects in 93
one specific location. Then, make a conscious effort to 104
always return them to their same location. 113

Anxiety is the number one cause of slips of memory. 123
There are several strategies that can help with recall. You 135
can reduce anxiety block by not drawing attention to it. 147
For example, if a word is at the tip of your tongue, keep 158
talking while your brain keeps searching for it. A helpful 170
way to remember numbers is by connecting them to a phrase, 182
such as the old adage about Columbus sailing the ocean blue 194
in fourteen hundred and ninety-two. You might also try to 206
remember numbers by connecting them with a birthday or by 217
making number patterns. Another approach to improve memory 229
could be aerobic exercising, which speeds the flow of blood 241
to the brain and also sharpens memory performance. 251

| 1 | 2 | 3 | 4 | 5 | 6 | 7 | 8 | 9 | 10 | 11 | 12 |

REFERENCE SECTION *(continued)*

PUNCTUATION

2. Hyphenate compound numbers (between twenty-one and ninety-nine) and fractions that are expressed as words.
   We observed twenty-nine fumbles during the football game.
   All teachers reduced their assignments by one-third.

3. Hyphenate words that are divided at the end of a line. Do not divide one-syllable words, contractions, or abbreviations; divide other words only between syllables.
   To appreciate the full significance of rain forests, you must see the entire documentary showing tomorrow in the library.

APOSTROPHES:

1. Use 's to form the possessive of singular nouns.
   The hurricane caused major damage to Georgia's coastline.

2. Use only an apostrophe to form the possessive of plural nouns that end in *s*.
   The investors' goals were outlined in the annual report.

3. Use 's to form the possessive of indefinite pronouns (such as someone's or anybody's); do not use an apostrophe with personal pronouns (such as *hers, his, its, ours, theirs,* and *yours*).
   She was instructed to select anybody's paper for a sample.
   Each computer comes carefully packed in its own container.

COLONS:

Use a colon to introduce explanatory material that follows an independent clause. (An independent clause is one that can stand alone as a complete sentence.)
A computer is useful for three reasons: speed, cost, and power.

DASHES:

Use a dash instead of a comma, semicolon, colon, or parenthesis when you want to convey a more forceful separation of words within a sentence. (If your keyboard has a special dash character, use it. Otherwise, form a dash by typing two hyphens, with no space before, between, or after.)
At this year's student council meeting, the speakers—and topics—were superb.

PERIODS:

Use a period to end a sentence that is a polite request. (Consider a sentence a polite request if you expect the reader to respond by doing as you ask rather than by giving a yes-or-no answer.)
Will you please call me.

SKILLBUILDING *(continued)*

TIMING 18

Do you live beyond your means? Are your expenses more 11
than your income? Are you quick to borrow money to pay off 23
debts? If you are, you are just like many other people. Our 35
government consistently operates on a deficit. In fact, it 47
runs two different deficits: one with its citizens, and the 59
other with the rest of the world. Some economists believe 70
these two deficits are related because if one of them were 82
not so large, the other would not be either. 91

Is all debt bad? No, deficit spending, within reason, 102
is healthy. It fuels the economy. When you buy a new car on 114
credit, you support the autoworkers. A problem arises when 126
the government borrows money to spend beyond its means. It 138
borrows from its citizens--you and me. It also borrows from 149
foreigners. Foreign countries purchase our treasury debt. 161
These investors certainly want to be compensated properly 173
for assuming the debt. The almost daily borrowing that the 184
government has to do often overwhelms credit markets. This 196
keeps interest rates high, which in turn creates appealing 208
investments. 211

Government debt is somewhat like individual debt. 221
The difference is that the government debt is much larger. 233
The moral of this story is that a little debt is okay, but 245
a lot of debt is not. 249

| 1 | 2 | 3 | 4 | 5 | 6 | 7 | 8 | 9 | 10 | 11 | 12 |

REFERENCE SECTION *(continued)*

PUNCTUATION

QUOTATION MARKS:

1. Use quotation marks around the titles of newspaper articles, magazine articles, chapters in a book, reports, conferences, and similar items.
The best article I found in my research was entitled "Multimedia for Everyone."

2. Use quotation marks around a direct quotation.
Harrison responded by saying, "This decision will not affect our class."

ITALIC (OR UNDERLINE):

Italicize (or underline) the titles of books, magazines, newspapers, and other complete published works.
I read *The Pelican Brief* last month. I read <u>The Pelican Brief</u> last month.

GRAMMAR

AGREEMENT:

1. Use singular verbs and pronouns with singular subjects and plural verbs and pronouns with plural subjects.
I was pleased with the performance of our team.
Reno and Phoenix were selected as the sites for our next two meetings.

2. Some pronouns (*anybody, each, either, everybody, everyone, much, neither, no one, nobody,* and *one*) are always singular and take a singular verb. Other pronouns (*all, any, more, most, none,* and *some*) may be singular or plural, depending on the noun to which they refer.
Each employee is responsible for summarizing the day's activities.
Most of the workers are going to get a substantial pay raise.

3. Disregard any intervening words that come between the subject and verb when establishing agreement.
The box containing the books and pencils has not been found.

4. If two subjects are joined by *or, either / or, nor, neither / nor,* or *not only / but also,* the verb should agree with the subject nearer to the verb.
Neither the players nor the coach is in favor of the decision.

5. The subject a number takes a plural verb; *the number* takes a singular verb.
The number of new students has increased to six.
We know that a number of students are in sports.

SKILLBUILDING *(continued)*

TIMING 17

Taking tests can be an ordeal. Even for students who 11
are well prepared and aware of the teacher's goals, testing 23
can be stressful. They can become victim to test anxiety. 34
It is perfectly natural for people to feel some anxiety 46
when confronted with a test. Anxiety can work as a positive 58
motivational factor. It can improve your concentration, 69
encourage you to do well, and sharpen your performance. 81
However, if it does cause stress, try to rid yourself of 92
sweaty palms, the fear of failure, and the tight knot in 104
your stomach. 107

It might help to realize that most teachers want their 118
students to do well on tests. They might discuss a test 129
ahead of time. Pay attention to such discussions. There are 141
strategies you can use to help reduce anxiety in a test 152
situation. You might use relaxation techniques before and 164
during a test when you feel yourself becoming anxious. You 176
could visualize yourself as being successful and keep a 187
confident attitude during the test. Also, you could remind 198
yourself that the test is not a life-threatening situation 210
and you can survive it. You need to recognize that the test 222
is important, but you might ask yourself just how much of 233
an effect it will have on your life five years from now. 244

| 1 | 2 | 3 | 4 | 5 | 6 | 7 | 8 | 9 | 10 | 11 | 12 |

REFERENCE SECTION *(continued)*

GRAMMAR

6. Subjects joined by and take a plural verb unless the compound subject is preceded by *each, every,* or *many a (an).*
   Every man, woman, and child is included in our survey.

7. Verbs that refer to conditions that are impossible or improbable (that is, verbs in the *subjunctive* mood) require the plural form.
   If the total eclipse were to occur tomorrow, it would be the second one this year.

PRONOUNS:

1. Use nominative pronouns (such as *I, he, she, we,* and *they*) as subjects of a sentence or clause.
   They traveled to Minnesota last week but will not return until next month.

2. Use objective pronouns (such as *me, him, her, us,* and *them*) as objects in a sentence or clause.
   The package has been sent to her.

ADJECTIVES AND ADVERBS:

Use comparative adjectives and adverbs (*-er, more,* and *less*) when referring to two nouns; use superlative adjectives and adverbs (*-est, most,* and *least*) when referring to more than two.
Of the two movies you have selected, the shorter one is the more interesting.
The highest of the three mountains is Mt. Everest.

WORD USAGE:

Do not confuse the following pairs of words:

- *Accept* means "to agree to"; *except* means "to leave out."
  We ***accept*** *your offer for developing the new product.*
  Everyone ***except*** *Sam and Lisa attended the rally.*

- *Affect* is most often used as a verb meaning "to influence"; *effect* is most often used as a noun meaning "result."
  Mr. Smith's decision will not ***affect*** *our music class.*
  It will be weeks before we can assess the ***effect*** *of this decision.*

- *Farther* refers to distance; *further* refers to extent or degree.
  Did we travel ***farther*** *today than yesterday?*
  We need to discuss our plans ***further****.*

- *Personal* means "private"; *personnel* means "employees."
  The letters were very ***personal*** *and should not have been read.*
  We hope that all ***personnel*** *will comply with the new rules.*

SKILLBUILDING *(continued)*

TIMING 16

Although heavy campaigning for a number of months now 11
leads up to a national convention for both parties, this 22
was not practiced in the early days of elections in our 34
country. Originally, candidates were selected by members of 46
their party congress. Selecting candidates in this manner 57
is called the caucus method. Caucusing was later dropped, 69
and nominations were made informally by state officials. 80

When the national convention process first started, it 91
brought much more national participation into the selection 103
process. When the first television camera was used, the 115
exposure increased even more. More citizens began to get 126
actively involved in politics. The use of the camera made 137
it seem as though they were at the convention. It has been 149
judged that over seventy million people watched during the 161
early years when conventions were televised. Today, most 172
Americans have likely watched at least one convention. 183

The expense of a national convention is quite high. 194
Citizens who are delegates feel that their participation is 206
worth whatever it costs to go. The parties do not pay for 218
television time. Sponsors pay for the commercials, and any 229
difference is paid for by the media itself. 238

| 1 | 2 | 3 | 4 | 5 | 6 | 7 | 8 | 9 | 10 | 11 | 12 |

REFERENCE SECTION *(continued)*

GRAMMAR

- *Principal* means "primary"; *principle* means "rule."
  *The **principal** means of research were interviewing and surveying.*
  *They must not violate the **principles** under which our country was founded.*

- *Passed* means "went by"; *past* means "before now."
  *We **passed** another car from our home state.*
  *In the **past**, we always took the same route.*

- *Advice* means "to provide guidance"; *advise* means "help."
  *The **advice** I gave her was simple.*
  *I **advise** you to finish your project.*

- *Council* is a group; *counsel* is a person who provides advice.
  *The student **council** met to discuss graduation.*
  *The court asked that **counsel** be present at the hearing.*

- *Then* means "at that time"; *than* is used for comparisons.
  *He read for a while; **then** he turned out the light.*
  *She reads more books **than** I do.*

- *Its* is the possessive form of it; *it's* is a contraction for it is.
  *We researched the country and **its** people.*
  ***It's** not too late to finish the story.*

- *Two* means "one more than one"; *too* means "also"; *to* means "in a direction."
  *There were **two** people in the boat.*
  *We wished we were on board, **too.***
  *The boat headed out **to** sea.*

- *Stationery* means "paper"; *stationary* means "fixed position."
  *Please buy some **stationery** so that I can write letters.*
  *The **stationary** bike at the health club provides a good workout.*

MECHANICS

CAPITALIZATION:

1. Capitalize the first word of a sentence.
   Please prepare a summary.

2. Capitalize proper nouns and adjectives derived from proper nouns. (A proper noun is the official name of a particular person, place, or thing.)
   Judy Hendrix drove to Albuquerque in her new car, a Pontiac.

SKILLBUILDING *(continued)*

TIMING 15

Before the middle of the twentieth century, workers 11
were treated as just additional elements of the production 22
process. Men and women worked under dismal conditions. Most 34
often, they were required to work twelve to sixteen hours a 46
day; and the work week was six days long. Wages were low. 58
Health and safety hazards were mostly ignored by employers. 70
When an employer provided any fringe benefits, they were 81
meager. Though workers were exploited, they were grateful 93
to have their jobs. Eventually, working conditions and the 105
treatment of workers have improved. 112

Effective management is a focus in today's work world. 123
A scientific approach in the management of employees may be 135
used. This scientific tool permits managers to motivate 146
workers by offering pay incentives to improve both product 158
quality and product quantity. For example, if a project 169
usually took an employee ten minutes to complete, a wage 181
incentive plan would pay a bonus for work finished in less 193
than ten minutes. Management has learned that workers will 204
produce more products as well as better products when the 216
working conditions are improved and wage incentives are 227
provided. 229

| 1 | 2 | 3 | 4 | 5 | 6 | 7 | 8 | 9 | 10 | 11 | 12 |

REFERENCE SECTION *(continued)*

MECHANICS

3. Capitalize the names of the days of the week, months, holidays, and religious days (but do not capitalize the names of the seasons).
   On Thursday, November 25, we will celebrate Thanksgiving, the most popular fall holiday.

4. Capitalize nouns followed by a number or letter (except for the nouns *line, note, page, paragraph,* and *size*).
   Please read Chapter 5, but not page 94.

5. Capitalize compass points (such as *north, south,* or *northeast*) only when they designate definite regions.
   The Crenshaws will vacation in the Northeast this summer.
   We will have to drive north to reach the closest Canadian border.

6. Capitalize common organizational terms (such as *advertising department* and *finance committee*) when they are the actual names of the units in the writer's own organization and when they are preceded by the word *the*.
   The quarterly report from the Advertising Department will be presented today.

7. Capitalize the names of specific course titles but not the names of subjects or areas of study.
   I have enrolled in Accounting 201 and will also take a marketing course.

NUMBER EXPRESSION:

1. In general, spell out numbers 1 through 10, and use figures for numbers above 10.
   We have rented two movies for tonight.
   The decision was reached after 27 precincts had sent in their results.

2. Use figures for:
   - Dates (use *st, d,* or *th* only if the day precedes the month).
     We will drive to the camp on the 23d of May.
     The tax report is due on April 15.
   - All numbers if two or more related numbers both above and below ten are used in the same sentence.
     Mr. Carter sent in 7 receipts; Ms. Cantrell sent in 22 receipts.
   - Measurements (time, money, distance, weight, and percentage).
     At 10 a.m. we delivered the $500 coin bank in a 17-pound container.
   - Mixed numbers.
     Our sales are up 9½ percent over last year.

SKILLBUILDING *(continued)*

TIMING 14

The Hawaiian Islands have much to offer the tourist. 11
One attraction is the amazing parks. The flora, fauna, and 23
buildings are all protected by federal law. Hawaii's state 34
bird, the nene, is endangered. When visitors feed these 46
birds, they attract them to parking lots and roadsides. 57
This puts the birds in danger from auto traffic that may 68
injure or kill them. Visitors must avoid feeding the birds 80
and animals. 83

The volcanoes of the Hawaiian Islands add mystery and 94
exotic scenery. A wonderful way to observe the raw power of 106
a volcano is by taking a helicopter tour. The helicopter is 118
well-suited for the air maneuvers needed to get a closer 129
view. Pilots usually fly directly over areas with the most 141
volcanic activity. They often dip low over huge lava pools, 153
skim still-glowing flows, and circle towering steam clouds 165
rising from where the lava enters the sea. You might like 176
to spend a full day at Kilauea to enjoy the sights. Atop 188
Kilauea, you can quietly appreciate the absolute beauty of 199
this impressive volcano. It is four thousand feet above sea 211
level and about ten degrees cooler than on the coast. 222

| 1 | 2 | 3 | 4 | 5 | 6 | 7 | 8 | 9 | 10 | 11 | 12 |

REFERENCE SECTION *(continued)*

MECHANICS

3. Spell out:

- Numbers used as the first word in a sentence.
  Seventy people attended the conference in San Diego last week.
- The smaller of two adjacent numbers.
  We have ordered two 5-pound packages for the meeting.
- The words millions and billions in even amounts (do not use decimals with even amounts).
  The lottery is worth 28 million this month.
- Fractions.
  About one-half of the audience responded to the questionnaire.

ABBREVIATIONS:

1. In nontechnical writing, do not abbreviate common nouns (such as *dept.* or *pkg.*), compass points, units of measure, or the names of months, days of the week, cities, or states (except in addresses).
The Sales Department will meet on Tuesday, March 7, in Tempe, Arizona.

2. In lowercase abbreviations made up of single initials, use a period after each initial but no internal spaces.
We will be including several states (e.g., Maine, New Hampshire, Vermont, Massachusetts, and Connecticut).

3. In all-capital abbreviations made up of single initials, do not use periods or internal spaces. (Exception: Keep the periods in most academic degrees and in abbreviations of geographic names other than two-letter state abbreviations.)
You need to call the EEO office for clarification on that issue.

SKILLBUILDING *(continued)*

TIMING 13

It is quite possible that Ellis Island is part of your 11
family history. For years, Ellis Island was an immigration 23
station. In the early part of the twentieth century, it 34
served as the main gateway to our country. Amazingly, over 46
twelve million foreigners had passed through its doors by 58
the middle of the twentieth century, when it closed. Ships 69
unloaded their passengers at the docks in New York. Then, 81
the passengers quickly transferred to boats and barges for 93
the trip to Ellis Island in New York Harbor. It was the 104
first place many of our forebears saw when they arrived in 116
America. 118

This country is comprised of immigrants, along with 128
native American Indians. An immigrant is someone who moves 140
from one country to another. An immigrant usually plans to 152
make the new country home. Millions of Americans can trace 163
their family history to ancestors who first arrived in the 175
United States through Ellis Island. Today, it is a museum. 187
Millions of dollars were raised to fix up the neglected 198
building. The museum is located only one mile from New York 210
City and a few hundred yards from the docks of New Jersey. 222

| 1 | 2 | 3 | 4 | 5 | 6 | 7 | 8 | 9 | 10 | 11 | 12 |

UNIT 1

Keyboarding

GOALS:

- Demonstrate which fingers control each key on the keyboard.
- Demonstrate correct touch-system techniques.
- Use home key anchors.
- Develop and practice correct keyboarding techniques.
- Key at a speed of 25 words per minute for 1 minute with 2 or fewer errors.
- Use proper spacing.
- Compose single word responses at the keyboard.

SKILLBUILDING *(continued)*

TIMING 12

Productivity measurement techniques are frequently 10
used in word processing installations today to evaluate the 22
output that is produced. This technique allows management 34
to compare workload effort in order to improve scheduling 46
and work dispersal. 50

Productivity measurement also can help a company by 60
recording, calculating, and tracking employee production 72
over a period of time. Supervisors are then able to create 83
performance standards designed for their organization. This 95
method of measurement can be used to assist managers in 107
making reliable decisions regarding salary increases and 118
promotion of word processing personnel. 126

A measure of production might also assist those who 136
are more capable in a number of ways. For example, when 148
compared to their peers, their abilities and skills will be 160
highlighted. Using this particular technique, all employees 172
can be evaluated on a parallel basis. Very talented workers 184
can be rewarded. Lastly, this measurement technique can 195
assist you in removing the subjectivity that is found in 206
company measurement systems used for evaluating employees. 218

| 1 | 2 | 3 | 4 | 5 | 6 | 7 | 8 | 9 | 10 | 11 | 12 |

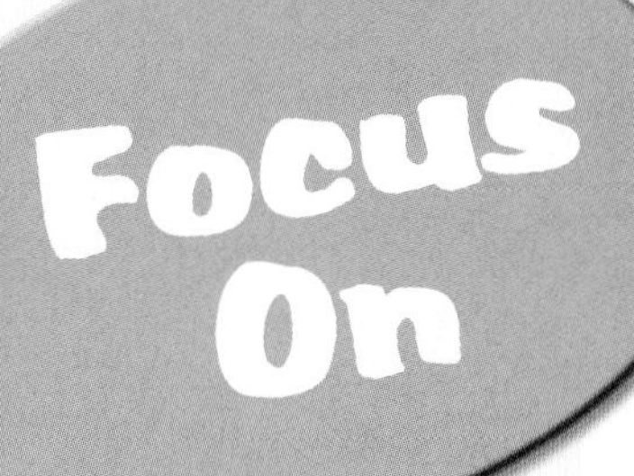

Good Keyboarding Habits

Practice perfect posture:

- **Center your body in front of the keyboard (body directly in front of the "J" key).**
- **Distance your abdomen approximately one hand's span from the keyboard.**
- **Keep your spine and abdomen straight.**

SKILLBUILDING *(continued)*

TIMING II

If you love mystery, you would certainly be amazed by 11
the speculation over how plants and animals first arrived 23
in Hawaii. Most people's thoughts of a Hawaiian paradise 34
include swaying palms, dense jungles, and luscious fruit 45
ready to be picked. For millions of years, the chain of 57
Hawaiian Islands were raw and barren places where no plants 69
or birds existed. These lush Pacific Ocean islands are a 80
geological mystery. They formed spontaneously more than two 92
thousand miles from any continental land, isolated from the 104
normal spread of plants and animals. Flora and fauna that 116
did reach them found a foreign ecosystem. They had to adapt 128
or perish in this environment. Many of the birds and plants 140
became so specialized that they were not only limited to 151
specific islands but also to specific isolated valleys. It 163
was fortunate that the soil was very rich. There were no 174
other plants or animals with which to compete. The climate 186
was nearly perfect for most of the entities growing on the 198
islands. The evolution of plants and animals on these small 210
islands took place quickly. 215

| 1 | 2 | 3 | 4 | 5 | 6 | 7 | 8 | 9 | 10 | 11 | 12 |

SECTION 1.1

New Keys: A S D F J K L ; Space Bar Enter

GOALS:

- Demonstrate correct posture and position at the keyboard.
- Learn the home keys, the SPACE BAR, and the ENTER key.

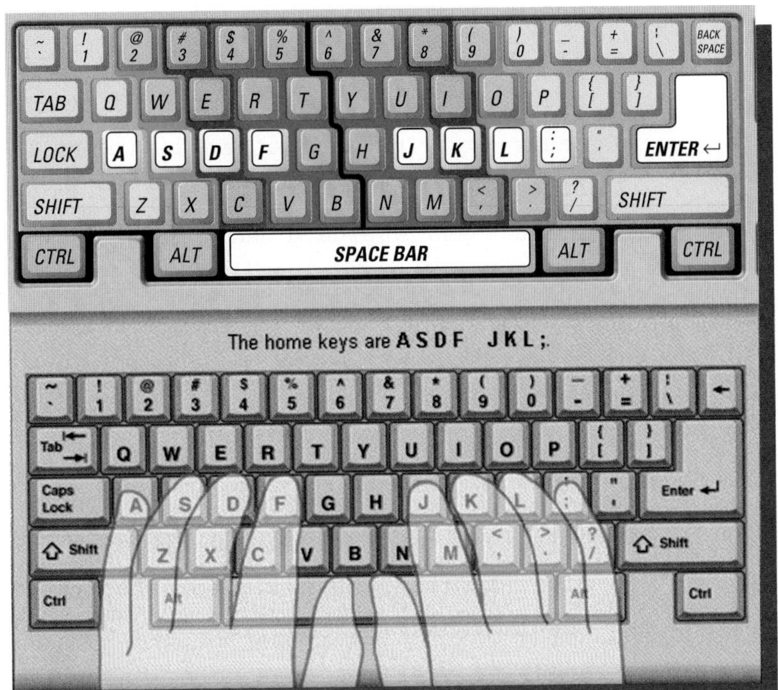

The home keys are A S D F J K L ;.

NEW KEYS

A. HOME-KEY POSITION

The A S D F J K L ; keys are called the home keys. Each finger controls a specific key and is named for its home key: A finger, S finger, D finger, and so on, ending with the Sem finger on the ; (semicolon) key.

1. Place the fingers of your left hand on A S D and F. Use the illustration as a guide.
2. Place the fingers of your right hand on J K L ;. Again, use the illustration as a guide. You will feel

SKILLBUILDING *(continued)*

TIMING 10

If you are not a classical music fan and do not often 11
go to the theater, you probably think, as do most concert 23
goers, that music before Bach is a mystery. Many music fans 35
see classical music as intensely lyrical, with madrigals 46
and dances that are accompanied by various horns, bells, 57
drums, violins, and other instruments. But, music and opera 69
have been listened to for almost five centuries. One way to 81
effectively approach this music is to just relax and enjoy 93
its strangeness. While you are listening, recognize what 105
sounds are pleasing to your ear and what sounds seem like 116
irradiating noise. You can train your ear to pick up the 128
music of the violin, cello, trumpet, clarinet, harp, piano, 140
piccolo, xylophone, tuba, and flute. Melodies played as 151
intended by the composer may sound quite peculiar to the 162
untrained ears of today's listeners. One reason for this 174
might be that the tuning of instruments has changed. Also, 185
the listeners of the fifteenth century likely had their own 197
ideas of what was considered enjoyable music, and their 209
preferences were different. 214

| 1 | 2 | 3 | 4 | 5 | 6 | 7 | 8 | 9 | 10 | 11 | 12 |

a raised marker on the F and J keys. These markers will help you keep your fingers on the home keys.

3. Curve your fingers.
4. Using the correct fingers, key each letter as you say it to yourself: a s d f j k l ;.
5. Remove your fingers from the keyboard and replace them on the home keys.
6. Key each letter again as you say it:
   a s d f j k l ;.

B. USING ANCHORS

An anchor is a home key that helps you return each finger to its home-key position after reaching for another key. Try to hold the anchors listed, but be sure to hold the first one, which is most important.

C. SPACE BAR

The SPACE BAR, located at the bottom of the keyboard, is used to insert spaces between letters and words, and after punctuation. Use the thumb of your writing hand (left or right) to press the SPACE BAR.

1. With your fingers on the home keys, key the letters a s d f. Then press the SPACE BAR 1 time.
2. Key j k l ;. Press the SPACE BAR 1 time.
3. Key a s d f. Press the SPACE BAR 1 time; then key j k l ;.
4. Repeat Steps 1–3.

SKILLBUILDING *(continued)*

TIMING 9

One of the many unique features of a democracy is that 11
everyone of legal age has the right to vote. Voting must be 23
taken seriously because it is our responsibility. It is 34
obvious that a government might not be representative if 46
citizens do not take an active part in choosing the people 58
to represent them. It is easy to pass judgment on our 69
leaders, but we also have to assume some responsibility 80
ourselves and participate in the voting process. 90

Citizens can vote for varying levels of government. 101
Federal, state, county, and city elections must be planned 112
for every year in which the terms of officials have ended. 124
Primaries are held to narrow the number of candidates. The 136
year in which a president is chosen can create a lot of 147
excitement, but citizens must be interested in and vote for 159
their choice each time. 164

A good voter should pay careful attention to the main 175
issues and the candidates. Newspapers, public debates, and 187
interviews are good sources of information. Choose those 198
officials who share your views and are best qualified. 209

| 1 | 2 | 3 | 4 | 5 | 6 | 7 | 8 | 9 | 10 | 11 | 12 |

D. ENTER KEY

Insertion Point: A vertical blinking bar on the computer screen that indicates where an action will begin.

The ENTER key moves the insertion point to the beginning of a new line. Reach to the ENTER key with the Sem finger. Lightly press the ENTER key. Return the Sem finger to home position.

Practice using the ENTER key. Key each line 1 time, pressing the SPACE BAR where you see a space and pressing the ENTER key at the end of a line.

```
asdf jkl; asdf jkl; asdf jkl;↵
asdf jkl; asdf jkl; asdf jkl;↵
asdf jkl; asdf jkl; asdf jkl;↵
asdf jkl; asdf jkl; asdf jkl;↵
```

E. F J KEYS

Key each line 1 time.

Use F and J fingers.

```
1 fff jjj fff jjj fff jjj ff jj ff jj f j↵
2 fff jjj fff jjj fff jjj ff jj ff jj f j↵
```

F. D K KEYS

Key each line 1 time.

Use D and K fingers.

```
3 ddd kkk ddd kkk ddd kkk dd kk dd kk d k↵
4 ddd kkk ddd kkk ddd kkk dd kk dd kk d k↵
```

SKILLBUILDING *(continued)*

TIMING 8

Genealogy has become a fascinating science to some 10
people. You do not need to be a scientist to get involved 22
in genealogy. You do not need a college degree to trace 33
your roots. There was a time when you may have wanted to 45
trace your family tree to prove that one or more of your 56
ancestors came over from Europe on the Mayflower. However, 68
today we often trace our roots as expressions of personal 79
and cultural pride and identity, no matter how humble a 91
person's origins may be. 96

There are many genealogical societies recognized in 106
this country. We all want to know where we came from and 118
how we arrived here. Genealogy can be a complex field. It 129
can include religion, demographics, geography, ethnic and 141
women's studies, legal history, photographic imaging, and 152
library research. Getting started at tracing your roots 164
does not have to be complicated. You just start with what 175
you know and then move toward the unknown. Inquire at your 187
school or city library to get you going with some research 199
you would like to do. 203

| 1 | 2 | 3 | 4 | 5 | 6 | 7 | 8 | 9 | 10 | 11 | 12 |

G. S L KEYS

S
L
KEYS
Use third fingers on S and L keys.

Key each line 1 time.

Use S and L fingers.

```
5 sss lll sss lll sss lll ss ll ss ll s l↵
6 sss lll sss lll sss lll ss ll ss ll s l↵
```

H. A ; KEYS

A
;
KEYS
Use fourth fingers on A and ; keys.

Key each line 1 time.

Use A and Sem fingers.

```
7 aaa ;;; aaa ;;; aaa ;;; aa ;; aa ;; a ;↵
8 aaa ;;; aaa ;;; aaa ;;; aa ;; aa ;; a ;↵
```

SKILLBUILDING

Technique Checkpoint

I. Technique Checkpoints enable you to practice new keys. They also give you and your teacher a chance to evaluate your keyboarding techniques. Focus on the techniques listed in the margin, such as:

- Use correct fingers.
- Keep your eyes on the copy.
- Press ENTER without pausing.
- Maintain correct posture.
- Maintain correct arm, hand, and finger position.

Continued on next page

SKILLBUILDING *(continued)*

TIMING 7

Did you ever look up at the sky during the night and 11
see a shooting star? Do you realize that what you saw was a 23
meteor racing across the sky? Sometimes meteor showers are 35
visible to the naked eye. At such times you do not need 46
special glasses or binoculars to view these space voyagers. 58
Between midnight and dawn is the best time to watch for 69
them. If you are watching outdoors, you get a much better 81
view. 82

Every year meteor showers are caused by extra scrap 92
matter of comets. When the comets are quite close to the 104
sun, more debris accumulates and there are likely to be 115
more meteors. Each summer, from around the middle of July 127
through the middle of August, a meteor show may light up 138
the night sky. At peak times, you may be able to see as 149
many as a hundred meteors in a night. In the city, a bright 161
meteor shower has to compete with the bright city lights. 173
From the ground, the meteors look as though they might be 184
coming from a constellation. 190

| 1 | 2 | 3 | 4 | 5 | 6 | 7 | 8 | 9 | 10 | 11 | 12 |

Focus on these techniques:
- ***Keep your eyes on the copy.***
- ***Keep fingers on home keys.***

Key lines 9–10 one time.

```
9  ff jj dd kk ss ll aa ;; f j d k s l a ;↵
10 ff jj dd kk ss ll aa ;; f j d k s l a ;↵
```

J. PRETEST

Key lines 11–12 for 1 minute. Repeat if time permits. Keep your eyes on the copy.

Hold anchor keys.

```
11 sad sad fad fad ask ask lad lad dad dad↵
12 as; as; fall fall alas alas flask flask↵
```

K. PRACTICE

Key lines 13–24 one time. Repeat if time permits.

Leave a blank line after each set of lines (13–14, 15–16, and so on) by pressing ENTER 2 times.

```
13 aaa ddd sad sad aaa sss lll lll all all↵
14 aaa ddd sad sad aaa sss lll lll all all↵↵

15 aaa sss kkk ask ask fff aaa ddd fad fad↵
16 aaa sss kkk ask ask fff aaa ddd fad fad↵↵

17 aaa ddd ddd add add lll aaa ddd lad lad↵
18 aaa ddd ddd add add lll aaa ddd lad lad↵↵

19 aaa sss ;;; as; as; ddd aaa ddd dad dad↵
20 aaa sss ;;; as; as; ddd aaa ddd dad dad↵↵

21 f fl fla flas flask; l la las lass lass↵
22 f fl fla flas flask; l la las lass lass↵↵

23 f fa fal fall falls; a al ala alas alas↵
24 f fa fal fall falls; a al ala alas alas↵↵
```

L. POSTTEST

Key lines 11–12 for 1 minute. Repeat if time permits. Keep your eyes on the copy. Compare your Posttest results with your Pretest results.

End-Of-Class Procedure

Refer to your *Student Guide* for keyboarding tips. Your teacher will tell you how to properly shut down your software.

SKILLBUILDING *(continued)*

TIMING 6

Many people have wondered what might possibly be the 11
greatest structure on earth. The tallest buildings, the 22
longest bridges, or the mightiest dams may all be examined 34
to find the answer to this difficult question. In the minds 46
of many people, one of the greatest structures ever built 57
was the Great Wall of China. It is a well-known fact that 69
its features are so impressive that astronauts have even 80
viewed the wall from their spaceships. 88

The structure was built primarily by mixing just earth 99
and bricks. It is wide enough at the top for several people 111
to walk abreast on it. It winds for miles through a large 123
part of the country, over mountains and across valleys. It 135
was constructed to keep out unwelcome tribes, and it is 146
believed that building the wall required the labor of many 158
thousands of persons for dozens of decades. The very first 170
sections of the Great Wall were built in the Age of Warring 182
States. 183

| 1 | 2 | 3 | 4 | 5 | 6 | 7 | 8 | 9 | 10 | 11 | 12 |

SECTION 1.2 New Keys: H E O

GOALS:

- Demonstrate correct touch-system techniques for alphabetic keys.
- Learn the H, E, and O keys.

A. WARMUP

Key each line 2 times. Leave 1 blank line after each set of lines.

Anchor Key Tips:
For H—anchor ; L K
For E—anchor A
For O—anchor J or ;

```
1 ff jj dd kk ss ll aa ;; f j d k s l a ;
2 adds adds fads fads asks asks lads lads
```

NEW KEYS

B.  KEY

Key each line 2 times.
Repeat if time permits.

Use J finger.
For H anchor ; L K.

```
3 jjj jhj jhj hjh jhj jjj jhj jhj hjh jhj
4 jhj ash ash jhj has has jhj had had jhj
5 jhj a lass has; adds a half; a lad had;
6 has a slash; half a sash dad shall dash
```

SKILLBUILDING *(continued)*

TIMING 5

Have you ever felt rundown, tired, and fatigued? The 11
symptoms listed above are common to many of us today. They 23
affect our job performance; they limit the fun we have with 35
our family and friends; and they can even affect our good 46
health. Here are a few of the ways by which we can quickly 58
minimize the problem and become more active in the things 70
we do daily. 72

It is critical that we get plenty of rest so that we 83
are rested when we get up each morning. We must eat a good 95
breakfast so that we can build up energy for the day that 106
follows. Physical exercise is a necessity, and it might be 118
the one most important ingredient in building up our energy 130
reserves. We must engage in vigorous exercise to make our 142
hearts beat faster and cause our breathing rate to increase 154
appreciably. These are things that can help us increase our 166
energy and make us healthier people. 174

| 1 | 2 | 3 | 4 | 5 | 6 | 7 | 8 | 9 | 10 | 11 | 12 |

C. E KEY

Key each line 2 times.
Repeat if time permits.

Use D finger.
For E anchor A S.

```
7  ddd ded ded ede ded ddd ded ded ede ded
8  ded led led ded she she ded he; ded he;
9  ded he led; she fell; he slashes sales;
10 he sees sheds ahead; she sealed a lease
```

D. O KEY

Key each line 2 times.
Repeat if time permits.

Use L finger.
For O anchor J K.

```
11 lll lol lol olo lol lll lol lol olo lol
12 lol odd odd lol hoe hoe lol foe foe lol
13 load sod; hold a foe; old oak hoes; lol
14 she sold odd hooks; he folded old hoses
```

SKILLBUILDING *(continued)*

TIMING 3

Businesses and individuals are free to write letters 11
to officials in Washington. There are dozens of people to 22
whom you might send a letter. These include the President, 34
senators, or representatives. People who are elected to go 46
to Washington take along their staff who answers most of 57
the mail from their constituents. Using the mail is just 69
one way legislators keep in touch with what is happening in 81
their individual congressional districts. 89

People send inquiries on many topics. They may want to 101
express a positive position or they may want to complain 113
about taxes, pollution, and foreign policy. Some letters 124
influence how lawmakers make their decisions. 133

| 1 | 2 | 3 | 4 | 5 | 6 | 7 | 8 | 9 | 10 | 11 | 12 |

TIMING 4

Autumn in the "northland" is very exciting. You jump 11
up in the early morning; walk out under a clear, blue sky; 23
and feel the strong chill in the air. The leaves have lost 34
their brilliant green. It appears that they may have been 46
tinted by someone passing by. The truth is that during the 58
night hours a frost has painted the green to hues of brown, 70
yellow, orange, and scarlet. It is a breathtaking panorama 82
in Technicolor. The leaves seem not to move in the quiet 92
breeze. Then, suddenly, a brisk puff lifts them from the 104
limbs and carries them gently like feathers to the ground 116
below. You watch as legions of leaves jump free and float 128
to the earth, covering it like a quilted blanket that looks 140
much like moss. When you walk on top of the blanket, it 151
cushions each step you take as though you are walking on 162
air. 163

| 1 | 2 | 3 | 4 | 5 | 6 | 7 | 8 | 9 | 10 | 11 | 12 |

SKILLBUILDING

Technique Checkpoint

E. ***Key each line 2 times. Repeat if time permits. Focus on the technique at the left.***

Focus on this technique: Press and release each key quickly.

```
15 ddd ded ded ede ded ddd ded ded ede ded
16 lll lol lol olo lol lll lol lol olo lol
17 jjj jhj jhj hjh jhj jjj jhj jhj hjh jhj
18 she has old jokes; he has half a salad;
```

F. PRETEST

Key lines 19–20 for 1 minute. Repeat if time permits. Keep your eyes on the copy.

Hold anchor keys.

```
19 heed jade hoof elf; hash folk head hole
20 seed lake look jell sash hold dead half
```

G. PRACTICE

Key each line 2 times. Repeat if time permits.

When you repeat a line:
- ***Speed up as you key the line.***
- ***Key it more smoothly.***
- ***Leave a blank line after the second line (press Enter 2 times).***

```
21 heed heed feed feed deed deed seed seed
22 jade jade fade fade fake fake lake lake
23 hoof hoof hood hood hook hook look look
24 elf; elf; self self sell sell jell jell

25 hash hash lash lash dash dash sash sash
26 folk folk fold fold sold sold hold hold
27 head head heal heal deal deal dead dead
28 hole hole hale hale hall hall half half
```

H. POSTTEST

Key lines 19–20 for 1 minute. Repeat if time permits. Keep your eyes on the copy. Compare your Posttest results with your Pretest results.

SKILLBUILDING *(continued)*

SUPPLEMENTARY TIMINGS

TIMING 1

Raising dogs can be a combination of both fun and hard 11
work. Before you even start, you should realize just which 23
breed can best adapt to your lifestyle. If you need a dog 35
to protect your house, a poodle might not give you enough 46
protection. If you are in your own apartment, a collie may 58
be too large. When you have chosen a dog for you, expect to 70
have to train it. This can be done quickly with a new puppy 82
that is willing to learn. 87

| 1 | 2 | 3 | 4 | 5 | 6 | 7 | 8 | 9 | 10 | 11 | 12 |

TIMING 2

For students who can speak a foreign language, there 11
is an amazing job market today. Many major companies in 22
other countries have been buying control of or investing in 34
American firms. The need for workers with foreign language 46
skills is seen in the large number of help wanted ads for 57
experts with language skills. 63

The fact that so many Americans cannot speak, read, or 75
write another language is tragic because the countries of 86
the world today are closely linked. International trade is 98
very important to business and government, and young people 110
cannot afford to be unequipped to meet the many changes and 122
challenges of the future. 127

| 1 | 2 | 3 | 4 | 5 | 6 | 7 | 8 | 9 | 10 | 11 | 12 |

SECTION 1.3 New Keys: M R I

GOALS:

- Demonstrate correct touch-system techniques for alphabetic keys.
- Learn the M, R, and I keys.

A. WARMUP

Key each line 2 times. Leave 1 blank line after each set of lines.

```
1 asdf jkl; heo; asdf jkl; heo; asdf jkl;
2 jade jade fake fake held held lose lose
```

NEW KEYS

B.  KEY

Key each line 2 times. Repeat if time permits.

Use J finger. For M anchor ; L K.

```
3 jjj jmj jmj mjm jmj jjj jmj jmj mjm jmj
4 jmj mom mom jmj mad mad jmj ham ham jmj
5 jmj make a jam; fold a hem; less flame;
6 messes make some moms mad; half a dome;
```

SKILLBUILDING *(continued)*

60 wpm

Many standard dictionaries give brief essays on topics such as the history of English, what is good usage, and the different dialects of English. Usage refers to how words are used in speaking and writing. A regional way of pronouncing a word is considered dialect. Quite frequently, a dictionary will give instructions on how to use the word. The most obvious information appears first. It is correct syllable division and spelling. When you type a paper, you need to be razor sharp on the correct way to hyphenate a word. Do not be lax in your writing. Use a dictionary to help check every report.

C.  KEY

Key each line 2 times.
Repeat if time permits.

Use F finger.
For R anchor A S D.

```
7  fff frf frf rfr frf fff frf frf rfr frf
8  frf far far frf for for frf err err frf
9  frf more rooms; for her marks; from me;
10 he reads ahead; more doors are far ajar
```

D. I KEY

Key each line 2 times.
Repeat if time permits.

Use K finger.
For I anchor ;.

```
11 kkk kik kik iki kik kkk kik kik iki kik
12 kik dim dim kik lid lid kik rim rim kik
13 kik if she did; for his risk; old mill;
14 more mirrors; his middle silo is filled
```

CARE AND OPERATION OF EQUIPMENT

For Discussion—Answer the following question. Refer to the Appendix for the Answer.

What is the proper way to turn on the computer? Demonstrate to your teacher.

SKILLBUILDING *(continued)*

56 wpm

Each June, July, or August, some firms put a closed sign at the front door. They let their employees have the entire month off. All of them like to zip out of town for a nice relaxing vacation. During this month, everyone can enjoy a little time in the sun, or in a boat. Some head for the mountains for a camping or hiking trip. In the summer, most of us usually do less indoors and spend quite a lot of time outside. Many winter resorts have summer activities. Their activities can be enjoyable and quite varied. They do a lot of business during the summer.

58 wpm

It has been more than a hundred years since the phone first touched our lives. It has modified the way all of us around the world converse. There are more ways than just a phone to help us quickly stay in touch with others. A computer connected to a modem or fax machine or a pager can be used to carry messages from place to place. The use of these carriers can be quicker and more cost-efficient than the use of the telephone. Today, using more than one of these communication devices is a common practice. We can choose to stay in touch by phone, fax, e-mail, page, or letter.

SKILLBUILDING

Technique Checkpoint

E. ***Key each line 2 times. Repeat if time permits. Focus on the techniques at the left.***

Focus on these techniques:
- ***Fingertips touching home keys.***
- ***Wrists up, off keyboard.***

```
15 jjj jmj jmj mjm jmj jjj jmj jmj mjm jmj
16 fff frf frf rfr frf fff frf frf rfr frf
17 kkk kik kik iki kik kkk kik kik iki kik
18 he did; his firm red desk lid is a joke
```

F. PRETEST

Key lines 19–20 for 1 minute. Repeat if time permits. Keep your eyes on the copy.

```
19 joke ride sale same roam aims sire more
20 jars aide dark lame foal elms hire mare
```

G. PRACTICE

Key each line 2 times. Repeat if time permits.

Keep eyes on copy. It will be easier to keep your eyes on the copy if you:
- ***Maintain an even pace.***
- ***Resist looking up from your copy.***

```
21 joke joke jade jade jams jams jars jars
22 ride ride hide hide side side aide aide
23 sale sale dale dale dare dare dark dark
24 same same fame fame dame dame lame lame

25 roam roam loam loam foam foam foal foal
26 aims aims arms arms alms alms elms elms
27 sire sire dire dire fire fire hire hire
28 more more mire mire mere mere mare mare
```

H. POSTTEST

Key lines 19–20 for 1 minute. Repeat if time permits. Keep your eyes on the copy. Compare your Posttest results with your Pretest results.

SKILLBUILDING *(continued)*

50 wpm

The Inca Indians lived hundreds of years ago near what is now called Peru. They were a great nation known for their many unique buildings. These buildings, in fact, are still visible in ruins deep in the jungle. The temples that remain can be scrutinized for clues about their religion, beliefs, culture, and way of life. Some knowledge already exists, for we have learned that they were a people of numerous skills. Perhaps in time we can uncover the answer to the secret of why the Incas vanished.

52 wpm

The brain controls conscious behavior like walking and thinking. It also controls involuntary behavior like the heartbeat and breathing. In humans, it is known to be the site of emotions, memory, and thought. It functions by receiving information through nerve cells from every part of the body. When the brain receives an influx of data, it needs to evaluate the data and then zip off commands to an area of the body like a muscle. Or, the brain might simply store the data. Neurons can process a large amount of data.

54 wpm

Working in a place where everyone gets along would be great. However, we all know that the chance of finding a job in a place like that really seldom happens. Each of us has a different personality. When we mix together all of those personalities, the results are quite varied. There will be those who get along with everyone and find no fault with anything. But, by and large, each of us can and will have a difference of opinion with someone at some point. We need to bring qualities like zeal and a good attitude to every job situation.

SECTION 1.4 Review

GOALS:

- Demonstrate correct posture and position at the keyboard and correct touch-system techniques for alphabetic keys.
- Improve keyboarding skill.

A. WARMUP

Key each line 2 times. Leave 1 blank line after each set of lines.

1 joke fade home jade mom lads lose less;
2 jell sods from jars adds half ash lead;

SKILLBUILDING

B. ENTER KEY

Use the **Sem** finger to press the **Enter** key.

Key each line 1 time. Repeat if time permits.

Press* Enter *after each semicolon and continue to key smoothly.

3 dad adds a home;↵ a sad lass sees ahead;↵
4 he led her here;↵ she folded old flames;↵
5 some lasses are moms;↵ he had less jade;↵
6 he sold old hooks;↵ she had jade flakes;↵

SKILLBUILDING *(continued)*

44 wpm

Most successful newspapers are large businesses with [1] an extensive staff and several readers. Now, though, [2] there is a growing number of smaller papers. Their aim is [3] to focus on a community or one subject. A small paper [4] that is well produced will concentrate on and promote a [5] local public. In addition, for those who are in the business, [6] operating it is challenging and rewarding. Moreover, [7] papers provide everyone a vehicle for free speech. [8]

46 wpm

Results of a citizenship test taken by a selected group [1] of high school students were surprising. The test was conducted [2] to determine how much knowledge young people have about [3] our system of government. Also, it questioned whether [4] they know how to split their ballot when they vote. Only [5] one-third of the students participating in the program knew [6] that a voter could divide his or her party choice. The [7] majority was ignorant of the political system altogether. [8]

48 wpm

Veterinarians are doctors who are trained to treat and to prevent [1] disease in animals. Although they attend different medical [2] schools than doctors trained to treat people, their program [3] of study and training are similar. Vets can limit their practice [4] to one kind of animal. If they choose to specialize [5] in horses, they can be highly paid because the patients might [6] be priceless race horses. Some vets, on the other hand, [7] would rather work with or conduct research on wild animals. [8]

C. SPACE BAR

Key each line 1 time.
Repeat if time permits.

Space between words without pausing.

```
7  as a sad lass; ask a lad; as a sad dad;
8  he had old sod; she made me mad; a door
9  mom hems; dad marked rare oak; mash ash
10 see her; make me; a sad lad; ash doors;
```

D. CONCENTRATION

Fill in the missing vowels shown at the left as you key each line 1 time.

Keep your eyes on the copy.

```
E  11 h- s--s s-al-d l-as-s; sh- h-ars a r--d
A  12 al-s - s-d l-d h-d - lo-d of f-ke smoke
O  13 ask her f-r a l-ad -f s-me -ld -ak m-ld
I  14 she sa-d d-m m-rrors make h-m look sl-m
```

E. *Key each line 2 times. Repeat if time permits. Focus on the techniques at the left.*

Focus on:
- ***Fingertips touching home keys.***
- ***Wrists up.***

```
15 his dark oak desk lid is a joke; he did
16 make a firm door from some rare red ash
17 a lad made a shed; he slashed odd sales
18 foals roam a farm; she sees a small elm
```

SKILLBUILDING *(continued)*

36 wpm

An interesting and exciting hobby for you could be working with plants. You have missed a joy if you have never waited with expectation for a tiny sprig to sprout into a plant. Actually, plants make wonderful pets for apartment dwellers. They neither bark nor meow, and the neighbors don't grumble about being kept awake or about being annoyed by a noisy pet.

38 wpm

Have you ever been on a fairly long trip by car only to find yourself bored because you didn't have much to do? You, the passenger, can engross yourself in a great book. This answer to the boredom can make time appear to pass more rapidly. You could purchase several paperbacks at a local bookstore; and as you read, you can capture numerous hours of entertainment and enjoyment.

40 wpm

Today, a quick way to get from one destination to another is by plane. For your flight, you can choose from among many airlines. In addition, airlines throughout the nation offer daily service to many cities here and abroad. Passengers on domestic and international flights should allow enough time before departure to secure seats on board the plane and to check in baggage at the airport terminal.

42 wpm

Every year when winter approaches, you might look up at the sky and see hundreds and maybe even thousands of birds flying toward warmer weather. Quite simply, they migrate south just to escape the severe days that come so soon. Some experts hypothesize that birds migrate because they physically cannot last in the harsh winters of the frigid north. Other experts think that birds migrate to locate better food sources.

F. PRETEST

Key lines 19–20 for 1 minute. Repeat if time permits. Keep your eyes on the copy.

```
19 more sire aims roam same sale ride joke
20 mare hire elms foal lame dark aide jars
```

G. PRACTICE

Key each line 2 times. Repeat if time permits. Keep your eyes on the copy.

It will be easier to keep your eyes on the copy if you:
- ***Maintain an even pace.***
- ***Concentrate on the copy.***

```
21 more more mire mire mere mere mare mare
22 sire sire dire dire fire fire hire hire
23 aims aims arms arms alms alms elms elms
24 roam roam loam loam foam foam foal foal

25 same same fame fame dame dame lame lame
26 sale sale dale dale dare dare dark dark
27 ride ride hide hide side side aide aide
28 jade jade made made mode mode mole mole
```

H. POSTTEST

Key lines 19–20 for 1 minute. Repeat if time permits. Keep your eyes on the copy. Compare your Posttest results with your Pretest results.

CARE AND OPERATION OF EQUIPMENT

For Discussion—answer the following question. Refer to the Appendix for the answer.

What is the proper way to turn off the computer? Demonstrate to your teacher.

SKILLBUILDING *(continued)*

28 wpm

When shopping in this country, we generally accept the price tag on merchandise for the final price the store will consider. If we really want an item, we pay the amount asked. In other nations, prices might vary each moment, depending on the ability of the purchaser to bargain.

30 wpm

National parks are owned by the people of America, and they are preserves for wildlife and timber. The parks are cared for by the government to be sure they remain protected and guarded resources. The rangers help prevent forest fires, analyze weather conditions, and keep watch on the wild animals.

32 wpm

You simply do not go rafting down the quick river flowing through the Grand Canyon without plenty of skill and help. The hazards can be just too severe. The beautiful canyon is rocky, thorny, and hot during summer months. At times, it is so windy that sand sprays may hit you in the face with a brisk and stinging jolt.

34 wpm

A batik is a dyed cloth that has hot wax placed on it to form a design. First the artist melts wax, tints it various colors, paints a design, and then dyes the cloth. Some artists prefer to paint the cloth with a clear wax. Then the batik is dyed again and again with many colors. Only the portion not covered with the wax becomes colored.

SECTION 1.5 New Keys: T N C

GOALS:

- Demonstrate correct touch-system techniques for alphabetic keys.
- Learn the T, N, and C keys.

A. WARMUP

Key each line 2 times. Leave 1 blank line after each set of lines.

```
1 asdf jkl; heo; mri; asdf jkl; heo; mri;
2 herd herd mild mild safe safe joke joke
```

NEW KEYS

B. 

KEY

Key each line 2 times. Repeat if time permits.

Use F finger. Anchor A S D.

```
3 fff ftf ftf tft ftf fff ftf ftf tft ftf
4 ftf kit kit ftf toe toe ftf ate ate ftf
5 ftf it is the; to them; for the; at it;
6 that hat is flat; it ate at least three
```

SKILLBUILDING *(continued)*

18 wpm

Each year, many Americans suffer a stroke. It can cause serious problems. For some, it can become difficult to walk or to use an arm. For others, a stroke can affect their speech.

20 wpm

Many people think angora is the wool of sheep but it comes from goats. The goats are sheared two times a year. The wool is washed through a special process. It can then be dyed and spun into strands.

20 wpm

The old woman who walks in the park always has a huge smile on her face. She talks to the people who cross her path. When she makes new friends, she offers assistance in her quiet way and is excited.

22 wpm

There is no substitute for the taste of ice cream on hot, humid days. Choices of all types are out to engage the eye, and the sharp clerks will fix just the mix and size to suit you best. A cup or a cone would be great.

24 wpm

To see the artists' pain is a joy. To watch the zeal with which they work to have the exact color show up on the pad is exciting. As they glide the new brush quickly across the pad, the radiant hues take form and bring smiles to our faces.

26 wpm

When you work with people every day, you get to know what it is that they like best. You also find out quickly what does make them frown. A bit of extra kind effort in a dozen little ways will make your office a pleasant place in which to complete all duties.

C.  N KEY

Key each line 2 times.
Repeat if time permits.

Use J finger.
Anchor ; L K.

```
7  jjj jnj jnj njn jnj jjj jnj jnj njn jnj
8  jnj ten ten jnj not not jnj and and jnj
9  jnj nine tones; none inside; on and on;
10 nine kind lines; ten done in an instant
```

D. C KEY

Key each line 2 times.
Repeat if time permits.

Use D finger.
Anchor A.

```
11 ddd dcd dcd cdc dcd ddd dcd dcd cdc dcd
12 dcd ace ace dcd can can dcd arc arc dcd
13 dcd on a deck; in each car; cannot act;
14 act at once; call to cancel the tickets
```

CARE AND OPERATION OF EQUIPMENT

For Discussion—answer the following question. Refer to the Appendix for the answer.

Computers would be useless without devices to help you input information. The most common input devices are the keyboard and the mouse. Demonstrate the proper use of the mouse and the keyboard.

SKILLBUILDING *(continued)*

PACED PRACTICE

The Paced Practice routine builds speed and accuracy in short, easy steps, using individualized goals and immediate feedback. You can use this routine any time after completing Section 1.18.

This section contains a series of 2-minute timings for speeds ranging from 14 wpm to 60 wpm. The first time you use these timings, take a 1-minute entry timing. Then, select a passage that is 2 wpm higher than your current keyboarding speed. Use a two-stage practice pattern to achieve each speed goal—first concentrate on speed, and then work on accuracy.

SPEED GOAL: Take three 2-minute timings on the same passage until you can complete it in 2 minutes (do not worry about the number of errors).

When you have achieved your speed goal, work on accuracy.

ACCURACY GOAL: To type accurately, you need to slow down—just a little bit. To reach your accuracy goal, drop back 2 wpm to the previous passage. Take three 2-minute timings on this passage until you can complete it in 2 minutes with no more than 2 errors.

For example, if you achieved a speed goal of 30 wpm, you should work on an accuracy goal of 28 wpm. When you have achieved the 28 wpm goal for accuracy, you would then move up 4 wpm (for example, to the 32 wpm passage) and work for speed again.

ENTRY TIMING

If your mailbox is full of mail that you do not want, 11
your name is on a mailing list. Firms buy mailing lists so 23
that they can send you their ads. Unless you write and ask 34
each company to take your name off its list, you will keep 46
getting junk mail. 50

14 wpm

Tourists like to[1] meander through the[2] Boston Gardens[3]
during the summer.[4] They stroll the[5] shady paths and then[6]
stop to ride[7] on the swan boats.[8]

16 wpm

Pleasure boats and[1] large tankers pass[2] through the
Cape Cod[3] canal every day. The[4] canal is spanned by[5] two
high bridges[6] for auto traffic and[7] by a railroad bridge.[8]

SKILLBUILDING

Technique Checkpoint

E. ***Key each line 2 times. Repeat if time permits. Focus on the technique at the left.***

Hold anchor keys. Keep your eyes on the copy.

```
15 fff ftf ftf tft ftf fff ftf ftf tft ftf
16 jjj jnj jnj njn jnj jjj jnj jnj njn jnj
17 ddd dcd dcd cdc dcd ddd dcd dcd cdc dcd
18 the carton of jam is here on this dock;
```

F. PRETEST

Key lines 19–20 for 1 minute. Repeat if time permits. Keep your eyes on the copy.

```
19 sail farm jets kick this none care ink;
20 rain hand jots tick then tone came sink
```

G. PRACTICE

Key each line 2 times. Repeat if time permits.

To increase skill:

- ***Keep your eyes on the copy.***
- ***Maintain good posture.***
- ***Speed up on the second keying.***

```
21 sail sail said said raid raid rain rain
22 farm farm harm harm hard hard hand hand
23 jets jets lets lets lots lots jots jots
24 kick kick sick sick lick lick tick tick

25 this this thin thin than than then then
26 none none lone lone done done tone tone
27 care care cake cake cane cane came came
28 ink; ink; link link rink rink sink sink
```

H. POSTTEST

Key lines 19–20 for 1 minute. Repeat if time permits. Compare your Posttest results with your Pretest results.

SKILLBUILDING *(continued)*

INDIVIDUAL REACHES

8

```
kik ki8k k8k 888 k8k 8/88 k8k 88.8 k8k ki8k 88.8 88,888 k8k
8 kegs, 88 kits, 888 kilns, 878 kickers, 876 knocks, or 8.8
The 8 keys fit 887 kits; Kim found 8,876 knots in the kits.
The 8 kind ladies got 882 kimonos for 188 kids in the play.
```

9

```
lol lo9l l9l 999 l9l 9/99 l9l 99.9 l9l lo9l 99.9 99,999 l9l
9 laps, 99 lots, 999 loops, 989 lilies, 987 lifters, or 9.9
Lillian said 9 times to leave 99 lilies for the 989 ladies.
My 9 lawyers had 19 leaky pens, 89 legal pads, and 9 limos.
```

10

```
;p; ;p0; ;0; 000 ;0; 0/00 ;0; 00.0 ;0; ;p0; 00.0 00,000 ;0;
10 pots, 20 pins, 300 parts, 400 plants, 500 parades or 0.0
The 10 party stores put 100 pots and 200 pans to pick from.
The 10 books had 23,000 pages in each; Paul read 500 pages.
```

All numbers

```
a1a s2s d3d f4f f5f j6j j7j k8k l9l ;0; Add 6 and 8 and 29.
That 534-page script called for 10 actors and 17 actresses.
After 1,374 miles in the car, she must then drive 185 more.
The 141 professors asked 4,690 sportscasters 230 questions.
```

All numbers

```
a1a s2s d3d f4f f5f j6j j7j k8k l9l ;0; Add 3 and 4 and 70.
They built 1,200 houses on 345 acres in just under 3 years.
Six boys arrived on May 26, 1994, and left on May 30, 1998.
Marlee bought 15 new books, 62 used books, and 47 new pens.
```

All numbers

```
a1a s2s d3d f4f f5f j6j j7j k8k l9l ;0; Add 5 and 7 and 68.
The 4 stores are open from 9:30 a.m. until 6:00 p.m. daily.
I gave away 2 pans, 4 plates, 8 glasses, and 25 containers.
She moved to 705 Garfield Street, not 507, on June 4, 2000.
```

SECTION 1.6

New Keys: V RIGHT SHIFT Period (.)

GOALS:

- Demonstrate correct touch-system techniques for alphabetic and command keys.
- Learn the V, RIGHT SHIFT, and period (.) keys, and spacing with the period.
- Determine speed (words per minute).

A. WARMUP

Key each line 2 times.

```
1 asdf jkl; jh de lo jm fr ki ft jn dc ;;
2 cash free dine jolt milk iron trim star
```

NEW KEYS

B.  KEY

Key each line 2 times. Repeat if time permits.

Use F finger. Anchor A S D.

```
3 fff fvf fvf vfv fvf fff fvf fvf vfv fvf
4 fvf vie vie fvf eve eve fvf via via fvf
5 fvf vie for love; move over; via a van;
6 vote to move; even vitamins have flavor
```

SKILLBUILDING *(continued)*

INDIVIDUAL REACHES

1 aqa aqla ala 111 ala 1/11 ala 11.1 ala aqla 11.1 11,111 ala
1 ant, 11 arms, 111 aunts, 101 apples, 131 animals, or 1.11
Henry read 111 pages in 1 hour and ate 1 apple in 1 minute.
Crystal wrote 1 story that was 1,111 pages long on 1 topic.

2 sws sw2s s2s 222 s2s 2/22 s2s 22.2 s2s sw2s 22.2 22,222 s2s
2 sips, 22 sets, 222 sites, 212 socks, 231 soldiers, or 2.2
She moved to Room 221 with 2,223 students for about 2 days.
Today 202 computer students were solving 322 math problems.

3 ded de3d d3d 333 d3d 3/33 d3d 33.3 d3d de3d 33.3 33,333 d3d
3 dots, 33 dogs, 333 drops, 323 dimes, 321 daisies, or 3.33
The 3 doctors and 3 nurses did the 3 surgeries in 33 hours.
Your 3 cats and 23 dogs liked to romp on the 330-acre farm.

4 frf fr4f f4f 444 f4f 4/44 f4f 44.4 f4f fr4f 44.4 44,444 f4f
4 figs, 44 fans, 444 farms, 434 finals, 431 friends, or 4.4
Meredith flew 444 miles to see 4 friends at 434 Oak Street.
Florence sold 41 fish dinners to the 44 customers at 4 p.m.

5 ftf ft5f f5f 555 f5f 5/55 f5f 55.5 f5f ft5f 55.5 55,555 f5f
5 foes, 55 facts, 555 foals, 545 fowls, 543 flights, or 5.5
Fred found 55 facts in 545 flights from 514 foreign places.
Theo found that flight 5253 leaves at 5 a.m. from gate 545.

6 jyj jy6j j6j 666 j6j 6/66 j6j 66.6 j6j jy6j 66.6 66,666 j6j
6 jaws, 66 jets, 666 jeeps, 656 jokes, 654 journals, or 6.6
She had 6 jobs to do in 66 hours. Julia worked 664 minutes.
Her 6 math tests had 165 problems to be done in 60 minutes.

7 juj ju7j j7j 777 j7j 7/77 j7j 77.7 j7j ju7j 77.7 77,777 j7j
7 jugs, 77 jars, 777 jumps, 767 joggers, 765 jewels, or 7.7
Joe saw 7 joggers run 177 miles across 7,777 acres of land.
The 7 suits were shipped to 7167 East 7th Avenue on July 7.

C. Right SHIFT Key

Key each line 2 times.
Repeat if time permits.

Use Sem finger.
Anchor J.

```
7  ;;; T;; T;; ;;; C;; C;; ;;; S;; S;; ;;;
8  ;;; Ted Ted ;;; Cal Cal ;;; Sam Sam ;;;
9  ;;; Ed likes Flint; Rick ran; save Tom;
10 Vera loved Florida; Aaron and Sam moved
```

D. . Key

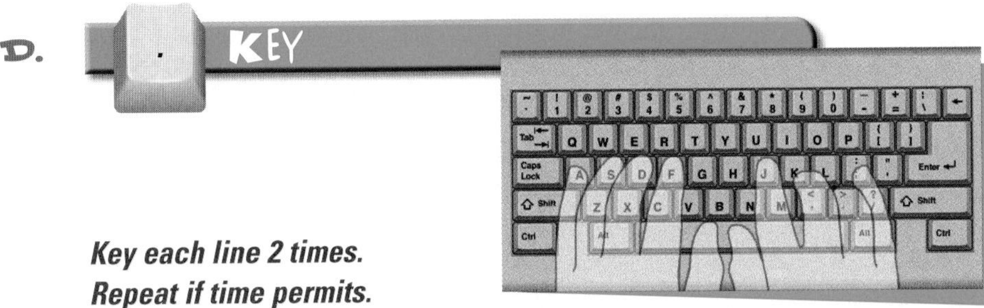

Key each line 2 times.
Repeat if time permits.

Use L finger.
Anchor ; or J.

```
11 l11 l.l l.l .l. l.l lll l.l l.l .l. lll
12 l.l Fr. Fr. l.l Sr. Sr. l.l Dr. Dr. l.l
13 l.l std. ctn. div. Ave. Rd. St. Co. vs.
14 Calif. Conn. Tenn. Colo. Fla. Del. Ark.
```

SKILLBUILDING

E. Spacing After Punctuation

Key each line 2 times. Repeat if time permits. Focus on the techniques at the left.

Space 1 time after:
- *A period at the end of a sentence.*
- *A period used with an abbreviation.*
- *A semicolon.*

```
15 The draft is too cold. Close this door.
16 Ask Vera to start a fire. Find a match.
17 Dr. T. Vincent sees me; he made a cast.
18 Ash Rd. is ahead; East Ave. veers left.
```

SKILLBUILDING *(continued)*

DIAGNOSTIC PRACTICE: NUMBERS

The Diagnostic Practice: Numbers routine is designed to diagnose and then correct your keystroking errors. You may use this program at any time throughout the course after you complete Unit 2.

DIRECTIONS:

1. Type one set of the Pretest/Posttest lines 1 time. Identify your errors.
2. Note your results—the number of errors you made on each key and your total number of errors. For example, if you typed *24* for *25,* that would count as 1 error on the number *5*.
3. For any number on which you made 2 or more errors, select the corresponding drill lines, on p. SB5 and p. SB6, and type them 2 times. If you made only 1 error, type the drill 1 time. If you made no errors on the Pretest/Posttest lines, type the drills that contain all numbers on page SB6 and type each line 1 time.
4. Finally, retype the Pretest/Posttest, and compare your performance with your Pretest.

PRETEST/POSTTEST

Set 1

```
ripe 4803, ire 843, wee 233, ore 943, pier 0834, wire 2843,
Silvio marked the chalkboard at 25, 30, and 45 centimeters.
Alice put markers at 10 km, 29 km, 38 km, 47 km, and 56 km.
Bob lost checks Nos. 234, 457, and 568. Mandy lost No. 901.
Please clean Rooms 340 and 380. Kerbey will clean Room 443.
Those five passengers are 25, 39, 42, 45, and 50 years old.
```

Set 2

```
wee 233, tie 583, toe 593, pure 0743, pour 0974, rout 4975,
Iva put 428 in group 1, 570 in group 2, and 396 in group 3.
The party governed during 1910, 1929, 1938, 1947, and 1956.
The total of 198, 384, 275, 470, and 672 is easy to figure.
They had 92 or 83. He has 10 or 74. We have 56 or maybe 57.
Check lockers 290, 471, 356, and 580 before school Tuesday.
```

Set 3

```
pie 083, rye 463, your 6974, tier 5834, eye 363, pipe 0803,
Read pages 100, 129, and 138; summarize Chapters 47 and 56.
By May 1, ship 29 seats, 38 stoves, 47 tents, and 56 coats.
The 29 females lived 180 days at 4387 South Parkview Court.
Janet read pages 105 through 120 and pages 387 through 469.
Marvin easily won the bulletins numbered 12,345 and 67,890.
```

F. ***Key each line 2 times. Focus on the techniques at the left.***

Hold anchor keys. Keep your eyes on the copy.

```
19 fff fvf fvf vfv fvf fff fvf fvf vfv fvf
20 ;;; T;; T;; ;;; C;; C;; ;;; S;; S;; ;;;
21 111 1.1 1.1 .1. 1.1 111 1.1 1.1 .1. 111
22 Dee voted for vivid vases on her visit.
```

G. DETERMINING SPEED

Speed is measured in words per minute (wpm). To determine your speed:

- Key for 1 minute.
- Determine the number of words you keyed. Every 5 strokes (characters and spaces) count as 1 word. Therefore, a 40-stroke line equals 8 words. Two 40-stroke lines equal 16 words.
- Use the cumulative word count at the end of lines to determine the number of words in a complete line.

To determine the number of words in an incomplete line:

- Use the word scale below the last line (below line 24 on this page).
- If you keyed line 23 and completed the word *vice* in line 24, you have keyed 14 words per minute (8 + 6 = 14).

```
23 fold hide fast came hold ride mast fame     8
24 hone rice mask fade none vice task jade    16
   | 1 | 2 | 3 | 4 | 5 | 6 | 7 | 8
```

CARE AND OPERATION OF EQUIPMENT

For Discussion—answer the following question. Refer to the Appendix for the answer.

Discuss why you should keep food and drinks away from your computer.

SKILLBUILDING *(continued)*

TROUBLESOME PAIRS

A/S	Sal said he asked Sara Ash for a sample of the raisins.
B/V	Vera very bravely was verbose with a bevy of beverages.
C/D	Candie decided the December calendar decal could decay.
E/W	Weni knew in weekday weather weak weeds grew elsewhere.
F/G	Goeff goofed by finding the gulf for the grateful frog.
H/J	Judith wore jodhpurs; she joshed with John and Johanna.
I/O	Iona totally foiled Olin's spoiled oily ointment plans.
K/L	Karl liked to walk seven kilometers quickly with Kelly.
M/N	Many have names of maidens among the main mason manors.
O/P	Opal and Polly phoned three opera pollsters in Phoenix.
Q/A	Quin quickly qualified this quality quart quartz quota.
R/T	Robert tried trading rations to three terrific skaters.
U/Y	If you are busy, buy your supply of yucca Yule in July.
X/C	Cal expected the excitement to exceed all expectations.
Z/A	The five sizable, lazy zebras zigzagged as Eliza gazed.

H. PRETEST

Key lines 23–24 for 1 minute. Repeat if time permits. Note your speed. Keep your eyes on the copy.

```
23 fold hide fast came hold ride mast fame     8
24 hone rice mask fade none vice task jade    16
   | 1  | 2  | 3  | 4  | 5  | 6  | 7  | 8
```

I. PRACTICE

Key each line 2 times. Repeat if time permits.

Build speed on repeated word patterns.

```
25 fold fold hold hold sold sold told told
26 hide hide ride ride rice rice vice vice
27 fast fast mast mast mask mask task task
28 came came fame fame fade fade jade jade

29 last last vast vast cast cast case case
30 mats mats mars mars cars cars jars jars
31 fell fell jell jell sell sell seal seal
32 dive dive five five live live love love
```

J. POSTTEST

Repeat the Pretest. Compare your Posttest results with your Pretest results.

K. THE BACKSPACE KEY

Use Sem finger to press the Backspace key.

Practice using the Backspace key to correct errors.

1. Key the following line:
   `Dee voted for vivid vases on her visit.`
2. Tap on the Backspace key six times to remove the word `visit`.
3. Key the new word `desk`.

SKILLBUILDING *(continued)*

INDIVIDUAL REACHES

A Ada and Anna had an allowance and always had adequate cash.
B Barbara grabbed back the brown bag Bob bought at a bargain.
C Charles can accept and cash any checks the church collects.
D David drove down and deducted the dividends he had divided.
E Everyone here exerted extra effort each week we were there.

F Fred Ford offered to find fresh food for five fine fellows.
G Guy suggested getting eight guys to bring George's luggage.
H Hank hoped that she had withheld the cash they had to have.
I Iris insists their idea is simply idiotic in this instance.
J Jack and Jerry joined Joe just to enjoy a journey to Japan.

K Kathy asked Ken to take a blank checkbook back to her bank.
L Larry helped several little fellows learn to play baseball.
M Mr. Ammon made many mistakes in estimating minimum markets.
N Nan never knew when any businessman wanted an announcement.
O One or two of those older tool orders ought to go out soon.

P Please provide proper paper supplies for plenty of persons.
Q Quentin quietly inquired what sequences required questions.
R Run over for another order from the firm across the street.
S She says she sold us some shiny scissors sometime Saturday.
T Try to get the truth when they talk about better attitudes.

U Unless you pour out your mixture, you could hurt our stuff.
V Vivian raved over violets and even saved several varieties.
W William will work well whenever we know where we will work.
X X-rays exceed examinations except for external exploration.
Y Yes, any day they say you may be ready, you may try to fly.
Z Zenith Franz realizes that he idealized the zigzag friezes.

SECTION 1.7

New Keys: W Comma (,) G

GOALS:

- Demonstrate correct touch-system techniques for alphabetic keys.
- Learn the W, comma (,), G keys, and spacing with a comma.

A. WARMUP

Key each line 2 times.

1 fail not; jest mist chin Rev. card sake
2 Rick did not join; Val loves that fame.

NEW KEYS

B. W KEY

Key each line 2 times.
Repeat if time permits.

Use S finger. Anchor F.

3 sss sws sws wsw sws sss sws sws wsw sws
4 sws was was sws own own sws saw saw sws
5 sws white swans swim; sow winter wheat;
6 We watched some whales while we walked.

SKILLBUILDING

DIAGNOSTIC PRACTICE: ALPHABET

The Diagnostic Practice: Alphabet routine is designed to diagnose and then correct your keystroking errors. You may use this program at any time throughout the course after you complete Section 1.18.

DIRECTIONS:

1. Type one set of the Pretest/Posttest lines 1 time. Identify your errors.
2. Note your results—the number of errors you made on each key and your total number of errors. For example, if you typed *rht* for *the*, that would count as 1 error on the letter *t*.
3. For any letter on which you made 2 or more errors, select the corresponding drill lines, on p. SB2, and type them 2 times. If you made only 1 error, type the drill 1 time.
4. If you made no errors on the Pretest/Posttest lines, turn to the practice on Troublesome Pairs on page SB3 and type each line 1 time. This section provides intensive practice on those pairs of keys commonly confused.
5. Finally, retype the same set of Pretest/Posttest lines, and compare your performance with your Pretest.

PRETEST/POSTTEST

Set 1

```
Buzz quickly designed five new projects for the wax museum.
John's wacky quip amazed but also vexed his new girlfriend.
Zed quickly jumped five huge barrels to warn Max and Teddy.
Orville quickly objected to Wes dumping five toxic hazards.
From the tower Dave saw six big jet planes quickly zoom by.
Beverly, has John kept that liquid oxygen frozen with care?
```

Set 2

```
Did Robert move that psychology quiz to next week for John?
Stanley, cover this oozy liquid wax before Jack mops again.
The six heavy guys jumped for eighty waltzing quarterbacks.
Skip was quite vexed by the seventeen jazzmen from Cologne.
The eight taxi drivers quickly zip by the jumble of wagons.
While having Joel wait, Ben quickly fixed the many zippers.
```

Set 3

```
Last week Jed McVey was quite busy fixing the frozen pipes.
Vic quickly mixed frozen strawberries into the grape juice.
Five big jet planes zoomed quickly by the six steel towers.
Jeff amazed the audience by quickly giving six new reports.
Sixty equals only five dozen, but we promised Jackie eight.
Joel quietly picked sixteen razors from the blue woven bag.
```

C. , Key

Key each line 2 times.
Repeat if time permits.

Use K finger.
Anchor ;.
Space 1 time after a comma.

7 kkk k,k k,k ,k, k,k kkk k,k k,k ,k, k,k
8 k,k it, it, k,k or, or, k,k an, an, k,k
9 k,k if it is, two, or three, as soon as
10 Vic, his friend, lives in Rich, Alaska.

D. G Key

Key each line 2 times.
Repeat if time permits.

Use F finger.
Anchor A S D.

11 fff fgf fgf gfg fgf fff fgf fgf gfg fgf
12 fgf leg leg fgf egg egg fgf get get fgf
13 fgf give a dog, saw a log, sing a song,
14 Gen gets a large sagging gift of games.

The Function Keys

For Discussion—answer the following question. Refer to the Appendix for the answer.

Where are the Function keys located on the computer keyboard?

PROJECT 12

Apply

Create a Database

Your business has really grown. You now have several clients, and you want to organize the information you have gathered for each client.

Your Turn

1. Create a database table to maintain the following information:

Last Name	Phone	Pet Name	Pet Type	Notes
Karnowski	555-0181	Lucky	dog	
Jorgensen	555-9089	Pepper	cat	
Carmody	555-7866	Coco	dog	
Raez	555-3454	Duke	dog	keep on leash at all times
Miller	555-2421	Yoda	hamster	nocturnal
Sandell	555-0087	Shaggy and Scooby	parakeets	
Glomski	555-1334	Taffy	dog	
Hotchkiss	555-0755	Chloe	cat	
Butcher	555-4590	Ranger	dog	
Van Gilder	555-3391	Princess	cat	does not go outside

2. Save the database table as ***urs*Clients**.
3. Spell-check, proofread, and correct errors.
4. Sort the records in ascending order by client last name.
5. Add the following new record: Coretti, 555-9887, Haley, dog.
6. Sort the records again in ascending order by client last name.
7. Change Glomski's phone number to 555-4318.
8. If necessary, save the changes. Print and close the file.

SKILLBUILDING

E. ***Key each line 2 times. Repeat if time permits. Focus on the techniques at the left.***

Hold anchor keys. Keep elbows in.

```
15 sss sws sws wsw sws sss sws sws wsw sws
16 kkk k,k k,k ,k, k,k kkk k,k k,k ,k, k,k
17 fff fgf fgf gfg fgf fff fgf fgf gfg fgf
18 Wanda watched the team jog to the glen.
```

F. **COUNTING ERRORS**

Count 1 error for each word, even if it contains several errors. Count as an error:

1. A word with incorrect spacing after it.
2. A word with an incorrect character.
3. A word with incorrect punctuation after it.
4. Each mistake in following directions for spacing or indenting.
5. A word with a space.
6. An omitted word.
7. A repeated word.
8. Transposed (switched in order) words.

Compare these incorrect lines with the correct lines (19–21). Each error is highlighted in color.

```
 Frank sold sold Dave old an washing mshcone .
    Carl joked with Al ice, Fran,  Edith.
Wamda wore redsocks; Sadie wore green,
```

Key each line 2 times. Proofread carefully and note your errors.

```
19 Frank sold Dave an old washing machine.
20 Carl joked with Alice, Fran, and Edith.
21 Wanda wore red socks; Sadie wore green.
```

APPLY

Create a Presentation

Needs to Be Loved!

Insert clip art.

Contact
Turtle Creek Animal Shelter

2023 North Lake Shore Drive
Fontana, WI 53125
Telephone: 262-555-5050
www.AnimalShelter.org

2. Save the document as ***urs*Pet of the Week**.
3. Spell-check, proofread, and correct errors.
4. Format slide transitions.
5. Save the changes. Print and close the file.

G. PRETEST

Take a 1-minute timing on lines 22–23. Note your speed and errors. Keep your eyes on the copy.

```
22 sag, mow, crew elf, down well scow king      8
23 hag, jot, glow ink, tows west snow ring     16
   | 1 | 2 | 3 | 4 | 5 | 6 | 7 | 8
```

H. PRACTICE

Key each line 2 times. Repeat if time permits.

Focus on:
- ***Wrists up; do not rest palms on keyboard.***
- ***Fingers curved; move from home position only when necessary.***

```
24 sag, sag, wag, wag, rag, rag, hag, hag,
25 mow, mow, how, how, hot, hot, jot, jot,
26 crew crew grew grew grow grow glow glow
27 elf, elf, elk, elk, ilk, ilk, ink, ink,

28 down down gown gown town town tows tows
29 well well welt welt went went west west
30 scow scow stow stow show show snow snow
31 king king sing sing wing wing ring ring
```

I. POSTTEST

Repeat the Pretest. Compare your Posttest results with your Pretest results.

J. THE BACKSPACE KEY

Practice using the BACKSPACE key to correct errors.

1. Key the following line:
   `Wanda watched the team jog to the glen.`
2. Tap on the BACKSPACE key five times to remove the word `glen`.
3. Key the new word `deck`.

Create a Presentation

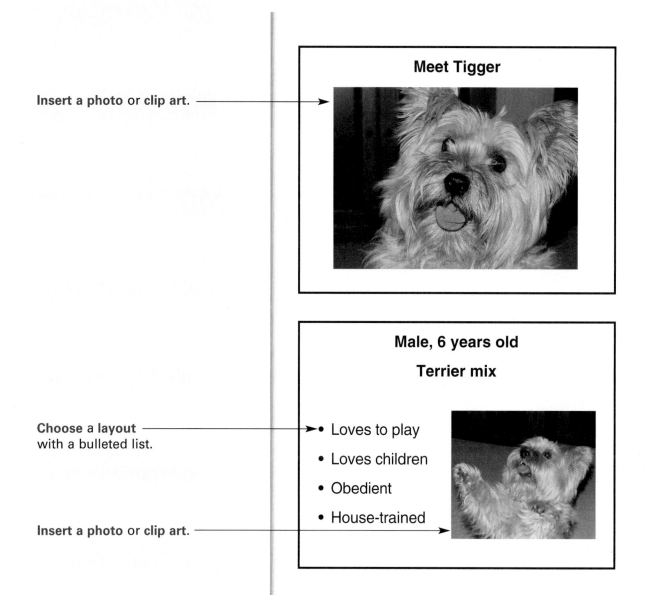

Meet Tigger

Insert a photo or clip art.

Male, 6 years old

Terrier mix

Choose a layout with a bulleted list.

- Loves to play
- Loves children
- Obedient
- House-trained

Insert a photo or clip art.

Continued on next page

SECTION 1.8 Review

GOALS:

- Demonstrate correct touch-system techniques and proper keyboarding skill.
- Improve speed and accuracy.
- Strengthen reaches to third, home, and bottom rows.

A. WARMUP

Key each line 2 times.

```
1 memo dock sink wave heed crag jolt jest
2 Tommi Ra has two free carnival tickets.
```

SKILLBUILDING

 RIGHT  KEY

Key each line 2 times. Repeat if time permits.

Anchor Right Shift with J. Keep your rhythm steady as you reach to the Shift key and back to home position.

```
3 Wade Dana Alda Sami Cata Devo Wane Glen
4 Vera Edie Fran Seth Adam Cara Rene Dave
5 Gene Vick Rick Coel Fran Dave Carl Sadi
6 Anna Wade Gino Sali Vida Theo Dean Eric
```

PROJECT 11

APPLY

Create a Presentation

You still volunteer at the animal shelter a few hours each week. Each week the shelter chooses one of the animals as the "Pet of the Week." You offer to create a slide show to promote this week's pet.

Your Turn

1. Create and format the slides shown below.

Key the title and the subtitle on the first slide.

Choose and **apply** a **design** to all slides.

Pet of the Week

Turtle Creek Animal Shelter

Continued on next page

C. CONCENTRATION

Fill in the missing letters shown at the left as you key each line 1 time.

```
O   7  S-me w-rk s- we make the w-rld cleaner.
E   8  W- hav- th-m saf-; V-ra l-ft to s-- it.
R   9  See, the -ive-s and st-eams a-e -ising.
H  10  A damaging c-emical mig-t -arm t-e men.
M  11  Their -o- -akes ja- and so-e sew ite-s.
I  12  W-ll-am -s -ll and w-ll l-ve -n Alaska.
```

D.

Key lines 13–16 two times. Remember to space 1 time after a comma. Focus on the technique at the left.

Right Shift Key. Keep your rhythm steady as you reach to the Shift key and back to home position.

```
13  Deloris sold red, tan, and orchid ties.
14  Dana had dogs, cats, and a tan hamster.
15  Todd ate mangoes, kiwis, and an orange.
16  Alicia worked on math, French, and law.
```

E. TECHNIQUE TIMINGS

Take two 30-second timings on each line. Focus on the techniques at the left.

Sit up straight and keep both feet flat on the floor.

```
17  Edie Victor saw the Alo Reed dress too.
18  Tom Salt and Arti Wiggs saw Sam and Di.
19  Rick saw Chris at three Eastmoor games.
20  Donna wrote to Anna, Ellen, and Rachel.
    |  1  |  2  |  3  |  4  |  5  |  6  |  7  |  8
```

PROJECT 10

APPLY

Create a Spreadsheet

You have been working for three months, and you kept notes about the money you earned. A spreadsheet will help you track your earnings.

Your Turn

1. Create a spreadsheet to track earnings, which are shown below.

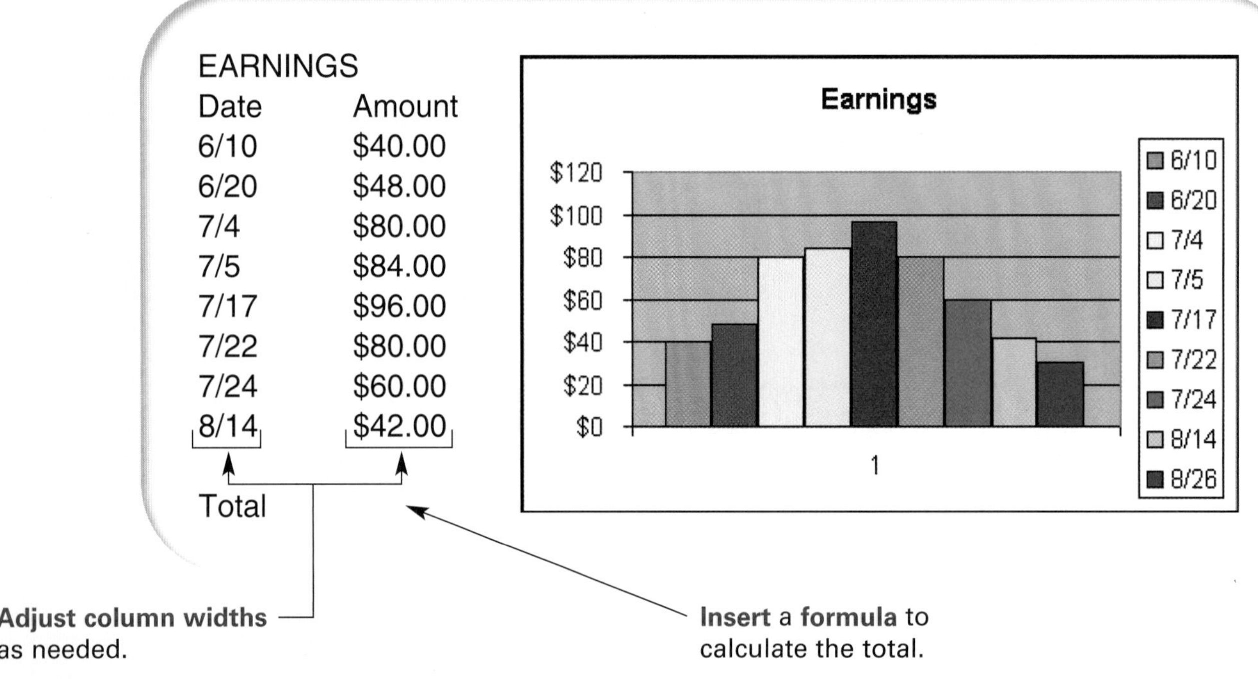

2. Save the spreadsheet as ***urs*Earnings**.
3. Edit the spreadsheet by adding a new entry dated 8/26 for $30.00.
4. Spell-check, proofread, and correct errors. Save the changes to the document.
5. Create a column bar chart to illustrate your summer's earnings.
6. Save the changes. Print and close the file.

F. 12-Second Sprints

Take three 12-second timings on each line. Try to increase your speed on each timing.

Each stroke in a 12-second timing is counted as 1 word. If you complete a line, your speed is 40 words per minute.

21 Al had one good mark and told me later.
22 We want to go west to work in the rain.
23 The snow fell one dark night last fall.
24 Watch the river flow over the dark dam.
| | | | 5 | | | | 10 | | | | 15 | | | | 20 | | | | 25 | | | | 30 | | | | 35 | | | | 40

G. Pretest

Take a 1-minute timing on lines 25–26. Note your speed and errors.

25 ring snow west tows ink, glow jot, hag, 8
26 king scow well down elf, crew mow, sag, 16
| 1 | 2 | 3 | 4 | 5 | 6 | 7 | 8

H. Practice

Key each line 2 times. Repeat if time permits.

Focus on:

- ***Wrists: do not rest palms on keyboard.***
- ***Fingers curved: move from the home position only when necessary.***

27 ring ring wing wing sing sing king king
28 snow snow show show stow stow scow scow
29 west west went went welt welt well well
30 tows tows town town gown gown down down

31 ink, ink, ilk, ilk, elk, elk, elf, elf,
32 glow glow grow grow grew grew crew crew
33 jot, jot, hot, hot, how, how, mow, mow,
34 hag, hag, rag, rag, wag, wag, sag, sag,

I. Posttest

Repeat the Pretest. Compare your Posttest results with your Pretest results.

PROJECT 9 Continued

Apply

Create a Web Page

5. Create a new Web page for your contact e-mail information.

Choose an appropriate layout and **apply a theme**.

Contact Information Page

A page displaying:

- Your contact information.
- A hyperlink to the home page.
- A hyperlink to the e-mail address.

Insert photos and/or **clip art**.

6. Save this page as ***urs*Contact Page**.
7. Open the home page, and create hyperlinks to the Fees Page and the Contact Page.
8. Spell-check, proofread, and correct errors.
9. Preview the Web pages, and test all hyperlinks. Make any necessary adjustments.
10. Save the changes. Print and close each file.

SECTION 1.9 New Keys: B U Left Shift

GOALS:

- Demonstrate correct touch-system techniques for alphabetic and command keys.
- Learn the B, U, and Left Shift keys.

A. WARMUP

Key each line 2 times.

1 dim logo wags jive foal corn them wags,
2 Wanda mailed the jewels that Carl made.

NEW KEYS

B.  KEY

Key each line 2 times.
Repeat if time permits.

Use F finger.
Anchor A and S.

3 fff fbf fbf bfb fbf fff fbf fbf bfb fbf
4 fbf rob rob fbf ebb ebb fbf bag bag fbf
5 fbf a bent bin, a back bend, a big bag,
6 That boat had been in a babbling brook.

PROJECT 9 Continued

APPLY

Create a Web Page

3. Create a new page to describe the fees.

Choose an appropriate layout and **apply a theme**.

Fees Page

A page displaying:

- A table with the fees you will charge per day.
- A hyperlink to the home page.

Insert photos and/or **clip art**.

4. Save the document as a Web page, ***urs*Fees Page**.

Continued on next page

C. U KEY

Key each line 2 times.
Repeat if time permits.

Use J finger.
Anchor ; L and K.

```
 7 jjj juj juj uju juj jjj juj juj uju juj
 8 juj jug jug juj urn urn juj flu flu juj
 9 juj jungle bugs, just a job, jumbo jets
10 Students show unusual business success.
```

D. LEFT SHIFT KEY

Key each line 2 times.
Repeat if time permits.

Use A finger.
Anchor F.

```
11 aaa Kaa Kaa aaa Jaa Jaa aaa Laa Laa aaa
12 aaa Kim Kim aaa Lee Lee aaa Joe Joe aaa
13 aaa Jan left; Nora ran; Uncle Lee fell;
14 Mari and Ula went to Kansas in October.
```

THE FUNCTION KEYS

For Discussion—answer the following question. Refer to the Appendix for the answer.

What is the purpose of the Function keys?

PROJECT 9 **APPLY**

Create a Web Page

Your business is growing. Your parents have offered to help you with transportation if you should get pet-sitting jobs outside of your neighborhood. A Web site would be another good way to promote your business.

Your Turn

1. Using the information provided in Projects 7 and 8, create a home page to display important information about the business.

Choose an appropriate layout and **apply a theme**.

Format a **horizontal border**.

Insert photos and/or **clip art**.

Home Page

A page displaying:

- Name of the business.
- Business slogan.
- List of services available.

2. Save the document as a Web page, ***urs*Home Page**.

Continued on next page

SKILLBUILDING

Technique Checkpoint

E. ***Key each line 2 times. Repeat if time permits. Focus on the technique at the left.***

Keep F or J anchored when shifting.

```
15 fff fbf fbf bfb fbf fff fbf fbf bfb fbf
16 jjj juj juj uju juj jjj juj juj uju juj
17 aaa Kaa Kaa aaa Jaa Jaa aaa Laa Laa aaa
18 Jo told Mike and Nel that she would go.
```

F. PRETEST

Take a 1-minute timing on lines 19–20. Note your speed and errors.

```
19 bran gist vast blot sun, bout just beef     8
20 craw just rest bran sum, dole hunk bear    16
   | 1  | 2  | 3  | 4  | 5  | 6  | 7  | 8
```

G. PRACTICE

Key each line 2 times. Repeat if time permits.

Place your feet:
- ***In front of the chair.***
- ***Flat on the floor.***
- ***Apart, with 6 or 7 inches between the ankles.***
- ***One foot a little ahead of the other.***

```
21 bran brad bred brew brow crow crew craw
22 gist list mist must gust dust rust just
23 vast vest jest lest best west nest rest
24 blot blob blow blew bled bred brad bran

25 sun, nun, run, bun, gun, gum, hum, sum,
26 bout boat boot blot bold boll doll dole
27 just dust dusk dunk bunk bulk hulk hunk
28 beef been bean bead beak beam beat bear
```

H. POSTTEST

Repeat the Pretest. Compare your Posttest results with your Pretest results.

PROJECT 8 APPLY

Create a Business Card

Several of your neighbors have expressed an interest in your pet-sitting services. In fact, you had your first job this week taking care of the neighbor's cat. You want to make it convenient for your neighbors to contact you when they need your help. You decide that a business card would be a good idea.

Your Turn

1. Use a template to create a business card. The business card should include information similar to that in the illustration.

Be creative and add borders and colors.

Home Alone Pet Care

While you're away,
I'll make sure your pets are okay.

Your Name
1719 Lakeview Drive
Fontana, WI 53125
Phone: 262-555-6978
E-mail: PetSitter@tyr.net

Insert clip art or **photo.**

2. Spell-check, proofread, and correct errors.
3. Save the document as ***urs*Home Alone Cards**. Print and close the file.

SECTION 1.10

New Keys: Q /

GOALS:

- Demonstrate correct touch-system techniques for alphabetic keys.
- Learn the Q and / (slash or diagonal) keys.

A. WARMUP

Key each line 2 times.

1 club face when silk mold brag java blue
2 Jana went biking, and Cila waved flags.

NEW KEYS

B.  KEY

Use the **A** finger to control the **Q** key.

Key each line 2 times. Repeat if time permits.

Use A finger. Anchor F.

3 aaa aqa aqa qaq aqa aaa aqa aqa qaq aqa
4 aqa quo quo aqa qui qui aqa que que aqa
5 aqa quail, quit quick quid, half quest,
6 The quints squabbled on a square quilt.

PROJECT 7 APPLY

Create a Flyer

You would like a summer job. You have decided to start a pet-sitting business. You decide to create a flyer that you can distribute in your neighborhood to promote your new pet-sitting business.

Your Turn

1. Design and create a flyer. The flyer should include information similar to that in the illustration.

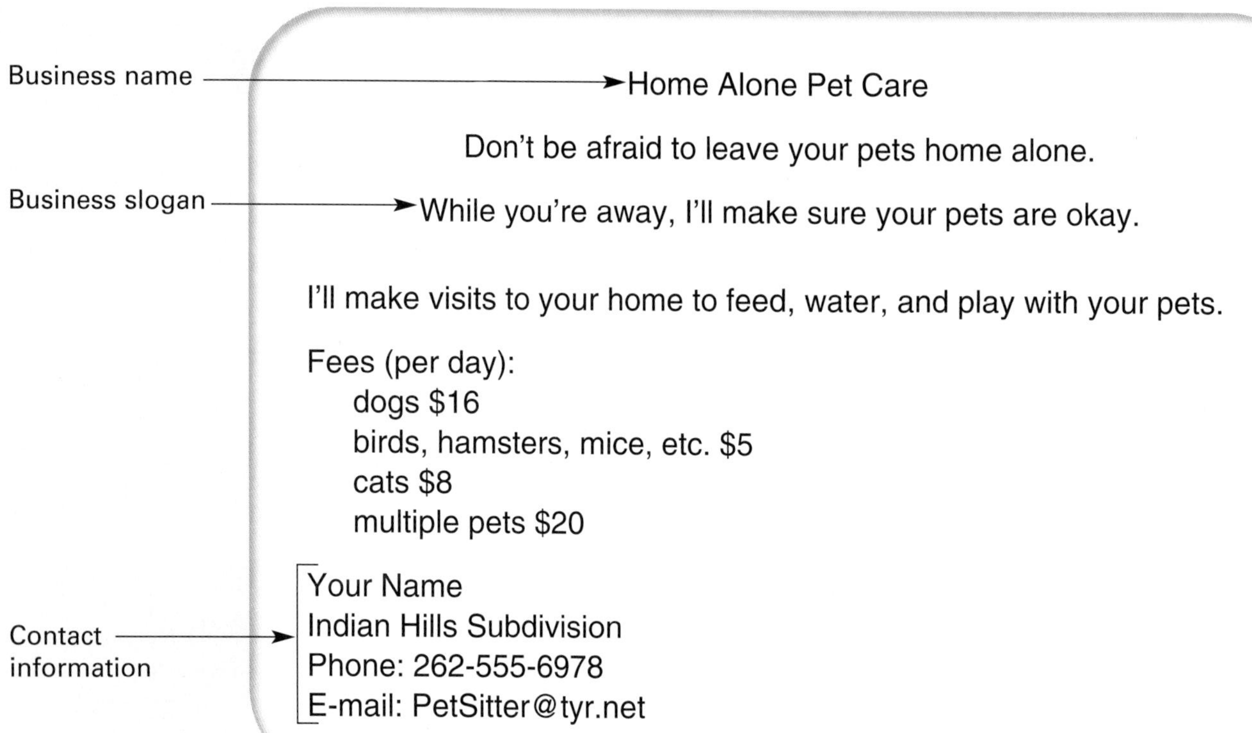

Business name
Home Alone Pet Care
Don't be afraid to leave your pets home alone.
Business slogan
While you're away, I'll make sure your pets are okay.
I'll make visits to your home to feed, water, and play with your pets.
Fees (per day):
dogs $16
birds, hamsters, mice, etc. $5
cats $8
multiple pets $20
Contact information
Your Name
Indian Hills Subdivision
Phone: 262-555-6978
E-mail: PetSitter@tyr.net

2. Spell-check, proofread, and correct errors.
3. Save the document as ***urs*Home Alone Flyer**. Print and close the file.

C. / KEY

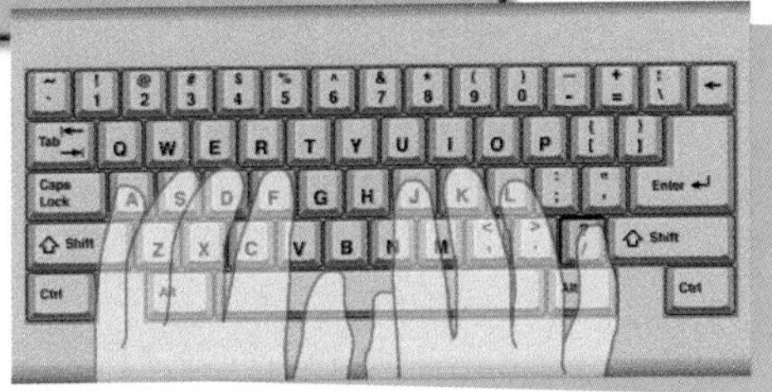

Key each line 2 times.
Repeat if time permits.

Use Sem finger. Anchor J. Do not space before or after a slash (diagonal).

```
7  ;;; ;/; ;/; /;/ ;/; ;;; ;/; ;/; /;/ ;/;
8  ;/; her/him ;/; us/them ;/; his/her ;/;
9  ;/; slow/fast, walk/ride, debit/credit,
10 The fall/winter catalog has new colors.
```

SKILLBUILDING

D.

Key each line 2 times. Repeat if time permits. Focus on the technique at the left.

Keep fingers curved and wrists level.

```
11 aaa aqa aqa qaq aqa aaa aqa aqa qaq aqa
12 ;;; ;/; ;/; /;/ ;/; ;;; ;/; ;/; /;/ ;/;
13 The quick squash squad requested quiet.
14 He/she said that we could do either/or.
```

E. TECHNIQUE TIMINGS

Take two 30-second timings on each line. Focus on the technique at the left.

Keep your eyes on the copy.

```
15 Louise will lead if she makes the team.
16 Their bands will march at the quadrant.
17 Brad just had time to finish his goals.
18 I was quiet as he glided over the wave.
   |  1  |  2  |  3  |  4  |  5  |  6  |  7  |  8
```

Create a Newsletter

Did you create a masthead at the top of the document?

Did you format a line between the columns?

Did you insert appropriate clip art or photos?

Did you format the two articles in two columns of equal width?

TURTLE CREEK ANIMAL SHELTER
2023 North Lake Shore Drive
Fontana, WI 53125
Telephone: 262-555-5050 *www.AnimalShelter.org*

VOLUNTEER OPPORTUNITIES

The success of Turtle Creek Animal Shelter relies on our volunteers to help manage the shelter and care for the animals. There are numerous areas where we need assistance in managing the shelter and caring for the animals.

Volunteer activities include the following:

- Adoption Day Volunteer
- Animal Foster Care Volunteer
- Fund-Raising Volunteer
- Grooming Volunteer
- Kennel Volunteer
- Lost and Found Volunteer
- Office Volunteer
- Pet Adoption Counselor
- Pet Pal Volunteer
- Special Events Volunteer
- Transportation Volunteer
- Volunteer Coordinator
- and much, much more!

You can schedule your volunteer hours at your convenience, and you determine how much time you want to contribute.

If you are interested in helping us, please contact Bonita at 555-4661 between 8 a.m. and 4 p.m., or e-mail us at AnimalShelter@tcas.org.

INTRODUCING THE NEW TEEN/JUNIOR PROGRAM

Teenagers have shown a great deal of interest in volunteering at TCAS. We recently established the Teen/Junior Program at TCAS to provide an opportunity for them to contribute. Students can choose from a variety of tasks, but they generally are most helpful socializing and playing with the animals. The animals really need this special attention, and it helps to prepare the animals for adoption.

Students can volunteer after school and on weekends. Before volunteering, teens must first attend an orientation. The orientation is offered each Saturday from 9 a.m. to 10 a.m. at the TACS office. Parents/guardians must sign a waiver for children under 18 years of age.

4. Save the changes. Print and close the file.

Hold those anchors.

F. PRETEST

Take a 1-minute timing on lines 19–20. Note your speed and errors.

```
19 find/seek boat fate jail cube brad swat    8
20 walk shut quid mile vane aqua slot quit   16
   | 1 | 2 | 3 | 4 | 5 | 6 | 7 | 8
```

G. PRACTICE

Key each line 2 times. Repeat if time permits.

To build skill:

- ***Key each line 2 times.***
- ***Speed up the second time you key the line.***

```
21 find/lose cats/dogs hike/bike walk/ride
22 seek/hide soft/hard mice/rats shut/ajar
23 boat goat moat mode rode rude ruin quid
24 fate face race rice nice Nile vile mile

25 jail fail fall gall mall male vale vane
26 cube Cuba tuba tube lube luau quad aqua
27 brad brat brag quag flag flat slat slot
28 swat swam swim slim slid slit suit quit
```

H. POSTTEST

Repeat the Pretest. Compare your Posttest results with your Pretest results.

I. THE BACKSPACE KEY

Practice using the Backspace key to correct errors.

1. Key the following line:
   `Brad just had time to finish his goals.`
2. Tap on the BACKSPACE key six times to remove the word `goals.`
3. Key the new word `walk.`

PROJECT 6 **APPLY**

Create a Newsletter

Format a one-page newsletter.

Your Turn

1. Open the file **12-1 Project 6**, and save the document as ***urs*Volunteer Newsletter**.
2. Format the document as indicated.

Create a masthead at the top of the document. Use the information provided in the inside address of the letter you created in Project 1 on page 433. The telephone number is 262-555-5050. The web site URL is www.AnimalShelter.org.

Format into two columns of equal width, with a line between columns.

Insert clip art or photos.

VOLUNTEER OPPORTUNITIES

The success of Turtle Creek Animal Shelter relies on our volunteers to help manage the shelter and care for the animals. There are numerous areas where we need assistance in managing the shelter and caring for the animals.

Volunteer activities include the following:

- Adoption Day Volunteer
- Animal Foster Care Volunteer
- Fund-Raising Volunteer
- Grooming Volunteer
- Kennel Volunteer
- Lost and Found Volunteer
- Office Volunteer
- Pet Adoption Counselor
- Pet Pal Volunteer
- Special Events Volunteer
- Transportation Volunteer
- Volunteer Coordinator
- and much, much more!

You can schedule your volunteer hours at your convenience, and you determine how much time you want to contribute.

If you are interested in helping us, please contact Bonita at 555-4661 between 8 a.m. and 4 p.m., or e-mail us at AnimalShelter@tcas.org.

3. Compare your document with the illustration on the next page.

Continued on next page

SECTION 1.11

New Keys: ' "

GOALS:

- Demonstrate correct touch-system techniques.
- Learn the apostrophe (') and the quotation mark (") keys.
- Improve speed and accuracy.

A. WARMUP

Key each line 2 times.

1 quill wagon cabin valued helms, and/or;
2 Jake is quite good in math but not Val.

NEW KEYS

B.   ' KEY

Key each line 2 times.
Repeat if time permits.

Use Sem finger.
Anchor J.
Do not space before or after an apostrophe within a word.

3 ;;; ;'; ;'; ';' ;'; ;;; ;'; ;'; ';' ;';
4 ;'; he's he's ;'; where's ;'; it's it's
5 ;'; ';' Kit's barn ;'; Ed's car ;'; ';'
6 Bill's car isn't running; it's at Li's.

PROJECT 5 APPLY

Create a Title Page

Include a title page for your report.

Your Turn

1. Open a new document.
2. Create an attractive title page for the report.

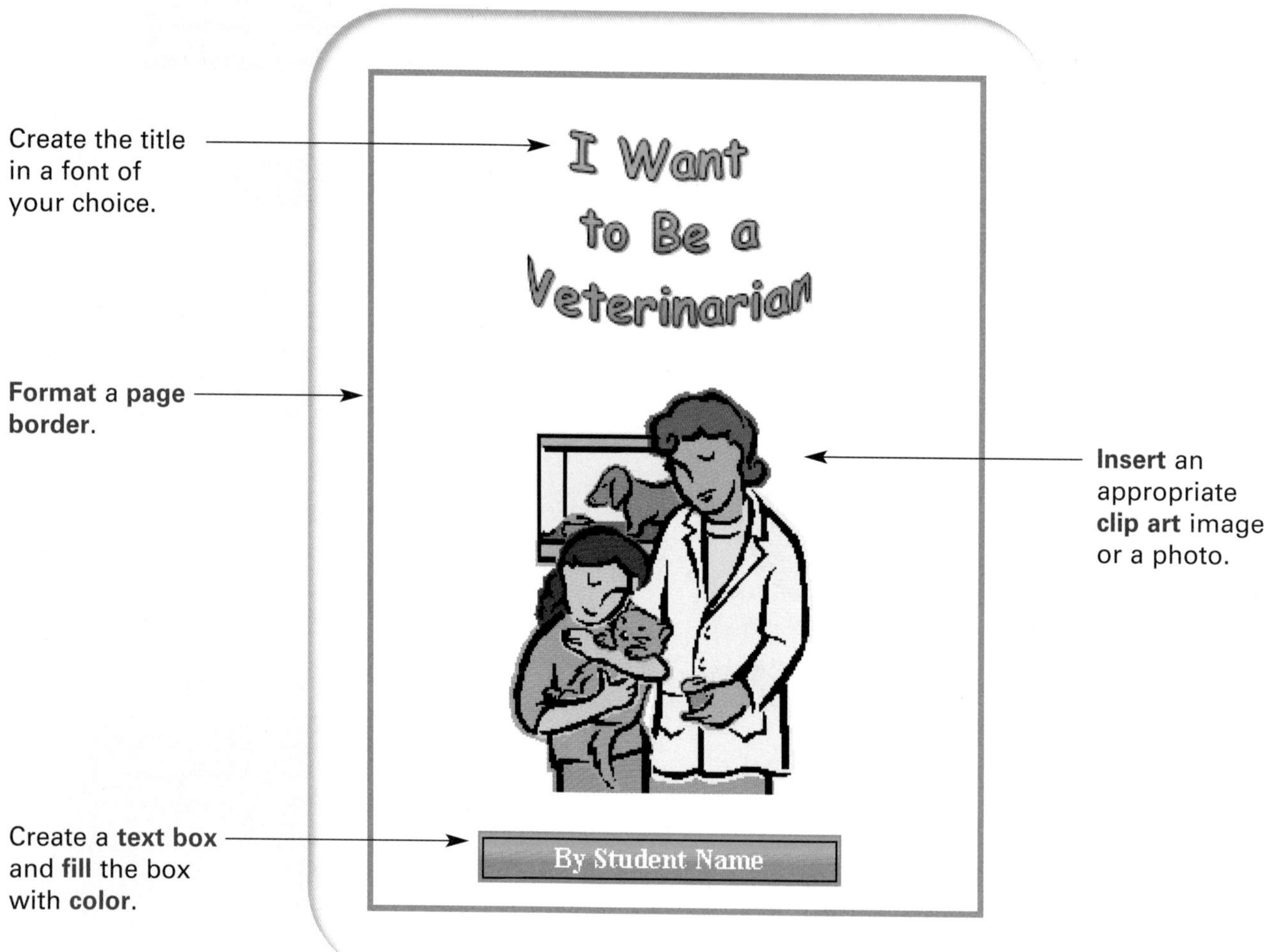

Create the title in a font of your choice.
I Want to Be a Veterinarian
Format a **page border**.
Insert an appropriate **clip art** image or a photo.
Create a **text box** and **fill** the box with **color**.
By Student Name

3. Save the document as ***urs*****Veterinarian Title Page**. Print and close the file.

C. " KEY

Key each line 2 times. Repeat if time permits.

SHIFT of apostrophe. Use Sem finger. Anchor J.

```
7  ;;; ;"; ;"; ";" ;"; ;;; ;"; ;"; ";" ;";
8  ;"; "win" "win" ;"; "big" "big" ;"; ";"
9  ;"; "mew" "oink" "woof" "moo" "baa" ";"
10 "Green" means "go"; "red" means "wait."
```

SKILLBUILDING

Technique Checkpoint

D. ***Key each line 2 times. Repeat if time permits. Focus on the technique at the left.***

Keep your eyes on the copy.

```
11 ;;; ;'; ;'; ';' ;'; ;;; ;'; ;'; ';' ;';
12 ;;; ;"; ;"; ";" ;"; ;;; ;"; ;"; ";" ;";
13 He said "no thanks," but it was "lame."
14 Rita "forgot," but Milo added "favors."
```

E. TECHNIQUE TIMINGS

Take two 30-second timings on each line. Focus on the technique at the left.

Keep your eyes on the copy.

```
15 Robb's clothes and image don't "match."
16 Mr. Quill said, "Wait." Lee did not go.
17 Jane's visit was "quick"; she ran back.
18 I haven't enough time to "quibble" now.
   | 1 | 2 | 3 | 4 | 5 | 6 | 7 | 8
```

PROJECT 4 Continued

APPLY

Create a Reference Page

7. Position the insertion point at the end of the document and insert a new page. Create a bibliography listing all the sources you cited within the report.

List all references here, using an appropriate report style.

BIBLIOGRAPHY

8. Spell-check, proofread, and correct errors.
9. Save the changes. Print and close the file.

F. 12-Second Sprints

Take three 12-second timings on each line. Try to increase your speed on each timing.

```
19 Go to the cabin and get us the dog now.
20 Now is the time to call all men for me.
21 She made a face when she lost the race.
22 Ask them if the vase is safe with them.
   | | | | 5 | | | | 10 | | | | 15 | | | | 20 | | | | 25 | | | | 30 | | | | 35 | | | | 40
```

G. Pretest

Take a 1-minute timing on lines 23–24. Note your speed and errors.

```
23 We can't "remember" how Bo got bruised.     8
24 Burt's dad "asked" Kurt to assist Ross.    16
   | 1 | 2 | 3 | 4 | 5 | 6 | 7 | 8
```

H. Practice

Key each line 2 times.

```
25 made fade face race lace lice nice mice
26 Burt Nora Will Mame Ross Kurt Olaf Elle
27 he's I've don't can't won't we've she's
28 Bo's dogs Lu's cows Mo's cats Di's rats

29 "mat" "bat" "west" "east" "gone" "tone"
30 He "quit"; she "tried." I hit a "wall."
31 sand/land vane/cane robe/lobe quit/suit
32 asks bask base vase case cast mast last
```

I. Posttest

Repeat the Pretest. Compare your Posttest results with your Pretest results.

PROJECT 4 Continued

APPLY

Format a Report

5. Also search the Internet for information about the job outlook for veterinarians. You can search for information on any of the following topics:
   - Number of veterinarians currently employed.
   - Average salaries for veterinarians.
   - Areas where veterinarians are needed.
   - Job responsibilities of veterinarians.
   - Advantages and disadvantages of a career in veterinary medicine.

   Complete the report by writing at least two paragraphs to summarize what you have learned about the job outlook for veterinarians. Be sure to cite your sources.

Since it takes a long time to prepare to be a veterinarian, I wanted to be sure there is a need for veterinarians. Here's what I learned.

Insert the new paragraphs of text here. Be sure to cite your sources, using a style of your choice.

6. Save the changes. Keep the file open for the next step.

Continued on next page

SECTION 1.12 Review

GOALS:

- Demonstrate proper keyboarding technique for alphabetic and command keys.
- Improve keyboarding skills.

A. WARMUP

Key each line 2 times.

```
1 java blue club face when brag silk mold
2 Geof went sailing, but Lin was at home.
```

SKILLBUILDING

 SHIFT KEYS 

Key each line 2 times. Repeat if time permits.

Keep your rhythm steady as you reach to the SHIFT keys. Anchor LEFT SHIFT with F. Anchor RIGHT SHIFT with J.

```
3 Seth Kebo Otis Fran Iris Edie Jose Dave
4 Hans Cara Nita Rene Uris Vera Mark Adam
5 Theo Jean Saul Hugh Eric Noel Vida Ivan
6 Gino Leah Burt Olla Anna Kris Wade Mike
```

Format a Report

Veterinarians can be very specialized in their work. For example, they can specialize in pet care or they can specialize in farm animals or exotic animals.

How to Become a Veterinarian

If you want to become a veterinarian, you must go to college. There are several colleges in the United States that will help you prepare to be a veterinarian. Each college has its own requirements, and so does each state. I researched the requirements in the state of XXXXXXX, and here is what I learned.

Indicate the state where you would choose to be a veterinarian.

3. Save the changes. Keep the document open for the next step.

4. Open your Web browser, and search the Internet for information about the educational requirements to become a veterinarian. Requirements will vary by state. Before you begin your search, choose a state where you would want to be a veterinarian. You can search for information about any of the following topics:
   - Universities that offer programs for veterinary careers.
   - Academic requirements for acceptance into veterinary programs.
   - Number of years required to complete a veterinary program.
   - Licensing for veterinary practice.
   - Areas of specialty.

   Then write at least two new paragraphs about what you have learned. Be sure to cite your sources.

Continued on next page

C. CONCENTRATION

Fill in the missing letters shown at the left as you key each line 1 time.

R	7	Ou- -ivers and oceans a-e being -uined.
EO	8	W- must w-rk t- mak- -ur w-rld cl-an-r.
H	9	-armful c-emicals fill muc- of t-e air.
ES	10	W- hav- lo-t u-ag- of -om- of our -oil.

D. ***Key each line 2 times. Repeat if time permits. Focus on the technique at the left.***

Sit up straight and keep your feet on the floor.

```
11 The cook went to work with cork boards.
12 Four foul jugs were left at the stream.
13 Toil in the weeds to get the seeds now.
14 Tell a joke, then gather other jesters.
```

E. TECHNIQUE TIMINGS

Take two 30-second timings on each line. Focus on the techniques at the left.

Keep your feet on the floor and sit up straight.

```
15 Ulan told Brian she would be glad to go.
16 In Boston one can see vast fish markets.
17 Bruce had this I/O switch changed again.
18 Treena saw quite a flock of "odd" birds.
   | 1 | 2 | 3 | 4 | 5 | 6 | 7 | 8
```

PROJECT 4 Continued

APPLY

Format a Report

For as long as
Since I can remember, I have always had a pet. When I was five years old I had a dwarf hamster named Bubbles. Then at When I was six years old I got had a turtle and some gold fish. When I turned eight we got a new puppy and I named him Rocky. Rocky is still my best friend. We also have two cats, tiger and Sam. I guess you could say our whole family loves animals.

Insert page numbers. → 1

When I was ten years old I was a member of the 4-H Club. For my state fair project I decided to raise a lamb. Before I selected my lamb, I had to learn a lot about the different breeds so I could make a good choice. I named my lamb Lolly. I fed her regularly and I kept the water trough clean. I wieghed Lolly every two weeks and kept a chart to monitor her growth. She weighed 110 pounds when we went to the fair. I groomed Lolly and showed her at the Fair. I was so excited when Lolly and and I won a blue ribbon. All my hard work paid off. I learned about the livestock industry and animal agriculture. I also learned to be responsible.

I talked with our veterinarian Dr. Durocher who owns her own animal clinic. Dr. Durocher said I would make a good veterinarian because I like animals and I like to take care of them. She said I need to study hard to be a veterinarian. She also said it would be a good idea if I volunteer at an animal shelter or a kennel. That way I can learn more about animal needs and how veterinarians help them.

Format all side headings **bold**. →

What a Veterinarian Does

Veterinarians protect the health and happiness of animals. They take care of sick and injured animals. Veterinarians help control animal diseases, and they advise owners on how to take care of their pets and livestock.

Continued on next page

F. PRETEST

Take a 1-minute timing on lines 19–20. Note your speed and errors.

```
19 Walter took a ride to the quiet street.        8
20 Quakes threw her around the trick door.       16
   | 1 | 2 | 3 | 4 | 5 | 6 | 7 | 8
```

G. PRACTICE

SPEED: If you made 2 or fewer errors on the Pretest, key lines 21–28 two times each.

ACCURACY: If you made more than 2 errors on the Pretest, key lines 21–24 as a group 2 times; then key lines 25–28 as a group 2 times.

Third Row Keys
Check hands:
- ***Curve fingers.***
- ***Hold home-key anchors.***

```
21 rook took cook cork work word ford fold
22 full fill file fire fore four foul fowl
23 jolt joke jets jerk jest just jugs jute
24 wire were went west jest quit quid quad

25 weed reed seed seat seal soil toil foil
26 dour sour sort tort tore wore sore lore
27 told hold sold sole hole role real teal
28 tire fire sire site suit quit whit with
```

H. POSTTEST

Repeat the Pretest. Compare your Posttest results with your Pretest results.

I. THE BACKSPACE KEY

Practice using the BACKSPACE key to correct errors.

1. Key the following line:
   `Bruce took a ride to the quiet street.`
2. Tap on the BACKSPACE key seven times to remove the word `street.`
3. Key the new word `stream.`

PROJECT 4 APPLY

Format a Report

You have started your report. You need to make some corrections and complete the report. Add information about educational requirements and job opportunities.

Your Turn

1. Open the file **12-1 Project 4**, and save the document as ***urs*Veterinarian**.

Change the left **margin** to 1.5 inches and the right margin to 1 inch.

2. Make the changes in the document as indicated below and on the next page.

Format all side headings **bold**.

I WANT TO BE A VETERINARIAN

Introduction

Have you ever wished you could play with a chimpanzee? Or, have you ever thought about what it would be like to touch a crocodile? Well, I have I love to be around animals. When I watch shows on television about exotic animals I wish I could be there, close to the animals, getting to know them, and learning all about them.

My Background

One of my most memorable experiences was ~~when I was~~ in second grade. A farmer ~~They~~ brought a llama named Charlie to our school. Charlie's face was fuzzy and he had big brown eyes. I got to pet Charlie. It was a really neat thing. When I touched Charlie's nose I felt him blow in my face. Charlie's owner said ~~that~~ it was a llama kiss. I also learned ~~that day~~ that llamas are remarkably intelligent ~~and~~ I knew then that some day I want ed to own a llama. ¶ I know it would be a lot of work to take care of a llama. But I still want to do it. I would like to learn about how to care for all kinds of animals. I want to do what I can to keep animals safe, healthy, and happy.

Continued on next page

SECTION 1.13 New Keys: P X

GOALS:

- Demonstrate correct touch-system techniques for alphabetic keys.
- Learn the P and X keys.

A. WARMUP

Key each line 2 times.

```
1 fade cave what swim quad blot king jars
2 Black liquids vanish from the jug I saw.
```

NEW KEYS

 B.  P KEY

Key each line 2 times.
Repeat if time permits.

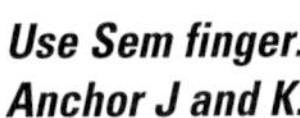
Use Sem finger. Anchor J and K.

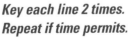

```
3 ;;; ;p; ;p; p;p ;p; ;;; ;p; ;p; p;p ;p;
4 ;p; nap nap ;p; pen pen ;p; ape ape ;p;
5 ;p; perfect plot, a pale page, pen pal,
6 Pam pulled a pouting pup past a puddle.
```

PROJECT 3 APPLY

Create an Outline

One of your class assignments is to research and write a report about becoming a veterinarian. Prepare an outline for the report.

Your Turn

1. Key the outline shown below.

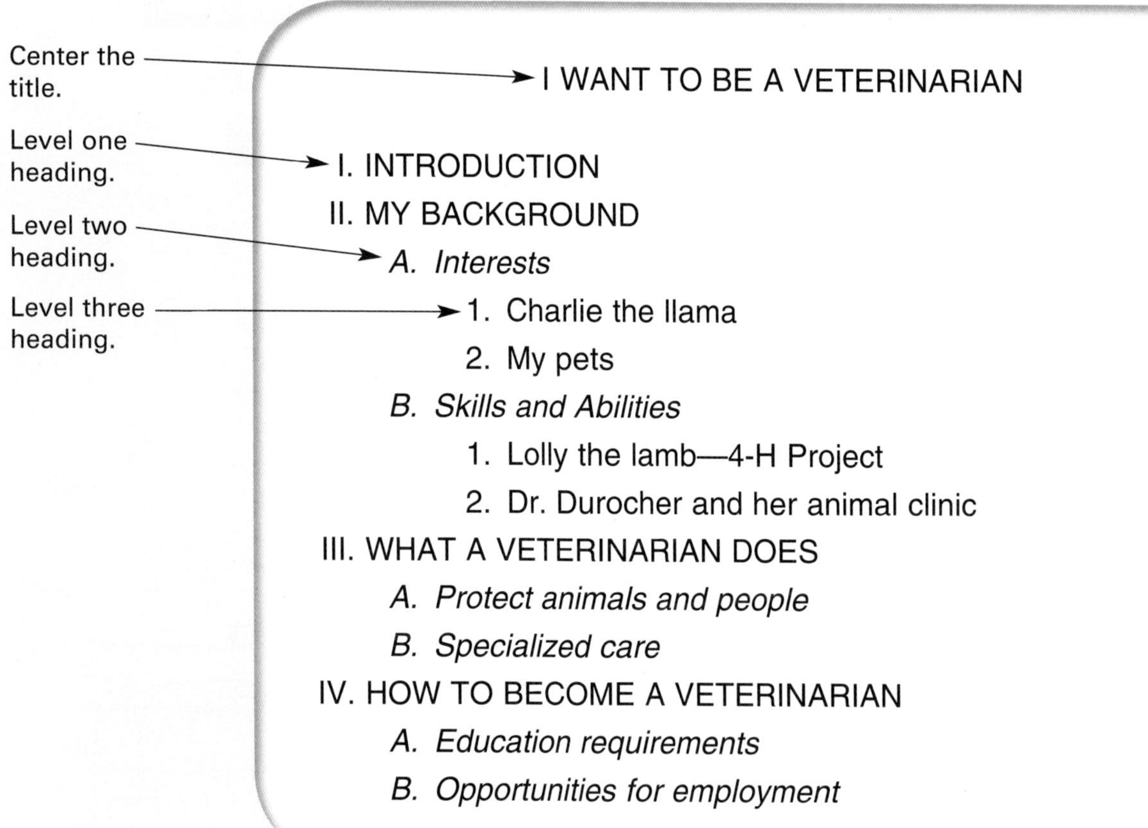

Center the title.
I WANT TO BE A VETERINARIAN
Level one heading.
I. INTRODUCTION
II. MY BACKGROUND
Level two heading.
A. Interests
Level three heading.
1. Charlie the llama
2. My pets
B. Skills and Abilities
1. Lolly the lamb—4-H Project
2. Dr. Durocher and her animal clinic
III. WHAT A VETERINARIAN DOES
A. Protect animals and people
B. Specialized care
IV. HOW TO BECOME A VETERINARIAN
A. Education requirements
B. Opportunities for employment

2. Apply the outline number feature and choose an appropriate outline style.
3. Spell-check, proofread, and correct errors.
4. Save the document as ***urs*Report Outline**. Print and close the file.

C. 

Key each line 2 times. Repeat if time permits.

Use S finger. Anchor A or F.

```
7  sss sxs sxs xsx sxs sss sxs sxs xsx sxs
8  sxs tax tax sxs mix mix sxs axe axe sxs
9  sxs lax taxes, vexed vixen, six Texans,
10 Fix the next six boxes on next weekend.
```

SKILLBUILDING

Technique Checkpoint

D. ***Key each line 2 times. Repeat if time permits. Focus on the techniques at the left.***

Remember to keep:
- ***Wrists up.***
- ***Fingers curved.***
- ***Feet flat on the floor.***

```
11 ;;; ;p; ;p; p;p ;p; ;;; ;p; ;p; p;p ;p;
12 sss sxs sxs xsx sxs sss sxs sxs xsx sxs
13 Phil will fix ripped carpets alone now.
14 Go see that duplex before next weekend.
```

E. **TECHNIQUE TIMINGS**

Take two 30-second timings on each line. Press ENTER at the end of each sentence. Focus on the technique at the left.

Keep your rhythm steady as you reach to the ENTER key and back to home position.

```
15 Pull on the tabs.↵ The box will open.↵
16 Speed is good.↵ Errors are not good.↵
17 Glue the picture.↵ The book is done.↵
18 Get the clothes.↵ Bring me their caps.↵
   |  1  |  2  |  3  |  4  |  5  |  6  |  7  |  8
```

PROJECT 2

APPLY

Create a Table

The Turtle Creek Animal Shelter welcomes your help. The office manager has asked you to create a list of all the dogs currently available for adoption from the shelter.

Your Turn

1. Create a table to organize the information shown below.

Center the table on the page **horizontally**.

Format the title and the column headings **bold** and **centered**.

Adjust the table to fit the contents.

Dogs for Adoption

Name	Date Arrived in Shelter	Description
Jack	April 11	5-year-old male; shepherd/lab mix; about 70 pounds; house-trained; good watchdog; great with kids.
Autumn	April 16	3-year-old female; golden retriever; about 75 pounds; house-trained; high energy; needs plenty of exercise.
Tigger	April 16	6-year-old male; terrier mix; about 20 pounds; sweet, friendly, and obedient; good with other dogs; loves to play.
Jasmine	April 18	9-year-old female; sheltie; about 25 pounds; gentle and calm; needs daily exercise and a quiet environment.
Max	April 20	3–4-year-old male; dalmatian mix; about 70 pounds; loves to play with other dogs and needs an area to run and play.
Billy Bob	April 21	5–6-year-old male; beagle; about 30 pounds; a very bright dog; house-trained, active, and good around kids.
Sophie	April 22	1–2-year-old female; collie; about 40 pounds; well-mannered; loves to run and play; short-to-medium hair and is a very pretty dog; gets along with dogs as well as cats.
Molly	April 23	1-year-old female; cocker spaniel mix; about 25 pounds; adorable and happy; playful and energetic; very bright and trainable.

2. Spell-check, proofread, and correct errors.
3. Save the document as ***urs*Dog Details**. Print and close the file.

F. PRETEST

Take a 1-minute timing on lines 19–20. Note your speed and errors.

```
19 slag chop gate plop tops bows veal dart    8
20 apex slab gave quit fix, hoax text jell   16
   | 1 | 2 | 3 | 4 | 5 | 6 | 7 | 8
```

G. PRACTICE

Key each line 2 times.

To key faster:
- ***Read copy before keying.***
- ***Key with smooth strokes.***

```
21 slag flag flap flax flux flex Alex apex
22 chop clop clap clan claw slaw slap slab
23 gate gale pale page pave have cave gave
24 plop flop flip slip ship whip quip quit

25 tops tips sips sits sit, six, mix, fix,
26 bows bowl jowl howl cowl coal coax hoax
27 veal real seal meal meat neat next text
28 dart part park bark balk ball bell jell
```

H. POSTTEST

Repeat the Pretest. Compare your Posttest results with your Pretest results.

I. THE BACKSPACE KEY

Practice using the BACKSPACE key to correct errors.

1. Key the following line:
   `Black liquids vanish from the jug I saw.`
2. Tap on the BACKSPACE key four times to remove the word `saw`.
3. Key the new word `opened`.

PROJECT 1 Continued

APPLY

Create a Personal Letter

I am available to help you on weekdays after school and on weekends. I would be willing to work up to six hours a week. I can start working next week.

Please call me at 555-6978 and let me know how I can help.

Sincerely,

Your Name

2. Spell-check, proofread, and correct errors.
3. Save the document as ***urs*Shelter Letter**. Print the letter.
4. Print an envelope for the letter. Close the file.

SECTION 1.14

New Keys: Y Tab

GOALS:

- Demonstrate correct touch-system techniques for alphabetic and command keys.
- Learn the Y and Tab keys.

A. WARMUP

Key each line 2 times.

```
1 jibe wing more vase deft lack hex; quid
2 Max just put a pale slab over the gate.
```

NEW KEYS

B. Y KEY

Key each line 2 times.
Repeat if time permits.

Use J finger. Anchor ; L K.

```
3 jjj jyj jyj yjy jyj jjj jyj jyj yjy jyj
4 jyj yes yes jyj joy joy jyj aye aye jyj
5 jyj yard of yarn, July joy, yellow yam,
6 Shelley yearns to yodel but only yells.
```

PROJECT 1 APPLY

Create a Personal Letter

After reading a newspaper article about animal shelters, you've decided to volunteer at an animal shelter in your community.

Your Turn

1. Create a personal letter in block style.

1719 Lakeview Drive
Fontana, WI 53125
March 21, 20--

Ms. Susan Yu, Director
Turtle Creek Animal Shelter
2023 North Lake Shore Drive
Fontana, WI 53125

Dear Ms. Yu:

I am interested in volunteering at your animal shelter. I love animals, and I have pets of my own, including a dog and a cat. I can help you feed, groom, and exercise the animals in your shelter.

Continued on next page

C. TAB KEY

The TAB key is used to indent paragraphs. The TAB key is located to the left of the Q key. Reach to the TAB key with the A finger. Keep your other fingers on home keys as you quickly press the TAB key.

Key each paragraph 2 times. Press ENTER only at the end of a paragraph. Repeat if time permits.

Word wrap automatically moves a word that does not fit on one line down to the next line.

```
     If you are happy, you will be able
to set goals. You will also smile more.
     The jury was out and no one could
leave the room. We all had to stay put.
```

SKILLBUILDING

D. ***Key each line 2 times. Focus on the technique at the left. Repeat if time permits.***

Keep your eyes on the copy.

```
jjj jyj jyj yjy jyj jjj jyj jyj yjy jyj
I saw yards of yellow fabric every day.
They happily played in the lonely yard.
Yes, the daily reports are ready today.
```

CARE AND OPERATION OF EQUIPMENT

For Discussion—answer the following question. Refer to the Appendix for the answer.

Demonstrate the proper way to insert and eject a disk from your computer.

SECTION 12.1 Capstone Projects

GOALS: Demonstrate the ability to:

- Format a personal letter, table, outline, report, newsletter, flyer, business card, Web page, spreadsheet, presentation, and database table.

WARMUP

Select Warmup from the Skillbuilding menu. Key each Warmup line 2 times.

Speed	1	You can stay in shape with a brisk walk three times a week.
Accuracy	2	Dr. Baxter was quick to analyze the four major food groups.
Numbers/Symbols	3	Donald and Darlene paid $5.08 for 4 pamphlets @ $1.27 each.
Language Link	4	We now have two kittens I adopted after they were deserted.

Making the Connection

In this unit, you will apply all the skills you have learned throughout this course. You will create each project as if you were running your own pet-sitting business.

The Pet Sitter projects simulate realistic tasks when one is volunteering at an animal shelter, completing a research report for a school assignment, and starting a pet-sitting business. As you complete these tasks, you will apply what you have learned and you will demonstrate use of your keyboarding and computer skills for personal use.

E. TECHNIQUE TIMINGS

Take two 30-second timings on each line. Focus on the technique at the left.

Keep your eyes on the copy as you take each timing.

15 Push your fingers to find the keys now.
16 You will see your typing speed improve.
17 Have a goal to type faster than before.
18 Try every day to achieve that new goal.
| 1 | 2 | 3 | 4 | 5 | 6 | 7 | 8

F. PRETEST

Take a 1-minute timing on lines 19–22. Note your speed and errors.

Remember: Press ENTER only at the end of the paragraph (line 22).

19   A jury will meet next January to 7
20 get a verdict. People stole costly fuel 15
21 from the boys. We found bags of cards 23
22 next to the mops in the broom closet. 30
| 1 | 2 | 3 | 4 | 5 | 6 | 7 | 8

G. PRACTICE

Key each line 2 times.

23 fuel duel duet suet suit quit quip quid
24 gape nape cape cave wave wage wags bags
25 mops pops maps hops tops toys joys boys
26 rope lope lops laps lips lids kids kiss

27 card cart curt hurt hurl furl fury jury
28 cost most lost lest best test text next
29 slab flab flap flaw flay slay clay play
30 pan, fan, tan, man, can, ran, Dan, Jan,

H. POSTTEST

Repeat the Pretest. Compare your Posttest results with your Pretest results.

Focus On

Good Keyboarding Habits

Focus on your knees.
To ensure proper position and posture at the keyboard:

- **Never cross your knees while at the computer.**
- **Knees should be bent at a 90-degree angle.**
- **Thighs should slope gently downward.**

SECTION 1.15 New Keys: Z Colon (:)

GOALS:

- Demonstrate correct touch-system techniques for alphabetic keys.
- Learn the Z and colon (:) keys.

A. WARMUP

Key each line 2 times.

1 bake chin jogs wave quip dome onyx left
2 His soft big lynx quickly jumped waves.

NEW KEYS

B.  Z KEY

Key each line 2 times.
Repeat if time permits.

Use A finger. Anchor F.

3 aaa aza aza zaz aza aaa aza aza zaz aza
4 aza zip zip aza zoo zoo aza zap zap aza
5 aza dozing zebu, he zags, dazed zebras,
6 Zachary ate frozen pizza in the gazebo.

UNIT 9

Capstone Projects

GOALS:

- Demonstrate the ability to create and format a letter and a table.
- Demonstrate the ability to format an outline, a report, a reference page, and a title page.
- Demonstrate the ability to create and format a newsletter, a flyer, and a business card.
- Demonstrate the ability to create a Web page.
- Demonstrate the ability to create a presentation.
- Demonstrate the ability to create a spreadsheet, a chart, and a database.

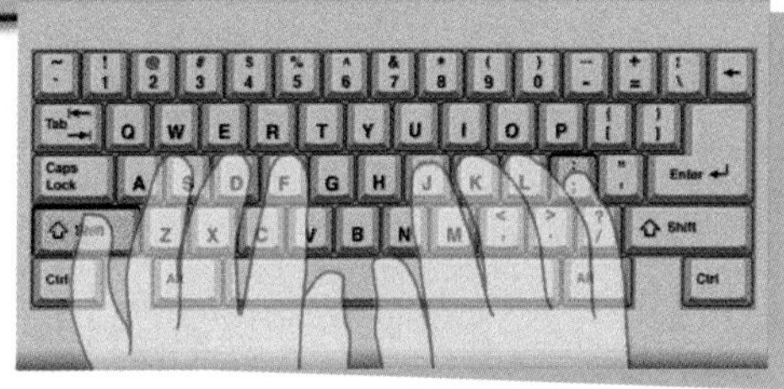

Key each line 2 times.
Repeat if time permits.

Shift of ;
Use LEFT SHIFT key.
Anchor J.
Space 1 time after a colon.

```
;:; ;:; ;:; :;: ;:; ;:; ;:; ;:; :;: ;:;
Dr. Webb: Mr. Que: Mrs. Downs: Ms. Lia:
Mr. Dode: Mrs. Chin: Ms. Finn: Dr. Mai:
To: From: Date: Subject: Attention: To:
```

CARE AND OPERATION OF EQUIPMENT

For Discussion—answer the following question. Refer to the Appendix for the answer.

Describe the proper care of a disk.

SKILLBUILDING

D. *Key each line 2 times. Repeat if time permits. Focus on the technique at the left.*

Keep your elbows close to your body.

```
aaa aza aza zaz aza aaa aza aza zaz aza
;:; ;:; ;:; :;: ;:; ;:; ;:; ;:; :;: ;:;
Zach and zany Hazel visited local zoos.
They saw: lazy zebras, apes, and lions.
```

COMPLETING UNIT 8 Continued

ENRICH

Curriculum Portfolio

LANGUAGE ARTS:

Create a music database table.

Create a database table of music CDs. Create columns for your favorite types of music, favorite titles, and favorite artists.

MATH:

Create a monetary exchange rate database.

Create a database of the exchange rates of ten countries. Include the name of the country, the monetary unit of the country, and the exchange rate for one U.S. dollar. Then sort the database alphabetically by the name of the country.

E. TECHNIQUE TIMINGS

Take two 30-second timings on each line. Focus on the technique at the left.

Keep your elbows close to your sides.

15 Type fast to reach the end of the line.
16 Keep your eyes on the copy as you type.
17 Tests are easy if you know the answers.
18 If they go to the zoo, invite them too.
| 1 | 2 | 3 | 4 | 5 | 6 | 7 | 8

F. PRETEST

Take a 1-minute timing on the paragraph. Note your speed and errors.

Remember to press ENTER only at the end of the paragraph.

19 As Inez roamed the ship, she told 7
20 fond tales. She slipped on that waxy 14
21 rung and fell to the deck. She hurt her 22
22 face and was dazed, but felt no pain. 30
| 1 | 2 | 3 | 4 | 5 | 6 | 7 | 8

G. PRACTICE

Key each line 2 times.

Check your posture.

23 waxy wavy wave save rave raze razz jazz
24 ship whip whop shop stop atop atoms At:
25 rung rang sang sing ring ping zing zinc
26 cure pure sure lure lyre byre bytes By:

27 tale kale Kate mate late lace face faze
28 fond pond bond binds bins inns Inez In:
29 gaze game fame same sale dale daze haze
30 roam loam loom zoom boom books took To:

H. POSTTEST

Repeat the Pretest. Compare your Posttest results with your Pretest results.

COMPLETING UNIT 8

ENRICH

Curriculum Portfolio

Use the database skills you have learned to create your curriculum portfolio project. Choose from one of the following topics.

SCIENCE:

Create a database table about planets.

Create a table listing each of the planets in our solar system, the average temperatures, and the distance from our Sun.

SOCIAL STUDIES:

Create a parks and recreation address database.

Create a database of recreation areas or parks in your community. Contact the parks or recreation department to find out the names, addresses, phone numbers, e-mail, and operating hours for these places. Then sort the database alphabetically by the park and recreation department name.

Continued on next page

SECTION 1.16 Review

GOALS:

- Demonstrate proper keyboarding skills and the ability to compose at the keyboard.
- Key 25/1′/2e (25 words per minute for 1 minute with 2 errors).

A. WARMUP

Key each line 2 times.

1 nest vote farm hail quid gaze coal waxy bake jeep
2 Gail must hold two jobs; she has had a hard life.
3 Kim, Ted has kept liquid oxygen frozen with care.

SKILLBUILDING

B. THIRD-ROW KEYS

Key each line 2 times. Repeat if time permits.

4 pest west test rest guest roast yeast toast totes
5 yarn yard ward word worry hurry query quirt quilt
6 Try to get an aqua shirt to wear for the picture.
7 We took your tire to the shop, but it was ruined.

Database Review

3. Alphabetize the database table as shown.

Sort the Last Name field in ascending order.

Review : Table

	First Name	Last Name	Age
	Jeff	Blessington	12
	Paraskevi	Brunson	11
	Sue	Cantor	11
	Suzann	Connell	13
	Patty	Cope	11
	Alexander	D'Anca	13
	Alissa	Hiraga	12
	Deanna	Johnson	12
	Mario	Leon	13
	Jordan	Miller	12
	Bethany	Schulenberg	11
	Tiffany	Smith	11
	Tashia	Stone	12
	Bill	Thill	11
	Rob	Wagman	13
▶	Amy	Spears	21

Add a new record for Amy Spears, age 21.

4. Change Amy Spears' age to 11. Delete the record for Jordan Miller.

5. Add a new record for the following classmate:

Pat Young, age 12.

6. Sort by the Last Name field again in ascending order. Create a query to filter all classmates who are age 11. Save the query as "Classmates Filter."

7. Save, print, and close the database.

C. PUNCTUATION SPACING

Space 1 time after a colon, a semicolon, a period at the end of a sentence, and a period used with initials and titles. Do not space after a period used within a.m. or p.m., geographic abbreviations, or academic degrees.

Key lines 8–12 one time. Note the spacing before and after each punctuation mark. Repeat if time permits.

```
8  Robb passed the test; he studied about two hours.
9  These courses are open: marketing, band, and art.
10 Karel wishes to type. Her cat is on the computer.
11 Dr. E. O. Anton was given the award in the U.S.A.
12 Gretchen received her B.S. and M.B.A. in the a.m.
```

D. TECHNIQUE TIMINGS

Take two 30-second timings on each line. Focus on the technique at the left.

Press ENTER at the end of each line and continue keying smoothly.

```
13 Ask Brenda about the summer sale. It's in Tucson.
14 Wil could buy socks there. The price was minimal.
15 Today, stationery is half off. Help me buy paper.
16 Even the books are reduced. We want to read more.
   | 1 | 2 | 3 | 4 | 5 | 6 | 7 | 8 | 9 | 10
```

CARE AND OPERATION OF EQUIPMENT

For Discussion—answer the following question. Refer to the Appendix for the answer.

Why should you protect your computer from computer viruses?

Database Review

You will apply the skills you have learned to create and edit a database table.

Your Turn

1. Open a blank database file and name the table *urs***Classmates**.
2. Key a database table, listing the first name, last name, and age of students in your class.

Name fields as shown.

Review : Table

First Name	Last Name	Age
Bill	Thill	11
Tashia	Stone	12
Suzann	Connell	13
Paraskevi	Brunson	11
Jordan	Miller	12
Bethany	Schulenberg	11
Alexander	D'Anca	13
Sue	Cantor	11
Alissa	Hiraga	12
Mario	Leon	13
Jeff	Blessington	12
Tiffany	Smith	11
Patty	Cope	11
Deanna	Johnson	12
Rob	Wagman	13
		0

List the first name, last name, and age of each student in your class.

Continued on next page

E. PRETEST

Take a 1-minute timing on the paragraph. Note your speed and errors.

17 My cousin, Vera, has been exercising for at 9
18 least seven weeks. I did my best to keep up with 19
19 her for at least one hour today, but it was much 29
20 too difficult. She is very strong and very quick. 39

| 1 | 2 | 3 | 4 | 5 | 6 | 7 | 8 | 9 | 10

F. PRACTICE

SPEED: If you made 2 or fewer errors on the Pretest, key lines 21–28 two times each.

ACCURACY: If you made more than 2 errors on the Pretest, key lines 21–24 as a group 2 times; then key lines 25–28 as a group 2 times.

Adjacent reaches are consecutive letters that are next to each other on the same row. **(weld)**

21 as base vases lasts haste taste fasts waste paste
22 po pole polar poems point poker polka spore spots
23 tr trade trips trace strut treat trend stray tray
24 re read real ream reel reeds breeds freed decreed

Jump reaches are consecutive letters on the top and bottom rows keyed with one hand. **(exam)**

25 br bran brush brute broth bring break bread brain
26 mu must munch murky mushy musty music mumps mulch
27 ze amaze gauze dozen prize blaze craze glaze size
28 cr crate crater create crack crab crib crow croak

G. POSTTEST

Repeat the Pretest. Compare your Posttest results with your Pretest results.

TOUCH-SYSTEM TECHNIQUES

Keep wrists straight and level while holding your mouse. Use your right index finger (if you are right handed) to left-click the mouse.

See Appendix for more on proper mousing.

PROJECT 4 **Reinforce**

Create a Table

In this project, you will sort the Presidents table, and then filter out any president with a first name other than George.

Your Turn

1. Open the database *urs***Presidents**.
2. **Create a new query**, using the Presidents table, **sorting the table** by "First Name" ascending and then by "Last Name" ascending.
3. Save the query as "President Sort" and close design view.
4. Run the query and print the results.
5. **Create a new query**, using the Presidents table, **filtering** the table by "First Name," and setting the criteria to "George."
6. Save the query as "President Filter" and close design view.
7. **Run the query** and print the results.
8. Save and close your database.

H. 1-MINUTE TIMINGS

Take two 1-minute timings on the paragraph. Note your speed and errors.

Goal: 25/1'/2e

```
     It is good that you have learned all of the       9
alphabet keys. With just some extra practice, you     19
will zip through work quickly.                        25
| 1 | 2 | 3 | 4 | 5 | 6 | 7 | 8 | 9 | 10   SI 1.22
```

I. COMPOSING AT THE KEYBOARD

Composing at the keyboard enables you to create documents without having to write them by hand. As you compose at the keyboard, key at a comfortable pace. Do not look at your hands, and do not worry about errors. Record your thoughts.

Answer each question with a single word. Press ENTER at the end of each answer.

Keep your eyes on the screen as you key; do not worry about errors.

Do you have a best friend?

What is your favorite sport?

Do you have a pet?

Have you ever ridden a horse?

What is your favorite color?

PROJECT 3 Continued

Practice

Database Queries—Filter Queries

5. In the Criteria box underneath the Last Name field, type "Smith." In the Criteria box underneath State, type "NV." This tells the query to show records only where a person has a last name of Smith and lives in Nevada.

Field:	First Name	Last Name	City	State	E-Mai
Table:	Friends	Friends	Friends	Friends	Frien
Sort:					
Show:	☑	☑	☑	☑	
Criteria:		"Smith"		"NV"	
or:					

6. Close the query window.
7. **Run the query.**
8. Examine your results to ensure that the only information listed is people with the last name of "Smith" who live in "NV."
9. Close the query window and the database, saving changes.

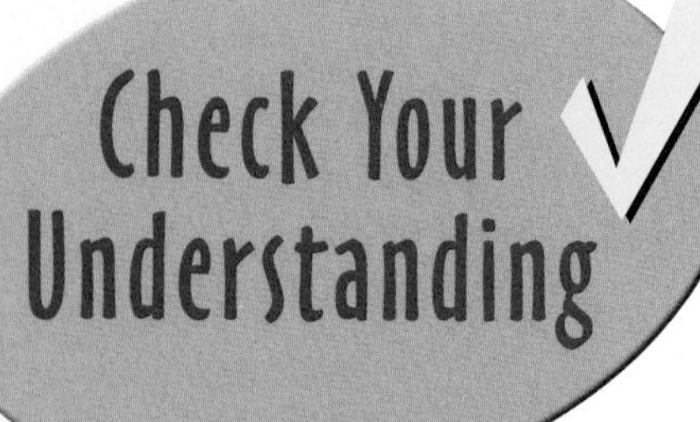

1. Open a word processing document and save as *urs*Sorting Basics.
2. Explain the difference between a simple sort and a multiple sort.
3. Explain the difference between a filter and a query.
4. Save the document. Print and close the file.

SECTION 1.17 New Keys: ? Caps Lock

GOALS:

- Learn the ? key.
- Use the Caps Lock key for all-capital letters.
- Demonstrate the ability to compose at the keyboard.

A. WARMUP

Key each line 2 times.

Hold those anchors.

1 herbs jinx gawk miff vest zinc ploy quad best zoo
2 Dozy oryx have quit jumping over the huge flocks.
3 Lax folks quickly judged the lazy dogs unfit now.

NEW KEYS

B. ? KEY

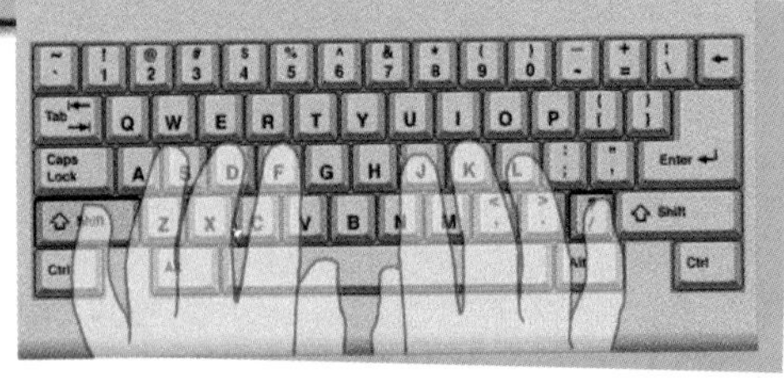

Key each line 2 times. Repeat if time permits.

Shift of /. Use Sem finger and Left Shift key. Anchor J. Space 1 time after a question mark.

4 ;;; ;/; ;/? ;?; ;?; ;;; ;/; ;/? ;?; ;?; ;;; ;/ ;?
5 ;/; ;?; now? now? ;?; how? how? ;?; who? who? ;?;
6 Who? What? Why? Where? When? Next? How many? Now?
7 How can Joe get there? Which way are the outlets?

PROJECT 3 **Practice**

Database Queries—Filter Queries

If you were searching a database for a specific set of criteria, there are faster ways to locate data than using multiple sorts. If you needed to locate all the people who live in Nevada who had a last name of "Smith," you could create a multiple sort by state and last name, then find the state section for "NV" and search down until you located the area that had last names of "Smith." A faster way of doing this is to ask our database to do the searching for us and display people *only* with a last name of "Smith" who live in "NV." Doing this creates a query known as a **Filter**. Here, we are going to filter our data to find all the Smiths who live in NV.

Your Turn

1. **Create a new query** by using the query wizard.
2. Select table Friends to be used in the query.
3. Select the fields to be used in the query. For this project, we will select all of the queries to be used.
4. Save the query as "Smith Filter" and choose the option to modify the query design after saving.

Continued on next page

C. CAPS LOCK KEY

Use the CAPS LOCK key to key letters or words in all-capital letters (all caps). You must press the SHIFT key to key symbols appearing on the top half of the number keys.

Key each line 2 times. Repeat if time permits.

Use A finger.

```
 8 A COMPUTER rapidly scanned most AIRMAIL packages.
 9 Another START/STOP safety lever was stuck lately.
10 Was JOSE elected CLASS PRESIDENT today or sooner?
11 You should not answer my door WHEN YOU ARE ALONE.
```

SKILLBUILDING

D.

Key each line 2 times. Repeat if time permits.

Quickly return fingers to home keys after reaching to other keys.

```
12 ;;; ;/; ;/? ;?; ;?; ;;; ;/; ;/? ;?; ;?; ;;; ;/ ;?
13 Did you see HELEN? Did you learn about her crash?
14 Her auto was hit by a TRAIN. She broke BOTH arms.
15 HOW will she manage while both arms are in casts?
```

E. TECHNIQUE TIMINGS

Take two 30-second timings on each line. Focus on the techniques at the left.

Hold those anchors. Quickly return your fingers to home-key position.

```
16 Tony was a better friend than Hope was to Salena.
17 Lu and I were at Camp Piney Forest in early fall.
18 I rode the Rocky Ford train to San Juan in March.
19 Maya, Sue, and Grace were there. It was exciting.
   | 1 | 2 | 3 | 4 | 5 | 6 | 7 | 8 | 9 | 10
```

PROJECT 2 **Practice**

Database Queries—Multiple Sorts

Congratulations! You have now created a Simple Sort. Now, let's try to do something a little more complicated. We are now going to sort our friends by the states in which they live, and then sort them by last name.

Your Turn

1. **Create a new query** by using the query wizard.
2. Select table Friends to be used in the query.
3. Select the fields to be used in the query. Once again, we will be using all of our fields, but we must be careful of the order in which we select them when constructing a multiple sort. Most database programs read from left to right, top to bottom. Sorting criteria is defined left to right, top to bottom. Select the state field first, then the last name field, then add the remaining fields using the ">>" button.
4. Save the query as "Friends Multiple Sort" and choose the option to modify the query design after saving.

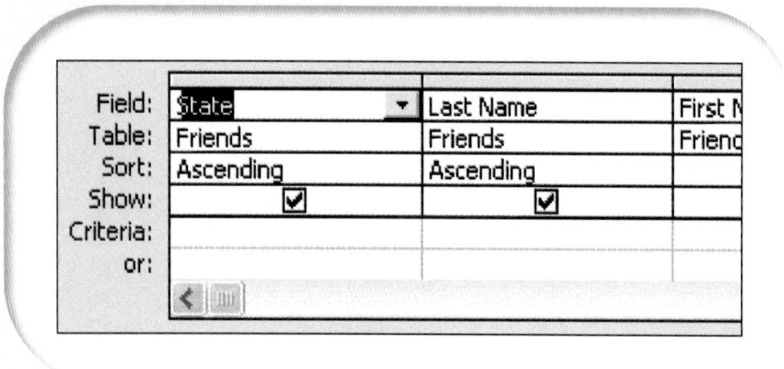

Field:	State	Last Name	First N
Table:	Friends	Friends	Frienc
Sort:	Ascending	Ascending	
Show:	☑	☑	
Criteria:			
or:			

5. **Sort the data** contained within the State and Last Name fields in ascending order. These fields should resemble the diagram at the left.
6. Close the query window.
7. **Run the query.**
8. Examine your results to ensure that your list is sorted alphabetically by state, and then by last name. If you do not have more than one person in a state, it will appear to be sorted only by state. If everyone on your list is from the same state, it will appear to be sorted only by last name.
9. Close the query window, leaving the database open.

F. PRETEST

Take a 1-minute timing on the paragraph. Note your speed and errors.

```
     The blind slats are broken. Can you fix the      9
broken ones? My WILY dog jumped out of the window    19
which is how this happened. There should be some     29
way to stop him. For a young dog, he is AMAZING.     39
| 1 | 2 | 3 | 4 | 5 | 6 | 7 | 8 | 9 | 10
```

G. PRACTICE

Key each line 2 times.

```
slat slit skit suit quit quid quip quiz whiz fizz
LASS bass BASE bake CAKE cage PAGE sage SAGA sags
maze mare more move wove cove core cure pure pore
mix; fix; fin; kin; kind wind wild wily will well

cape cane vane sane same sale pale pals pats bats
jump pump bump lump limp limb lamb jamb jams hams
slow BLOW blot SLOT plot PLOP flop FLIP blip BLOB
mite more wire tire hire hide hive jive give five
```

H. POSTTEST

Repeat the Pretest. Compare your Posttest results with your Pretest results.

I. COMPOSING AT THE KEYBOARD

Answer each question with a single word. Press ENTER at the end of each answer.

Keep your eyes on the screen as you key.

What day of the week is today?
What is your favorite animal?
What is your favorite food?
What is your favorite ice cream flavor?
What month is your birthday?

PROJECT 1 Continued

Practice

Database Queries—Simple and Multiple Sorts

Field:	First Name	Last Name	City	State	Birthday	E-M
Table:	Friends	Friends	Friends	Friends	Friends	Frie
Sort:						
Show:	☑	☑	☑	☑	☑	
Criteria:						
or:						

You should now be able to view information about the query. The tables (complete with a listing of the fields contained within) should be displayed as well as the fields you specifically have selected for use in the sort. In addition, you should be able to modify the field name, table from which the field is selected, sorting criteria—whether or not the field is shown, and criteria for the fields.

6. **Sort the data** contained within the Last Name field in ascending order by selecting Ascending in the sort box underneath Last Name. When sorting alphanumeric data, ascending means A–Z, 0–9. Descending means Z–A, 9–0.
7. Close the query window.
8. **Run the query.**
9. Examine your results to ensure that your list is in fact sorted alphabetically by last name.
10. Close the query window, leaving the database open.

SECTION 1.18

New Keys: - _

GOALS:

- Demonstrate correct touch-system techniques.
- Learn the hyphen (-) and underscore (_) keys.
- Key 25/1'/2e.

A. WARMUP

Key each line 2 times.

1 rave jinx tact safe mind glib quit yelp hawk doze
2 We all must be good friends to have good friends.
3 We have quickly gained sixty prizes for best jam.

NEW KEYS

B.   - KEY

Key each line 2 times.
Repeat if time permits.

Use Sem finger. Anchor J. Do not space before or after hyphens.

4 ;;; ;p; ;p-; ;-; -;- ;;; ;p; ;p-; ;-; -;- ;;; ;-;
5 ;p- ;-; self-made ;-; one-third ;p- one-sixth ;-;
6 ;p- ;-; part-time ;-; one-tenth ;p- two-party ;-;
7 Self-made Jim stopped at an out-of-the-way place.

PROJECT 1 Practice

Database Queries—Simple and Multiple Sorts

For a search in a random database of several hundred (or as is often the case, several hundred thousand) people, finding a specific person or group of people manually would be very difficult. To help us read and reference our Friends database more easily, we are going to sort our friends alphabetically by last name.

Your Turn

1. Open the database *urs***Friends** created in Section 11.1 and open the Friends table.
2. **Create a new query** by using the query wizard.
3. Select the Friends table as the table/query to be used.
4. Select the fields to be used in the query. To select fields, choose the field to be used in the query and click the ">" button. For this project, select all fields to be used in the query.
5. Save the query as "Friends Simple Sort" and choose the option to modify the query design after saving.

Continued on next page

C. 

Key each line 2 times. Repeat if time permits.

Use Sem finger and the LEFT SHIFT key. Anchor J.

```
8  ;p; ;p- ;-; ;-_; ;-_; ;p-_ _;_ ;p-_ ;-_; ;_; ;p-_
9  ;;; ;p; ;p_; ;_; _;_ ;;; ;p; ;p_; ;_; _;_ ;;; ;_;
10 Quick, create this seven-character line: _______.
11 Be sure to use her e-mail name, jennifer_cochran.
```

SKILLBUILDING

D. ***Key each line 2 times. Repeat if time permits. Focus on the techniques at the left.***

Keep your feet on the floor, back straight, elbows in.

```
12 ;;; ;p; ;p-; ;-; -;- ;;; ;p; ;p-; ;-; -;- ;;; ;-;
13 ;;; ;p; ;p_; ;_; _;_ ;;; ;p; ;p_; ;_; _;_ ;;; ;_;
14 Are you an easy-going person who gets along well?
15 The new name he now uses for e-mail is jute_rope.
```

E. **TECHNIQUE TIMINGS**

Take two 30-second timings on each line. Focus on the techniques at the left.

Sit up straight, keep your elbows in, and keep your feet flat on the floor.

```
16 Steward and Phon drove a car down to the shelter.
17 Ten people helped serve meals to thirty children.
18 They said it was hard work. Jung felt happy then.
19 This might help solve these problems in our city.
   | 1 | 2 | 3 | 4 | 5 | 6 | 7 | 8 | 9 | 10
```

Sorts and Queries

GOALS: Demonstrate the ability to:

- Create a simple query.
- Use queries to do simple sorts.
- Use queries to do multiple sorts.
- Use queries to filter data sets.

WARMUP

Select Warmup from the Skillbuilding menu. Key each Warmup line 2 times.

Speed	1	It was a good idea to start to write your report this week.
Accuracy	2	My ax just zipped through the fine black wood quite evenly.
Numbers/Symbols	3	What a sight! Good luck! Watch out! At last! No way! Never!
Language Link	4	The accident was distressing; however, no one was impaired.

Making the Connection

So far, you've entered data into something that feels a lot like a spreadsheet. What is it then that makes databases so special? In addition to storing vast amounts of data, databases have the ability to search this information and display a desired result. To do this, we construct what is known as a **query**. Queries are questions we ask our database.

In addition to queries, we can display the information a database contains in many different ways. For instance, we can print our list of friends alphabetically, by state, or alphabetically by state. When we sort based on a single criteria (alphabetically OR by state), we call this a **Simple Sort**. When we sort based on a number of criteria (alphabetically AND by state), we call this a **Multiple Sort**.

F. PRETEST

Take a 1-minute timing on the paragraph. Note your speed and errors.

```
20      Look up in the western sky and see how it is     9
21 filled with magnificent pinks and reds as the sun    19
22 begins to set. As the sun sinks below the clouds,    29
23 you will see an amazing display of great colors.     39
   | 1 | 2 | 3 | 4 | 5 | 6 | 7 | 8 | 9 | 10
```

G. PRACTICE

SPEED: If you made 2 or fewer errors on the Pretest, key lines 24–31 two times each.

ACCURACY: If you made more than 2 errors on the Pretest, key lines 24–27 as a group 2 times. Then, key lines 28–31 as a group 2 times.

***Left and right reaches are a sequence of at least three letters keyed by fingers on either the left or the right hand.* (lease, think)**

```
24 was raged wheat serve force carts bears cages age
25 tag exact vases rests crank enter greet moves ear
26 was raged wheat serve force carts bears cages age
27 tag exact vases rests crank enter greet moves ear

28 get table stage hired diets gears wages warts rat
29 hop mouth union input polka alone moors tunic joy
30 him looms pumps nouns joked pound allow pours hip
31 lip mopes loose equip moods unite fills alike mop
```

H. POSTTEST

Repeat the Pretest. Compare your Posttest results with your Pretest results.

I. 1-MINUTE TIMINGS

Take two 1-minute timings on the paragraph. Note your speed and errors.

Goal: 25/1′/2e

```
32      We saw where gray lava flowed down a path.       9
33 At the exit, Justin saw trees with no bark and a     19
34 quiet, fuzzy duck looking at me.                     25
   | 1 | 2 | 3 | 4 | 5 | 6 | 7 | 8 | 9 | 10   SI 1.23
```

PROJECT 3 Reinforce

Create and Edit Database Tables

Create a table about some of the presidents of the United States.

Field Name	Data Type
First Name	Text
Last Name	Text
Start	Text
End	Text

Your Turn

1. **Open a new database.** Name the database *urs*Presidents.
2. **Create a table** and name the fields as shown.
3. Enter the following data into the table.

Resize the columns so the data can be easily seen.

First Name	Last Name	Start	End
James	Polk	1845	1849
Theodore	Roosevelt	1901	1909
George	Bush	1989	1993
John	Adams	1797	1801
George	Washington	1789	1797
Woodrow	Wilson	1913	1921

4. Change the last name of George Bush to Bush, Sr.
5. **Add new records** for the following presidents:

   Abraham Lincoln – 1861-1865; John Kennedy – 1961-1963
6. **Delete** the **record** about James Polk.
7. **Add a new field** after "End" and name it # President. Research the # Presidency for each person. For example, George Washington was the 1st.
8. Print the table. Save and close the database table.

SECTION 1.19 Skillbuilding

GOALS:

- Demonstrate proper keyboarding skills.
- Use correct spacing before and after punctuation.

A. WARMUP

Key each line 2 times.

Words	1 fuzz busy flat apex gash avow junk quad czar mink
Speed	2 A good first impression must be made immediately.
Accuracy	3 Rob moved a psychology quiz to next week for Jay.

SKILLBUILDING

B. SPACE BAR

Key each line 2 times. Repeat if time permits.

Space between words without pausing.

4 up by rod hub cue dry mow zip elk jaw van era ark
5 do we fad wet tab boy hid lug mug zap box kid fog
6 in my car zoo tag pop vat jar lid yam fix war qua
7 so to add fun joy run sew lad man did nip was hop

PROJECT 2 Practice

Editing a Database

One of your friends has a new e-mail address and phone number. As information changes, you need to be able to delete old records and add new ones to a database.

Your Turn

1. Use the illustration to edit the database table.

First Name	Last Name	City	State	Birthday	E-Mail	Phone
Janet	Jones	Houston	TX	May 9	jjones@hotmail.com	(713) 555-3115
Sasha	Smith	Las Vegas	NV	March 10	sasha421@aol.com	(702) 555-0444
Bob	Thompson	Seattle	WA	July 12	kpxracer719@aol.com	(206) 555-0100
Edwin	Jones	Los Angeles	CA	August 8	eddiej@rr.com	(213) 555-7000

Add a new field, "Birthday."
Key the data shown.

2. Change the e-mail address of Janet Jones to jjones@rr.com.
3. **Add a new record** for a new friend as follows:

   Jamie Kent lives in Austin, TX. His birthday is August 10.
   E-mail is kentj@hotmail.com. Phone # is (512) 555-8934.
4. **Delete** the **record** about Edwin Jones.
5. Fill in the Birthday field for your own friends you have added.
6. Print the table.
7. Save and close the database table.

C.

Key each line 2 times. Repeat if time permits.

Key smoothly as you use the SHIFT keys.

8 Quinton Robert Farris Cheryl Eunice Xavier George
9 Juliet Noelle Ulysses Ingmar Hunter Yasmin Melvin
10 Tamara Zachary Quenna Aurora Bryant Dawson Salome
11 Mignon Jeffrey Yvette Olinda Harold Joanna Lionel

D.

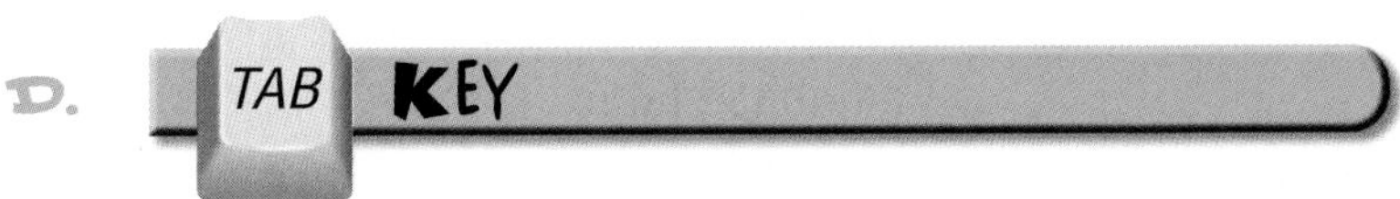

Key each line 2 times. Press the TAB key to indent the first line; press ENTER only at the end of lines 13 and 15.

12   We read the daily newspaper to learn what is
13 going on in other countries. Do you also read it?

14   Do you read or watch the news? If you don't,
15 you should. How will you learn what is happening?

E. CONCENTRATION

Fill in the missing vowels as you key each line 1 time. Repeat if time permits.

16 E-ch d-y thos- fing-rs w-ll m-ve a l-ttl- f-st-r.
17 Y-u m-st le-rn to th-nk wh-re all thos- k-ys ar-.
18 D- y-u ke-p yo-r ey-s on th- c-py y-u ar- key-ng?
19 On- d-y so-n yo-r f-ng-rs w-ll fly ov-r th- k-ys.

F. PUNCTUATION SPACING

Key lines 20–24 one time. Note the spacing before and after each punctuation mark. Repeat if time permits.

20 Accounting is a good course. I am taking it soon.
21 Dr. Tim Bellio, Ph.D., is in the U.S. or the U.K.
22 Please turn on the TV; my favorite program is on.
23 Mr. C. L. Brickmann and his son, T. J., are home.
24 We must talk to two people: Anthony and Consuela.

PROJECT 1 Continued

Practice

Create a Table and Enter Data

6. Use the illustration below to help you identify the parts of a database table. Add the following records to your database table.

A column or **field** is a specific category of information. Here, the fields (in order) are First Name, Last Name, City, State, E-Mail, and Phone.

First Name	Last Name	City	State	E-Mail	Phone
Janet	Jones	Houston	TX	jjones@hotmail.com	(713) 555-3115
Sasha	Smith	Las Vegas	NV	sasha421@aol.com	(702) 555-0444
Bob	Thompson	Seattle	WA	kpxracer719@aol.com	(206) 555-0100
Edwin	Jones	Los Angeles	CA	eddiej@rr.com	(213) 555-7000

A row or **record** is a group of fields that give information about a given topic, idea, or object. The first record in the example above gives Janet's name, the city and state where she lives, e-mail address, and telephone number.

When records are entered into fields, they form an object called a **table**. A table is a combination of the fields (First Name, City, State, etc.) and the records they contain (Janet's information, Sasha's information, etc.).

7. Enter the information you gathered about your friends in the Making the Connection section to your database table.

8. **Resize** the columns so the data can be easily seen.

9. **Print the table.**

10. Close the table.

G. TECHNIQUE TIMINGS

Take two 30-second timings on each line. Focus on the techniques at the left.

Lines 25 and 26: Concentrate on efficient, smooth operation of the SHIFT keys.
Lines 27 and 28: Space quickly without pausing.

```
25 Jay and Ed were on time. Iva liked doing Tai Chi.
26 Alberto, set the clock. It is good to be on time.
27 Both Y. O. Fox and T. C. Ole had a Ph.D. in math.
28 Mr. Vasquez and Mr. Mayer were not in the office.
   | 1 | 2 | 3 | 4 | 5 | 6 | 7 | 8 | 9 | 10
```

H. PRETEST

Take a 1-minute timing on the paragraph. Note your speed and errors.

```
29      Have you tried to get a project completed by     9
30 a deadline only to realize that you simply will      19
31 not be able to finish it? What you do next will      29
32 depend on the project and how soon you need it.      38
   | 1 | 2 | 3 | 4 | 5 | 6 | 7 | 8 | 9 | 10
```

I. PRACTICE

SPEED: If you made 2 or fewer errors on the Pretest, key lines 33–40 two times each.

ACCURACY: If you made more than 2 errors on the Pretest, key lines 33–36 as a group 2 times. Then key lines 37–40 as a group 2 times.

Up reaches are consecutive letters on the home row and third row keyed by one hand. **(task)**

Down reaches are consecutive letters on the home row and bottom row keyed by one hand. **(call)**

```
33 se seats seal pulse lease seams eases sedan mouse
34 gr great gray grows grain grade grass groan grave
35 lo love glove ploys clock locks flock block lobes
36 dr draft drift drive dress drama drums drab drape

37 av lava paved avert favor shave avoid brave raven
38 nk drink pink links crank plank sinks honks blank
39 sc scar scare scant scrap scent scoot scold scone
40 ba barks bare barns barb baby back bang bald bath
```

J. POSTTEST

Repeat the Pretest. Compare your Posttest results with your Pretest results.

PROJECT 1

Practice

Create a Table and Enter Data

When we look up a friend's phone number in the school directory, search for something on the Internet, or look up a topic in an encyclopedia, we are finding and using information. A **database** is an organized collection of information on a given subject or topic. Databases allow you to store and manage a collection of information.

Your Turn

1. **Open a new database.** Name the database *urs*Friends.
2. **Create a database table.**
3. **Name the fields** as follows: First Name, Last Name, City, State, E-Mail, and Phone.
4. **Set the field type** for each of the fields to "Text." It is important to note that while a text field can hold a number (or a combination of letters and numbers), a number or integer field can hold **only** numbers (no letters!). Check the field names and types with the illustration at left.
5. Save the table, naming it "Friends." If prompted about the lack of a "Primary Key," choose the option that will prevent one from being created (most often "No" or "Ignore").

Field Name	Data Type
First Name	Text
Last Name	Text
City	Text
State	Text
E-Mail	Text
Phone	Text

Continued on next page

SECTION 1.20 Skillbuilding

GOALS:

- Demonstrate proper keyboarding skills.
- Use correct spacing before and after punctuation.
- Key 25/1'/2e.

A. WARMUP

Key each line 2 times.

Words	1	itch plum jilt waxy fizz next clod quad brag skit
Speed	2	It is good to meet new people as soon as you can.
Accuracy	3	Cover the cozy liquid wax before Jack mops again.

SKILLBUILDING

B. ALPHABET REVIEW

Key each line 2 times. Repeat if time permits.

4 baffle quartz toxic veins major whack gaudy equip
5 banjo wizard rhyme heaven steep affix laugh quack
6 matrix shady squaw venom jacket spill zebra fudge
7 Be quick to move them up/down; jinx lazy fingers.

Create Database Tables and Enter Data

GOALS: Demonstrate the ability to:

- Create a table.
- Identify database parts.
- Define fields.
- Enter data into a table.

WARMUP

Select Warmup from the Skillbuilding menu. Key each Warmup line 2 times.

Speed	1	We have to learn to make introductions with poise and ease.
Accuracy	2	Mo brought back five or six dozen pieces of quaint jewelry.
Numbers/Symbols	3	She will visit our top offices (#1 & #2): DALLAS 7 EL PASO?
Language Link	4	The trip to Grandma's house was farther than they expected.

Making the Connection

What types of information would you keep about your friends in a telephone book? Some categories might include name, address, and telephone number. The information you collect can be organized so it is easy to find and use.

Your Turn

1. On a sheet of paper, make six columns as shown with the following headings: first name, last name, city, state, e-mail address, and phone number.

First Name	Last Name	City	State	E-Mail	Phone
1					
2					
3					
4					
5					

2. Fill each column with information about five friends.
3. Save your information for Project 1.

C.

Key each line 2 times. Repeat if time permits.

Key smoothly as you use the SHIFT keys.

```
8  Querida Arthur Donata Regina Gwynne Warden Samuel
9  Leilani Ursula Javier Margot Phoebe Irving Oliver
10 Timothy Carlos Elliot Felice Zenina Vernon Winona
11 Nokomis Isabel Hayley Pascal Justin Latham Kameko
```

D.

Key each line 1 time. Repeat if time permits.

Press the TAB key to begin each sentence, and press ENTER at the end of each sentence.

```
12 Did you meet your goals? I did not. They all did.
13 My car is stuck. I need it towed. Will you do it?
14 Let's see a movie. What's playing? I do not know.
15 Look at that. It is quite amazing. I am thrilled.
```

E. CONCENTRATION

Fill in the missing vowels as you key each line 1 time. Repeat if time permits.

```
16 K--p all f-ng-rs curv-d -nd y--r wr-sts up a b-t.
17 Ke-p yo-r b-ck er-ct, b-t le-n yo-r b-dy forw-rd.
18 Ke-p y-ur elb-ws r-lax-d and cl-se to y-ur s-des.
19 K-ep y-ur h-ad up -nd t-rned tow-rd th- textb--k.
20 K-ep b-th fe-t on th- flo-r, on- aft-r th- oth-r.
```

F. PUNCTUATION SPACING

Key lines 21–25 one time. Note the spacing before and after each punctuation mark. Repeat if time permits.

```
21 Tom's flowers--especially the tulips--are lovely.
22 Have you seen her gloves? Are they in the drawer?
23 If Leilani can go tomorrow, we will go then also.
24 Estes Park has roads as well as hike/bike trails.
25 That fly-by-night business was selling old disks.
```

Good Keyboarding Habits

Focus on your feet.
To keep your body positioned properly while at the keyboard—place your feet:

- **Apart, with 6 or 7 inches between the ankles.**
- **In front of the chair.**
- **One foot a little ahead of the other.**
- **Flat on the floor.**

G. TECHNIQUE TIMINGS

Take two 30-second timings on each line. Focus on the technique at the left.

Try to key smoothly as you operate the Shift keys.

26 Oliver let Margo answer the Gopher Internet quiz.
27 Connecting with the World Wide Web was difficult.
28 Janice learned about URLs, FTP, and Gopher sites.
29 Sam, Jo, and Di were fluent in German and French.
| 1 | 2 | 3 | 4 | 5 | 6 | 7 | 8 | 9 | 10

H. PRETEST

Take a 1-minute timing on the paragraph. Note your speed and errors.

30 There are fewer golf courses in Clark County 9
31 than in Milton County. One reason is the need for 19
32 rich soil to grow grass. Clark County has mostly 29
33 clay soil, which does not absorb water well. 38
| 1 | 2 | 3 | 4 | 5 | 6 | 7 | 8 | 9 | 10

I. PRACTICE

SPEED: If you made 2 or fewer errors on the Pretest, key lines 34–41 two times each.

ACCURACY: If you made more than 2 errors on the Pretest, key lines 34–37 as a group 2 times; then key lines 38–41 as a group 2 times.

Discrimination reaches are keys that are commonly substituted and easily confused. **(wear)**

34 asa aside sadly flask sails saved trash masks sas
35 fgf fight goofs golfs fugue gaffe foggy frogs gfg
36 wew weans sweet swell sweat sewer fewer weeks ewe
37 rtr art part port sort fort worth trade title rtr

38 klk kilns kilts kills keels flock block locks lkl
39 nmn means lemon minor numbs names money hymns mnm
40 oio boils soils joins coins lions toils spoil ioi
41 jhj joy jewels judge huge hugs jugs just jury jhj

J. POSTTEST

Repeat the Pretest. Compare your Posttest results with your Pretest results.

UNIT 8 Database

GOALS:

- Demonstrate how to create a database table and enter data.
- Demonstrate how to add database fields and records.
- Demonstrate how to delete database records.
- Demonstrate how to edit database records.
- Demonstrate how to sort a database.

K. 1-MINUTE TIMINGS

Take two 1-minute timings on the paragraph. Note your speed and errors.

Goal: 25/1′/2e

42 Paul bought five quartz watches. He expects 9
43 to give me one just to show his thanks. He will 19
44 also give me a large dog today. 25

| 1 | 2 | 3 | 4 | 5 | 6 | 7 | 8 | 9 | 10 *SI 1.16*

CARE AND OPERATION OF EQUIPMENT

For Discussion—answer the following question. Refer to the Appendix for the answer.

Describe how computer viruses can infect your computer and what precautions you can take to prevent infections. Demonstrate how to protect a disk from computer viruses.

COMPLETING UNIT 7 Continued

ENRICH

Curriculum Portfolio

LANGUAGE ARTS:

Create a reading minutes spreadsheet.

Create a spreadsheet to keep track of how many minutes you read each day of the week for a one-month period. Calculate the average number of minutes you read each week. Then create a line chart comparing the number of weekly minutes read.

MATH:

Create a budget spreadsheet.

Create a spreadsheet to keep track of how you spend your money for a six-month period. Calculate how much money you have left at the end of each month. Then create a bar chart comparing your monthly expenses.

UNIT 2 Keyboarding Skills

GOALS:

- Refine and improve keyboarding techniques.
- Demonstrate correct touch-system techniques for numeric keys.
- Demonstrate correct touch-system techniques for symbol keys.
- Key at a speed of 31 words per minute for 3 minutes with 5 or fewer errors.
- Compose multiple words/short phrases at the keyboard.
- Demonstrate capitalization rules.

COMPLETING UNIT 7

Enrich

Curriculum Portfolio

Use the spreadsheet skills you have learned to create your curriculum portfolio project. Choose from one of the following topics:

Science:

Create a temperature spreadsheet.

Create a spreadsheet to keep track of the daily temperature for a one-week period. Calculate the average, high, and low temperatures for the week. Then create a line chart comparing the daily temperatures for the week.

Social Studies:

Create a sales spreadsheet.

Create a spreadsheet to keep track of the weekly sales of a school fundraiser. Calculate the total weekly sales. Then create a bar chart comparing the sales for one week.

Continued on next page

Focus On

Good Keyboarding Habits

Focus on your back.
To support your back:

- **The chair should support your upper and lower back.**
- **Your back should rest against the back of the chair.**
- **Your hips should be toward the back of the chair.**
- **Make sure your chair is adjustable.**

Apply

Spreadsheet Review

8. Open a new spreadsheet file. Save as ***urs*Animal Speeds**.
9. Key the data as shown in the illustration below.

	A	B
1	**SPEED OF ANIMALS**	
2		
3	**Type**	**MPH**
4	Housefly	5
5	Cheetah	70
6	Race Horse	45
7	Goldfish	4
8	Whale	20

10. Create a pie chart from the data.
11. Show the percentage labels for each animal type.
12. Save the changes.
13. Print the spreadsheet and the pie chart. Keep the spreadsheet open.
14. Change the pie chart to a column bar chart by selecting the appropriate data.
15. Save the changes.
16. Print the spreadsheet and the column bar chart. Keep the spreadsheet open.
17. Change the column bar chart to a line chart by selecting the appropriate data.
18. Include the data labels.
19. Save the changes. Print the spreadsheet and the line chart. Close the file.

SECTION 2.1

New Keys: 4 $ 7 &

GOALS:

- Demonstrate correct techniques for numeric and symbol keys.
- Learn the 4, $, 7, and & keys.
- Demonstrate proper keyboarding techniques.
- Key 27/2'/4e.

A. WARMUP

Key each line 2 times.

Words 1 shot idea jobs corn quip give flex whey maze elks

Speed 2 It is not a good idea to play ball in the street.

Accuracy 3 My joke expert amazed five huge clowns in Quebec.

NEW KEYS

B. 4 AND $ KEY

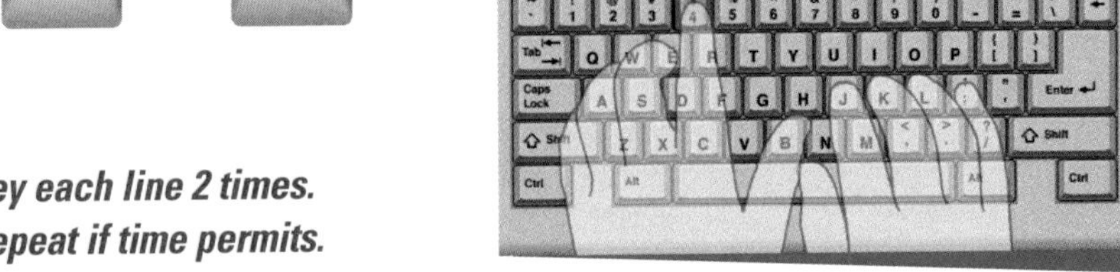

Key each line 2 times. Repeat if time permits.

Use F finger. Anchor A.

4 frf fr4f f4f 444 f4f 4/44 f4f 44.4 f4f 44,444 f4f

5 44 films, 44 foes, 44 flukes, 44 folders, or 4.44

6 I saw 44 ducks, 4 geese, and 4 swans on the lake.

7 Today, our team had 4 runs, 4 hits, and 4 errors.

REVIEW Continued

APPLY

Spreadsheet Review

6. Key the formula shown.

To figure the speed of each runner, divide the meters by the seconds. Use the Fill Down command to copy the formula to the rest of the cells.

	A	B	C	D	E
1	**WORLD TRACK RECORDS**				
2					
3	**Holder**	**Country**	**Speed**	**Distance**	**Record**
4			(Meter/Second)	(Meters)	(Seconds)
5					
6	Deratu Tulu	Ethiopia	=D6/E6	10,000	1,800.17
7	Gabriela Szabo	Romania		5,000	840.41
8	Cathy Freeman	Australia		400	49.11
9	Florence Griffith-Joyner	USA		100	10.49
10	Florence Griffith-Joyner	USA		200	21.34
11	Donovan Bailey	USA		100	9.84
12	Michael Johnson	USA		200	19.32
13	Michael Johnson	USA		400	43.49
14	Noah Ngeny	Kenya		1,500	180.32
15	Marie-Jose Perec	France		400	48.25
16					
17	Highest Speed				
18	Lowest Speed				

Use the Max and Min function formulas to find the highest and lowest speeds.

Format the Speed column to 2 decimal places.

7. Save the changes. Print and close the file.

Continued on next page

$ is the SHIFT of 4. Do not space between the $ and the number.

```
8  frf fr4 f4f f4$f f$f f$f $4 $44 $444 f$f f4f $444
9  $444, 44 fish, 4 fans, $44, 444 fellows, $4, $444
10 Jo paid $44 for the oranges and $4 for the pears.
11 They had $444 and spent $44 of it for 4 presents.
```

C. 7 AND & KEY

Key each line 2 times. Repeat if time permits.

Use J finger. Anchor ;.

```
12 juj ju7j j7j 777 j7j 7/77 j7j 77.7 j7j 77,777 j7j
13 77 jokers, 77 joggers, 77 jets, or 7.77, 77 jumps
14 Hank will perform July 4 and 7, not June 4 and 7.
15 On July 4, we celebrated; on August 7, we rested.
```

Use J finger and LEFT SHIFT. Anchor ;. Space before and after the ampersand (&).

```
16 juj ju7 j7j j7&j j&j j&j j& &j& ju7& j&j j7j ju7&
17 7 jugs & 7 jars & 7 jewels & 7 jurors & 7 jungles
18 He thinks he paid $44 & $77 instead of $47 & $74.
19 B & C ordered 744 from Dixon & Sons on January 7.
```

SKILLBUILDING

D. TECHNIQUE TIMINGS

Take two 30-second timings on each line. Focus on the techniques at the left.

Lines 20 and 21: Keep your eyes on the copy. Lines 22 and 23: Space without pausing.

```
20 Kara saw a ship as she was walking over the hill.
21 Ned says he can mend the urn that fell and broke.
22 The five of us had to get to the bus before noon.
23 Lou said he would be at the game to see us later.
   | 1 | 2 | 3 | 4 | 5 | 6 | 7 | 8 | 9 | 10
```

REVIEW Continued

APPLY

Spreadsheet Review

5. Edit the spreadsheet as shown.

Insert a column before column "Distance." Format the title "Speed." Add the subheading (Meter/Second).

	A	B	C	D	E
1	**WORLD TRACK RECORDS**				
2					
3	**Holder**	**Country**	**Speed**	**Distance**	**Record**
4			(Meter/Second)	(Meters)	(Seconds)
5					
6	Deratu Tulu	Ethiopia		10,000	1,800.17
7	Gabriela Szabo	Romania		5,000	840.41
8	Cathy Freeman	Australia		400	49.11
9	Florence Griffith-Joyner	USA		100	10.49
10	Florence Griffith-Joyner	USA		200	21.34
11	Donovan Bailey	USA		100	9.84
12	Michael Johnson	USA		200	19.32
13	Michael Johnson	USA		400	43.49
14	Noah Ngeny	Kenya		1,500	180.32
15	Marie-Jose Perec	France		400	48.25
16					
17	Highest Speed				
18	Lowest Speed				

Add the two rows shown.

Continued on next page

E. PRETEST

Take a 1-minute timing on the paragraph. Note your speed and errors.

```
24      Each of us should try to eat healthful food,   9
25 get proper rest, and exercise moderately. All of   19
26 these things will help each of us face life with   29
27 more enthusiasm and more energy.                   35
   | 1 | 2 | 3 | 4 | 5 | 6 | 7 | 8 | 9 | 10
```

F. PRACTICE

SPEED: If you made 2 or fewer errors on the Pretest, key lines 28–35 two times each.

ACCURACY: If you made more than 2 errors on the Pretest, key lines 28–31 as a group 2 times. Then key lines 32–35 as a group 2 times.

Adjacent Reaches

```
28 tr train tree tried truth troop strum strip stray
29 op open slope opera sloop moped scoop hoped opine
30 er were loner every steer error veers sewer verge
31 po port porter pole pods potter potion pound pout
```

Jump Reaches

```
32 on onion ozone upon honor front spoon phone wrong
33 ex exams exist exact flex exits exalt vexed Texas
34 ve even veers vests verbs leave every verge heave
35 ni nine ninth night nimble nifty nice nickel nigh
```

G. POSTTEST

Repeat the Pretest. Compare your Posttest results with your Pretest results.

H. 1-MINUTE ALPHANUMERIC TIMING

Take a 1-minute timing on the paragraph. Note your speed and errors.

```
36      Luke sent a $47 check to Computers & Such to   9
37 get a disk with 44 games & 4 special programs for  19
38 7 friends. He saw 47 of his friends at 4 p.m.      28
   | 1 | 2 | 3 | 4 | 5 | 6 | 7 | 8 | 9 | 10
```

REVIEW Continued

APPLY

Spreadsheet Review

3. Edit the spreadsheet as indicated.

Insert a column before column B "Distance."

	A	B	C
1	**WORLD TRACK RECORDS**		
2			
3	**Holder**	**Distance**	**Record**
4		(Meters)	(Seconds)
5			
6	Deratu Tulu	10,000	1,800.17
7	Gabriela Szabo	5,000	840.41
8	Carl Lewis	100	9.86
9	Cathy Freeman	400	49.11
10	Florence Griffith-Joyner	100	10.49
11	Florence Griffith-Joyner	200	21.34
12	Donovan Bailey	100	9.84
13	Michael Johnson	200	19.32
14	Noah Ngeny	1,500	180.32
15	Marie-Jose Perec	400	48.25

Delete row 8 containing information about Carl Lewis.

Insert one row under the row containing information about Michael Johnson.

4. Add the data as indicated.

	A	B	C	D
1	**WORLD TRACK RECORDS**			
2				
3	**Holder**	**Country**	**Distance**	**Record**
4			(Meters)	(Seconds)
5				
6	Deratu Tulu	Ethiopia	10,000	1,800.17
7	Gabriela Szabo	Romania	5,000	840.41
8	Cathy Freeman	Australia	400	49.11
9	Florence Griffith-Joyner	USA	100	10.49
10	Florence Griffith-Joyner	USA	200	21.34
11	Donovan Bailey	USA	100	9.84
12	Michael Johnson	USA	200	19.32
13	Michael Johnson	USA	400	43.49
14	Noah Ngeny	Kenya	1,500	180.32
15	Marie-Jose Perec	France	400	48.25

Key the title "Country." Format bold. Change the font size to 12 pt. Align center the title. Key the data shown.

Key in the additional information about Michael Johnson.

Continued on next page

I. 2-MINUTE TIMINGS

Take two 2-minute timings on lines 39–44. Note your speed and errors.

Goal: 27/2′/4e

39 Have you been to see our zoo? It is a fun 9
40 thing to do in the summer. Bring your lunch to 18
41 eat in the park by the lake. You can watch a bear 28
42 cub perform or just view the zebras. Then explore 38
43 this place and see all the quail and ducks. Take 48
44 some photos to capture the day. 54
| 1 | 2 | 3 | 4 | 5 | 6 | 7 | 8 | 9 | 10 *SI 1.10*

CARE AND OPERATION OF EQUIPMENT

The cursor-movement (arrow) keys help you move around the screen without using a mouse.

Depending on the program, you may be able to press Home to move the insertion point to the beginning of a line, and End to move to the end of a line.

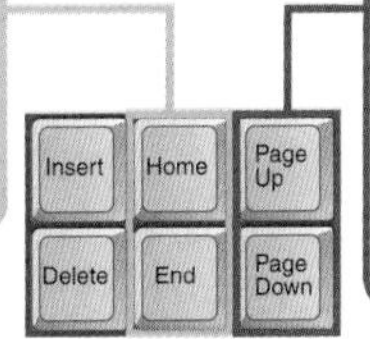

The Page Up and Page Down keys let you "flip"through a document, screen by screen, like turning the pages of a book. Press Page Up to jump to the previous screen; press Page Down to jump to the next.

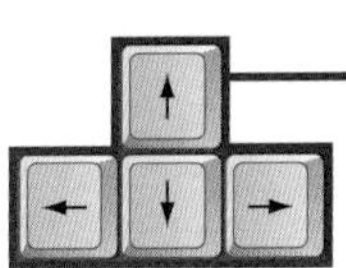

The arrow keys move the insertion point up or down a single line, or left or right one character space.

REVIEW SECTION 10

APPLY

Spreadsheet Review

In this review project you will apply the skills you have learned to create and edit a spreadsheet. You will also calculate with simple and function formulas, then create a chart. Refer to previous projects as needed.

Your Turn

1. Open a new spreadsheet file, and save as *urs***Track Records**.
2. Key and format the information shown.

Format the title bold and change the font size to 12 pt.

Center align the headings and format bold.

	A	B	C
1	**WORLD TRACK RECORDS**		
2			
3	**Holder**	**Distance**	**Record**
4		(Meters)	(Seconds)
5			
6	Deratu Tulu	10,000	1,800.17
7	Gabriela Szabo	5,000	840.41
8	Carl Lewis	100	9.86
9	Cathy Freeman	400	49.11
10	Florence Griffith-Joyner	100	10.49
11	Florence Griffith-Joyner	200	21.34
12	Donovan Bailey	100	9.84
13	Michael Johnson	200	19.32
14	Noah Ngeny	1,500	180.32
15	Marie-Jose Perec	400	48.25

Change the column width so the cell with the most data fits.

Format the numbers to separate the thousands with a comma.

Continued on next page

SECTION 2.2 New Keys: 3 # 8 *

GOALS:

- Demonstrate correct techniques for numeric and symbol keys.
- Learn the 3, #, 8, and * keys.
- Demonstrate proper keyboarding skills.
- Key 27/2'/4e.

A. WARMUP

Key each line 2 times.

Speed	1 The time for Andrew to stop is when the sun sets.
Accuracy	2 Ten foxes quickly jumped high over twelve zebras.
Numbers	3 Lines 47, 77, and 44 were right; line 74 was not.
Symbols	4 Bakes & Deli pays $4, $4.77, and $7.44 for dimes.

NEW KEYS

B. 3 AND # KEY

Key each line 2 times.
Repeat if time permits.

Use D finger. Anchor A or F.

5 ded de3d d3d 333 d3d 3/33 d3d 33.3 d3d 33,333 d3d
6 33 dimes, 33 dishes, 33 dots, 33 daisies, or 3.33
7 Draw 33 squares, 3,333 rectangles, and 3 circles.
8 They had 333 dogs in 33 kennels for over 3 weeks.

PROJECT 4 Reinforce

Create a Chart

In this project you will reinforce what you have learned by creating a chart.

Your Turn

1. Open a new spreadsheet file, and save as ***urs*****Zoo Animals**.

	A	B
1	**ANIMALS IN THE ZOO**	
2		
3	**Type**	**Number**
4	Birds	125
5	Reptiles	56
6	Amphibians	145
7	Herd Animals	91
8	Predators	43

2. Key the data as shown in the illustration at left.
3. **Create a pie chart** from the data.
4. **Show the percentage labels** for each animal type.
5. Save the changes to the spreadsheet.
6. Print the spreadsheet and the pie chart. Keep the spreadsheet open.
7. Change the pie chart to a **column bar chart** by selecting the appropriate data.
8. Save the changes to the spreadsheet.
9. Print the spreadsheet and the bar chart. Keep the spreadsheet open.
10. Change the bar chart to a **line chart** by selecting the appropriate data.
11. Include the **data labels**.
12. Save the changes to the spreadsheet.
13. Print the spreadsheet and the line chart. Close the file.

The # (number or pound sign) is the SHIFT of 3. Anchor A or F. Do not space between the number and #.

Key each line 2 times.

9 ded de3 d3d d3#d d#d d#d #3 #33 #333 d#d d3d #333
10 #3, 3 dots, #33, 33 dogs, #333, 333 ditches, #333
11 Is Invoice #373 for 344#, 433#, or 343# of fruit?
12 The group used 43# of grade #3 potatoes at lunch.

Key each line 2 times. Key smoothly as you use the SHIFT keys. Repeat if time permits.

Use K finger. Anchor ;.

13 kik ki8k k8k 888 k8k 8/88 k8k 88.8 k8k 88,888 k8k
14 88 kegs, 88 kilns, 88 knocks, 88 kickers, or 8.88
15 Our zoo has 88 zebras, 38 snakes, and 33 monkeys.
16 The house is at 88 Lake Street, 8 blocks farther.

*The * (asterisk) is the SHIFT of 8. Do not space between the word and *.*

17 kik ki8 k8k k8*k k*k k*k *8 *88 *888 k*k k8k *888
18 *8, 88 kits, *88, 88 keys, *888, 88 kimonos, *888
19 This manual* and this report* are in the library.
20 Reports* are due in 8 weeks* and should be typed.

CARE AND OPERATION OF EQUIPMENT

When pressed along with an alphanumeric key, Shift forces the computer to output a capital letter or symbol. Shift is also a modifier key in some programs; for example, you can press Shift along with arrow keys to select text for editing.

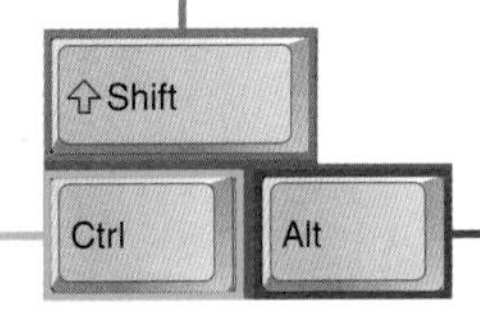

The Ctrl (Control) key produces different results depending on the program you are using. In many Windows-based programs, Ctrl-key combinations provide shortcuts for menu commands. For example, the combination Ctrl+O enables you to open a new file.

The Alt (Alternate) key operates like the Ctrl key, but produces a different set of results. In Windows programs, Alt-key combinations enable you to navigate menus and dialog boxes without using the mouse.

PROJECT 3 Continued

Practice

Create a Pie Chart

2. Open the file **10-5 Project 3**, and save it as ***urs*Rainfall Season**.
3. **Create a pie chart** from the spreadsheet data shown.

	A	B
1	RAINFALL BY SEASON	
2		
3		Inches
4	Winter	10
5	Spring	15
6	Summer	6
7	Fall	8
8	Total	39

Include cells A4 through B7 in the range selected for the chart.

4. Key RAINFALL BY SEASON for the chart title.
5. Include the **show percentage labels**.
6. If your chart appears on the same page with the spreadsheet, position the chart under the spreadsheet data. Resize the chart as needed so that all the information displays clearly.
7. Save the changes to the spreadsheet.
8. Print the spreadsheet and the pie chart. Close the file.

D. PRETEST

Take a 1-minute timing on the paragraph. Note your speed and errors.

```
21      Do you brood when you make errors on papers?   9
22 It would be better to figure out what causes the   19
23 errors and to look for corrective drills to help   29
24 you make fewer errors in the future.               36
   | 1 | 2 | 3 | 4 | 5 | 6 | 7 | 8 | 9 | 10
```

E. PRACTICE

SPEED: If you made 2 or fewer errors on the Pretest, key lines 25–32 two times each.

ACCURACY: If you made more than 2 errors on the Pretest, key lines 25–28 as a group 2 times. Then key lines 29–32 as a group 2 times.

Double Reaches

```
25 rr errs hurry error furry berry worry terry carry
26 ll bill allay hills chill stall small shell smell
27 tt attar jetty otter utter putty witty butte Otto
28 ff stuff stiff cliff sniff offer scuff fluff buff
```

Alternate Reaches

```
29 is this list fist wish visit whist island raisins
30 so sons some soap sort soles sound bosses costume
31 go gone goat pogo logo bogus agora pagoda doggone
32 fu fun fume fund full fuel fuss furor furry fuzzy
```

F. POSTTEST

Repeat the Pretest. Compare your Posttest results with your Pretest results.

PROJECT 3 Practice

Create a Pie Chart

A **pie chart** uses a circle divided into pieces or slices to graphically show the relationship among values in a spreadsheet. All the values make up the entire circle or "pie."

Your Turn

1. Use the illustration to help you identify the parts of the pie chart.

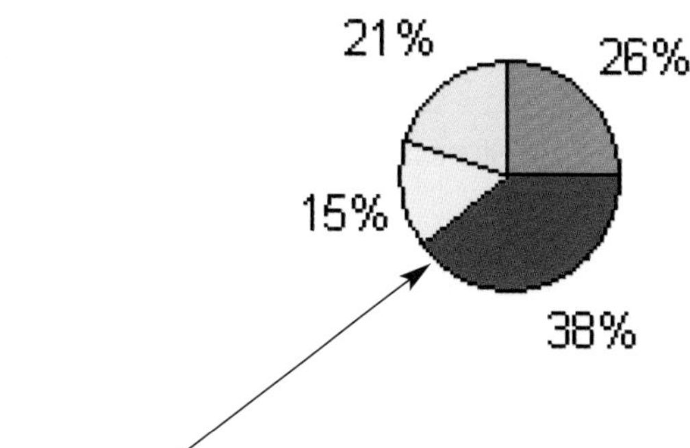

Each piece of the pie represents one of the values in the spreadsheet.

Continued on next page

G. NUMBER AND SYMBOL PRACTICE

Key each line 1 time. Repeat if time permits.

33 83 doubts, 38 cubs, 37 shrubs, 33 clubs, 34 stubs
34 87 aims, 83 maids, 88 brains, 73 braids, 84 raids

35 78 drinks, 48 brinks, 43 inks, 83 minks, 33 links
36 88 canes, 78 planes, 73 manes, 34 cans, 84 cranes

37 #7 blue, 4# roast, $3 paint, 77 books,* 3 & 4 & 8
38 7# boxes, 38 lists, $4 horse, #8 tree,* 7 & 3 & 4

39 Seek & Find Research sells this book* for $37.84.
40 The geometry test grades were 88, 87, 84, and 83.

H. 1-MINUTE ALPHANUMERIC TIMING

Take a 1-minute timing on the paragraph. Note your speed and errors.

41 B. Warmsly & J. Barnet paid the $847 charges 9
42 for the closing costs of their home at 3487 Cliff 19
43 Road; claim #47* shows the charge. 26

| 1 | 2 | 3 | 4 | 5 | 6 | 7 | 8 | 9 | 10

I. 2-MINUTE TIMINGS

Take two 2-minute timings on lines 44–49. Note your speed and errors.

Goal: 27/2'/4e

44 We just want to stay all day in the store to 9
45 see the very new shoe styles. Sue quickly saw the 19
46 mix of zany colors. Jo put on a yellow and green 29
47 pair and looked in a mirror. The shoes had wide 39
48 strips on the soles. We were certain of the good 48
49 brand, so I bought two pair. 54

| 1 | 2 | 3 | 4 | 5 | 6 | 7 | 8 | 9 | 10 SI1.12

PROJECT 2 Continued

Practice

Create a Line Chart

2. Open the data file **10-5 Project 2**, and save it as *urs***Temperatures**.
3. **Create a line chart** from the spreadsheet data shown.

	A	B	C
1	**AVERAGE TEMPERATURES**		
2			
3	**Month**	**Degree**	
4	January	32	
5	February	38	
6	March	54	
7	April	65	
8	May	78	

Include cells A3 through B8 in the range selected for the chart.

4. Key AVERAGE TEMPERATURES for the chart title.
5. Include the **data labels** to show the spreadsheet values.
6. If your chart appears on the same page with the spreadsheet, position the chart under the spreadsheet data. Resize the chart as needed so that all the information displays clearly.
7. Save the changes to the spreadsheet.
8. Print the spreadsheet and the line chart. Close the file.

SECTION 2.3 New Keys: 2 @ 9 (

GOALS:

- Demonstrate correct techniques for numeric and symbol keys.
- Learn the 2, @, 9, and (keys.
- Demonstrate proper keyboarding skills.
- Key 27/2'/4e.

A. WARMUP

Key each line 2 times.

Speed	1 The big lake was filled with many ducks and fish.
Accuracy	2 Lazy Jaques picked five boxes of oranges with me.
Numbers	3 The answer is 78 when you add 44 and 34 together.
Symbols	4 Invoices #73 and #48 from C & M Supply were $438.

NEW KEYS

B. 2 AND @ KEY

Key each line 2 times. Repeat if time permits.

Use S finger. For 2 and @, anchor F.

5 sws sw2s s2s 222 s2s 22.2 s2s 2/22 s2s 22,222 s2s
6 22 sips, 22 swings, 22 signals, 22 sites, or 2.22
7 Our class used 22 pens, 23 disks, and 24 ribbons.
8 There were 22 people waiting for Bus 22 on May 2.

PROJECT 2 Practice

Create a Line Chart

A **line chart** uses points on a grid connected by lines to represent the spreadsheet values. A line chart is often the best choice for showing trends or changes in values over time.

Your Turn

1. Use the illustration to help you identify the parts of the line chart.

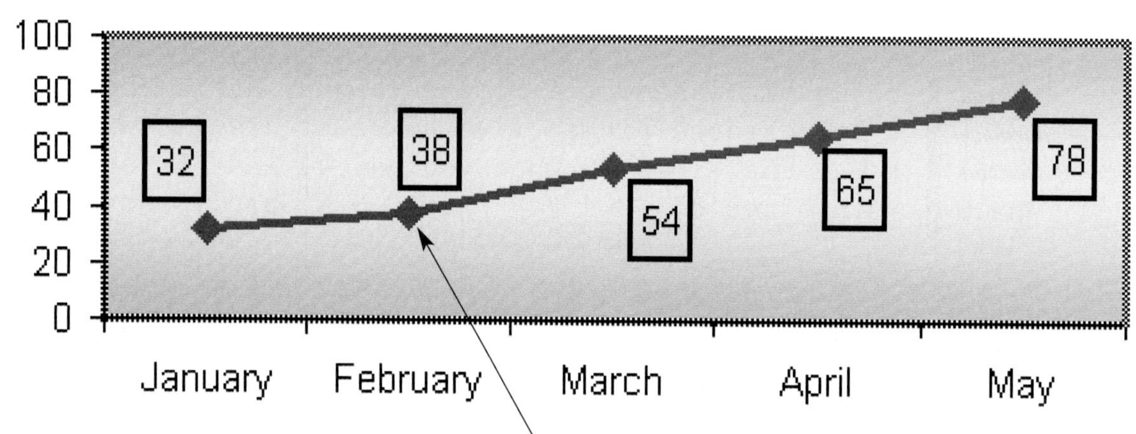

The chart values are represented by points on the grid. Lines connect the points.

Continued on next page

Key each line 2 times.

@ (at) is the SHIFT of 2. Space 1 time before and after @ except when it is used in an e-mail address.

```
9  sws sw2 s2s s2@s s@s s@s @2 @22 @222 s@s s2s @222
10 @2, 2 sons, @22, 22 sets, @222, 222 sensors, @222
11 Paul said his e-mail address was smith@acc.co.us.
12 She bought 2 @ 22 and sold 22 @ 223 before 2 p.m.
```

C. 9 AND (KEY

Key each line 2 times. Repeat if time permits.

Use L finger. For 9 and (, anchor J.

```
13 lol lo91 191 999 191 9/99 191 99.9 191 99,999 191
14 99 laps, 99 loops, 99 lilies, 99 lifters, or 9.99
15 He said 99 times not to ask for the 99 fair fans.
16 They traveled 999 miles on Route 99 over 9 weeks.
```

The ((left parenthesis) is the SHIFT of 9. Space 1 time before an opening parenthesis; do not space after it.

```
17 lol lo9 191 19(1 1(1 1(1 (9 (99 (999 1(1 191 (999
18 (9, 9 lots, (99, 99 logs, (999, 999 latches, (999
19 lo9( (99( (9 lo9(1 lo( 9( 9(9 (9( 9(9 1( lo9(1 9(
20 lo9( 19(1 9(91 1((1 (9ol 99 lambs, (999, 999 lads
```

SKILLBUILDING

Technique Checkpoint

D. *Key each line 2 times. Focus on the technique at the left.*

Keep your eyes on the copy when keying numbers and symbols.

```
21 sws sw2s s2s 222 s2s 22.2 s2s 2/22 s2s 22,222 s2s
22 sws sw2 s2s s2@s s@s s@s @2 @22 @222 s@s s2s @222
23 lol lo91 191 999 191 9/99 191 99.9 191 99,999 191
24 lol lo9 191 19(1 1(1 1(1 (9 (99 (999 1(1 191 (999
```

PROJECT 1 Continued

Practice

Create a Bar Chart

2. **Create a column bar chart** from the spreadsheet data shown.

	A	B	C	D	E
1	**STUDENT COUNCIL ELECTION**				
2	**Votes Received**				
3					
4		**Grade 6**	**Grade 7**	**Grade 8**	**Total Votes**
5	Janis Roberts	20	12	10	42
6	Tomas Perez	12	24	31	67
7	Kim Yung	18	23	15	56

Include cells A4 through E7 in the range selected for the chart.

3. Key STUDENT COUNCIL ELECTION for the chart title.
4. If your chart appears on the same page with the spreadsheet, position the chart under the spreadsheet data. Resize the chart as needed so that all the information displays clearly.
5. Save the changes to the spreadsheet.
6. Print the spreadsheet and the bar chart. Close the file.

E. PRETEST

Take a 1-minute timing on the paragraph. Note your speed and errors.

25 Were you in the biology group that mixed the 9
26 ragweed seeds with some vegetable seeds? Jon and 19
27 Kim sneezed all month because of that. All of us 29
28 agreed that we must be more careful in the lab. 38
| 1 | 2 | 3 | 4 | 5 | 6 | 7 | 8 | 9 | 10

F. PRACTICE

SPEED: If you made 2 or fewer errors on the Pretest, key lines 29–36 two times each.

ACCURACY: If you made more than 2 errors on the Pretest, key lines 29–32 as a group 2 times. Then key lines 33–36 as a group 2 times.

Left Reaches

29 tab wards grace serve wears farce beast crate car
30 far weeds tests seeds tread graze vexed vests saw
31 bar crest feast refer cease dated verge bread gas
32 car career grasses bread creases faded vested tad

Right Reaches

33 you Yukon mummy ninon jolly union minim pylon hum
34 mom nylon milky lumpy puppy holly pulpy plink oil
35 pop oomph jumpy unpin nippy imply hippo pupil nip
36 you union bumpy upon holly hill moon pink ill mop

G. POSTTEST

Repeat the Pretest. Compare your Posttest results with your Pretest results.

H. 1-MINUTE ALPHANUMERIC TIMING

Take a 1-minute timing on the paragraph. Note your speed and errors.

37 The planned ski tour #4 begins at 2:43 p.m., 9
38 and tour #3 begins at noon. Every tour costs $43, 19
39 and everyone will end at 7:38 p.m. 26
| 1 | 2 | 3 | 4 | 5 | 6 | 7 | 8 | 9 | 10

PROJECT 1 Practice

Create a Bar Chart

Spreadsheet programs allow you to create charts from data in a spreadsheet. Spreadsheets provide many different chart types, such as bar, line, and pie charts. A **bar chart** has vertical or horizontal bars representing spreadsheet values.

Your Turn

1. Use the illustration to help you identify the parts of the column bar chart.

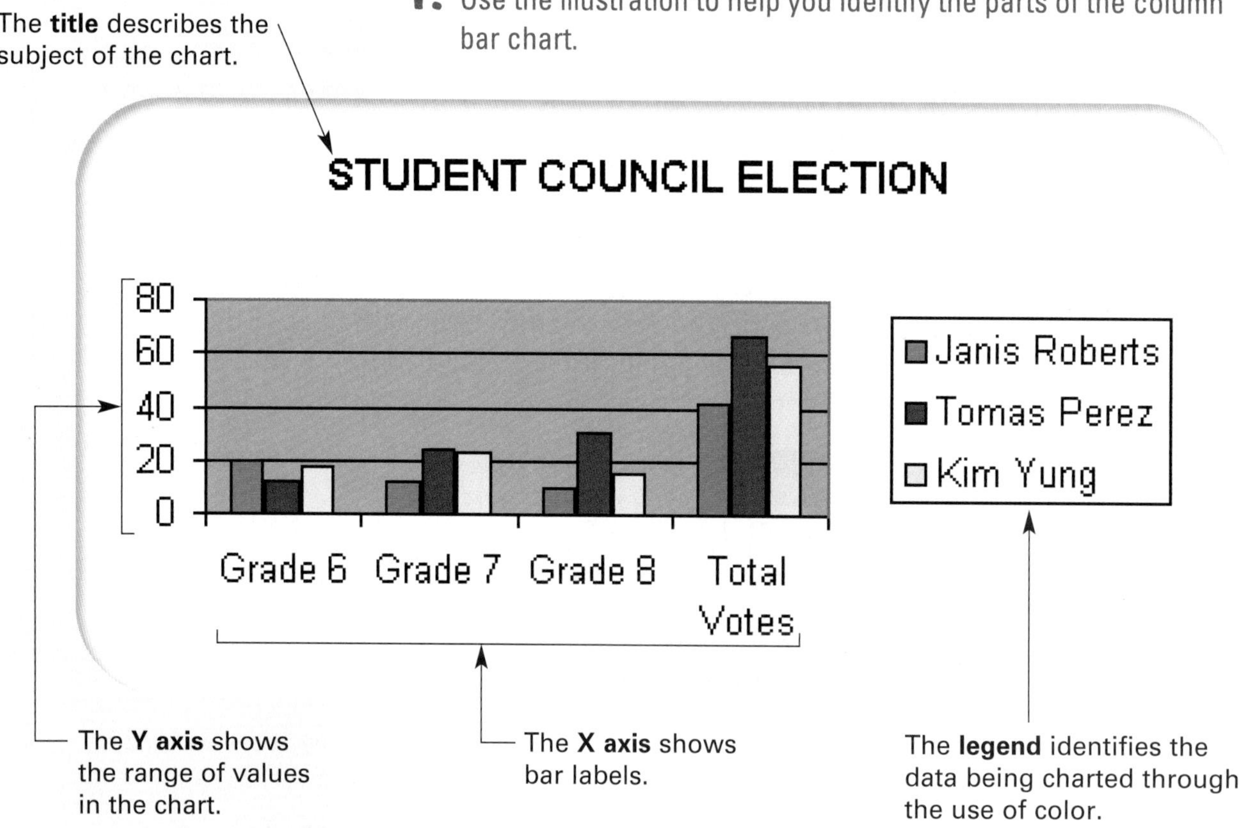

The **title** describes the subject of the chart.
STUDENT COUNCIL ELECTION
80
60
40
20
0
Grade 6
Grade 7
Grade 8
Total Votes
Janis Roberts
Tomas Perez
Kim Yung
The **Y axis** shows the range of values in the chart.
The **X axis** shows bar labels.
The **legend** identifies the data being charted through the use of color.

Continued on next page

I. 2-MINUTE TIMINGS

Take two 2-minute timings on lines 40–45. Note your speed and errors.

Goal: 27/2'/4e

```
     It is a joy to end a term with good grades.     9
Fall term could be very nice if it were not for     19
exams and quizzes. Jan, though, likes to study to   29
show how much she has learned. She places great     38
value in having high marks. She knows her peers     48
admire the grades she achieved.                     54
| 1 | 2 | 3 | 4 | 5 | 6 | 7 | 8 | 9 | 10          SI 1.17
```

TOUCH-SYSTEM TECHNIQUES

While holding the mouse, keep your wrist straight.

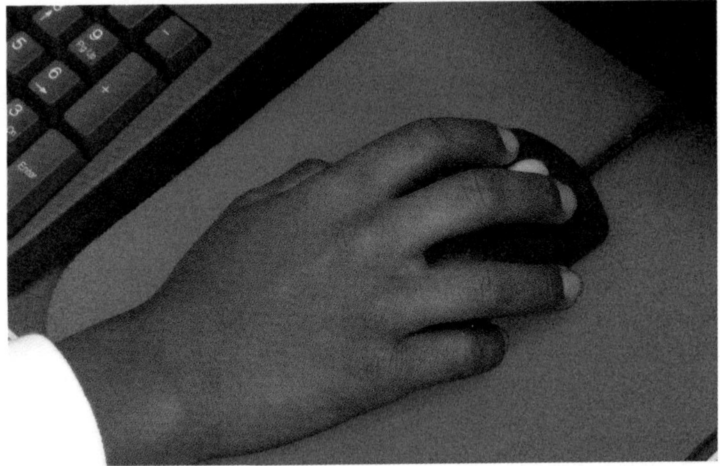

Hold the mouse lightly. Do not squeeze tightly or grip it too hard. Place the mouse close to the keyboard so you don't have to strain your wrist or arm to reach up or over.

SECTION 10.5 Create Charts

GOALS: Demonstrate the ability to:

- Understand the parts of a chart.
- Create a bar chart.
- Create a line chart.
- Create a pie chart.

WARMUP

Select Warmup from the Skillbuilding menu. Key each Warmup line 2 times.

Speed	1	Some people seem to have more hours in the day than others.
Accuracy	2	Jeff quietly moved a dozen boxes last night by power truck.
Numbers/Symbols	3	The invoice #740 for $189.32 is subject to a 6.5% discount?
Language Link	4	First we washed our hands, then it was time to enjoy lunch.

Making the Connection

You can create a chart to graphically display your spreadsheet data. Charts allow you to easily compare data.

Your Turn

1. Open the file **10-5 Project 1**, and save it as ***urs*Student Council**.
2. Keep the spreadsheet open for Project 1.

Student Council Election
Votes Received

	Grade 6	Grade 7	Grade 8	Total Votes
Janis Roberts	20	12	10	42
Tomas Perez	12	24	31	67
Kim Yung	18	23	15	56

SECTION 2.4 Review

GOALS:

- Demonstrate correct touch-system techniques.
- Key 27/2'/4e.
- Demonstrate ability to compose at the keyboard.

A. WARMUP

Key each line 2 times.

Speed	1 The first time Alf drove a car, he hit a pothole.
Accuracy	2 Zigzag through the zebu with zip to avoid injury.
Numbers	3 Room 43 holds 87 people, but only 29 are present.
Symbols	4 Buy 78 gross* of #2 pencils @ $3.94 at the store.

SKILLBUILDING

B. TAB KEY

Key each paragraph 2 times. Press the TAB key to indent the first line; press ENTER only at the end of lines 6 and 8. Repeat if time permits.

5 We found 99 gnats, 44 flies, 33 fleas, and
6 77 seals beside the 33 trees at the 2-acre beach.

7 Bo & Son bought 88 axles @ $42.98. They said
8 Rule #37 on page 88 was now Rule #42 on page 93.

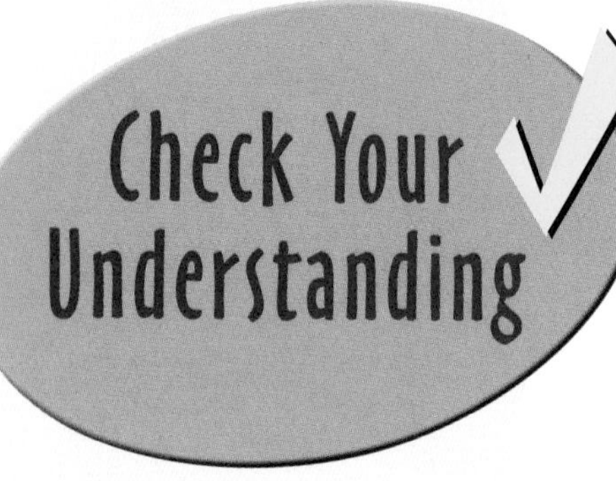

1. Open a new word processing document, and save it as ***urs*Function Formulas**.
2. Explain how the function formula can save you time.
3. Discuss how the Sum function adds numbers.
4. Discuss how the Average function averages numbers.
5. Discuss how the Fill Down and Fill Right commands can save you time.

	A	B	C	D	E	F	G
1							**Student**
2	**Name**	**Test 1**	**Test 2**	**Test 3**	**Test 4**	**Test 5**	**Average**
3	Janet	95	85	100	92	88	92.0
4	Ramon	96	90	95	83	91	91.0
5	Sam	84	88	94	81	93	88.0
6	Laura	74	88	90	78	85	83.0
7	Irma	89	93	87	88	92	89.8
8	Dan	88	84	92	80	91	87.0
9	Jacob	80	88	91	93	84	87.2
10	Ali	93	87	90	98	92	92.0
11	Nora	96	93	90	93	100	94.4
12							
13	**Test Average**	88.3	88.4	92.1	87.3	90.7	
14	**Lowest Grade**	74.0	84.0	87.0	78.0	84.0	
15	**Highest Grade**	96.0	93.0	100.0	98.0	100.0	

Compare urs*Grades with the illustration.*

C. ENTER KEY

Key each line 2 times. Press ENTER at the end of every sentence. Continue keying smoothly. Repeat if time permits.

Remember to press ENTER at the end of every sentence.

```
9  Study all of Chapter 29. It covers pages 234-249.
10 Chelsea lives at 778 Cherokee. That's in Paducah.
11 Write Jo at pets@coyote.com. Jo's address is new.
12 That text* is at B & B Printing. It is makeready.
```

D. TECHNIQUE TIMINGS

Take two 30-second timings on each line. Focus on the technique at the left.

Keep elbows in.

```
13 She works for Mr. D. N. Logan at Logan Locksmith.
14 Is the May/June issue late? My copy has not come.
15 Find these colors: pink, blue, green, and purple.
16 My hoity-toity behavior was rude, extremely rude.
   | 1 | 2 | 3 | 4 | 5 | 6 | 7 | 8 | 9 | 10
```

THE FUNCTION KEYS

The function keys are F1, F2, F3, and so on. They are most often arranged on the top row of the keyboard and allow you to input a command with a single stroke. For example, F1 has become the standard for Help. Press the F1 function key on your keyboard to access Help.

PROJECT 5 Reinforce

Calculate Formulas

In this project you will reinforce what you have learned by entering simple function formulas to calculate student averages.

Your Turn

1. Open the file **10-4 Project 5**, and save it as *urs***Grades**.
2. Enter **function formulas** to complete the student averages shown below.

Find the test average with the **Average function formula.** Use the **Min function formula** to find the lowest grade. Use the **Max function formula** to find the highest grade.

Find the student average with the **Average function formula.**

	A	B	C	D	E	F	G
1							Student
2	Name	Test 1	Test 2	Test 3	Test 4	Test 5	Average
3	Janet	95	85	100	92	88	
4	Ramon	96	90	95	83	91	
5	Sam	84	88	94	81	93	
6	Laura	74	88	90	78	85	
7	Irma	89	93	87	88	92	
8	Dan	88	84	92	80	91	
9	Jacob	80	88	91	93	84	
10	Ali	93	87	90	98	92	
11	Nora	96	93	90	93	100	
12							
13	Test Average						
14	Lowest Grade						
15	Highest Grade						

Use the **Fill Down command** to copy the formulas to the rest of the cells.

Use the **Fill Right command** to copy the formulas to the rest of the cells.

3. **Format** the average **numbers** to one decimal place.
4. **Format** the lowest- and highest-grade **numbers** to one decimal place.
5. Save the changes. Print and close the file.

E. PRETEST

Take a 1-minute timing on the paragraph. Note your speed and errors.

17 Ed's prize-winning ewe stays on Mario's farm 9

18 until the petting zoo opens. Every day Skip takes 19

19 that ewe and her lamb to the fair. It's amazing 28

20 to see how much time is spent caring for animals. 38

| 1 | 2 | 3 | 4 | 5 | 6 | 7 | 8 | 9 | 10

F. PRACTICE

SPEED: If you made 2 or fewer errors on the Pretest, key lines 21–28 two times each.

ACCURACY: If you made more than 2 errors on the Pretest, key lines 21–24 as a group 2 times. Then key lines 25–28 as a group 2 times.

Adjacent Reaches	21	io trio riot pious Mario ew ewes mews sewer views
Jump Reaches	22	un tune dune under bound ze zeal zest prize seize
Double Reaches	23	ss hiss boss dress gloss ll fall tall small jolly
Up Reaches	24	dr drip drive dream drab ho hope hole hold hollow
Alternate Reaches	25	ro rode rote crows throw do doze judo kudos docks
Left Reaches	26	fa farm fast favor fazed er errs were erase terms
Right Reaches	27	ki kiln skip skill skimp pl plot plum plows plugs
Down Reaches	28	ca call caps cards caper ni niece nine nick night

G. POSTTEST

Repeat the Pretest. Compare your Posttest results with your Pretest results.

H. 1-MINUTE ALPHANUMERIC TIMING

Take a 1-minute timing on lines 29–31. Note your speed and errors.

29 Our black cat, Beauty, weighed 9#. She had a 9

30 checkup at Paws & Claws on June 23. Her shots and 19

31 exam cost $48, but she's worth it all. 27

| 1 | 2 | 3 | 4 | 5 | 6 | 7 | 8 | 9 | 10

PROJECT 4 Continued

Practice

Using the Fill Right and Fill Down Command

4. Use the **Fill Down command** to copy the total formula in cell F2 to cells F3 through F10. The answers appear as shown in the illustration below.

	A	B	C	D	E	F
1	**Name**	**Week 1**	**Week 2**	**Week 3**	**Week 4**	**Total Sales**
2	Ben	$21.65	$43.00	$22.73	$19.84	$107.22
3	Haris	$25.89	$28.86	$18.15	$35.23	$108.13
4	Leticia	$18.00	$29.19	$27.65	$31.00	$105.84
5	Erin	$11.87	$29.76	$41.00	$16.50	$99.13
6	Diana	$23.87	$17.44	$20.65	$22.00	$83.96
7	Trang	$33.45	$24.86	$29.65	$25.83	$113.79
8	Katie	$13.75	$21.00	$26.75	$28.24	$89.74
9	Clay	$22.55	$14.89	$24.75	$18.65	$80.84
10	Scott	$16.50	$38.73	$23.45	$20.25	$98.93

5. Click in cell F3, and notice the formula. The cells that are referenced have changed. Now the formula reads =SUM(B3:E3). **Cell references** identify a cell in a spreadsheet, such as A1, A2, etc.
6. Click in cell B17, and key the number 9.
7. Hold down the SHIFT key, and click in cell E17. The row is highlighted as shown in the illustration below.

17	**Enrollment**	9			

8. Use the **Fill Right command** to copy the number in cell B17 to cells C17, D17, and E17. The numbers appear as shown in the illustration below.

17	**Enrollment**	9	9	9	9

9. Save the changes. Print and close the file.

I. 2-MINUTE TIMINGS

Take two 2-minute timings on lines 32–37. Note your speed and errors.

Goal: 27/2′/4e

```
32      Why use proper grammar when you speak? One         9
33 of the best reasons is that others will judge you      19
34 by your speech. Fair or not, people examine words      29
35 you use and how you use them. You have to speak        38
36 well daily. Avoid buzzwords and slang. People          48
37 will be very quick to judge you.                       54
   | 1 | 2 | 3 | 4 | 5 | 6 | 7 | 8 | 9 | 10         SI 1.23
```

J. COMPOSING AT THE KEYBOARD

Answer each question with a few words or short phrase. Press ENTER after each answer.

38 Who is your best friend?

39 Who are two people who have been in the news this week?

40 What is your favorite snack?

41 What is your favorite type of music?

42 What is your favorite song?

PROJECT 4 Practice

Using the Fill Right and Fill Down Command

You can reduce the number of keystrokes to produce a formula by using a fill command. The **Fill Down command** copies data or formulas in columns. The **Fill Right command** copies data or formulas in rows.

Your Turn

1. Click in cell F2, and key the Sum function formula =SUM(B2:E2). Compare your spreadsheet with the illustration shown below.

SUM | =SUM(B2:E2)

	A	B	C	D	E	F
1	**Name**	**Week 1**	**Week 2**	**Week 3**	**Week 4**	**Total Sales**
2	Ben	$21.65	$43.00	$22.73	$19.84	=SUM(B2:E2)
3	Haris	$25.89	$28.86	$18.15	$35.23	

2. Press ENTER. The answer $107.22 appears.
3. Hold down the SHIFT key and click in cell F10. The column is highlighted as shown in the illustration at right.

Continued on next page

SECTION 2.5 New Keys: 1 ! 0)

GOALS:

- Demonstrate correct techniques for numeric and symbol keys.
- Learn the 1, !, 0, and) keys.
- Demonstrate proper keyboarding skills.
- Key 27/2'/4e.

A. WARMUP

Key each line 2 times.

Speed	1 The goal of trade schools is to teach job skills.
Accuracy	2 Jess Mendoza quickly plowed six bright vineyards.
Numbers	3 Nate took this new order: 78, 74, 83, 29, and 23.
Symbols	4 Purchase 32# of grass seed today @ $2.98 a pound.

NEW KEYS

B. 1 AND ! KEY

Key each line 2 times.

For 1 and !, anchor F. Use A finger. Do not use the lower-case letter l (el) for 1.

```
5 aqa aq1a a1a 111 a1a 1/11 a1a 11.1 a1a 11,111 a1a
6 11 arms, 11 areas, 11 adages, 11 animals, or 1.11
7 My 11 aides can type 111 pages within 11 minutes.
8 Joann used 11 gallons of gas to travel 111 miles.
```

PROJECT 3 Continued

Practice

Enter the MINIMUM and MAXIMUM Function Formulas

4. Click in cell B15, and key the Maximum function formula =MAX(B2:B10). Compare your spreadsheet with the illustration shown below.

MAX | =MAX(B2:B10)

	A	B	C	D	E
1	**Name**	**Week 1**	**Week 2**	**Week 3**	**Week 4**
2	Ben	$21.65	$43.00	$22.73	$19.84
3	Haris	$25.89	$28.86	$18.15	$35.23
4	Leticia	$18.00	$29.19	$27.65	$31.00
5	Erin	$11.87	$29.76	$41.00	$16.50
6	Diana	$23.87	$17.44	$20.65	$22.00
7	Trang	$33.45	$24.86	$29.65	$25.83
8	Katie	$13.75	$21.00	$26.75	$28.24
9	Clay	$22.55	$14.89	$24.75	$18.65
10	Scott	$16.50	$38.73	$23.45	$20.25
11					
12	**Total Sales**	$187.53	$247.73	$234.78	$217.54
13	**Average Sales**	$20.84	$27.53	$26.09	$24.17
14	**Lowest Sales**	$11.87	$14.89	$18.15	$16.50
15	**Highest Sales**	=MAX(B2:B10)			

The Maximum function formula =MAX(B2:B10) finds the largest number in cells B2, B3, B4, B5, B6, B7, B8, B9, and B10.

5. Press ENTER. The answer $33.45 appears.

6. Enter a **Maximum function formula** to find the highest total sales for Week 2, Week 3, and Week 4.

7. Save the changes. Keep the spreadsheet open for Project 4.

Key each line 2 times.

***!** is the* SHIFT *of 1.*
Space 1 time after an exclamation point.

```
9  aqa aql ala al!a a!a a!a 1! 11! 111! a!a ala 111!
10 1!, 1 ant, 11! 11 acres, 111! 111 adverbs, 1 area
11 Listen! There was a cry for help! They need help!
12 Look! It's moving! I'm frightened! Run very fast!
```

C. 0 AND) KEY

Key each line 2 times.
Repeat if time permits.

Use Sem finger.
For 0 and), anchor J.
Do not use the capital letter O for 0 (zero).

) is the* SHIFT *of 0 (zero).
Space 1 time after a closing parenthesis except when it is followed by punctuation; do not space before it.

```
13 ;p; ;p0; ;0; 000 ;0; 1.00 ;0; 20.0 ;0; 30,000 ;0;
14 300 parts, 700 planks, 800 parades, 900 particles
15 Can you add these: 80, 10, 90, 40, 20, 70, & 130?
16 Some emoticons such as :-( or :( use parentheses.

17 ;p; ;p0 ;0; ;0); ;); ;); );; );;; ;); ;0; );;; ;)
18 ;0; ;0) ;); ;); 10) 20) 30) 40) 70) 80) 90) 1001)
19 The box (the big red one) is just the right size.
20 My friend (you know which one) is arriving early.
```

SKILLBUILDING

Technique Checkpoint

D. ***Key each line 2 times. Focus on the techniques at the left.***

Keep your eyes on the copy; hold home-key anchors.

```
21 aqa aqla ala 111 ala 1/11 ala 11.1 ala 11,111 ala
22 aqa aql ala al!a a!a a!a 1! 11! 111! a!a ala 111!
23 ;p; ;p0; ;0; 000 ;0; 1.00 ;0; 20.0 ;0; 30,000 ;0;
24 p;p p;0 ;0; ;0); ;); ;); );; );;; ;); ;0; );;; ;)
```

PROJECT 3 Practice

Enter the MINIMUM and MAXIMUM Function Formulas

The **MINIMUM and MAXIMUM functions** find the largest or smallest number in a range of cells.

Your Turn

1. Click in cell B14, and key the Minimum function formula =MIN(B2:B10). Compare your spreadsheet with the illustration shown below.

MIN =MIN(B2:B10)

	A	B	C	D	E
1	**Name**	**Week 1**	**Week 2**	**Week 3**	**Week 4**
2	Ben	$21.65	$43.00	$22.73	$19.84
3	Haris	$25.89	$28.86	$18.15	$35.23
4	Leticia	$18.00	$29.19	$27.65	$31.00
5	Erin	$11.87	$29.76	$41.00	$16.50
6	Diana	$23.87	$17.44	$20.65	$22.00
7	Trang	$33.45	$24.86	$29.65	$25.83
8	Katie	$13.75	$21.00	$26.75	$28.24
9	Clay	$22.55	$14.89	$24.75	$18.65
10	Scott	$16.50	$38.73	$23.45	$20.25
11					
12	**Total Sales**	$187.53	$247.73	$234.78	$217.54
13	**Average Sales**	$20.84	$27.53	$26.09	$24.17
14	**Lowest Sales**	=MIN(B2:B10)			

The Minimum function formula =MIN(B2:B10) finds the smallest number in cells B2, B3, B4, B5, B6, B7, B8, B9, and B10.

2. Press ENTER. The answer $11.87 appears.
3. Enter a **Minimum function formula** to find the lowest total sales for Week 2, Week 3, and Week 4.

Continued on next page

E. PRETEST

Take a 1-minute timing on the paragraph. Note your speed and errors.

25 Dave and I took our backpacks and started up 9
26 the old mountain trail. Around sunset, we stopped 19
27 to set up camp and have a hot meal. We were very 29
28 tired after such a long day hiking uphill. 37

| 1 | 2 | 3 | 4 | 5 | 6 | 7 | 8 | 9 | 10

F. PRACTICE

SPEED: If you made 2 or fewer errors on the Pretest, key lines 29–36 two times each.

ACCURACY: If you made more than 2 errors on the Pretest, key lines 29–32 as a group 2 times. Then key lines 33–36 as a group 2 times.

Up Reaches

29 ho shock chose phone shove hover holly homes shot
30 st stair guest stone blast nasty start casts step
31 il lilac filed drill build spill child trail pail
32 de dear redeem warden tide render chide rode dead

Down Reaches

33 ab squab labor habit cabin cable abate about able
34 ca pecan recap catch carve cable scale scamp camp
35 av ravel gavel avert knave waved paved shave have
36 in ruin invent winner bring shin chin shrink pine

G. POSTTEST

Repeat the Pretest. Compare your Posttest results with your Pretest results.

H. 1-MINUTE ALPHANUMERIC TIMING

Take a 1-minute timing on lines 37–39. Note your speed and errors.

37 Joy wanted to get a dozen (12) baseball bats 9
38 @ $4.29 from the sports store at 718 Miner Place. 19
39 When I went, only 10 bats were left. 26

| 1 | 2 | 3 | 4 | 5 | 6 | 7 | 8 | 9 | 10

PROJECT 2 Practice

Enter the AVERAGE Function Formula

The **AVERAGE function** adds the values in a selected range of cells and divides the sum by the number of values in the range.

Your Turn

1. Click in cell B13, and key the Average function formula =AVERAGE(B2:B10). Compare your spreadsheet with the illustration shown below.

AVERAGE | =AVERAGE(B2:B10)

	A	B	C	D	E
1	**Name**	**Week 1**	**Week 2**	**Week 3**	**Week 4**
2	Ben	$21.65	$43.00	$22.73	$19.84
3	Haris	$25.89	$28.86	$18.15	$35.23
4	Leticia	$18.00	$29.19	$27.65	$31.00
5	Erin	$11.87	$29.76	$41.00	$16.50
6	Diana	$23.87	$17.44	$20.65	$22.00
7	Trang	$33.45	$24.86	$29.65	$25.83
8	Katie	$13.75	$21.00	$26.75	$28.24
9	Clay	$22.55	$14.89	$24.75	$18.65
10	Scott	$16.50	$38.73	$23.45	$20.25
11					
12	**Total Sales**	$187.53	$247.73	$234.78	$217.54
13	**Average Sales**	=AVERAGE(B2:B10)			

The Average function formula =AVERAGE(B2:B10) adds the values in cells B2, B3, B4, B5, B6, B7, B8, B9, and B10, then divides the sum by 9.

2. Press ENTER. The answer $20.84 appears.
3. Enter an **Average function formula** to average the total sales for Week 2, Week 3, and Week 4.
4. Save the changes. Keep the spreadsheet open for Project 3.

I. 2-MINUTE TIMINGS

Take two 2-minute timings on lines 40–45. Note your speed and errors.

Goal: 27/2′/4e

In the fall of the year, I find pleasure in 9
zipping up to the foothills to quietly view the 19
trees changing colors. Most all aspens turn to 28
shades of gold. Oak trees exude tones of red and 38
orange. The plants change colors each fall, but 47
all the changes are just amazing. 54

| 1 | 2 | 3 | 4 | 5 | 6 | 7 | 8 | 9 | 10 SI 1.27

CARE AND OPERATION OF EQUIPMENT

KEYBOARD SHORTCUTS	
Press	**To access**
ALT + H	Glencoe Keyboarding Software Help
ALT + O	Glencoe Keyboarding Software Options
ALT + F	Glencoe Keyboarding Software File Menu
CTRL + X	Exit Glencoe Keyboarding Software dialog box

PROJECT 1 Practice

Enter the SUM Function Formula

The **SUM function** allows you to add an entire row or column instantly. Functions are convenient to use because they reduce keystrokes. **Functions** are built-in formulas that the spreadsheet provides.

Your Turn

1. Click in cell B12, and key the Sum function formula =SUM(B2:B10). A colon (:) in a formula represents a range of cells. Compare your spreadsheet with the illustration shown below.

SUM =SUM(B2:B10)

	A	B	C	D	E
1	**Name**	**Week 1**	**Week 2**	**Week 3**	**Week 4**
2	Ben	$21.65	$43.00	$22.73	$19.84
3	Haris	$25.89	$28.86	$18.15	$35.23
4	Leticia	$18.00	$29.19	$27.65	$31.00
5	Erin	$11.87	$29.76	$41.00	$16.50
6	Diana	$23.87	$17.44	$20.65	$22.00
7	Trang	$33.45	$24.86	$29.65	$25.83
8	Katie	$13.75	$21.00	$26.75	$28.24
9	Clay	$22.55	$14.89	$24.75	$18.65
10	Scott	$16.50	$38.73	$23.45	$20.25
11					
12	**Total Sales**	=SUM(B2:B10)			

The Sum function formula =SUM(B2:B10) adds the values in cells B2, B3, B4, B5, B6, B7, B8, B9, and B10.

2. Press ENTER. The answer $187.53 appears.
3. Enter a **Sum function formula** to sum the total sales for Week 2, Week 3, and Week 4.
4. Save the changes. Keep the spreadsheet open for Project 2.

SECTION 2.6 New Keys: 5 % 6 ^

GOALS:

- Demonstrate correct techniques for numeric and symbol keys.
- Learn the 5, %, 6, and ^ keys.
- Demonstrate proper keyboarding skills.
- Key 27/2'/4e.

A. WARMUP

Key each line 2 times.

Speed	1 Our team at band camp did a new drill for guests.
Accuracy	2 Two jobs require packing five dozen axes monthly.
Numbers	3 Mark read the winning numbers: 190, 874, and 732.
Symbols	4 The shop (J & B) has #10 envelopes* @ $.24 a doz.

NEW KEYS

B. 5 AND % KEY

Key each line 2 times.

Use F finger. For 5 and %, anchor A.

5 ftf ft5f f5f 555 f5f 5/55 f5f 55.5 f5f 55,555 f5f
6 55 fins, 55 facts, 55 fields, 55 futures, or 5.55
7 Jo saw 55 bulls, 14 cows, 155 sheep, and 5 goats.
8 I just sold 55 items; his total for today is 555.

SECTION 10.4 Enter Functions

GOALS: Demonstrate the ability to:

- Use simple functions in formulas.
- Use the Fill Right command.
- Use the Fill Down command.

WARMUP

Select Warmup from the Skillbuilding menu. Key each Warmup line 2 times.

Speed	1	We can all speak well if we think about what we are saying.
Accuracy	2	Because he was very lazy, Jake paid for six games and quit.
Numbers/Symbols	3	Hasn't our July Check #830 for $149.56 been mailed to them?
Language Link	4	The chapter was much longer than she had expected it to be.

Making the Connection

How long would it take you to add a list of numbers?

Your Turn

1. Open the file **10-4 Project 1**, and save it as ***urs*Fundraiser**.
2. Keep the file open for Project 1.

Week 1

$21.65
$25.89
$18.00
$11.87
$23.87
$33.45
$13.75
$22.55
$16.50

Key each line 2 times.

% is the SHIFT of 5. The % (percent) is used in statistical data. Do not space between numbers and %.

9 ftf ft5 f5f f5%f f%f f%f 5% 55% 555% f%f f5f 555%
10 5%, 5 foes, 55%, 55 fees, 555%, 555 fiddles, 555%
11 The meal is 55% protein, 20% starch, and 25% fat.
12 On June 5, 55% of the students had 5% more skill.

C. 6 AND ^ KEY

Key each line 2 times. Repeat if time permits.

Use J finger. For 6 and ^, anchor ;.

13 jyj jy6j j6j 666 j6j 6/66 j6j 66.6 j6j 66,666 j6j
14 66 jaws, 66 jokes, 66 jewels, 66 jackets, or 6.66
15 Her averages were 76.46, 81.66, 86.56, and 96.36.
16 Multiply .66 by .51; the correct answer is .3366.

^ is the SHIFT of 6. The ^ (caret) is used in some programming languages. Do not space between the caret and numbers.

17 jyj jy6 j6j j6^j j^j j^j ^j ^jj ^jjj j^j j6j ^jjj
18 6^, 6 jams, 66^, 66 jets, 666^, 666 jingles, 666^
19 The test problems included these: 75^2, 4^3, 8^6.
20 The ^ (caret) appeared 6 times in a line of code.

SKILLBUILDING

D. TECHNIQUE TIMINGS

Take two 30-second timings on each line. Focus on the technique at the left.

Sit up straight with your feet on the floor.

21 Snow leopards are graceful animals with soft fur.
22 They live in the high, rugged mountains of Tibet.
23 These big cats are adept at climbing and leaping.
24 They use their tails to balance on narrow ledges.
| 1 | 2 | 3 | 4 | 5 | 6 | 7 | 8 | 9 | 10

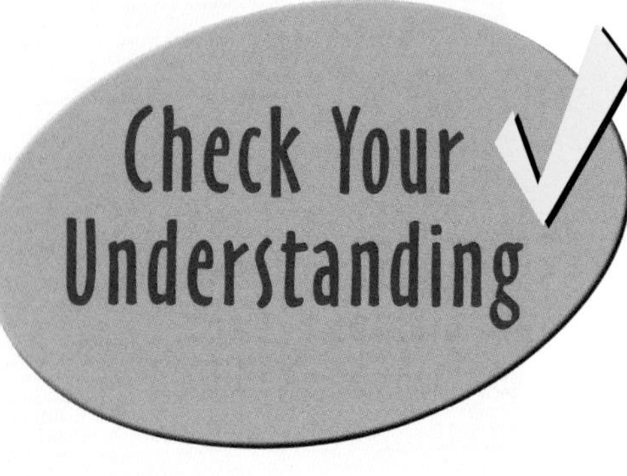

1. Open a new word processing document, and save it as *urs*Spreadsheet Formulas.
2. Discuss why formulas must begin with an equal sign (=).
3. Describe the four kinds of symbols used to create simple formulas.
4. Discuss why the cell location is used to create a formula.
5. Save the changes. Print and close the file.

	A	B	C	D
1	Item	Quantity	Price	Amount
2	pencils	5	$0.50	$2.50
3	pens	6	$1.45	$8.70
4	ruled paper	5	$0.95	$4.75
5	folders	6	$1.25	$7.50
6	spiral notebook	1	$8.50	$8.50
7	three-ring binders	5	$1.25	$6.25
8	**Total Amount Spent**			$38.20
9				
10	**Budgeted Amount**	$40.00		
11	**Difference from Budget**	$1.80		
12	**Percentage of Budget Spent**	95.50%		

Compare urs*School Supplies with the illustration.*

E. PRETEST

Take a 1-minute timing on lines 25–28. Note your speed and errors.

25 As a flock, the crows flew to some clumps of 9
26 stalks near the eddy. They seemed to eat the pods 19
27 joyfully as they fed in the field. We like to 28
28 watch them, especially in the morning. 36
| 1 | 2 | 3 | 4 | 5 | 6 | 7 | 8 | 9 | 10

F. PRACTICE

SPEED: If you made 2 or fewer errors on the Pretest, key lines 29–36 two times each.

ACCURACY: If you made more than 2 errors on the Pretest, key lines 29–32 as a group 2 times. Then key lines 33–36 as a group 2 times.

Adjacent	29	po pods poem point poise lk hulk silk polka stalk
Jump	30	mp jump pump trump clump cr cram crow crawl creed
Double	31	dd odds eddy daddy caddy tt mitt mutt utter ditto
Consecutive	32	un unit punk funny bunch gr grab agree angry grip
Alternate	33	iv give dive drive wives gl glad glee ogled gland
Left/Right	34	fe fear feat ferns fetal jo joys join joker jolly
Up/Down	35	sw swan sway sweat swift k, ark, ask, tick, wick,
In/Out	36	lu luck blunt fluid lush da dash date sedan panda

G. POSTTEST

Repeat the Pretest. Compare your Posttest results with your Pretest results.

H. 1-MINUTE ALPHANUMERIC TIMING

Take a 1-minute timing on lines 37–39. Note your speed and errors.

37 Kim ran the 7.96-mile race last week. Yanni 9
38 ran 14.80 miles. Zeke said the next 5K run will 19
39 be held on August 14 or August 23. 26
| 1 | 2 | 3 | 4 | 5 | 6 | 7 | 8 | 9 | 10

PROJECT 5 **Reinforce**

Create Formulas

In this project you will reinforce what you have learned by entering simple formulas in a spreadsheet to calculate the cost of school supplies.

Your Turn

1. Open the file **10-3 Project 5**, and save it as ***urs*School Supplies**.
2. **Create formulas** to complete the budget shown below.

	A	B	C	D
1	**Item**	**Quantity**	**Price**	**Amount**
2	pencils	5	$0.50	
3	pens	6	$1.45	
4	ruled paper	3	$0.95	
5	folders	6	$1.25	
6	spiral notebook	1	$8.50	
7	three-ring binders	4	$1.25	
8	**Total Amount Spent**			
9				
10	**Budgeted Amount**	$40.00		
11	**Difference from Budget**			
12	**Percentage of Budget Spent**			
13				
14				

To figure the amount of each item, multiply the Quantity by the Price.

To figure the total amount spent on school supplies, add the prices in the Amount column.

To see if you spent within the budgeted amount, subtract the Total Amount Spent from the Budgeted Amount.

To see what percentage of the budget was spent, divide the Total Amount Spent by the Budgeted Amount.

3. You decided that you will need five, 3-ring binders and five packages of ruled paper. Change the quantity of each of those items to 5.
4. Save the changes. Print and close the file.

I. 2-MINUTE TIMINGS

Take two 2-minute timings on lines 40–45. Note your speed and errors.

Goal: 27/2'/4e

40 As you look for jobs, be quite sure that the 9
41 way you dress depicts the position that you want. 19
42 If you desire to obtain an office job, a zippy 29
43 fashion is not for you. Expect to arrive in a 38
44 clean, pressed business suit. Your clothes should 48
45 match that job you are seeking. 54
| 1 | 2 | 3 | 4 | 5 | 6 | 7 | 8 | 9 | 10 SI 1.23

CARE AND OPERATION OF EQUIPMENT

Hold your CD carefully by the edges. Fingerprints on the CD can scratch or damage the CD. Store CDs away from heat and return them to their case when not in use.

PROJECT 4

Practice

Enter a Division Formula

Another simple formula is dividing a cell value by another cell value. The symbol for division is the forward slash (/).

Your Turn

1. Open the file **10-3 Project 4**, and save it as *urs***Baseball**.
2. Click in cell E2, and key the **formula** =c2/b2. Compare your spreadsheet with the illustration shown below.

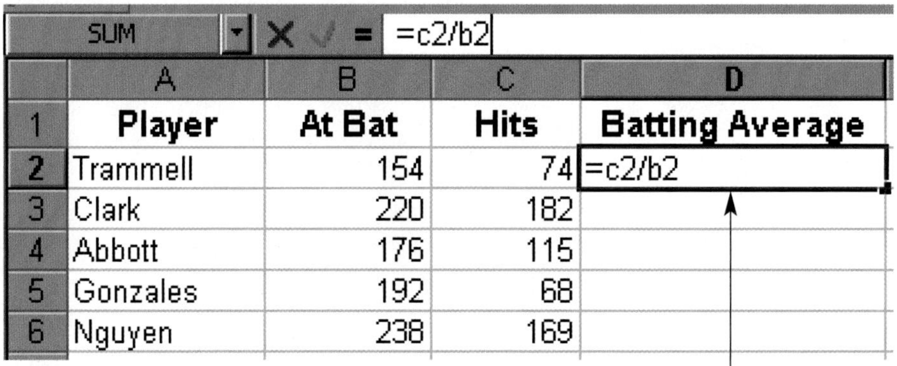

SUM =c2/b2

	A	B	C	D
1	Player	At Bat	Hits	Batting Average
2	Trammell	154	74	=c2/b2
3	Clark	220	182	
4	Abbott	176	115	
5	Gonzales	192	68	
6	Nguyen	238	169	

The formula =c2/b2 divides the value 74 in cell c2 by the value 154 in cell b2.

3. Press Enter. The answer 0.481 appears. This means a player earned a hit 48% of the times he came to bat.
4. **Create formulas** to calculate the rest of the batting averages.
5. Save the changes. Print and close the file.

SECTION 2.7 Special Symbols

GOALS:

- Demonstrate correct techniques for symbols.
- Learn the <, >, \, +, =, {, }, [,], and ~ keys.
- Demonstrate proper keyboarding skills.
- Key 27/2'/4e.

A. WARMUP

Key each line 2 times.

Speed	1	Brent hurt his arm today and is in a lot of pain.
Accuracy	2	The tax is zero on these dozen tax-exempt pizzas.
Numbers	3	The population of Cooper is 216,974, not 326,815.
Symbols	4	Stop & Shop has 25% off reams of 24# paper @ $13.

NEW KEYS

B. SPECIAL SYMBOLS

You have learned to key many frequently used symbols by touch. Less frequently used symbols also appear on the keyboard. Although it is not necessary to learn these symbols by touch, you should know what they are, how they are used, where they are located, and which fingers to use for keying them.

PROJECT 3 Continued

Practice

Enter a Multiplication Formula

5. Click in cell E2, and key the **formula** =b2−d2. Compare your spreadsheet with the illustration shown below.

SUM | =b2-d2

	A	B	C	D	E
1	**Item**	**Price**	**% of Discount**	**$ of Discount**	**Sale Price**
2	Shirt	$25.00	20%	$5.00	=b2-d2
3	Shorts	$32.00	15%		
4	Pants	$38.00	25%		
5	Shoes	$45.00	10%		

The formula =b2−d2 subtracts the value $5.00 in cell d2 from the value $25.00 in cell b2.

6. Press ENTER. The answer $20.00 appears.
7. **Create formulas** to calculate the rest of the Sale Price column.
8. Save the changes. Print and close the file.

Find each of the symbols shown below on your keyboard. Note which finger controls each key and the spacing used with the symbol. In the example column, study how the symbol is used.

Key	Name	Use	Finger	Spacing	Example
\	Back Slash	Naming files and directories	Sem	No space before and after	`a:\Medical\ Doctor.cgs`
<	Less Than	Math	K	One space before and after	`15 < 25`
>	Greater Than	Math	L	One space before and after	`31 > 19`
=	Equal	Math	Sem	One space before and after	`A = 27`
+	Plus	Math	Sem	One space before and after	`3 + 3 = 6`
[ ]	Left and Right Brackets	Enclose special text	Sem	No space after [or before]	`"He [Twain] wrote . . . "`
{ }	Left and Right Curly Braces	Math and Internet searches	Sem	No space after { or before }	`{4, 2, 6}`
~	Tilde	Internet addresses	A	No space before and after	`www.isp.com/~jon`

PROJECT 3 Practice

Enter a Multiplication Formula

Another simple formula is multiplication of a cell value by another value. The mathematical sign for multiplication is the asterisk symbol (*).

Your Turn

1. Open the file **10-3 Project 3**, and save it as ***urs*Sale**.
2. Click in cell D2, and key the **formula** =b2*c2. Compare your spreadsheet with the illustration shown below.

SUM =b2*c2

	A	B	C	D	E
1	**Item**	**Price**	**% of Discount**	**$ of Discount**	**Sale Price**
2	Shirt	$25.00	20%	=b2*c2	
3	Shorts	$32.00	15%		
4	Pants	$38.00	25%		
5	Shoes	$45.00	10%		

The formula =b2*c2 multiplies the value $25.00 in cell b2 by the value 20% in cell c2.

3. Press ENTER. The answer $5.00 appears.
4. **Create formulas** to calculate the rest of the "$ of Discount" column.

Continued on next page

Key each line 2 times. Repeat if time permits.

5 Dakota typed "C:\DATABASE\FRESHMEN\OFFICERS.SEP."
6 If X < Z and Y > X but < Z, then Z > X and Z > Y.
7 Please see if 7.13 + 5.21 = 12.34 and 9 + 2 = 11.

8 "They [Americans] captured Trenton [New Jersey]."
9 Search for these: {New York}, Ohio, {New Mexico}.
10 Use this format: http://www.server.com/~username.

SKILLBUILDING

C. PRETEST

Take a 1-minute timing on lines 11–14. Note your speed and errors.

11 A news report said that the trash will be 9
12 collected next week. Many county roads are still 19
13 covered with too much snow. The county officials 29
14 will discuss this problem for a few more days. 38
| 1 | 2 | 3 | 4 | 5 | 6 | 7 | 8 | 9 | 10

D. PRACTICE

SPEED: If you made 2 or fewer errors on the Pretest, key lines 15–22 two times each.

ACCURACY: If you made more than 2 errors on the Pretest, key lines 15–18 as a group 2 times. Then key lines 19–22 as a group 2 times.

Discrimination reaches are keys that are commonly substituted and easily confused. Example: wear.

15 asa flask aside sails saved masks sadly trash sas
16 fgf frogs foggy gaffe fugue golfs goofs fight gfg
17 ewe weeks fewer sewer sweat swell sweet weans wew
18 ded deal heeded dent need debate feed student ede

19 ioi spoil toils lions coins joins soils boils oio
20 mnm hymns money names numbs minor lemon means nmn
21 klk locks block flock keels kills kilts kilns lkl
22 yuy yule young unduly pulley bully ruby jumpy uyu

PROJECT 2 Practice

Enter a Subtraction Formula

Another simple formula is subtracting one cell value from another. The mathematical sign for subtraction is the minus sign (−).

	A	B
1		**Week 1**
2	**Income**	
3	mowed lawn	$15.00
4	baby-sat	$10.00
5	**Total**	$25.00
6		
7	**Expenses**	
8	movie rental	$4.00
9	game rental	$3.00
10	snacks	$1.50
11	**Total**	$8.50
12		
13	**Amount Left**	=b5-b11

The formula =b5−b11 subtracts the value $8.50 in cell b11 from the value $25.00 in cell b5.

Your Turn

1. Click in cell A13 and key Amount Left.
2. Click in cell B13 and key the **formula** =b5−b11. Compare your spreadsheet with the illustration shown at the left.
3. Press Enter. The answer $16.50 appears.
4. Compare your paper calculation with the spreadsheet answer.
5. **Create a formula** to calculate the Amount Left for Weeks 2, 3, and 4 as shown below.

12						
13	**Amount Left**	$16.50				

Subtract Expense Total from Income Total.

6. Oops! You just realized that you have a mistake. The cost of the game rental for Week 3 was $3.00 instead of $2.50. Change the amount in cell D9 to $3.00. Notice the Total Expenses and the Amount Left for Week 3 change.
7. Save the changes. Print and close the file.

E. POSTTEST

Repeat the Pretest. Compare your Posttest results with your Pretest results.

F. ALPHABET REVIEW

Key each line 1 time. Repeat if time permits.

23 aa alas also again after bb bake blow begin black

24 cc came coat charm clear dd drop door dream dated

25 ee ever each eager enemy ff five foal frame flute

26 gg game give grate guard hh hope hall heavy human

27 ii iced into ideal ionic jj jail joke jewel juice

28 kk keep kick knife knock ll long lace lower lever

29 mm mope mail merit music nn name none never night

30 oo over open order occur pp pure pain piece plump

31 qq quit quad quest quote rr roar rain rhyme rural

32 ss sing soap saber sense tt time talk tooth trait

33 uu us urge upon vv via vase vine ww wag west warm

34 xx ox axis exit yy yen year yank zz zoo zany zinc

G. NUMBER AND SYMBOL REVIEW

Key each line 1 time. Repeat if time permits.

35 46 maps, 69 snaps, 65 traps, 15 drapes, 63 grapes

36 57 lots, 85 plots, 16 slots, 50 floats, 86 clocks

37 53 hams, 46 trams, 95 slams, 62 flames, 67 blames

38 58 ails, 60 sails, 96 nails, 45 snails, 47 trails

39 (1) 32% of $17, (2) 2^9, (3) 15 @ $.81, (4) Wait!

40 (5) the key,* (6) A & W, (7) 56 @ $.10, (8) 40^3*

Continued on next page

PROJECT 1 Continued

Practice

Introduction to Formulas

5. **Create a formula** to add the rest of the Income and Expenses Totals for each week.

Format cells B3 through F11 with currency format.

B5 | f_x =B3+B4

	A	B	C	D	E	F
1		**Week 1**	**Week 2**	**Week 3**	**Week 4**	**Total**
2	**Income**					
3	mowed lawn	$15.00	$15.00	$15.00	$15.00	
4	baby-sat	$10.00	$12.00	$8.00	$10.00	
5	**Total**	$25.00				
6						
7	**Expenses**					
8	movie rental	$4.00	$1.99	$4.00	$4.00	
9	game rental	$3.00	$3.00	$2.50	$3.00	
10	snacks	$1.50	$1.00	$2.35	$3.25	
11	**Total**					
12						

Add total amount for each week.

Add total amount for all four weeks.

6. Save the changes. Keep the spreadsheet open for Project 2.

Key each line 1 time.

41 Tony said 3^2 and 20% of 40 have the same answer.
42 He rented 56 vases, 239 tables, and 4,078 chairs.

43 A & Z billed us for 79 pens @ $.23 on Invoice #8.
44 Dan collected 98 flowers, 39 bugs, and 47 leaves.

45 Nice & Clean (formerly #1 Laundry) is in Memphis.
46 The 743 people were served 980 rolls by 12 girls.

H. 1-MINUTE ALPHANUMERIC TIMING

Take a 1-minute timing on lines 47–79. Note your speed and errors.

47 Jason paid Invoice #75 with Check #2301. He 9
48 mailed it June 24, but he forgot the $.39 stamp. 19
49 Stop & Go's bill needs to be paid July 1. 27
| 1 | 2 | 3 | 4 | 5 | 6 | 7 | 8 | 9 | 10

I. 2-MINUTE TIMINGS

Take two 2-minute timings on lines 50–55. Note your speed and errors.

Goal: 27/2'/4e

50 The Cherokee had no desire to leave the land 9
51 of their fathers. Troops required them to move to 19
52 the west. Many of them froze to death during the 29
53 brutal winter journey. They were not equipped to 39
54 exist through the cold winter as they moved along 49
55 the tragic Trail of Tears. 54
| 1 | 2 | 3 | 4 | 5 | 6 | 7 | 8 | 9 | 10 SI 1.30

PROJECT 1 Practice

Introduction to Formulas

To add, subtract, multiply, and divide, create a spreadsheet **formula**, which is a mathematical equation. All formulas must begin with an equal sign (=).

Your Turn

1. Open the file **10-3 Project 1**, and save it as *urs***Budget**.
2. Click in cell B5, and key the formula =b3+b4. Compare your spreadsheet with the illustration shown below.

The **formula bar** displays the formula for the cell.

SUM =b3+b4

	A	B	C	D	E	F
1		**Week 1**	**Week 2**	**Week 3**	**Week 4**	**Total**
2	**Income**					
3	mowed lawn	$15.00	$15.00	$15.00	$15.00	
4	baby-sat	$10.00	$12.00	$8.00	$10.00	
5	**Total**	=b3+b4				
6						

The formula =b3+b4 adds the value $15.00 in cell b3 and the value $10.00 in cell b4.

3. Press ENTER. The answer $25.00 appears.
4. Compare your paper calculation with the spreadsheet answer.

Continued on next page

SECTION 2.8

Numeric Keypad: 4 5 6 Enter

Goals:

- Demonstrate correct numeric keypad techniques.
- Learn the 4, 5, 6, and Enter keys on the numeric keypad.
- Learn capitalization rules.
- Demonstrate proper keyboarding skills.
- Key 30/2'/4e.

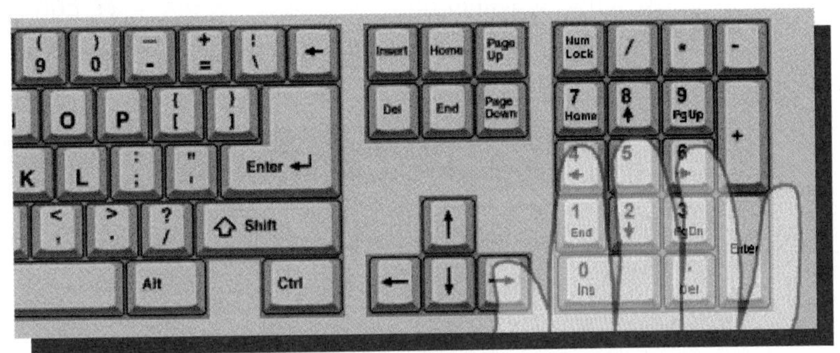

A. Warmup

Key each line 2 times.

Speed	1 We will be out for spring break in two more days.
Accuracy	2 Skip was quite vexed by the jazzman from Cologne.
Numbers	3 Your fingers can now find 10, 29, 38, 47, and 56.
Symbols	4 If T > Z, then explain (please!) why {T + H = Z}.

Touch-System Techniques

The numeric keypad is usually located on the right side of the keyboard. It contains symbols (+, -, *, and /) just like a calculator. Use these symbols to show addition (+), subtraction (-), multiplication (*), or division (/).

SECTION **10.3**

Use Simple Formulas

GOALS: Demonstrate the ability to:

- Enter a simple formula to add.
- Enter a simple formula to subtract.
- Enter a simple formula to multiply.
- Enter a simple formula to divide.

WARMUP

Select Warmup from the Skillbuilding menu. Key each Warmup line 2 times.

Speed	1	`The temperature last night dropped below the freezing mark.`
Accuracy	2	`Jack typed four dozen requisitions for hollow moving boxes.`
Numbers/Symbols	3	`The citation for the case is 795 F.2D 1423 (9th Cir. 1996).`
Language Link	4	`Then Coach said the prize went to whoever ran the farthest.`

Making the Connection

Peter has been keeping a monthly budget plan on paper. When he needs to keep track of his money, he uses pencil, paper, and a calculator to figure it out.

Your Turn

1. Use a sheet of paper to calculate the amount of money Peter has left over each week.

	Week 1	Week 2	Week 3	Week 4	Total
Income					
mowed lawn	$15.00	$15.00	$15.00	$15.00	
baby-sat	$10.00	$12.00	$8.00	$10.00	
Total					
Expenses					
movie rental	$4.00	$1.99	$4.00	$4.00	
game rental	$3.00	$3.00	$2.50	$3.00	
snacks	$1.50	$1.00	$2.35	$3.25	
Total					
Amount left					

Add total amount for each week. → (Income Total and Expenses Total)

Add total amount for all four weeks. → (Total column)

Subtract Expenses Total from Income Total. → (Amount left)

B. Capitalization

Study the rules and the examples below. Then edit lines 5–8 to correct any errors in capitalization.

Rule 1 Capitalize the first word of a sentence.

The weather bureau predicted a winter storm. It was severe.

Rule 2 Capitalize the names of the days of the week, months, holidays, and religious days. Do not capitalize the names of the seasons.

In the fall, we celebrate Thanksgiving on Thursday, November 24.

Edit the lines to correct any errors in capitalization.

```
5 memorial day this year will fall on monday, may 27.
6 why wait until wednesday? we can leave later today.
7 during the Winter, they skied and skated every day.
8 Offices are closed on memorial day and on thursday.
```

C. Keypad Home-Key Position

The NUM LOCK key must be active before you can enter numbers on the keypad. If the NUM LOCK light is not on, press the NUM LOCK key.

The 4, 5, and 6 are the home keys for the numeric keypad.

1. Place your J, K, and L fingers on 4, 5, and 6 on the numeric keypad. You will feel a raised marker on the 5 key. This marker will help you keep your fingers on the home keys.
2. Place your Sem finger over the ENTER key. The ENTER key on the numeric keypad functions just like the ENTER key on the alphabetic keyboard.

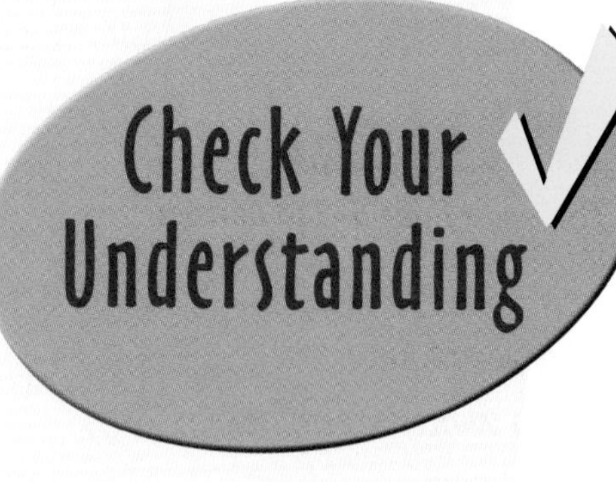

1. Open a new word processing document, and save it as *urs*Spreadsheet Editing.
2. Describe when it would be necessary to change a column width.
3. Describe why ### symbols sometimes appear in a column.
4. Describe how to insert a column or row.
5. Describe how to delete a column or row.
6. Describe how to organize information alphabetically.
7. Save the changes. Print and close the file.

	A	B	C
1	**COUNTRY INFORMATION**		
2			
3	**Country**	**Capital**	**Population**
4			
5	Brazil	Brasilia	176,029,560
6	China	Beijing	1,284,303,705
7	Germany	Berlin	83,251,887
8	South Korea	Seoul	10,432,774
9	United States	Washington, D.C.	278,058,881
10	Vietnam	Hanoi	81,098,416

Compare urs*Country with the illustration.*

D. 4 5 6 KEYS

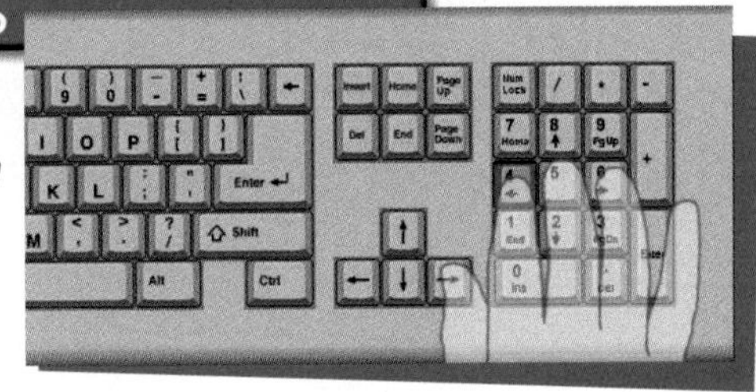

Enter the following numbers column by column. Use the proper finger for each key. Press ENTER after the final digit of each number. Repeat if time permits.

Use J, K, and L fingers. Keep your eyes on the copy. Accuracy is very important when entering numbers.

9	444	456	454
10	555	654	464
11	666	445	546
12	455	446	564
13	466	554	654
14	544	556	645
15	566	664	666
16	644	665	555
17	655	456	444
18	456	654	456

SKILLBUILDING

E. KEYPAD PRACTICE

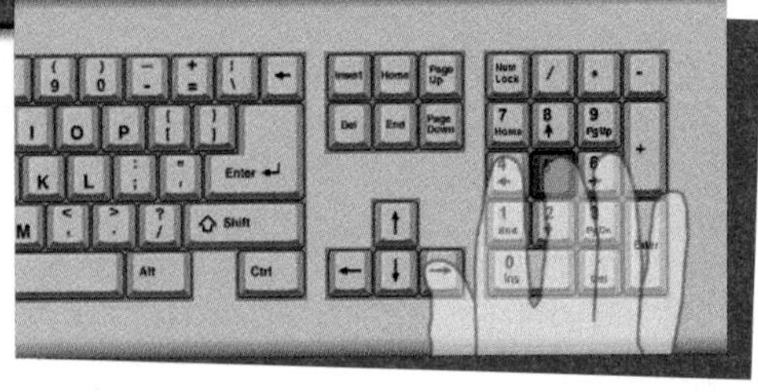

Enter the following numbers column by column. Press ENTER after the final digit of each number. Keep your eyes on the copy. Repeat if time permits.

Use J, K, and L fingers. Keep your eyes on the copy. Accuracy is very important when entering numbers.

19	444	455	464	555	466	646	666	544	456	445	644
20	546	554	556	454	645	664	545	654	665	565	465
21	445	446	455	466	456	454	465	464	554	556	544
22	644	655	645	646	654	656	666	464	555	665	456
23	654	456	564	465	646	656	464	456	546	564	465

PROJECT 4 Continued **Reinforce**

Create a Spreadsheet

5. Edit the spreadsheet as shown.

Insert 2 rows above "Country." Key the title shown. Format bold. Change the font size to 12 pt.

	A	B	C	D
1	**COUNTRY INFORMATION**			
2				
3	**Country**	**Area (sq. mi.)**	**Capital**	**Population**
4				
5	China	3,705,386	Beijing	1,284,303,705
6	Brazil	3,286,470	Brasilia	176,029,560
7	South Korea	38,450	Seoul	10,432,774
8	Germany	137,823	Berlin	83,251,887
9	United States	3,679,192	Washington, D.C.	278,058,881
10	Vietnam	127,243	Hanoi	81,098,416

Delete the column named "Area (sq. mi.)."

6. Use the sort feature to alphabetize the "Country" column as shown.

	A	B	C	D
1	**COUNTRY INFORMATION**			
2				
3	**Country**	**Capital**	**Population**	
4				
5	China	Beijing	1,284,303,705	
6	Brazil	Brasilia	176,029,560	
7	South Korea	Seoul	10,432,774	
8	Germany	Berlin	83,251,887	
9	United States	Washington, D.C.	278,058,881	
10	Vietnam	Hanoi	81,098,416	
11				

Sort the **list** in **ascending order.**

7. Save the changes. Print and close the file.

F. TECHNIQUE TIMINGS

Take two 30-second timings on each line. Focus on the techniques at the left.

Concentrate on efficient and smooth operation of the ENTER key.

```
24 Will Zeb and Vern work Zone Two with Cam and Nic?
25 Miriam and Dolores saw Broadway and Main Streets.
26 Did Ben Milo fix that off/on switch? Did it work?
27 Ivan is grateful that it is ready for the winter.
   | 1 | 2 | 3 | 4 | 5 | 6 | 7 | 8 | 9 | 10
```

G. DIAGNOSTIC PRACTICE: ALPHABET

Turn to the Diagnostic Practice: Alphabet routine on page SB1. Key one of the Pretest/Posttest paragraphs and identify any errors. Then key the corresponding drill lines on page SB2 two times for each letter on which you made 2 or more errors and 1 time for each letter on which you made only 1 error. Finally, repeat the same Pretest paragraph and compare your performance.

H. 12-SECOND SPRINTS

Take three 12-second timings on each line. Try to increase your speed on each timing.

```
28 Walking can pick you up if you are feeling tired.
29 Your heart and lungs can work harder as you walk.
30 It may be that a walk is often better than a nap.
31 You will keep fit if you walk each and every day.
   ||||5||||10||||15||||20||||25||||30||||35||||40||||45||||50
```

PROJECT 4 Continued

Reinforce

Create a Spreadsheet

3. Edit the spreadsheet as shown in the illustration.

	A	B	C
1	**Country**	**Area (sq. mi.)**	**Population**
2			
3	China	3,705,386	1,284,303,705
4	Brazil	3,286,470	176,029,560
5	Germany	137,823	83,251,887
6	United States	3,679,192	278,058,881
7	Czech Republic	30,450	10,432,774

Insert one **row** above row 5 containing information about the country Germany.

Delete the row containing information about the country Czech Republic.

Insert a column before column C, "Population."

4. Add the data as indicated.

	A	B	C	D
1	**Country**	**Area (sq. mi.)**	**Capital**	**Population**
2				
3	China	3,705,386	Beijing	1,284,303,705
4	Brazil	3,286,470	Brasilia	176,029,560
5	South Korea	38,450	Seoul	10,432,774
6	Germany	137,823	Berlin	83,251,887
7	United States	3,679,192	Washington, D.C.	278,058,881
8	Vietnam	127,243	Hanoi	81,098,416

Key the information about South Korea and Vietnam.

Key the title "Capital." Format bold. Change the font size to 12 pt. Align center the title. Key the remaining data as shown.

Continued on next page

I. 2-MINUTE TIMINGS

Take two 2-minute timings on lines 32–38. Note your speed and errors.

Goal: 30/2'/4e

```
32      Some senior students realize that once they     9
33 leave school, they must plan for more education.    19
34 Most might not know exactly what their first job    29
35 will be or what skills will equip them to move      38
36 ahead in a job or to change to another job. You     48
37 should make plans for your future now while you     57
38 have the time.                                      60
   | 1 | 2 | 3 | 4 | 5 | 6 | 7 | 8 | 9 | 10       SI 1.25
```

TOUCH-SYSTEM TECHNIQUES

Return your fingers to home-key position after reaching for upper or lower keys.

PROJECT 4 **Reinforce**

Create a Spreadsheet

In this project you will reinforce what you have learned by creating and editing a spreadsheet about the area, population, and capital cities of several countries.

Your Turn

1. Open a **new** spreadsheet **file**, and save as *urs***Country**.
2. Key and format the information shown.

Click and drag the column boundaries to **change** the **column width** so the cell with the most data fits.

Align center the headings, format bold, and change the font size to 12 pt.

	A	B	C
1	**Country**	**Area (sq. mi.)**	**Population**
2			
3	China	3,705,386	1,284,303,705
4	Brazil	3,286,470	176,029,560
5	Germany	137,823	83,251,887
6	United States	3,679,192	278,058,881
7	Czech Republic	30,450	10,432,774

Format the numbers to separate the thousands with a comma.

Continued on next page

SECTION 2.9 Numeric Keypad: 7 8 9

GOALS:

- Demonstrate correct numeric keypad techniques.
- Learn the 7, 8, and 9 keys on the numeric keypad.
- Demonstrate proper keyboarding skills.
- Key 30/2′/4e.

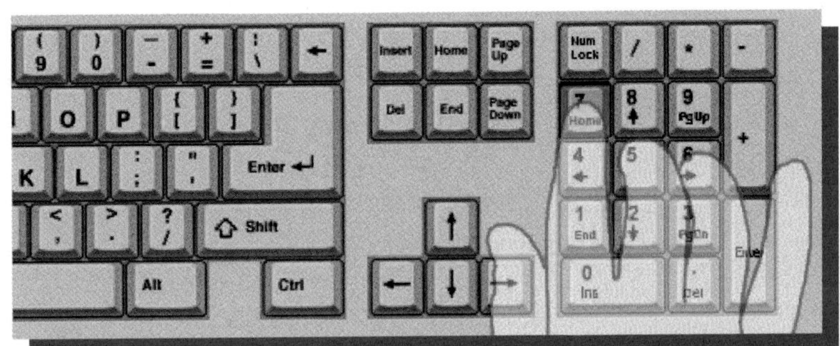

A. WARMUP

Key each line 2 times.

Speed	1	No one can say that he is not giving full effort.
Accuracy	2	Alex was puzzled by the czar's quip about oxygen.
Language Link	3	He and Molly traveled to Iowa on Saturday by bus.
Numbers	4	Without looking I can type 67, 89, 23, 14, and 5.

The numeric keypad contains a NUM LOCK key. The NUM LOCK key works like the CAPS LOCK key on the alphabet side of the keyboard—when the NUM LOCK key is activated—it forces the numeric keys to input numbers.

You know the NUM LOCK key is activated when the light appears by the key.

PROJECT 3 Practice

Sort a List of Data

You can **sort** your data in a spreadsheet either alphabetically or numerically. This is helpful when you want to organize your information.

Your Turn

1. Select cells A4 through B13 as shown.
2. Sort in ascending order the "Length of Life" column.

Sort the list in ascending order.

	A	B
1	**My Research**	
2		
3	**Length of Life**	**Years**
4	Blue jay	4
5	Canada goose	32
6	Penguin	26
7	Raven	25
8	Ostrich	50
9	Whale	20
10	Alligator	56
11	Crocodile	13
12	Bullfrog	15
13	Rattlesnake	18

3. Save the changes. Print and close the file.

NEW KEYS

B. 7 8 9 KEYS

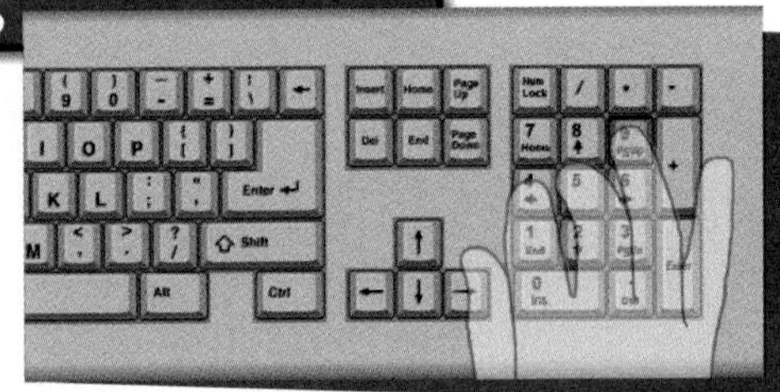

Enter the following numbers column by column. Use the proper finger for each key. Press ENTER after the final digit of each number. Keep your eyes on the copy. Repeat if time permits.

Use J, K, and L fingers. Be sure NUM LOCK is on. Concentrate on accuracy as you enter the numbers.

```
474   585   696
747   858   969
774   885   996
447   558   669
744   855   966
477   588   699
444   555   666
747   858   969
774   885   996
747   858   969
```

SKILLBUILDING

C. KEYPAD PRACTICE

Enter the following numbers column by column. Use the proper finger for each key. Press ENTER after the final digit of each number. Keep your eyes on the copy. Repeat if time permits.

Use proper fingers. Concentrate on accuracy.

```
456   556   474   699   477   577   677   748   847   947
654   664   585   747   488   588   688   749   849   948
445   665   696   858   499   599   699   758   857   957
446   456   477   969   478   578   678   759   859   958
554   654   588   789   489   589   689   767   868   969
```

PROJECT 2 Continued

Practice

Insert and Delete Columns and Rows

3. Add the data as indicated.

	A	B	C
1	**Length of Life**	**Years**	**Months**
2	Blue jay	4	48
3	Canada goose	32	384
4	Penguin	26	312
5	Raven	25	300
6	Ostrich	50	600
7	Whale	20	240
8	Alligator	56	672
9	Crocodile	13	156
10	Bullfrog	15	180
11	Rattlesnake	18	216

Key the title "Years." Format bold. Change the font size to 12 pt., and align center. Enter the data shown.

Key the information about the ostrich.

4. Edit the spreadsheet as shown.

	A	B	C
1	**My Research**		
2			
3	**Length of Life**	**Years**	**Months**
4	Blue jay	4	48
5	Canada goose	32	384
6	Penguin	26	312
7	Raven	25	300
8	Ostrich	50	600
9	Whale	20	240
10	Alligator	56	672
11	Crocodile	13	156
12	Bullfrog	15	180
13	Rattlesnake	18	216

Insert 2 rows above "Length of Life." Key the title shown. Format bold. Change the font size to 12 pt.

Delete the column named "Months."

5. Save the changes. Keep the file open for Project 3.

D. PACED PRACTICE

Turn to the Paced Practice routine beginning on page SB7. Take a 1-minute timing on the Entry Timing paragraph. Then follow directions at the top of page SB7 for completing the activity.

E. 30-SECOND OK TIMINGS

Take two 30-second OK timings on lines 20–21. Then take two 30-second OK timings on lines 22–23. Goal: No errors.

```
20      He wants to work for a company that provides
21 benefits to workers. Jay's benefits are terrific.

22      Flat computer screen means that I can set up
23 my computer on my desk because the parts all fit.
   | 1 | 2 | 3 | 4 | 5 | 6 | 7 | 8 | 9 | 10
```

CARE AND OPERATION OF EQUIPMENT

Use a small, soft brush to clean dust from the keyboard.

PROJECT 2 Practice

Insert and Delete Columns and Rows

You can delete a row or column to remove data you no longer want in your spreadsheet. You can also add a row or column to insert additional data.

Your Turn

1. Open the file **10-2 Project 2**, and save it as ***urs*Animals**.
2. Edit the spreadsheet as indicated.

	A	B
1	**Length of Life**	**Months**
2	Blue jay	48
3	Canada goose	384
4	Penguin	312
5	Raven	300
6	Whale	240
7	Alligator	672
8	Crocodile	156
9	Gila Monster	240
10	Bullfrog	180
11	Rattlesnake	216

Insert a column before column B "Months."

Insert one **row** above row 6 about the whale.

Delete the **row** containing information about the gila monster.

Continued on next page

F. PRETEST

Take a 1-minute timing on the paragraph. Note your speed and errors.

24 Jenny loved most all of the opera music that 9
25 the kids sang. No one could deny how funny they 19
26 looked in muffs and emu feathers. Everyone had a 29
27 blast that afternoon. 33
| 1 | 2 | 3 | 4 | 5 | 6 | 7 | 8 | 9 | 10

G. PRACTICE

SPEED: If you made 2 or fewer errors on the Pretest, key lines 28–35 two times each.

ACCURACY: If you made more than 2 errors on the Pretest, key lines 28–31 as a group 2 times. Then key lines 32–35 as a group 2 times.

Adjacent Reaches

28 as mast blast phase clash ashes atlas brash hasty
29 op crop opera flops opens poppy drops opals mopes
30 ds kids spuds grids bonds birds brads leads holds
31 lk milk talks walks balks milky silky bulky sulky

Jump Reaches

32 mu mute music muffs munch murky mulls musty muddy
33 ve cove verse serve curve verve wives chive sieve
34 ny deny funny phony shiny sunny irony corny agony
35 in sink blink slink whine shine winds pines inlet

H. POSTTEST

Repeat the Pretest. Compare your Posttest results with your Pretest results.

I. 2-MINUTE TIMINGS

Take two 2-minute timings on lines 36–42. Note your speed and errors.

Goal: 30/2'/4e

36 The end of a school program is a great feat 9
37 for most students. Some believe it might be the 19
38 last time for a test. This may not be so, as a 28
39 number of exams may be taken in their lifetime. 38
40 It is quite puzzling to some why tests should be 47
41 given when they have already been judged by their 57
42 achievements. 60
| 1 | 2 | 3 | 4 | 5 | 6 | 7 | 8 | 9 | 10 SI 1.22

PROJECT 1 Continued

Practice

Create a New Spreadsheet and Change Column Width

	A	B	C
1	Region	Population	
2			
3	Asia	3674863000	
4	Africa	778997999	
5	Europe	732855000	
6	North America	483211000	
7	South America	342841000	
8	Australia/Oceania	31643000	
9	Antarctica	0	
10			

4. Enter the Population data. Make the changes indicated.

Align center the headings, format bold, and change the font size to 12 pt.

Format the numbers to separate the thousands with a comma.

	A	B	C
1	**Region**	**Population**	
2			
3	Asia	###########	
4	Africa	778,997,999	
5	Europe	732,855,000	
6	North America	483,211,000	
7	South America	342,841,000	
8	Australia/Oceania	31,643,000	
9	Antarctica	0	
10			

5. If necessary, widen the column borders as shown.

Change the **column width** to remove the number symbols and display the data.

6. Save the changes. Print and close the file.

SECTION 2.10

Review

GOALS:

- Demonstrate correct touch-system for techniques and proper numeric keypad and keyboarding skills.
- Key 30/2′/4e.
- Demonstrate the ability to compose at the keyboard.

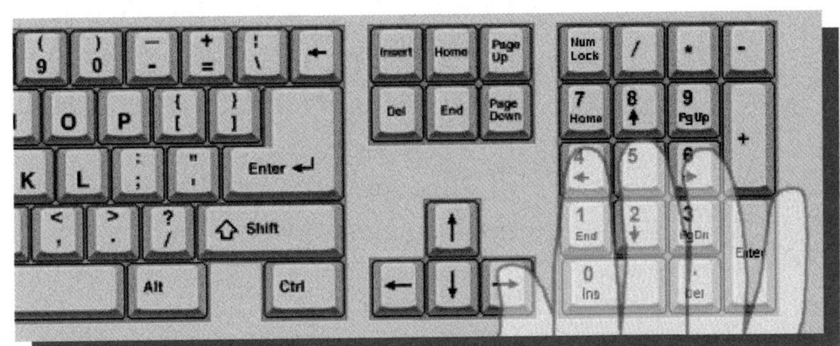

A. WARMUP

Key each line 2 times.

Speed	1	Tish dances with grace and seems to float on air.
Accuracy	2	Zudora and Javan are amazed by the tranquil pool.
Language Link	3	We took Ms. Verhetsel to the airport on Thursday.
Numbers/Symbols	4	Movies 7 (on Highway 59) charges $2 on Thursdays.

SKILLBUILDING

B. KEYPAD REVIEW

Enter the following numbers column by column. Use the proper finger for each key. Press ENTER after the final digit of each number. Keep your eyes on the copy. Repeat if time permits.

Use the correct fingers as you enter each set of numbers. Operate the numeric keypad smoothly.

5	444	999	657	547	557	985	968	897	766	687
6	555	489	658	548	558	986	969	898	768	697
7	666	589	659	549	559	964	894	899	769	567
8	777	689	654	554	987	965	895	764	684	459
9	888	789	655	556	984	967	896	765	685	648

PROJECT 1 Practice

Create a New Spreadsheet and Change Column Width

Create a new spreadsheet to enter data. You can easily adjust column widths to display the data.

Your Turn

1. Open a **new** spreadsheet **file**, and save as ***urs*Population**.

2. Key the column headings as shown.

	A	B	C
1	Region	Population	
2			
3			

3. Enter each Region, and change the column border as shown.

	A	B	C
1	Region	Population	
2			
3	Asia		
4	Africa		
5	Europe		
6	North America		
7	South America		
8	Australia/Oceania		
9	Antarctica		
10			

Click and drag the column boundary to **change** the **column width** so the cell with the most data fits.

Continued on next page

C. ***Key each line 2 times. Focus on the technique at the left.***

Concentrate on smooth operation of the Shift keys.

10 Benji typed a report on New Guinea and Australia.
11 Kodi said that all of us should meet after class.
12 I bought yards of flannel at Sew Easy this month.
13 Oren donated his profit to the Find-a-Child Fund.

D. ALPHABET REVIEW

Key each line 1 time. Concentrate on efficient and smooth operation of the Shift keys. Repeat if time permits.

14 A Anna Aram Alan B Bel Bern Beth C Curt Chan Cleo
15 D Desi Dino Dona E Ean Erin Egan F Fifi Finn Faye
16 G Gaby Gian Gena H Ham Hank Hedy I Ilse Ilya Iris

17 J Jess Jori Jojo K Kia Kern Kwan L Luke Lars Lyda
18 M Miki Marc Mara N Noe Niki Noel O Olin Otto Olga
19 P Pace Pita Powa Q Qam Quin Quan R Rani Reid Rory

20 S Suni Saul Shan T Tov Taio Tobi U Ulma Urie Ushi
21 V Vera Vick Vala W Web Wren Wilt X Xann Xela Xuxa
22 Y Yoki York Ynez Yusif Z Zizi Zane Zena Zeke Zara

E. TECHNIQUE TIMINGS

Take two 30-second timings on each line. Focus on the technique at the left.

Concentrate on smooth operation of the Shift keys.

23 David and Ian still work at B. K. Dry Goods, Inc.
24 Mrs. R. K. Dunn taught Spanish at Jefferson High.
25 Rory, Anna, and Han ran the Mile-High Race today.
26 She is at the top in her new job at the car wash.
| 1 | 2 | 3 | 4 | 5 | 6 | 7 | 8 | 9 | 10

SECTION 10.2

Create and Edit a Spreadsheet

GOALS: Demonstrate the ability to:

- Create a new spreadsheet.
- Change column widths.
- Insert rows and columns.
- Delete rows and columns.
- Sort data.

WARMUP

Select Warmup from the Skillbuilding menu. Key each Warmup line 2 times.

Speed	1	Elaine invited several of her friends over for the evening.
Accuracy	2	Why would quick brown foxes want to jump over any lazy dog?
Numbers/Symbols	3	Only 4% of our current PCs are equipped with CD-ROM drives.
Language Link	4	Rather than go any farther, they stopped to get directions.

Making the Connection

Ingrid would like to create an attractive spreadsheet to display her research about world populations.

Your Turn

1. Think of some ways Ingrid might organize the data in a spreadsheet.
2. Share your answers with a partner.
3. Launch your spreadsheet software for Project 1.

Region	Population
Asia	3,674,863,000
Africa	778,997,999
Europe	732,855,000
North America	438,211,000
South America	342,841,000
Australia/Oceania	31,643,000
Antarctica	0

F. PRETEST

Take a 1-minute timing on the paragraph. Note your speed and errors.

27 Buzz did research about the history of tidal 9
28 waves. The doom and gloom of his essay threw our 19
29 class into a tizzy. The wild storm outside didn't 29
30 help matters. We were all upset that day. 37
| 1 | 2 | 3 | 4 | 5 | 6 | 7 | 8 | 9 | 10

G. PRACTICE

SPEED: If you made 2 or fewer errors on the Pretest, key lines 31–38 two times each.

ACCURACY: If you made more than 2 errors on the Pretest, key lines 31–34 as a group 2 times. Then key lines 35–38 as a group 2 times.

Double Reaches

31 ss pass floss guess essay lasso fussy abyss issue
32 oo doom gloom igloo roomy roost afoot bloom scoot
33 zz buzz pizza dizzy jazzy fuzzy dizzy tizzy fizzy
34 ll will silly hello jelly wells drill kills walls

Alternate Reaches

35 ti tidy ticks tight optic title tidal stick stiff
36 or fork odors storm world coral works adorn stork
37 wi wiry wield twice widow swift wicks swish twirl
38 sl slap slick isles aisle slant slams slips slows

H. POSTTEST

Repeat the Pretest. Compare your Posttest results with your Pretest results.

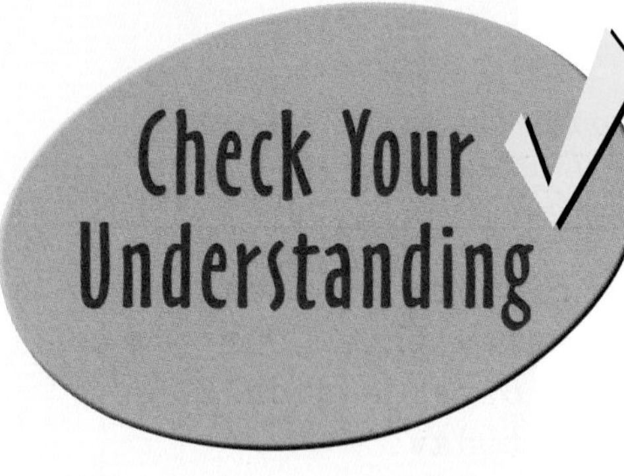

1. Open a new word processing document, and save it as *urs***Spreadsheet Parts**.
2. Describe the difference between a row and a column.
3. Describe what cell D4 stands for.
4. Describe ways you can move to each cell and enter data.
5. Discuss the benefits of formatting data with commas.
6. Save the changes. Print and close the file.

	A	B	C	D
1	**River**	**Continent**	**Miles (Approx.)**	**Kilometers (Approx.)**
2				
3	*Nile*	Africa	4,160	6,693
4	*Amazon*	South America	4,000	6,436
5	*Yangtze*	Asia	3,964	6,378
6	*Mississippi*	North America	3,740	6,017
7	*Yenisei-Angara*	Asia	2,543	4,091
8				

Compare urs*Rivers with the illustration.*

I. 2-MINUTE TIMINGS

Take two 2-minute timings on lines 39–45. Note your speed and errors.

Goal: 30/2′/4e

39 Good workers will be quick to discover what 9
40 others on the job like or dislike. Just a bit of 19
41 extra effort by them will make the office a more 29
42 pleasing place in which to work. A cheerful card 38
43 once in a while can bring a smile to one in need 48
44 of support at work. It is amazing how one kind 58
45 act spreads. 60
| 1 | 2 | 3 | 4 | 5 | 6 | 7 | 8 | 9 | 10 SI 1.21

J. COMPOSING AT THE KEYBOARD

Answer each question with a few words or a short phrase. Keep your eyes on the screen as you compose; do not look at your hands.

46 What career interests you?
47 What kind of animal do you think makes a good pet?
48 What are two states you would like to visit?
49 What are three things you would like to change about yourself?
50 Who are three people you admire?

PROJECT 3 Continued Reinforce

Edit and Format Data

Select the column headings. **Align center** and format in **bold**. Change the **font size** to 12 pt.

3. Format the data as indicated so your spreadsheet will look like the one illustrated.

	A	B	C	D
1	**River**	**Continent**	**Miles (Approx.)**	**Kilometers (Approx.)**
2				
3	*Nile*	Africa	4,145	6,669
4	*Amazon*	South America	4,000	6,436
5	*Yangtze*	Asia	3,964	6,378
6	*Mississippi*	North America	3,740	6,017
7	*Yenisei-Angara*	Asia	3,442	5,538
8				

Select the names of rivers. Format in **italic**. Change the **font size** to 11 pt.

Select all the **cells** containing numbers. Format the numbers to **separate the thousands with a comma.**

4. Edit the additional spreadsheet data as follows:

- **a.** Change cell C3 to 4160.
- **b.** Change cell D3 to 6693.
- **c.** Change cell C7 to 2543.
- **d.** Change cell D7 to 4091.

5. Save the changes. Print and close the file.

SECTION 2.11 Numeric Keypad: 1 2 3

GOALS:

- Demonstrate correct touch-system techniques.
- Learn the 1, 2, and 3 keys on the numeric keypad.
- Demonstrate proper keypad and keyboarding skills.
- Key 30/2'/4e.
- Demonstrate the ability to compose at the keyboard.

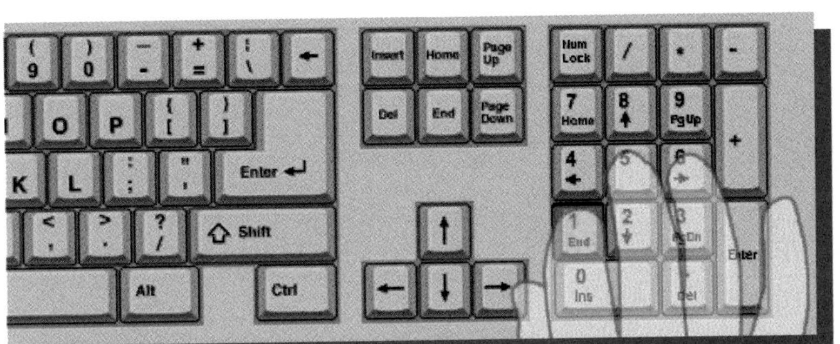

A. WARMUP

Key each line 2 times.

Speed	1	The rain will stop soon; then the sun will shine.
Accuracy	2	Zeke exhibits exuberance on quizzes about quakes.
Language Link	3	Shalena will meet us Saturday at Happy Rock Park.
Numbers/Symbols	4	Paige added 7 + 1 + 24 + 13 + 22 + 11 and got 78.

TOUCH-SYSTEM TECHNIQUES

Notice the words and arrows on the numeric keypad. When the Num Lock key is not activated, pressing the 7 key or the Home key on the numeric keypad will position the insertion point at the beginning of a line. Pressing 1 or the End key will position the insertion point at the end of a line.

PROJECT 3 **Reinforce**

Edit and Format Data

In this project you will reinforce what you have learned by editing and formatting a spreadsheet.

Your Turn

1. Open the file **10-1 Project 3**, and save it as ***urs*Rivers**.
2. Use the TAB key or arrow keys to move to each cell, and enter the data shown.

	A	B	C	D
1	River	Continent	Miles (Approx.)	Kilometers (Approx.)
2				
3	Nile	Africa	4145	6669
4	Amazon	South America	4000	6436
5	Yangtze	Asia	3964	6378
6	Mississippi	North America	3740	6017
7	Yenisei-Angara	Asia	3442	5538
8				

Continued on next page

NEW KEYS

B. 1 2 3 KEYS

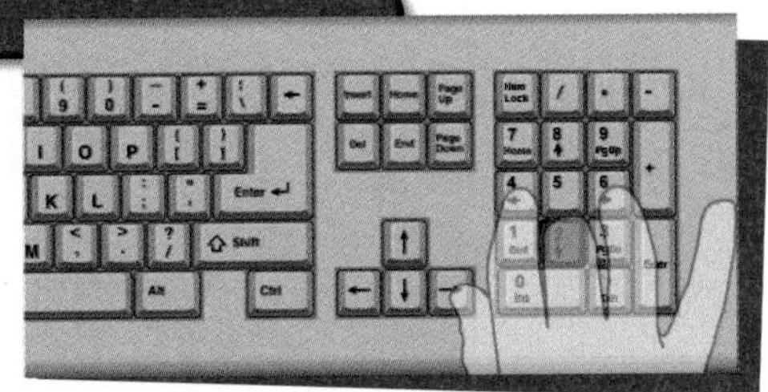

Enter the following numbers column by column. Use the proper finger for each key. Press* Enter *after the final digit of each number. Keep your eyes on the copy. Repeat if time permits.

Use J, K, and L fingers. Keep your eyes on the copy. Concentrate on accuracy.

5	444	555	666
6	111	222	333
7	144	225	336
8	441	552	663
9	144	255	366
10	411	522	633
11	444	555	666
12	414	525	636
13	141	252	363
14	411	525	636

SKILLBUILDING

C. KEYPAD PRACTICE

Enter the following numbers column by column. Press* Enter *after the final digit of each number. Keep your eyes on the copy. Repeat if time permits.

Keep your eyes on the copy.

15	476	167	754	531	746	334	568	829	957	146
16	372	426	193	942	853	712	149	637	486	329
17	551	789	592	726	962	365	438	218	582	381
18	983	238	812	861	147	819	129	341	673	247
19	421	945	638	397	285	654	247	759	149	655

PROJECT 2 Practice

Edit and Format Data

You can change the way information is displayed in a cell by formatting the data. Information can be quickly and easily edited.

Your Turn

1. Format the data as indicated so your spreadsheet will look like the one illustrated.

Select the column headings. **Align center** and format in **bold**. Change the **font size** to 12 pt.

	A	B	C	D	E	F
1	**Country**	**East**	**Midwest**	**South**	**West**	
2						
3	*Argentina*	9,498	1,046	15,266	35,855	
4	*Honduras*	4,233	789	28,754	21,743	
5	*India*	15,940	5,821	8,474	12,840	
6	*Mexico*	14,833	52,830	229,731	718,992	
7	*Philippines*	10,583	3,581	1,947	16,884	
8						

Select the names of countries. Format in **italic.**

Select all the **cells** containing numbers. Format the numbers to **separate the thousands with a comma.**

2. **Select** cell B5, and key the new data 14,875.
3. Edit the additional spreadsheet data as follows:
   a. Change cell D4 to 33,018.
   b. Change cell D7 to 2,196.
   c. Change cell C3 to 2,742.
   d. Change cell E6 to 802,451.
4. Save the changes. Print and close the file.

D. TECHNIQUE TIMINGS

Take two 30-second timings on each line. Focus on the technique at the left.

Keep your eyes on the copy.

```
20 The high school students will visit other places.
21 I toured an art museum that was west of the city.
22 Twenty letters were addressed to the three of us.
23 My car (the blue convertible) is hard to keep up.
   | 1 | 2 | 3 | 4 | 5 | 6 | 7 | 8 | 9 | 10
```

E. PRETEST

Take a 1-minute timing on the paragraph. Note your speed and errors.

```
24      Molly and Abe took water to the barn for the    9
25 horses to drink. Half an hour later, Ralph filled   19
26 the hay racks. It was he who discovered Star, our   29
27 very best horse, was ill.                           34
   | 1 | 2 | 3 | 4 | 5 | 6 | 7 | 8 | 9 | 10
```

F. PRACTICE

SPEED: If you made 2 or fewer errors on the Pretest, key lines 28–35 two times each.

ACCURACY: If you made more than 2 errors on the Pretest, key lines 28–31 as a group 2 times. Then key lines 32–35 as a group 2 times.

Left Reaches

```
28 Abe purse bases debts large match ocean nurse Tad
29 red urban water yearn Jerry trays racks horse set
30 war rated tubes upset verbs Xerox quart image cad
31 car fears raven carts froze graze exact grave sad
```

Right Reaches

```
32 Lon pilot linen Molly hours Louis zooms films Jim
33 mop jumps knows plugs Naomi quill flint drink hum
34 nip human flood Ralph mound joins yolks co-op poi
35 mop polka plums homey plump mound limps money Lou
```

G. POSTTEST

Repeat the Pretest. Compare your Posttest results with your Pretest results.

PROJECT 1 Continued

Practice

Identify Spreadsheet Parts

3. Key the number 9498 in cell B3.

The number you enter in the cell appears in the formula bar.

B3 fx 9498

	A	B	C	D	E
1	Country	East	Midwest	South	West
2					
3	Argentina	9498			
4	Honduras				
5	India				
6	Mexico				
7	Philippines				

4. Use the TAB key or arrow keys to move to each cell.
5. Enter the remaining data shown.

	A	B	C	D	E	F
1	Country	East	Midwest	South	West	
2						
3	Argentina	9498	1046	15266	35855	
4	Honduras	4233	789	28754	21743	
5	India	15940	5821	8474	12840	
6	Mexico	14833	52830	229731	718992	
7	Philippines	10583	3581	1947	16884	
8						

6. Save the changes. Keep the spreadsheet open for Project 2.

H. 2-MINUTE TIMINGS

Take two 2-minute timings on lines 36–42. Note your speed and errors.

Goal: 30/2′/4e

36 A good way to earn extra money is by taking 9
37 care of children. It is not a job for the lazy. 19
38 Being in charge of small children requires hard 28
39 work and savvy. You can take workshops to learn 38
40 the basics of child care, and you should take a 47
41 course in first aid so you are prepared for any 57
42 medical crisis. 60
| 1 | 2 | 3 | 4 | 5 | 6 | 7 | 8 | 9 | 10 SI 1.27

I. COMPOSING AT THE KEYBOARD

Answer each question with a short phrase. Keep your eyes on the monitor as you compose.

43 What are three things you should know before you agree to baby-sit?

44 Why should you keep your eyes on the copy when you key?

45 What three things do you admire most about your best friend?

PROJECT 1 Practice

Identify Spreadsheet Parts

Software programs with **spreadsheets** help you manage and store numbers and text. Rows and columns are used to organize information. Each column is identified by a letter such as A, B, or C. Each row is identified by a number such as 1, 2, or 3. When a column and row form a rectangle, it is called a **cell**.

Your Turn

1. Use the illustration to help you identify the parts of the spreadsheet.
2. Click in cell B3 to **select** the **cell**.

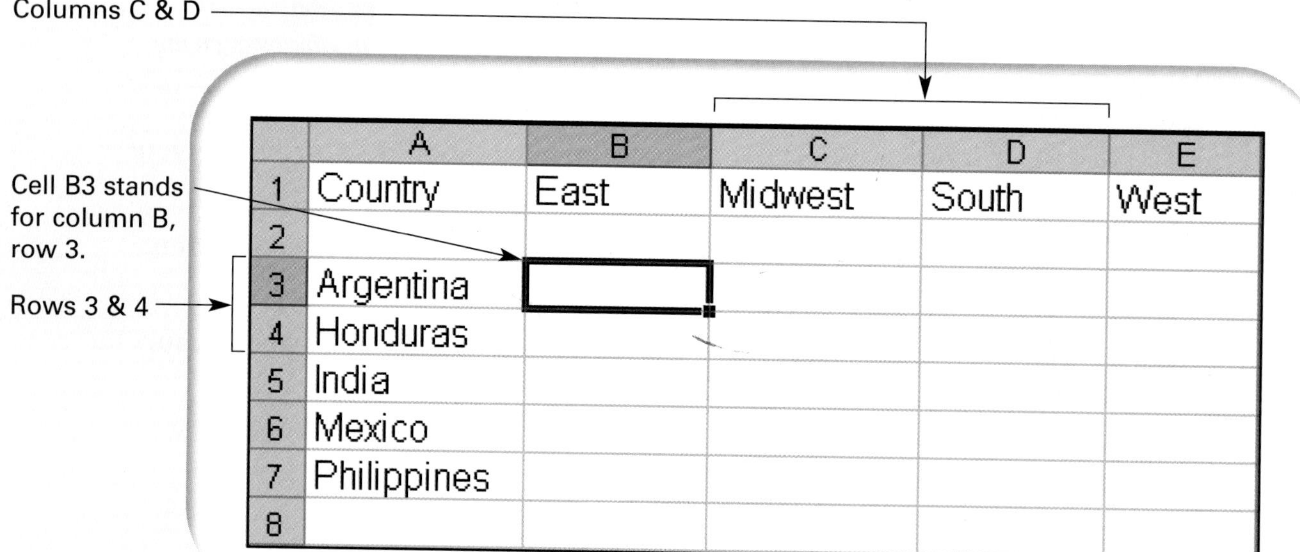

Continued on next page

SECTION 2.12

Numeric Keypad: 0 .

GOALS:

- Demonstrate correct touch-system techniques.
- Learn the 0 and (.) decimal keys on the numeric keypad.
- Demonstrate proper keypad skills.
- Key 30/2'/4e.

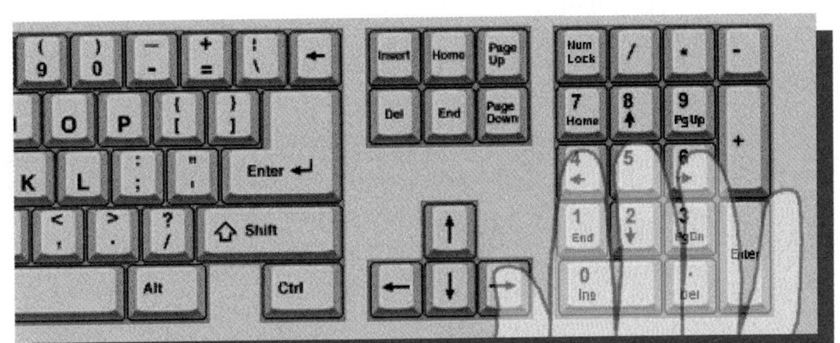

A. WARMUP

Key each line 2 times.

Speed	1	To have more pep, walk one or two miles each day.
Accuracy	2	Zorba has cichlids imported from Lake Tanganyika.
Language Link	3	She watches while I write it out and he signs it.
Numbers/Symbols	4	S & A closed at 3 7/16, up 5/8, a +14.71% change.

TOUCH-SYSTEM TECHNIQUES

When the Num Lock key is not activated, the Numeric Keypad works in conjunction with your alphabetic keys. You can delete text by pressing the (.) Del key. You can also use the Enter key from the Numeric Keypad.

SECTION 10.1 Spreadsheet Basics

GOALS: Demonstrate the ability to:

- Identify spreadsheet parts.
- Enter data.
- Select cells.
- Format and edit data.

WARMUP

Select Warmup from the Skillbuilding menu. Key each Warmup line 2 times.

Speed	1	We are planning to have a cookout when we meet at the lake.
Accuracy	2	All four mixtures in the deep brown jug froze very quickly.
Numbers/Symbols	3	Invoice #70-2 read: 653# "Extra" @ $4.89 per lb., less 10%.
Language Link	4	We usually vacation at a place that is south of the border.

Making the Connection

Mark researched United States immigration data for his history fair project. He would like to organize his information, shown below, so it is easier to read.

Your Turn

1. Open the file **10-1 Project 1** from your spreadsheet software and save it as ***urs*****Immigration**.
2. Keep the spreadsheet open for Project 1.

Country	East	Midwest	South	West
Argentina	9498	1046	15266	35855
Honduras	4233	789	28754	21743
India	15940	5821	8474	12840
Mexico	14833	52830	229731	718992
Philippines	10583	3581	1947	16884

NEW KEYS

B. 0 KEY

Enter the following numbers column by column. Press Enter after the final digit of each number. Keep your eyes on the copy. Repeat if time permits.

Use the right thumb. Keep your eyes on the copy. Concentrate on accuracy.

404	470	502
505	500	603
606	690	140
707	410	250
808	520	360
909	630	701
101	407	802
202	508	903
303	609	405
505	401	506

C.  KEY

Enter the following numbers column by column. Press Enter after the final digit of each number. Keep your eyes on the copy. Repeat if time permits.

Use L finger. Keep K finger anchored on the 5 key as you reach down to the decimal.

4.5	7.8	1.2
6.5	9.8	3.2
4.4	7.7	1.1
4.4	7.7	1.1
5.5	8.8	2.2
5.5	8.8	2.2
6.6	9.9	3.3
6.5	9.9	3.3
4.5	7.8	1.2
6.5	8.9	1.3

Focus On Good Keyboarding Habits

Focus on your neck. To avoid neck strain:

- **Looking slightly downward is better for your neck than constantly looking upward.**
- **Do not twist your neck too far right or left.**
- **Position your book next to the monitor and place it on a stand.**

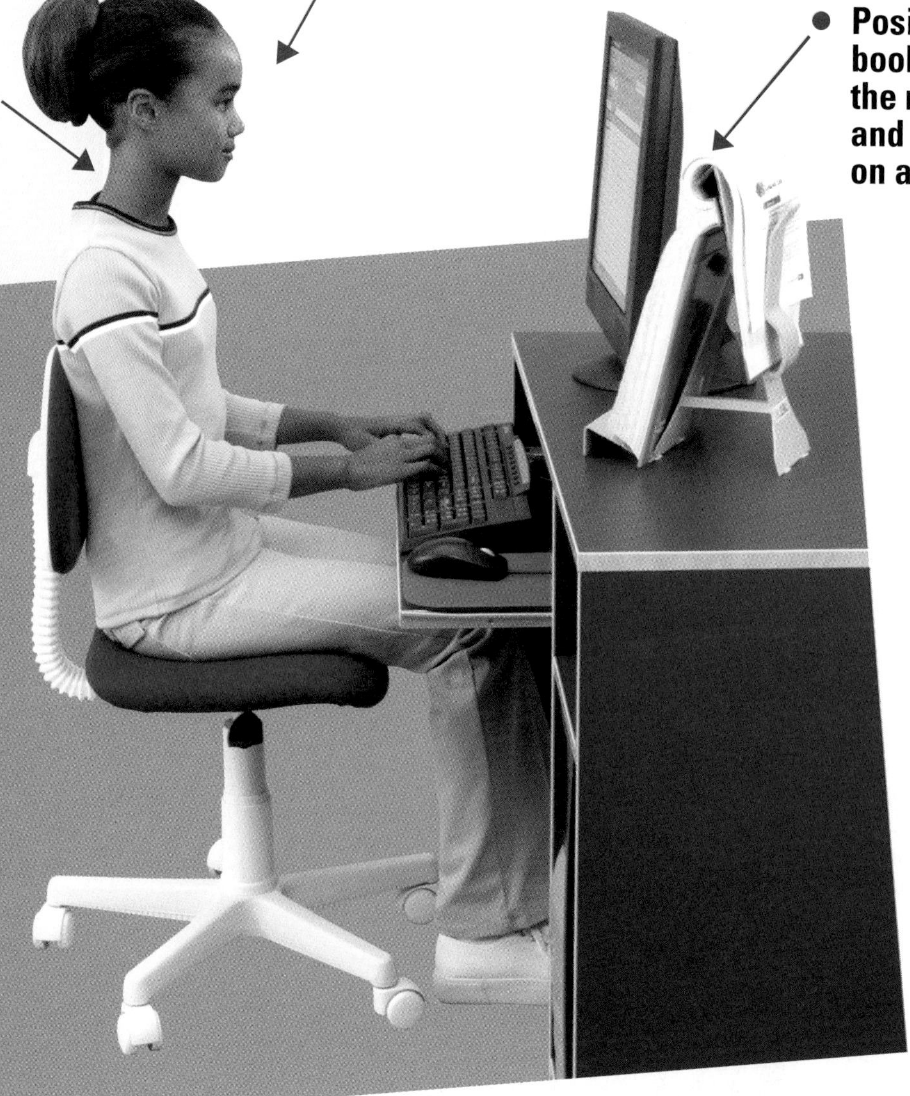

SKILLBUILDING

D. KEYPAD PRACTICE

Enter the following numbers column by column. Press Enter after the final digit of each number. Keep your eyes on the copy. Repeat if time permits.

1.7	7.5	7.6	5.0	6.2	6.0	6.7	4.5	3.0	6.4
5.8	2.4	2.3	2.8	3.5	9.1	5.1	3.0	7.6	2.8
1.6	8.3	1.7	9.9	5.0	2.7	1.6	9.3	1.3	5.9
3.0	4.2	3.4	8.1	7.4	1.8	2.8	8.0	8.2	5.1
6.9	9.0	6.5	4.0	4.6	8.9	7.2	4.9	4.7	9.0

E. 12-SECOND SPRINTS

Take three 12-second timings on each line. Try to increase your speed on each timing.

If nothing nice can be said, do not say anything.
Be kind if you want others to be kind toward you.
You won't smell like roses if you play with pigs.
Keep the dog away from the cats to avoid a fight.

| | | | 5 | | | | 10 | | | | 15 | | | | 20 | | | | 25 | | | | 30 | | | | 35 | | | | 40 | | | | 45 | | | | 50

F. PRETEST

Take a 1-minute timing on lines 34–37. Note your speed and errors.

Unless they are crazy, most humans prefer to 9
be free, not in jail. That is why laws that take 19
away our freedom for illegal acts we perform are 29
created and are effective. 34

| 1 | 2 | 3 | 4 | 5 | 6 | 7 | 8 | 9 | 10

UNIT 7

Spreadsheets

GOALS:

- Demonstrate how to create, edit, and format a spreadsheet.
- Demonstrate how to calculate in a spreadsheet using simple formulas.
- Demonstrate how to calculate in a spreadsheet using function formulas.
- Demonstrate how to copy formulas.
- Demonstrate how to create a spreadsheet chart.

G. PRACTICE

***SPEED:** If you made 2 or fewer errors on the Pretest, key lines 38–45 two times each.*

***ACCURACY:** If you made more than 2 errors on the Pretest, key lines 38–41 as a group 2 times. Then key lines 42–45 as a group 2 times.*

Up Reaches

```
38 hu hunt shuts churn hunch human husky huffs hulls
39 de deck bride depth order wader adept video decay
40 fr free frock frame frost fryer fruit frail fresh
41 li line flies blind click slick limes light flier
```

Down Reaches

```
42 ac acre poach whack acrid actor tract slack enact
43 l. pal. hill. jail. nail. yowl. dial. peel. till.
44 az raze graze craze glaze dazed blaze gazed jazzy
45 on once ponds fonts stone clone alone don't front
```

H. POSTTEST

Repeat the Pretest. Compare your Posttest results with your Pretest results.

I. 2-MINUTE TIMINGS

Take two 2-minute timings on lines 46–52. Note your speed and errors.

Goal: 30/2'/4e

```
46      Poachers hunt and kill game against the law.   9
47 Many species such as big cats, caimans, quetzal    19
48 birds, and whales may become extinct from being    28
49 killed for their fur, hides, or feathers. Laws     38
50 have been passed to save wildlife. Parks have      47
51 been jointly set up in all parts of the world to   57
52 serve as havens.                                   60
   | 1 | 2 | 3 | 4 | 5 | 6 | 7 | 8 | 9 | 10      SI 1.22
```

COMPLETING UNIT 6 Continued

Enrich

Curriculum Portfolio

Math:

Create geometrical art.

Shapes are in everything around us. Using a digital camera, capture images of the following shapes that you can find in objects around your school.

a. Triangle
b. Hexagon
c. Trapezoid
d. Pentagon
e. Rectangle
f. Square
g. Octagon
h. Parallelogram
i. Quadrilateral
j. Diamond

Create a presentation to illustrate the shapes. Use the arrow draw tool to point to the shape in the photo.

Language Arts:

Create an autobiography.

An autobiography is the life story a person has written about himself or herself. Create an autobiography presentation to tell your life story. Include at least six of the following points about yourself in the presentation:

1. Your name and age (mandatory)
2. Where you were born
3. Where you grew up
4. Your interests
5. Your goals
6. A person or experience that influenced you
7. Interesting places to which you have traveled
8. Favorite sports or hobbies
9. Books you read and liked
10. How you spend your spare time

SECTION 2.13 Review

GOALS:

- Demonstrate proper keyboarding skills.
- Key 30/2'/4e.

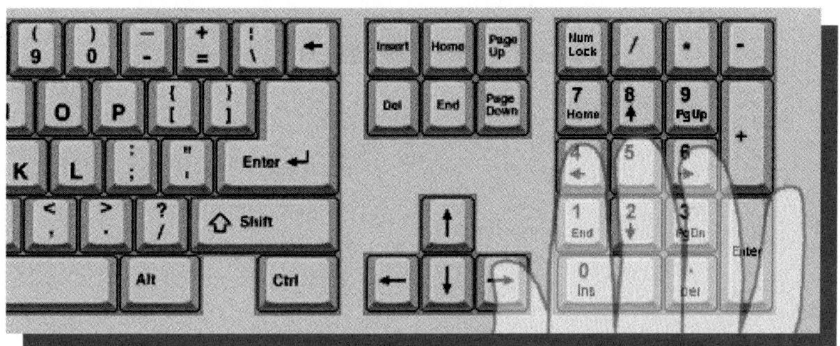

A. WARMUP

Key each line 2 times.

Speed	1	`Think about this: If it is to be, it is up to me.`
Accuracy	2	`Vladimir Kosma Zworykin made the television tube.`
Language Link	3	`Syd catches a plane at O'Hare Airport in Chicago.`
Numbers/Symbols	4	`Nashville has *985,026 people; Miami, *1,192,582.`

SKILLBUILDING

B. KEYPAD PRACTICE: 3-DIGIT NUMBERS

Enter the following numbers column by column. Press ENTER after the final digit of each number. Keep your eyes on the copy, and use the proper finger for each key. Repeat if time permits.

Enter numbers smoothly. Use correct fingers.

5	136	964	806	295	597	628	728	627	959	172
6	940	250	275	407	426	519	546	341	241	859
7	852	173	394	718	618	537	639	730	862	931
8	710	982	180	363	304	405	410	859	730	604
9	788	829	903	120	311	441	349	555	668	776

COMPLETING UNIT 6

ENRICH

Curriculum Portfolio

Use the presentation skills you have learned to help you create your curriculum portfolio project. Choose from any of the following to help you illustrate your presentation:

a. Clip art
b. Scanned pictures
c. Digital photos
d. Sound/narration
e. Animation
f. Internet photos/images

Choose from one of the following topics:

SCIENCE:

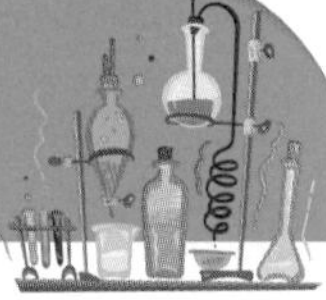

Create a timeline.

Have you ever wondered who invented the Frisbee® Flying Discs or who invented blue jeans? Use the Internet to research about an invention. The invention can be from ancient times to the present. Create a timeline presentation of your findings. Be sure to cite your sources at the end of the presentation.

SOCIAL STUDIES:

Create a geography presentation.

Create a presentation about a country of your choice. You should illustrate and tell about the major cities, rivers, landforms, surrounding bodies of water, and any interesting geographical landmarks. Use the Internet to research the country you chose. Be sure to cite your sources at the end of the presentation.

Continued on next page

C. KEYPAD PRACTICE: DECIMALS

Enter the following numbers column by column. Press ENTER after the final digit of each number. Keep your eyes on the copy, and use the proper finger for each key. Repeat if time permits.

Enter numbers smoothly. Use correct fingers.

10	1.97	5.08	6.19	3.52	4.33	17.44	52.28	68.61
11	3.85	6.44	9.37	8.10	2.19	14.20	23.85	60.97
12	6.55	6.65	7.87	9.00	3.10	20.49	88.47	19.39
13	2.10	2.81	2.33	7.06	7.68	67.99	44.53	45.54
14	8.83	7.90	4.16	8.20	1.49	55.20	15.62	37.39

D. TECHNIQUE TIMINGS

Take two 30-second timings on each line. Focus on the techniques at the left.

Lines 15–16: Key without pausing. Lines 17–18: Key end-of-sentence punctuation smoothly.

```
15 Roy and Bob did their best to study for the test.
16 My two cats are eager to sit in my lap as I work.
17 If you are to make friends, you must be friendly.
18 Who me? Oh no! I can. What time? Look out! Did I?
   | 1 | 2 | 3 | 4 | 5 | 6 | 7 | 8 | 9 | 10
```

REVIEW Continued

APPLY

Presentation Review

7. Use the Spelling feature to identify any errors; then correct them.
8. Apply an appropriate design template.
9. Change the slide layout, and choose appropriate clip art or photos as shown.

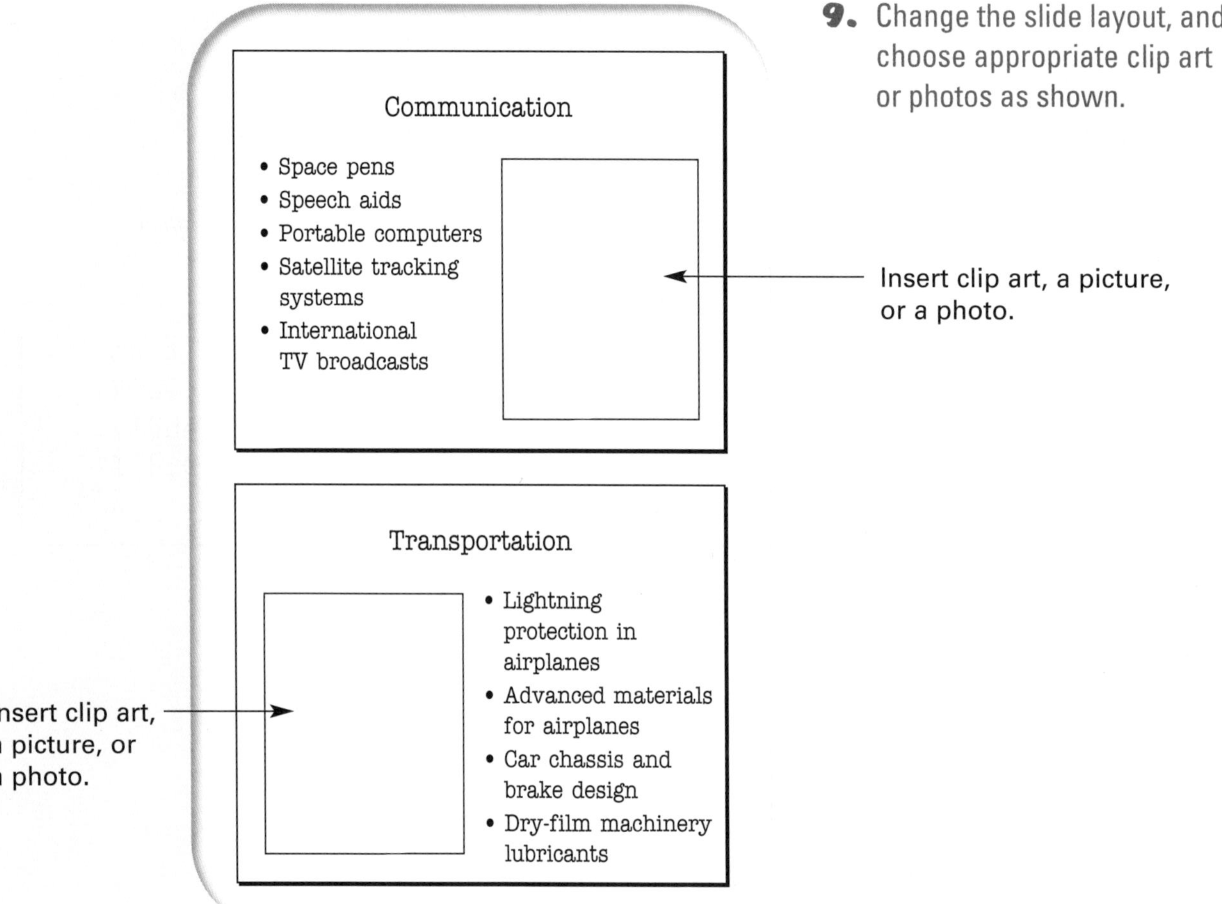

Communication
• Space pens
• Speech aids
• Portable computers
• Satellite tracking systems
• International TV broadcasts
Insert clip art, a picture, or a photo.
Transportation
• Lightning protection in airplanes
• Advanced materials for airplanes
• Car chassis and brake design
• Dry-film machinery lubricants
Insert clip art, a picture, or a photo.

10. Choose an animation and sound effect for each slide.
11. Change to Slide Show View, and preview the presentation.
12. Save the changes. Print and close the file.

E. PRETEST

Take a 1-minute timing on lines 19–22. Note your speed and errors.

19 Joy's niece darted in front of a car, but 9
20 the driver was able to stop quickly. She was only 19
21 dazed. She did not want us to cheer or make a 29
22 fuss over her. 32

| 1 | 2 | 3 | 4 | 5 | 6 | 7 | 8 | 9 | 10

F. PRACTICE

SPEED: If you made 2 or fewer errors on the Pretest, key lines 23–30 two times each.

ACCURACY: If you made more than 2 errors on the Pretest, key lines 23–26 as a group 2 times. Then key lines 27–30 as a group 2 times.

Adjacent Reaches	23 rt sort part heart start ui quit suit quiet quick
Jump Reaches	24 mo most move among money ce aced race cease niece
Double Reaches	25 ee glee weed keeps cheer ss sass fuss grass cross
In Reaches	26 st stay stop stray state pi pint pile pines spine
Alternate Reaches	27 to tofu torn storm torso pa paid pals pause pants
Left/Right Reaches	28 da dart dabs dazed dates jo joys join enjoy jolly
Up/Down Reaches	29 st star stop first coast h? ash? huh? Noah? dish?
Out Reaches	30 fa fall sofa loofa farms ho hose hone hoist phone

G. POSTTEST

Repeat the Pretest. Compare your Posttest results with your Pretest results.

H. 1-MINUTE ALPHANUMERIC TIMING

Take a 1-minute timing on lines 31–34. Note your speed and errors.

31 In 1929 stock prices passed $350 per share. 9
32 By 1932, they had dropped under $100, forcing 18
33 9,000 banks to close. People without jobs climbed 28
34 above 25%. 30

| 1 | 2 | 3 | 4 | 5 | 6 | 7 | 8 | 9 | 10

REVIEW Continued

APPLY

Presentation Review

4. After Slide 7, add two new slides as shown.

Transportation

- Lightning protection in airplanes
- Advanced materials for airplanes
- Car chassis and brake design
- Dry-film machinery lubricants

Slide 8

General

- Shock-absorbing football helmets
- Ski boots
- Fail-safe flashlights
- Joystick game controllers
- Infrared cameras
- Digital clocks
- Polarized sunglasses
- Aerodynamic golf balls
- Firefighter breathing systems
- Bar coding
- Thermal gloves and boots

Slide 9

5. **Change** the **slide order** as follows:

a. Move Slide "Transportation" to come after Slide "Communication."

b. Move Slide "Home" to come after Slide "Food and Nutrition."

6. Edit Slide 3 as shown.

Types of Spin-Offs

- Communication
- Transportation ← Add text.
- Food–Nutrition
- Home ← Add text.
- Health–Medicine
- Home ← Delete text.
- General ← Add text.

Continued on next page

I. 2-MINUTE TIMINGS

Take two 2-minute timings on lines 35–41. Note your speed and errors.

Goal: 30/2′/4e

Zebras are members of the horse family and 9
are well known for their unique stripes. They 18
enjoy life on the plains and foothills of Africa 28
where they feed on grass and trees. Attempts to 37
use them for work and to ride have failed. The 47
quagga, which is now extinct due to hunting, was 57
kin to the zebra. 60

| 1 | 2 | 3 | 4 | 5 | 6 | 7 | 8 | 9 | 10 *SI 1.25*

CARE AND OPERATION OF EQUIPMENT

These buttons give you quick access to the Internet, and they can be programmed to perform specific tasks.

APPLY

Presentation Review

3. Edit the slides as shown.

Communication

- Space pens
- Speech aids
- Portable computers
- Satellite tracking systems
- Satellite dishes ← Add text.
- International TV broadcasts

Food–Nutrition

- Food additives
- Food packaging ← Delete text.
- Heat-resistant substances
- Aluminum foil for preserving food
- Freeze-dried foods ← Add text.
- Plastics for food and beverages

Home

- Home insulation materials
- Cordless tools
- Water purification systems
- Flat-panel televisions
- Wireless alarms ← Delete text.
- Energy-saving air conditioners
- Safe sewage treatments

Continued on next page

SECTION 2.14 Skillbuilding

GOALS:

- Demonstrate correct touch-system techniques.
- Demonstrate proper numeric and keyboarding skills.
- Key 31/3'/5e.

A. WARMUP

Key each line 2 times.

Speed	1	All of us have bad days now and then, but they do not last.
Accuracy	2	The quetzal, a superb green and gold bird, lives in Mexico.
Language Link	3	The exchange students arrived in winter and left in spring.
Numbers/Symbols	4	When Tip & Toe has a sale, buy 24 pairs of socks @ 25% off.

SKILLBUILDING

B. KEYPAD PRACTICE: 4-DIGIT NUMBERS

Enter the following numbers column by column. Press ENTER after the final digit of each number. Keep your eyes on the copy, and use the proper finger for each key. Repeat if time permits.

Use correct fingers. Input accurately.

5	8964	8073	6182	8090	2401	3159	5361	6047
6	3103	2619	5079	9324	5561	8252	6873	7984
7	5295	5302	6416	7451	8564	2785	9790	1021
8	7206	6195	2840	5327	4963	7548	2080	1976
9	1847	8443	3594	1686	1378	9029	4303	4267

REVIEW Continued

APPLY

Presentation Review

Communication

- Space pens
- Speech aids
- Portable computers
- Satellite tracking systems
- International TV broadcasts

Slide 4

Food–Nutrition

- Food additives
- Food packaging
- Heat-resistant substances
- Aluminum foil for preserving food
- Plastics for food and beverages

Slide 5

Health–Medicine

- Programmable heart pacemaker
- EZ chair lift
- Digital image processing
- Cancer detection
- Invisible braces
- Ear thermometer
- Heart monitoring techniques
- Movable artificial limbs
- Lasers for eye and brain surgery
- Robotic surgery
- Computer reader for the blind

Slide 6

Home

- Home insulation materials
- Cordless tools
- Water purification systems
- Flat-panel televisions
- Wireless alarms
- Energy-saving air conditioners
- Safe sewage treatments

Slide 7

Continued on next page

C. KEYPAD PRACTICE: DECIMALS

Enter the following numbers column by column. Press ENTER after the final digit of each number. Keep your eyes on the copy, and use the proper finger for each key. Repeat if time permits.

10	80.5	9.72	67.04	4387.90	98.10	86.17
11	724.16	15.39	904.32	128.50	6524.01	349.05
12	7512.41	4607.09	583.55	95.63	141.16	2508.96
13	1204.78	672.80	808.23	379.94	6.39	677.28
14	339.45	453.92	1.62	4.63	7813.25	1.96

D. 12-SECOND SPRINTS

Take three 12-second timings on each line. Try to increase your speed on each timing.

15 You must repress your fears, or you will not be in control.
16 Our failures can teach us good lessons if we will let them.
17 When you have a dream, you must never, never give up on it.
18 You should give your best effort to everything that you do.
| | | | 5 | | | | 10 | | | | 15 | | | | 20 | | | | 25 | | | | 30 | | | | 35 | | | | 40 | | | | 45 | | | | 50 | | | | 55 | | | | 60

E. TECHNIQUE TIMINGS

Take two 30-second timings on each line. Focus on the technique at the left.

Keep your eyes on the copy.

19 Lau went to the cafe in the city to have a good dinner out.
20 She and Travis left the band and saw the parade in Detroit.
21 Isau moved the desk over to my right side during our class.
22 People who work at the desk like to keep paper on the left.
| 1 | 2 | 3 | 4 | 5 | 6 | 7 | 8 | 9 | 10 | 11 | 12

REVIEW SECTION 9

APPLY

Presentation Review

In this project, you will apply the skills you have learned to create a presentation. You will also edit slides and enhance the presentation with clip art and animations.

Your Turn

1. Open a **new presentation**, and create the slides as shown.
2. Save the presentation as ***urs*Spin-Offs**.

Spin-Offs From Space

Your name

Slide 1

What Are Spin-Offs?

- Technology originally developed for space
- Space technology adapted and used to make our lives better

Slide 2

Types of Spin-Offs

- Communication
- Food–Nutrition
- Health–Medicine
- Home

Slide 3

Continued on next page

F. ALPHABET REVIEW

Key each line 1 time. Repeat if time permits.

23 Alf is able to add; Bill bikes by Beth; Cal can call Carli.
24 Darla's dad is Dale; Evi eats eggs; Flo's farm is far away.
25 Gary's grass is green; Hans has his hats; Ilse is innocent.

26 Just jump, Jeff; Kylie knows knives; Lyle loves Louisville.
27 Marta manages a mall; Nona noted nothing; Orion owns opals.
28 Pat pinches pennies; Quinn quietly quit; Rez reads rapidly.

29 Suni serves sushi; Tara tells tall tales; Uriah uses umber.
30 Val visits Vermont; Wilma washes windows; Xan x-rays Xylia.
31 Yvonne yearns for a yellow yo-yo; Zachariah's zest is zero.

G. PACED PRACTICE

Turn to the Paced Practice routine beginning on page SB7. Take three 2-minute timings, starting at the point where you left off the last time.

H. 3-MINUTE TIMINGS

Take two 3-minute timings on lines 32–40. Note your speed and errors.

Goal: 31/3′/5e

32 A rain forest and a jungle are not quite the same. A 11
33 rain forest has very lofty trees that form a canopy for 22
34 shorter trees as well as vines and other plants that grow 34
35 in the shade. The floor is more or less open. A jungle, on 45
36 the other hand, is the dense, scrubby brush that exists on 57
37 the floor after a rain forest has been cut. 66
38 Large rain forests are found in the Amazon basin. Rain 78
39 forests give us timber and sites for crops like tea and 89
40 house many species. 93

| 1 | 2 | 3 | 4 | 5 | 6 | 7 | 8 | 9 | 10 | 11 | 12 SI 1.26

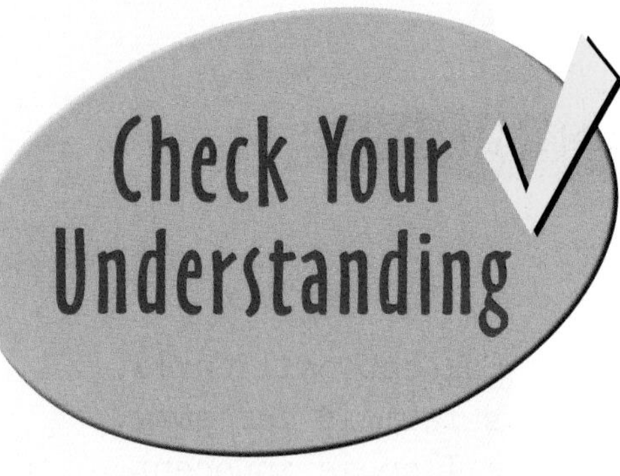
Check Your Understanding

1. Open a new word processing document, and save it as *urs*Adding Animation.
2. Explain the purpose of adding animation and sound to a presentation.
3. Describe when you would want to change the animation order.
4. Save the changes. Print and close the file.

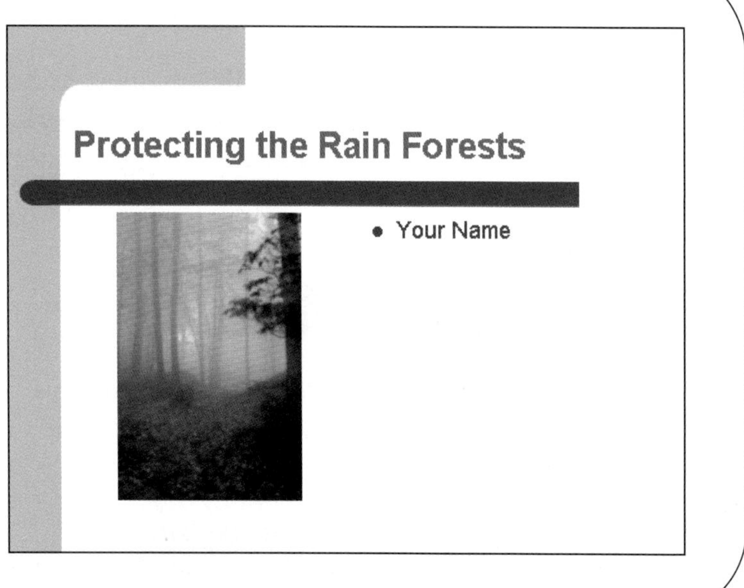
Protecting the Rain Forests
• Your Name

interNET CONNECTION

1. Open one of your previous presentations ("Alexander the Great" or "Protecting the Rain Forests").
2. Explore the Clips Online and/or the Motion Clips feature of your software.
3. Do a Web search on "free video clips Alexander the Great" or "free video clips rainforest" to find additional clips to enhance your presentation.
4. Add your new clips to one of the slides.
5. Save the changes, view the presentation, and close the file.

UNIT 3

Computer Basics

GOALS:

- Demonstrate correct use of command, shortcut, and function keys.
- Demonstrate how to use the Help feature.
- Demonstrate how to create and organize electronic files and folders.
- Demonstrate basic editing skills.
- Demonstrate how to use search engines and collect and utilize data from the Internet.

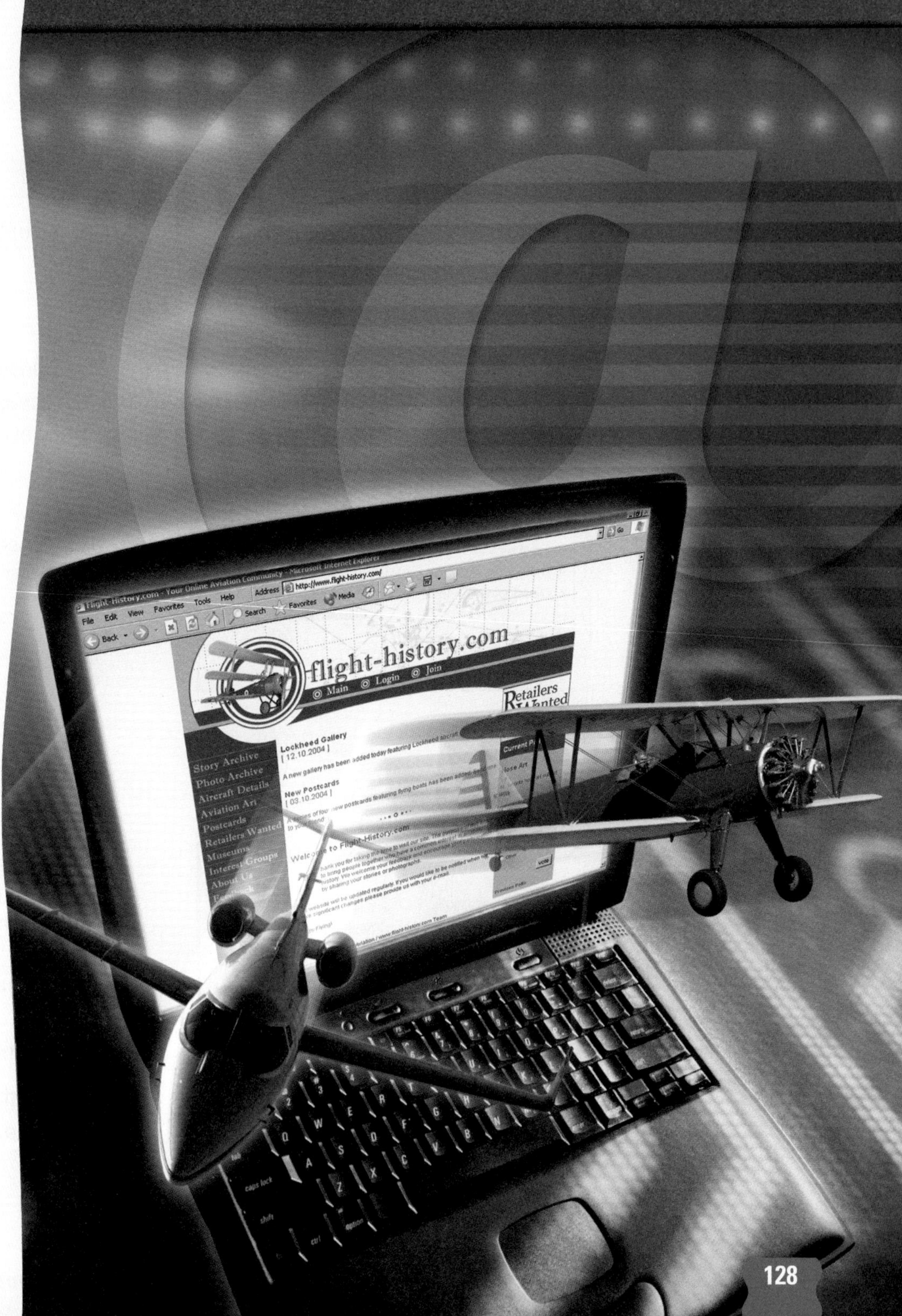

PROJECT 3 Reinforce

Animation

In this project you will reinforce what you have learned by adding animation to a presentation.

Your Turn

1. Open the file ***urs*Rain Forest-Art** you created in Section 9.3, and save it as ***urs*Rain Forest-Animation**.

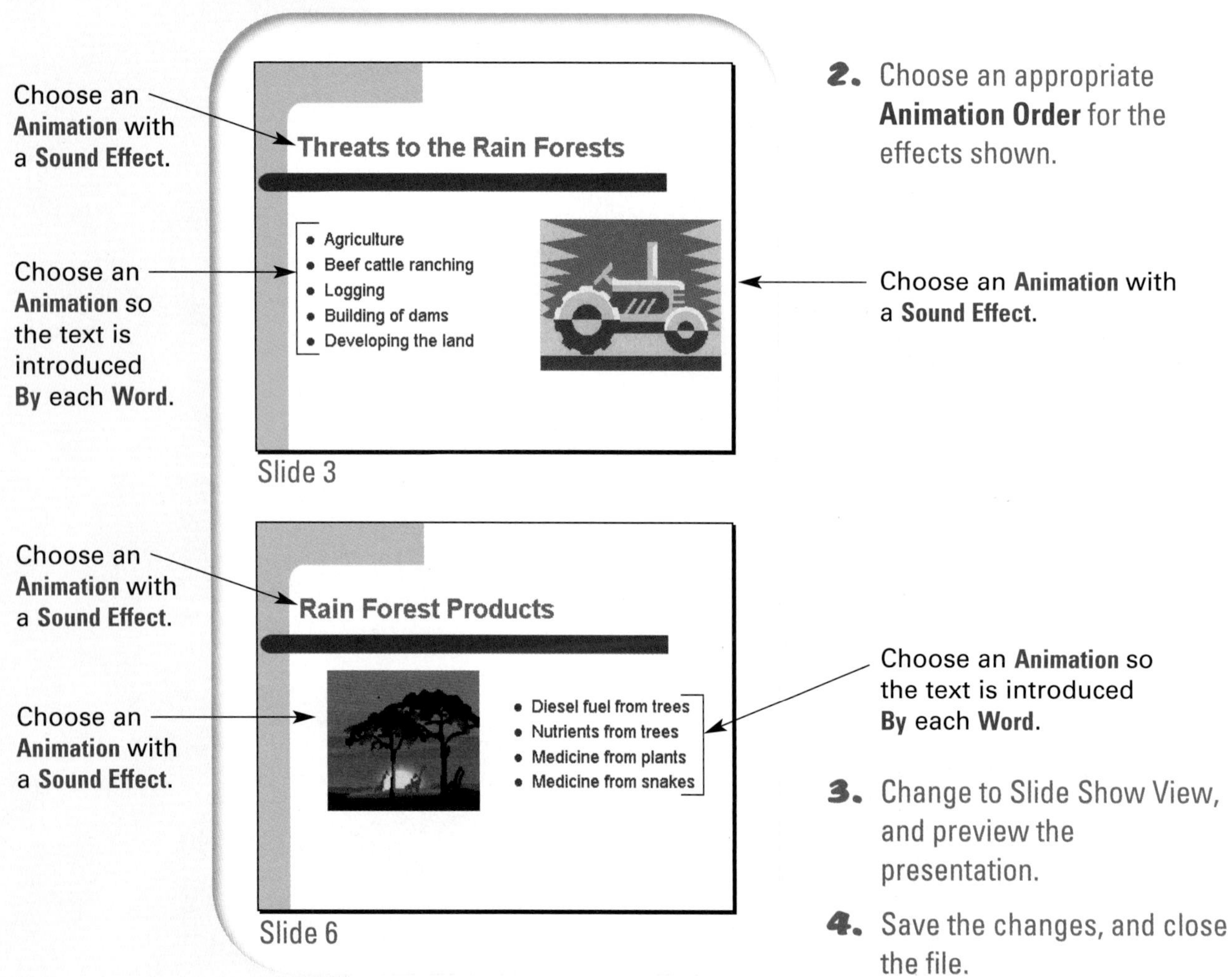

Choose an **Animation** with a **Sound Effect.**
Threats to the Rain Forests
Choose an **Animation** so the text is introduced **By** each **Word.**
Agriculture
Beef cattle ranching
Logging
Building of dams
Developing the land
Choose an **Animation** with a **Sound Effect.**
Slide 3
Choose an **Animation** with a **Sound Effect.**
Rain Forest Products
Choose an **Animation** with a **Sound Effect.**
Diesel fuel from trees
Nutrients from trees
Medicine from plants
Medicine from snakes
Choose an **Animation** so the text is introduced **By** each **Word.**
Slide 6

2. Choose an appropriate **Animation Order** for the effects shown.

3. Change to Slide Show View, and preview the presentation.

4. Save the changes, and close the file.

Focus On

Good Keyboarding Habits

Focus on your eye distance from the monitor. To avoid eyestrain:

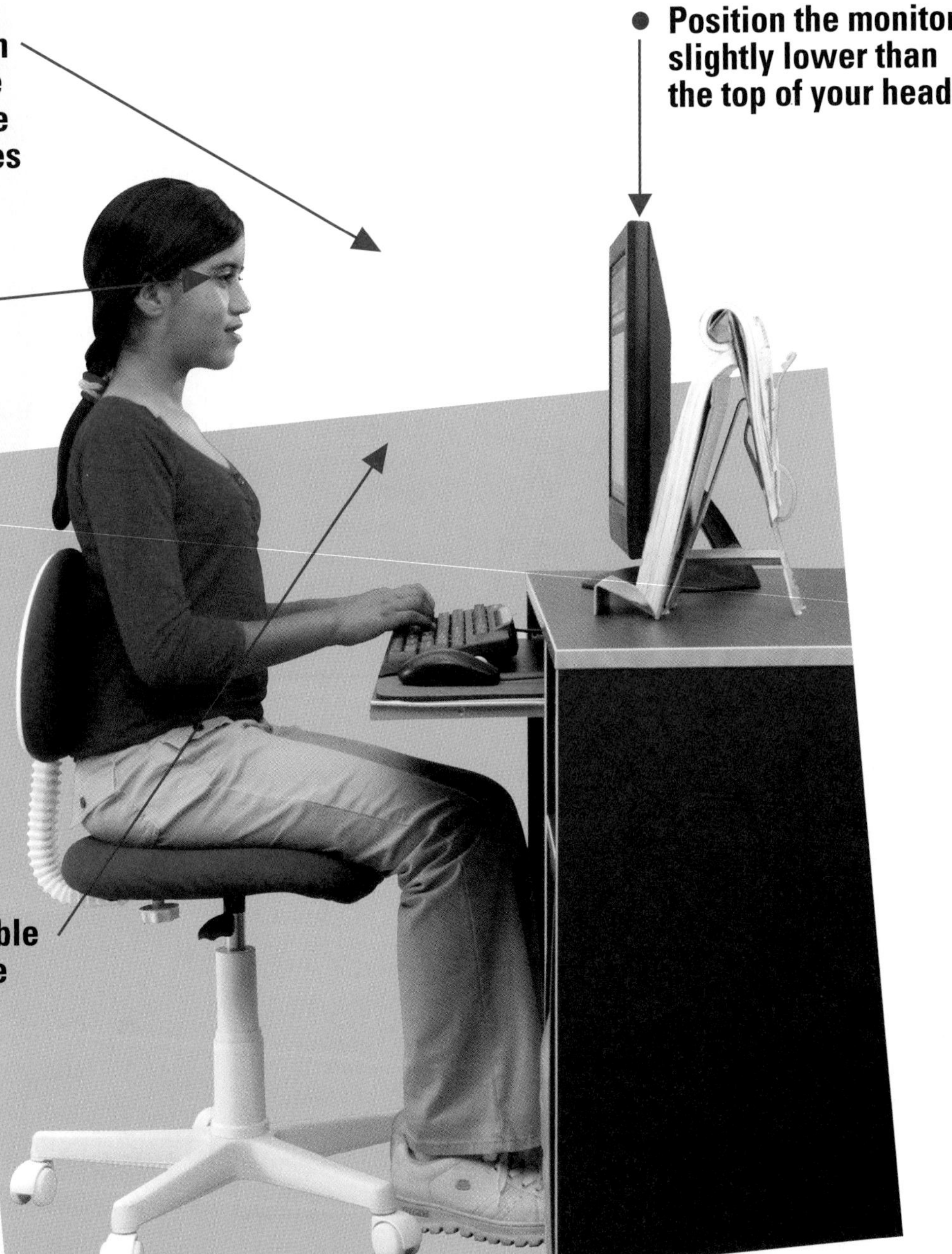

• The distance from your eyes and the monitor should be between 20 inches and 24 inches.
• Position the monitor slightly lower than the top of your head.
• Eye gaze should be slightly down.
• Sit at a comfortable distance from the monitor.

PROJECT 2 Practice

Add Sound and Change the Animation Order

You can add additional special effect animations to create more interest in your presentation.

Your Turn

1. Go to Slide 3 of the presentation, and choose an **Animation** for each part of the slide as shown.

Click the Title text box, and choose an **Animation** with a **Sound Effect**.

Click the clip art, and choose an **Animation** with a **Sound Effect**.

Young Alexander

- Educated by Aristotle
- Good at every sport
- Commanded men in battle
- Enjoyed the study of science

Click on the Bulleted List text box, and choose an **Animation** so the text is introduced **By** each **Word**.

2. Change to Slide Show View, and preview the presentation. Click the slide to make the animations appear.

The title appears first on a mouse click.

The clip art appears third and automatically.

Young Alexander

- Educated by Aristotle
- Good at every sport
- Commanded men in battle
- Enjoyed the study of science

3. Go to Slide 3 again, and **Change** the **Animation Order** as shown.

The bulleted list appears second and automatically.

4. Change to Slide Show View, and preview the presentation. Click the slide to make the animations appear.
5. Save the changes, and close the file.

SECTION 3.1 Software Basics

GOALS: Demonstrate the ability to:

- Open a new document.
- Identify menu commands, shortcut keys, and function keys.
- Use the Help feature.
- Save and close a document.

WARMUP

Select Warmup from the Skillbuilding menu. Key each Warmup line 2 times.

```
Speed     1 Set your goals, and then make plans to achieve those goals.
Accuracy  2 messes make some moms mad; half a dome; for his risk; mills
Speed     3 he reads ahead; his middle silo is filled; more old mirrors
Accuracy  4 jade fake held lose messes make some moms mad; half a dome;
```

Making the Connection

An easy way to learn software is to explore and use the features. You can learn about many software features by using the online Help feature.

Your Turn

1. Open a new word processing document.
2. Key a list of all the software features that you find. For example, can you find the button for Bold? Do you see the word Help?
3. Keep the document open for Project 1.

LIST OF SOFTWARE FEATURES

Bold
Help

PROJECT 1 Practice

Add Animation

You can animate any of the objects on your slides. **Animation** is how text and graphics appear on a slide.

Your Turn

1. Open the file ***urs*AlexanderArt** you created in Section 9.3, and save it as ***urs*Alexander-Animation**.

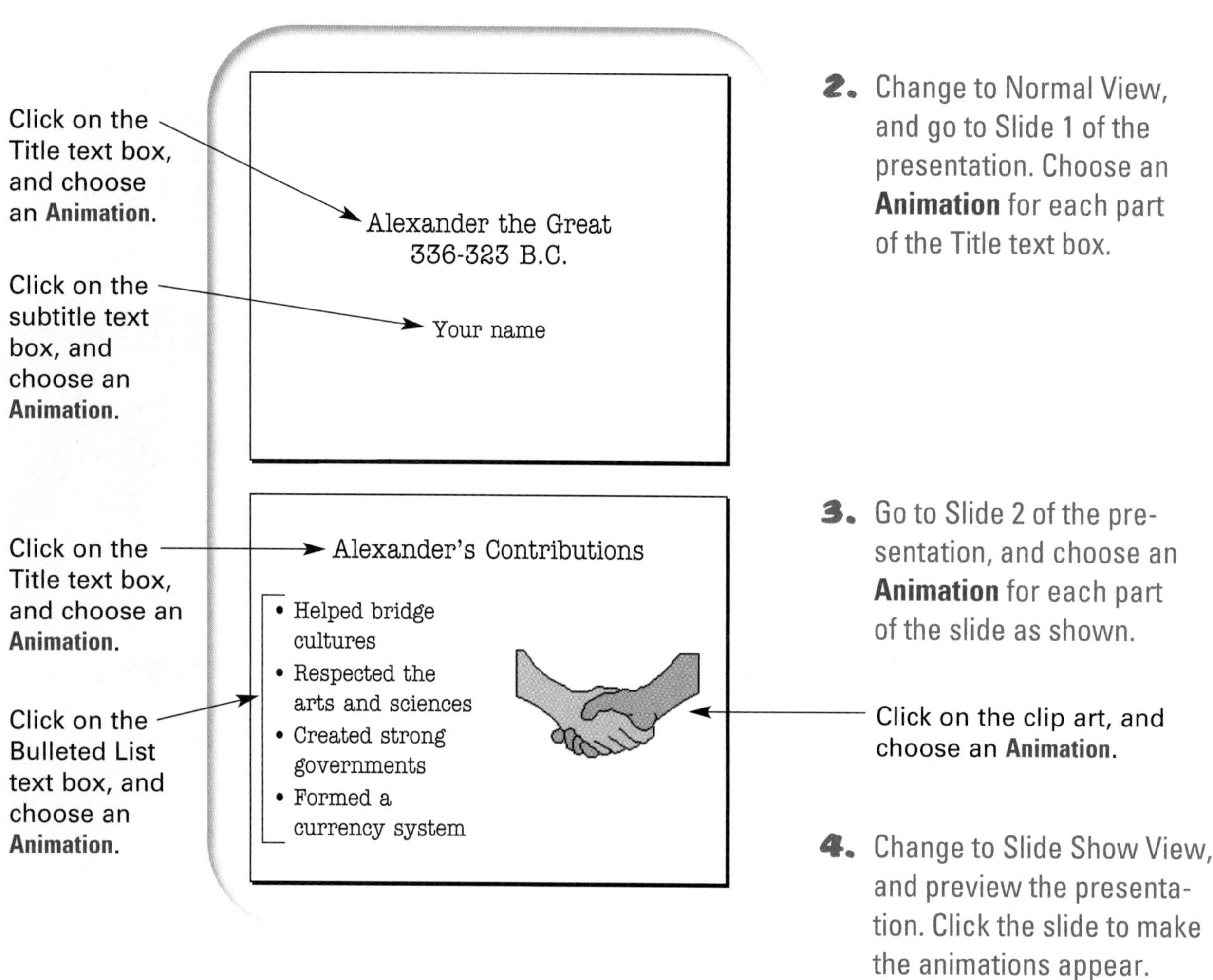

Click on the Title text box, and choose an **Animation**.
Alexander the Great
336-323 B.C.
Click on the subtitle text box, and choose an **Animation**.
Your name
Click on the Title text box, and choose an **Animation**.
Alexander's Contributions
• Helped bridge cultures
• Respected the arts and sciences
• Created strong governments
• Formed a currency system
Click on the Bulleted List text box, and choose an **Animation**.
Click on the clip art, and choose an **Animation**.

2. Change to Normal View, and go to Slide 1 of the presentation. Choose an **Animation** for each part of the Title text box.

3. Go to Slide 2 of the presentation, and choose an **Animation** for each part of the slide as shown.

4. Change to Slide Show View, and preview the presentation. Click the slide to make the animations appear.

5. Save the changes, and keep the presentation open for Project 2.

PROJECT 1 Practice

Identify Word Processing Software Functions and Use Software Commands

You will learn that no matter which software you use, you will become familiar with a core set of software features. Find the following screen parts (listed in bold) with a partner. You can find the bolded words in the glossary.

Your Turn

1. Find and point to the **title bar** on your screen.
2. Find and point to the **menu bar** on your screen.
3. Find and point to the **toolbar** on your screen.
4. Find and point to the **insertion point** on your screen.
5. Position the mouse pointer over the word File in the menu bar. Click 1 time.
   a. A drop-down menu appears. Each item in the menu indicates a different task.
   b. Find the command to open a new word processing document.
   c. Click anywhere outside the drop-down menu. The menu is no longer displayed.
6. Key your first and last name. Where is the insertion point? It should be at the end of your last name.
7. Use the mouse or the left arrow key on the keyboard to move the insertion point between your first and last name.
8. Key your middle name. Where is the insertion point? It should be at the end of your middle name.
9. Open the File menu, and select the Close command. When you are prompted to save the changes to your document, click No.
10. Open the File menu, and select the Open command to open a new document. Keep the document open for Project 2.

SECTION 9.4 Add Animation

GOALS: Demonstrate the ability to:

- Add animation to slides.
- Add sounds.
- Change the animation order.

WARMUP

Select Warmup from the Skillbuilding menu. Key each Warmup line 2 times.

Speed	1	A strong dollar makes it easier for interest to be lowered.
Accuracy	2	An aqueous liquid was used externally to prevent abscesses.
Numbers/Symbols	3	Tell each student to get his/her parents/guardians on 9/17.
Language Link	4	We bought seven pies and seven dozen cookies for the party.

Making the Connection

Are you familiar with the poet Shel Silverstein? One way you can find out about him is by reading the information on the jacket of one of his books.

Let's look at another way to learn about Shel Silverstein. Open the file **9-4 Project 1** and view the presentation about the poet Shel Silverstein. Think about your responses to the questions that follow.

Shel Silverstein

- Born in 1932
- Couldn't play ball
- Couldn't dance
- Liked to draw
- Liked to dance

Your Turn

1. When you viewed the presentation about Shel Silverstein, what held your attention?
2. What did you learn about Shel Silverstein?
3. Was the information interesting?
4. Is viewing the presentation more effective than reading the book jacket?
5. Which method helped you remember the information?
6. Close the presentation without saving.

PROJECT 2 Practice

Use Help

You can learn many features of your word processing software by using online Help or the *Student Guide*. Important words and phrases that are listed in the Help feature or in the *Student Guide* are shown in red. Key the red word in your online Help; if you have a *Student Guide*, look up the words in red.

Your Turn

1. Open your online software Help.
2. Position the insertion point in the Help text window and key in **shortcut key** as shown below. If you are using the *Student Guide*, go to Unit 3 and look up the term **shortcut key**.

shortcut key

Look up words in **red** in the online Help feature or in the *Student Guide*.

3. Read about shortcut keys. Click in your document to key your answer. Give an example of how a shortcut key is used.
4. Look up **print a document**. What are the steps to print a document? Key your answers.
5. Look up **navigate**. What are two ways to navigate or scroll in a document? Key your answers.
6. Look up **keyboard shortcuts**. What are two keyboard shortcuts that allow you to navigate through a document with the keyboard? Key your answers.
7. Look up **function keys**. What are the function keys? Find examples of function keys for the following: help, save, and check spelling.
8. Look up **Save As**. Read how to save a document.
9. **Save** the document **As** *urs***Help**. **Close** the document.

Replace **urs** with your own initials.

Check Your Understanding

1. Open a new word processing document, and save it as *urs*Adding Art.
2. Describe when it would be necessary to change the slide layout.
3. Describe the purpose of adding clip art and pictures to a presentation.
4. Save the changes, print, and close the file.

*inter*NET CONNECTION

1. **Open one of your previous presentations ("Alexander the Great" or "Protecting the Rain Forests").**
2. **Open your Web browser, and search for free clip art on the Internet.**
3. **When you find a free clip art site, look for additional clip art to enhance your presentation.**
4. **Add your new clip art to one of the slides.**
5. **Save the changes, view the presentation, and close the file.**
6. **On your own: Create a Web page with links to a few of the best free clip art sites. Make sure to describe them on the page so you will know what they contain.**

PROJECT 3 Reinforce

Software Commands and Help

Your Turn

1. **Open** a new word processing document.
2. Key the sentence shown below in yellow.

When you see words highlighted in **yellow**, key the words as shown.

Franklin owned his own newspaper in Philadelphia.

3. Move the insertion point in front of the word Franklin, and key the word Ben.
4. Move the insertion point to the end of the line, and press ENTER 2 times.
5. Explore the command menus and the Help feature of your software to respond to the following questions. Key your answers.
   a. What menu name would you use to find the **Save** command?
   b. What menu name would you use if you wanted to change the **Font**?
   c. What shortcut keys would you use to **Open** a document?
   d. What does the Toolbar button look like for checking **Spelling and Grammar**?
   e. Describe what theToolbar button looks like to **print** a document.
6. **Save As** *urs*Software. **Close** the document.

PROJECT 3 **Reinforce**

Add Clip Art and Pictures

Reinforce what you have learned by enhancing a presentation with clip art and pictures.

Your Turn

1. Open the file ***urs*Rain Forest-Edits**, and save it as ***urs*Rain Forest-Art**.
2. Change the slide layout; then choose an appropriate clip art layout as shown.

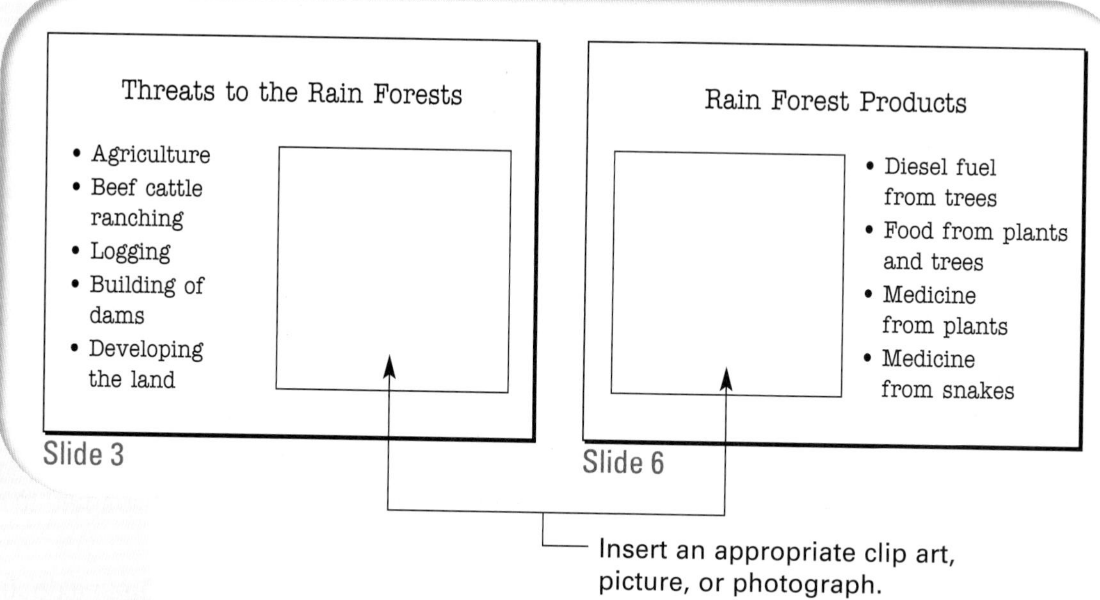

Threats to the Rain Forests
• Agriculture
• Beef cattle ranching
• Logging
• Building of dams
• Developing the land
Slide 3
Rain Forest Products
• Diesel fuel from trees
• Food from plants and trees
• Medicine from plants
• Medicine from snakes
Slide 6
Insert an appropriate clip art, picture, or photograph.

3. Save the changes, view the presentation, and close the file.

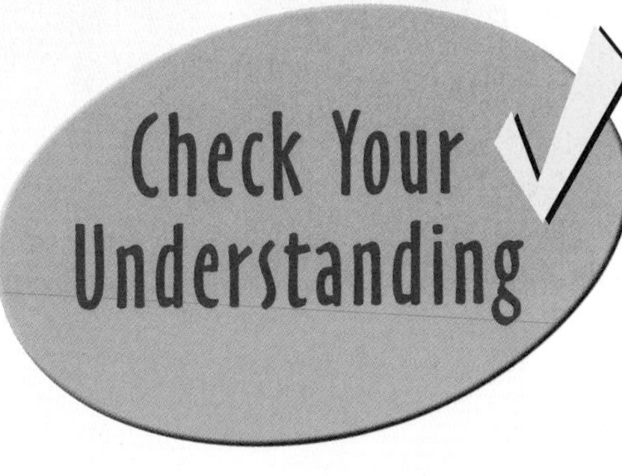

1. Open a new word processing document.
2. Describe where on the screen you see the name of the document.
3. Describe where on the screen you see menu options.
4. Describe where on the screen you find shortcut keys and function keys displayed.
5. Name three different ways you can open a new word processing document.
6. Save the document as *urs*Screen. Close the file.

CD-ROMs store many forms of data, including text, music, audio, and full-motion video.

PROJECT 2 Practice

Add Pictures and Clip Art

Pictures and photographs can also be used to communicate your message. Remember the picture you choose will likely be what your audience looks at first.

Your Turn

1. Change to Normal View, and go to Slide 3 of the presentation.
2. Choose the **Slide Layout** command; then choose an appropriate clip art and text layout as shown.

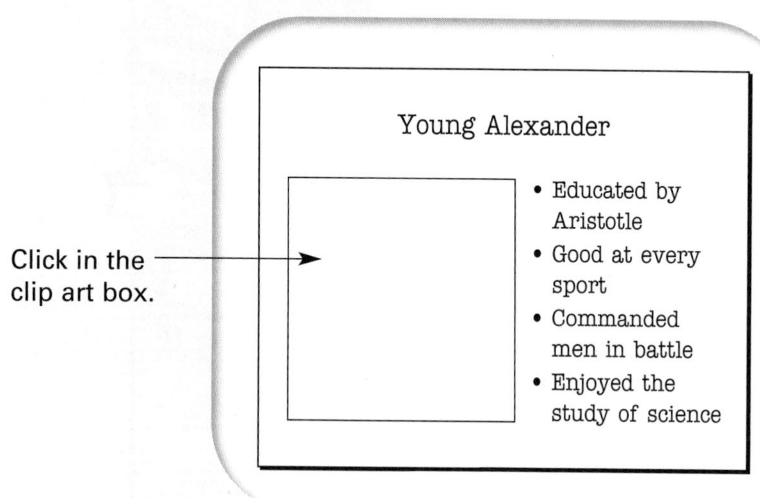
Young Alexander
• Educated by Aristotle
• Good at every sport
• Commanded men in battle
• Enjoyed the study of science

Click in the clip art box.

3. Search for an appropriate picture or photograph as shown.
4. Save the changes, view the presentation, and close the file.

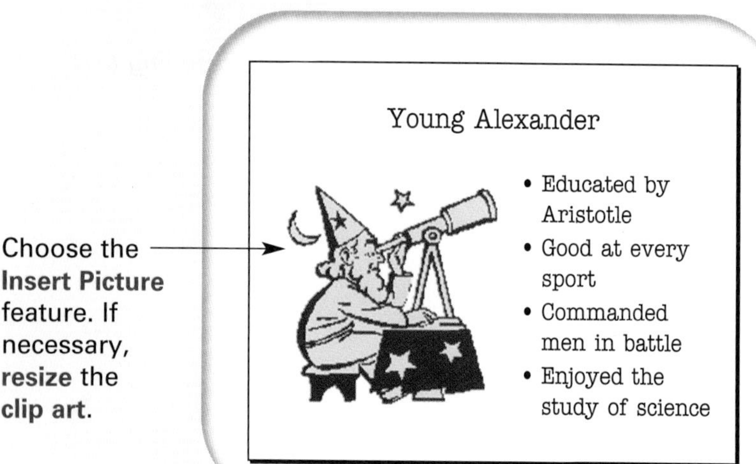
Young Alexander
• Educated by Aristotle
• Good at every sport
• Commanded men in battle
• Enjoyed the study of science

Choose the **Insert Picture** feature. If necessary, **resize the clip art.**

SECTION 3.2 Manage Files

GOALS: Demonstrate the ability to:

- Create a folder.
- Open an existing file.
- Find a file.
- Delete a file.

WARMUP

Select Warmup from the Skillbuilding menu. Key each Warmup line 2 times.

Speed	1	We may make a nice profit if all of the work is done right.
Accuracy	2	From the tower Dave saw six big jet planes quickly zoom by.
Speed	3	foal elms hire mare jell sods from jars adds half ash head;
Accuracy	4	joke ride sale same roam aims sire more jars aide dark lame

Making the Connection

Have you ever lost your homework? Putting your papers in folders for each class is similar to creating folders for your computer. You can store whatever documents you create and save them in folders on your computer.

Your Turn

1. Open a new word processing document.
2. Think about some tips that will help you organize your school papers. Key your ideas.
3. Keep the document open for Project 1.

ORGANIZING TIPS

Make one folder for each class.
Label each folder.

PROJECT 1 Practice

Change the Slide Layout and Add Clip Art

You can add clip art to help make your presentation more interesting and entertaining. The clip art you choose should match your message.

Your Turn

1. Change to Normal view, and go to Slide 2 of the presentation.

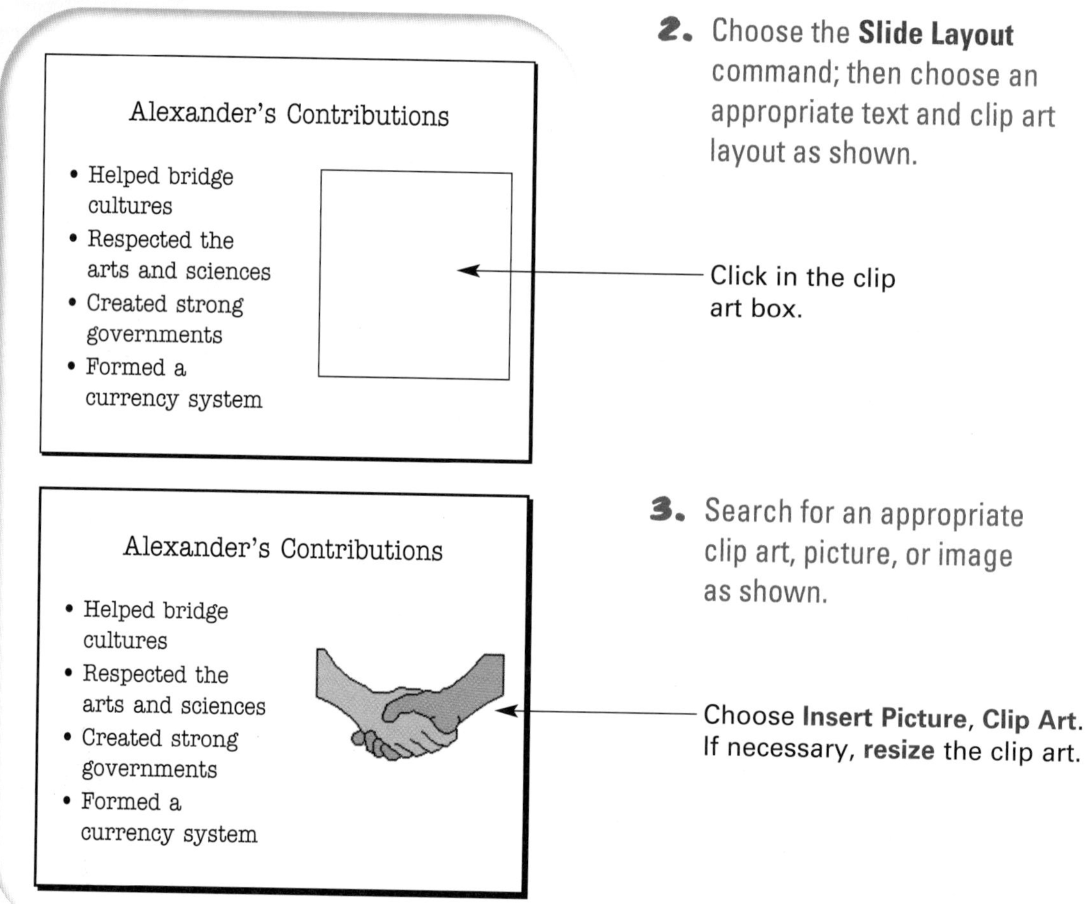
Alexander's Contributions
• Helped bridge cultures
• Respected the arts and sciences
• Created strong governments
• Formed a currency system
Click in the clip art box.
Alexander's Contributions
• Helped bridge cultures
• Respected the arts and sciences
• Created strong governments
• Formed a currency system
Choose Insert Picture, Clip Art. If necessary, resize the clip art.

2. Choose the **Slide Layout** command; then choose an appropriate text and clip art layout as shown.
3. Search for an appropriate clip art, picture, or image as shown.
4. Save the changes, and keep the presentation open for Project 2.

PROJECT 1 Practice

Organize Files and Create Folders

Documents you create using your software are called **files**. Use **folders** to organize files so you can find them easily.

To create a folder and save the file you created in *Making the Connection*, follow these steps:

Your Turn

1. Choose the **Save As** command.
2. Create a **New folder**.
3. Name the new folder Unit 3.
4. Open the **new folder**.
5. Save the document with the filename ***urs*Organizing**.
6. **Close** the file.
7. **Open** the file **3-2 Project 1**, and read the paragraph.

Replace **urs** with your own initials.

The documents you create and use are called files. When you save the file, you save it to a drive—such as the hard drive, the network drive, or a floppy disk or CD—on your computer. To help you keep things neatly organized on the drives, you can create folders to store your files. To avoid losing your work, you should save changes you make to your document regularly.

8. Position the insertion point at the end of the paragraph; then key the highlighted sentence shown in the paragraph above.
9. Choose the Save As command and, if necessary, open the Unit 3 folder.
10. Save the document as ***urs*File**.
11. Close the file.

Notice the filename on the software Title Bar changes to *urs*File.

SECTION 9.3 Add Clip Art to Slides

GOALS: Demonstrate the ability to:

- Change the slide layout.
- Insert clip art and pictures.
- Resize clip art and pictures.

WARMUP

Select Warmup from the Skillbuilding menu. Key each Warmup line 2 times.

Speed	1	We must drive cautiously during the rush hours in the city.
Accuracy	2	Gazelles are Bovidae herbivores living from India to Egypt.
Numbers/Symbols	3	Martin & Wills sent a check for $2,195; the bill is $3,468.
Language Link	4	We need to buy 16 bars of soap. We have seven bars on hand.

Making the Connection

Have you ever given a report and wanted to use a visual display to help your audience understand what you were talking about? By adding clip art and pictures to your presentation, you can help communicate your message. The images will help your audience remember the information you present.

Your Turn

1. Open the file ***urs*AlexanderEdits** you created in Section 9.2, and save it as *urs*AlexanderArt.
2. Keep the presentation open for Project 1.

Alexander's Contributions

- Helped bridge cultures
- Respected the arts and sciences
- Created strong governments
- Formed a currency system

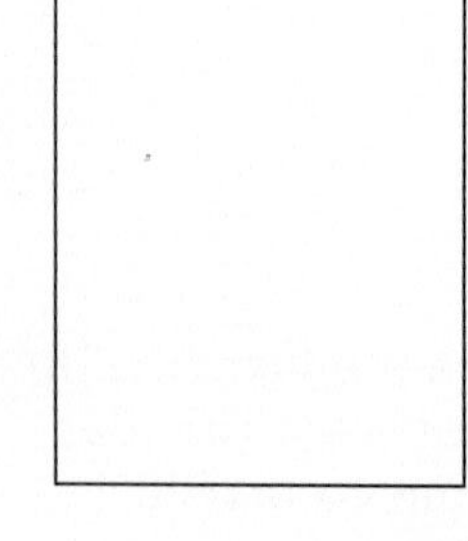

PROJECT 2 Practice

Find and Delete Files

Sometimes you might forget where you saved your file. If this happens, you can locate the file by using the **Search** feature in the operating system software.

Your Turn

1. Choose the **Find** (or **Search**) command. (Use the command from your word processing or your operating system software.)
2. Find the file ***urs*File**.
3. When the filename appears, click on the filename 1 time and press the DELETE key.
4. Close the Find (or Search) feature.

If you do not know where your file is, choose the Find command from your word processing software.

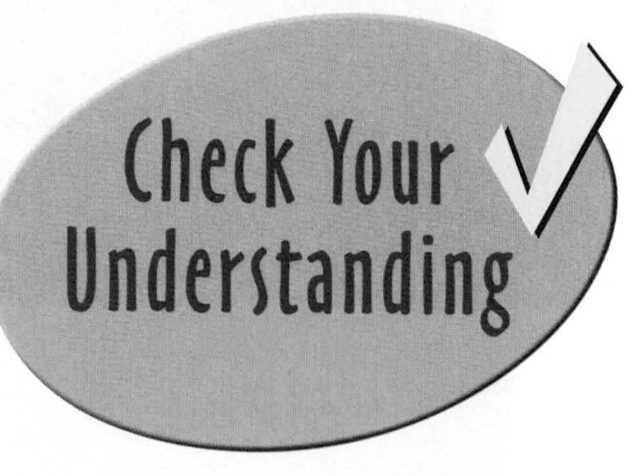

1. Open the presentation *urs*AlexanderEdits.
2. Does your presentation match the illustration shown?
3. Make any necessary corrections.
4. Print and close the file.

*urs*AlexanderEdits

Alexander the Great
336-323 B.C.

Your name

1

Alexander's Contributions

- Helped bridge cultures
- Respected the arts and sciences
- Created strong governments
- Formed a currency system

2

Young Alexander

- Educated by Aristotle
- Good at every sport
- Commanded men in battle
- Enjoyed the study of science

3

Old and New World Empires

Macedon	Turkistan	Persian
Greece	Russia	Syria
Bulgaria	Afghanistan	Israel
Macedonia	China	Lebanon

4

PROJECT 3

Reinforce

Manage Files

Reinforce what you have learned about managing files.

Your Turn

1. Find and open the file ***urs*Organizing**.
2. Save the file as ***urs*Filetips** in a new folder named Managing Files.
3. Close the file.
4. Find and delete the file ***urs*Organizing** in the Unit 3 folder.

Check Your Understanding

1. Open a new word processing document.
2. Describe how to create a folder.
3. Describe how to use the Find command to find a file.
4. Save the document as ***urs*Files**.
5. Close the file.

Reinforce

Edit the Presentations

3. After Slide 4, add two **New Slides** as shown.

Rain Forest Foods	
• Bananas	• Lemons
• Pineapples	• Peppers
• Coconuts	• Avocados
• Papayas	• Sugarcane

Threats to the Rain Forests

- Agriculture
- Beef cattle ranching
- Logging
- Building of dams
- Developing the land

4. Change the **slide order** as follows

  a. Move Slide 6 ("Threats to the Rain Forests") to come after Slide 2 ("Rain Forest Facts").

  b. Move Slide 4 ("Rain Forest Products") to the end of the presentation.

5. Use the **Spelling** feature to identify any errors; then correct them.

6. Change to Slide Show View, and preview the presentation.

7. Save the changes, and close the file.

SECTION 3.3 Editing Basics

GOALS: Demonstrate the ability to:

- Edit sentences with proofreaders' marks.
- Use the BACKSPACE, INSERT, and DELETE keys.
- Select text and insert text.
- Use the Cut, Copy and Paste commands, and the Undo command.

WARMUP

Select Warmup from the Skillbuilding menu. Key each Warmup line 2 times.

Speed	1	`I did not see her take the pencil, but I know that she did.`
Accuracy	2	`Taxi drivers are quick to zip by the huge jumble of wagons.`
Speed	3	`It's the secretary who accepted the stationery on Thursday.`
Accuracy	4	`nine kind lines; ten done in an instant; act at once; lines`

Making the Connection

When you create your work in a word processing document, you will find that it is easy to correct your mistakes.

Your Turn

1. Open the file **3-3 Project 1**, and save it as *urs*Proofermarks.
2. Notice that your document contains ten sentences. These sentences require corrections. What kinds of errors do you see?
3. Keep the document open for Project 1.

PROOFREADERS' MARKS

1. The club officer is very busy.
2. He gave the final estimate for the bike repair.
3. They find all him funny.

PROJECT 4

Reinforce

Edit the Presentations

Reinforce what you have learned by editing a presentation.

Your Turn

1. Open the file ***urs*Rain Forest** you created in Section 9.1, and save it as *urs*Rain Forest-Edits.
2. Edit the slides as shown.

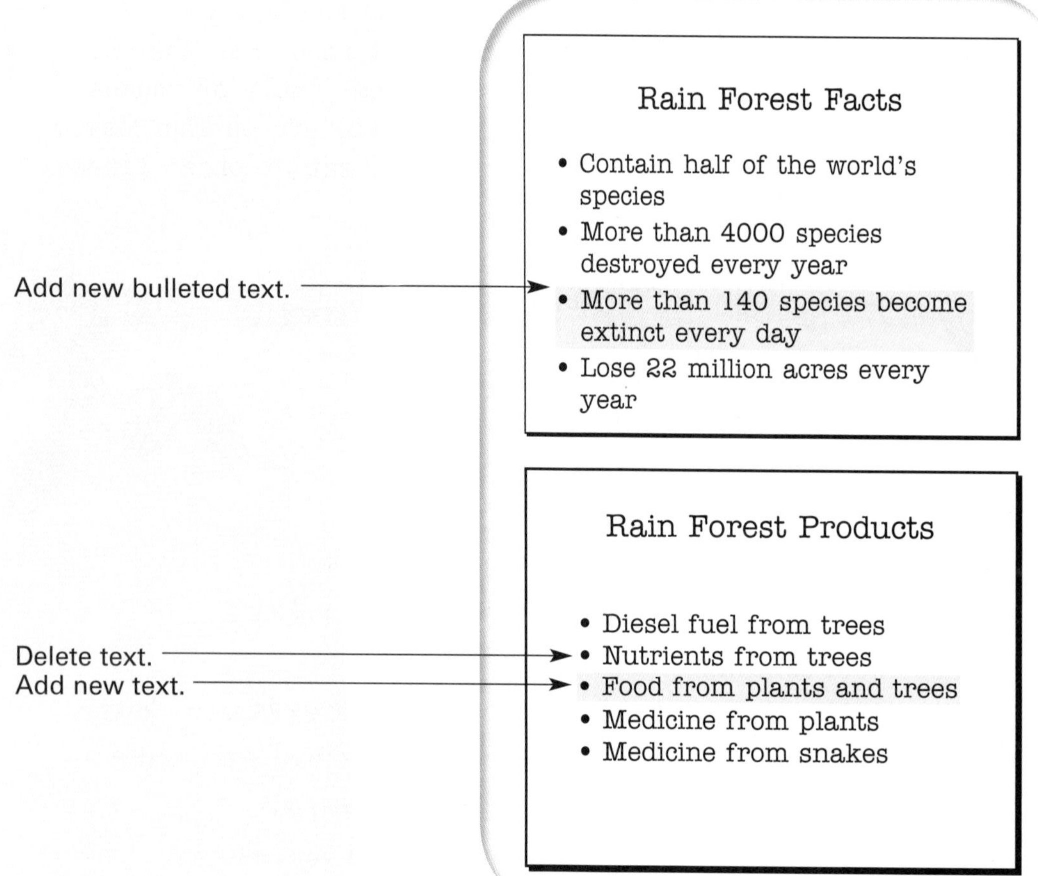

Rain Forest Facts
• Contain half of the world's species
• More than 4000 species destroyed every year
• More than 140 species become extinct every day
• Lose 22 million acres every year
Add new bulleted text.
Rain Forest Products
• Diesel fuel from trees
• Nutrients from trees
• Food from plants and trees
• Medicine from plants
• Medicine from snakes
Delete text.
Add new text.

Continued on next page

Insert and Delete Text

When you edit your work, you can use proofreaders' marks to show exactly how a document should be revised. **Proofreaders' marks** are symbols that are used to mark changes that need to be made.

Your Turn

PROOFREADERS' MARKS		
Symbol	**Draft Copy**	**Final Copy**
^ Insert	1. The ^student club officer is very busy.	The student club officer is very busy.
Delete	2. He gave the ~~final~~ estimate for the bike repair.	He gave the estimate for the bike repair.
Transpose	3. They find all him funny.	They all find him funny.

1. In Sentence 1, position the insertion point between "The" and "club" and key the text student.
2. In Sentence 2, position the insertion point after the letter "l" in the word "final." Press the **Backspace Key** until the entire word is erased. The **backspace key** erases the characters to the left of the insertion point.
3. In Sentence 3, position the insertion point before the letter "f" in the word "find." Press the **Insert Key** on your keyboard; this key is sometimes called the **Overtype key**. Key the text all find. The text is keyed over the existing words. Press Insert again to turn the feature off.

Continued on next page

PROJECT 3 Continued

Practice

Change the Slide Order

4. Choose the Paste command. The slide order is rearranged as shown.

Alexander the Great
336-323 B.C.
Your name
1
Young Alexander
• Educated by Aristotle
• Good at every sport
• Commanded men in battle
• Enjoyed the study of science
2
Alexander's Contributions
• Helped bridge cultures
• Respected the arts and sciences
• Created strong governments
• Formed a currency system
3
Old and New World Empires

Macedon	Turkistan	Persian
Greece	Russia	Syria
Bulgaria	Afghanistan	Israel
Macedonia	China	Lebanon

4

5. Change the **Slide Order** again by moving Slide 2 ("Young Alexander") after Slide 3 ("Alexander's Contributions").
6. Change to Slide Show View, and preview the presentation.
7. Save the changes, and close the file.

PROJECT 1 Continued

Practice

Insert and Delete Text

PROOFREADERS' MARKS		
Symbol	**Draft Copy**	**Final Copy**
¶ New Paragraph	4. I can't wait to finish.¶They want to leave soon.	I can't wait to finish. They want to leave soon.
⊙ Insert a period	5. She left⊙He followed her.	She left. He followed her.
^ Insert a comma	6. If I go^so will he.	If I go, so will he.
≡ Capitalize	7. president Lincoln was a tall man.	President Lincoln was a tall man.
/ Lowercase	8. Our club President met with the school staff.	Our club president met with the school staff.

4. In Sentence 4, position the insertion point between the period after "finish" and before "They." Press ENTER to create a new paragraph. If necessary, press TAB to indent the new paragraph.
5. In Sentence 5, position the insertion point after the word "left" and key a period.
6. In Sentence 6, position the insertion point after the word "go" and key a comma.
7. In Sentence 7, position the insertion point before the letter "p" in the word "president." Press the **DELETE KEY**. The **delete key** erases the characters to the right of the insertion point. Then key a capital P.
8. In Sentence 8, position the insertion point after the "P" in "President." Press BACKSPACE; then key a lowercase letter p.
9. **Save** the changes to the document. Keep the file open for Project 2.

PROJECT 3 **Practice**

Change the Slide Order

If you want to change the order of your presentation, you can quickly rearrange the slides.

Your Turn

1. Change to Slide Sorter View, and click on Slide 4 ("Alexander's Contributions") to select it.
2. Choose the Cut command.
3. Place the insertion point between Slides 2 and 3 as shown.

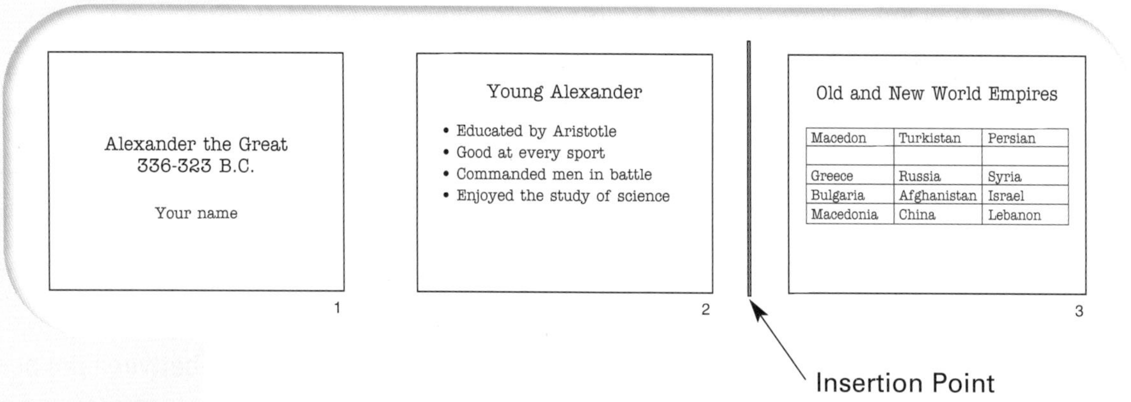

Alexander the Great
336-323 B.C.

Your name

1

Young Alexander

- Educated by Aristotle
- Good at every sport
- Commanded men in battle
- Enjoyed the study of science

2

Old and New World Empires

Macedon	Turkistan	Persian
Greece	Russia	Syria
Bulgaria	Afghanistan	Israel
Macedonia	China	Lebanon

3

Insertion Point

Continued on next page

PROJECT 2 Practice

Cut and Paste Text

A quick way to change text is to use the Cut and Paste commands. When text is cut, it is stored in the **clipboard**. The **clipboard** is a temporary storage area in your software. The text on the clipboard can be placed in another location.

In order to move text, you must first select a portion of the document you want to change. An easy way to **select text** is to use the "click-Shift-click" method.

Your Turn

Symbol	Draft Copy	Final Copy
move Move text	9. Lauren carefully swam (move)	Lauren swam carefully.

1. In Sentence 9, position the insertion point before the letter "c" in the word "carefully."
2. Hold down the SHIFT key and move the insertion point to after the letter "y" in "carefully." The entire word is highlighted as shown in the illustration below.

Selected text is text that is highlighted by a colored or shaded box. → 9. Lauren carefully swam.

3. Choose the **Cut** command. The word "carefully" disappears.
4. Position the insertion point after the letter "m" in the word "swam."
5. Choose the **Paste** command. The word "carefully" appears again.

If you accidentally remove more text than you want to delete, be sure to use the Undo command immediately.

6. Choose the **Undo** command until the word "carefully" is back in its original position.
7. Save the changes. Keep the file open for Project 3.

PROJECT 2 Practice

Add and Delete Slides

You can easily change the content of your presentation by adding and deleting slides.

Your Turn

1. Change to Slide sorter view, and delete the slide shown.

Alexander the Great
336-323 B.C.

Your name

1

Young Alexander

- Educated by Aristotle
- Good at every sport
- Commanded men in battle
- Enjoyed the study of science

2

Alexander's Empire
336-323 B.C.

- Macedonia
- Greece
- Bulgaria
- Russia
- Lebanon
- China
- Syria
- Israel
- Iran
- Afghanistan

3

Alexander's Contributions

- Helped bridge cultures
- Respected the arts and sciences
- Created strong governments
- Formed a currency system

4

Click on Slide 3 to select it, and press DELETE.

2. Change to Normal view, **add a new slide**, and choose a Table layout.

Old and New World Empires

Macedon	Turkistan	Persian
Greece	Russia	Syria
Bulgaria	Afghanistan	Israel
Macedonia	China	Lebanon

Create a table with 3 columns and 5 rows. Then key the text.

3. Save the changes, and keep the presentation open for Project 3.

PROJECT 3 Practice

Copy and Paste Text

If you want the same text to appear in different places in a document, use the Copy and Paste commands. Copying text allows you to repeat information in your document without having to key the text again.

Your Turn

Symbol	Draft Copy	Final Copy
COPY Copy text	10. The girl (is fast.) The boy (COPY)	The girl is fast. The boy is fast.

1. In Sentence 10, position the insertion point before the letter "i" in the word "is."
2. Hold down the SHIFT key and move the insertion point to after the period following the word "fast." The group of words is highlighted as shown in the illustration below.

Selected text → The girl is fast.

3. Choose the **Copy** command.
4. Position the insertion point after the letter "y" in the word "boy."
5. Choose the **Paste** command. The words "is fast." are copied.
6. Choose the **Undo** command to delete the words "is fast."
7. Save the changes to the file.
8. Close the file.

If you change your mind about copying the text, be sure to use the Undo command immediately.

PROJECT 1
Continued

Practice

Edit Text and Use Proofing Tools

3. Go to Slide 2 and edit as shown.

Young Alexander

- Educated by Aristotle
- Good at every sport
- Loved poetry and music ← Delete the third bulleted line.
- Commanded men in battle
- Enjoyed the study of science ← Key the new line of text.

4. Use the **Spelling** feature to identify any errors; then correct them.

5. Save the changes, and keep the presentation open for Project 2.

PROJECT 4

Reinforce

Editing Basics

Reinforce using your editing skills by making the necessary corrections to the essay.

Your Turn

1. Open the file **3-3 Project 4** and save it as ***urs*Jefferson**.
2. Study the illustration. Make the changes indicated by the proofreaders' marks.

Thomas Jefferson was born on April 13 1743. He was born on a small farm in Virginia called shadwall. Thomas had red hair and hazel eyes. He was very skinny and pretty tall. When he was a young lad, he would go to school like all the other kids. Thomas had four brothers and six sisters It was pretty hard living in a big family. Jefferson spent his time reading as a little kid. When he got older, he liked to farm and invent things. He loved music and loved to play the Violin. Thomas Jefferson got married on January 1, 1772. He got married to Martha Skelton Wayles. had six children.

3. Save the changes to the file.
4. Close the file.

PROJECT 1 Practice

Edit Text and Use Proofing Tools

You can easily edit and correct your text.

Your Turn

1. Go to Slide 1 and edit as shown.

Alexander the Great
336-323 B.C.

Your name

Place the insertion point at the end of the last letter in the title and press ENTER.

Key the new line of text.

2. Go to Slide 4 and edit as shown.

Alexander's Contributions

- Helped bridge cultures
- Respected the arts and sciences
- Created strong governments
- Formed a currency system

Place the insertion point at the end of the last line and press ENTER.

Key the new line of text.

Continued on next page

1. Open ***urs*****Jefferson**.
2. Check to see if you interpreted the proofreaders' marks correctly by comparing your document with the illustration below. Make any necessary corrections.
3. Close the file.

Thomas Jefferson was born on April 13, 1743. He was born on a farm in Virginia called Shadwall. Thomas had red hair and hazel eyes. He was also very skinny and pretty tall. Thomas had four brothers and six sisters. It was pretty hard living in a big family. When he was a young lad, he would go to school like all the other kids. Jefferson spent his time reading as a little kid. When he got older, he liked to farm and invent things. He loved music and loved to play the violin.

Thomas Jefferson got married on January 1, 1772. He got married to Martha Wayles Skelton. Martha had six children.

SECTION 9.2

Edit Slides

GOALS: Demonstrate the ability to:

- Edit slide text.
- Use proofing tools.
- Add and delete slides.
- Change the slide order.

WARMUP

Select Warmup from the Skillbuilding menu. Key each Warmup line 2 times.

Speed	1	Four students from our school will run in the state finals.
Accuracy	2	The quadrant has been a survey device since medieval times.
Numbers/Symbols	3	Invoice 836-259 for $1,274.50 is subject to a 12% discount.
Language Link	4	The accountant had 100 five-column pads in his desk drawer.

Making the Connection

When you prepare an oral report, you may need to make some corrections and changes on your notes. You can easily make changes or correct your mistakes without starting over with presentation software.

Your Turn

1. Open the file ***urs*Alexander** you created in Section 9.1, and save it as *urs*AlexanderEdits.
2. Keep the file open for Project 1.

Alexander the Great

Your name

SECTION 3.4 Editing Basics

GOALS: Demonstrate the ability to:

- Format fonts, and font sizes and styles.
- Change alignment of text in a document.
- Preview and print a document.
- Use the spelling and grammar feature.

WARMUP

Select Warmup from the Skillbuilding menu. Key each Warmup line 2 times.

Speed	1	I did not see her take the pencil, but I know that she did.
Accuracy	2	Taxi drivers are quick to zip by the huge jumble of wagons.
Language Link	3	It's the secretary who accepted the stationery on Thursday.
Numbers/Symbols	4	Lee cut the pieces of twine 9 1/2, 7 3/4, and 6 5/8 inches.

Making the Connection

Your friend Ryan has lost his dog, and he has asked you to help him make a sign that you can distribute around the neighborhood. You want to help Ryan create a sign that will grab people's attention. Begin creating the sign by determining how you will display the information that will be printed on the sign.

Lost Dog

Reward!
$50.00

Yellow Lab
About 70 lbs.
4 yrs. old
Purple collar with name tag
Male

His name is Ringo.

Ashton Woods
Subdivision

Contact:
555-5555

Your Turn

1. Open the file **3-4 Project 1**, and save it as ***urs*Lostdog**.
2. Keep the file open for Project 1.

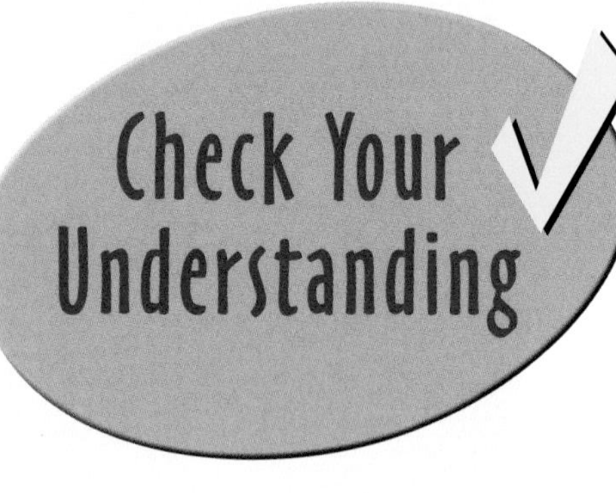
Check Your Understanding

1. Open a word processing document, and save it as *urs***Presentation Basics**.
2. Describe the difference between Outline view and Normal view.
3. Describe the difference between Slide Sorter view and Slide show view.
4. Describe three types of slide layouts.
5. Describe the purpose of using a design template.
6. Save the changes.
7. Print and close the file.

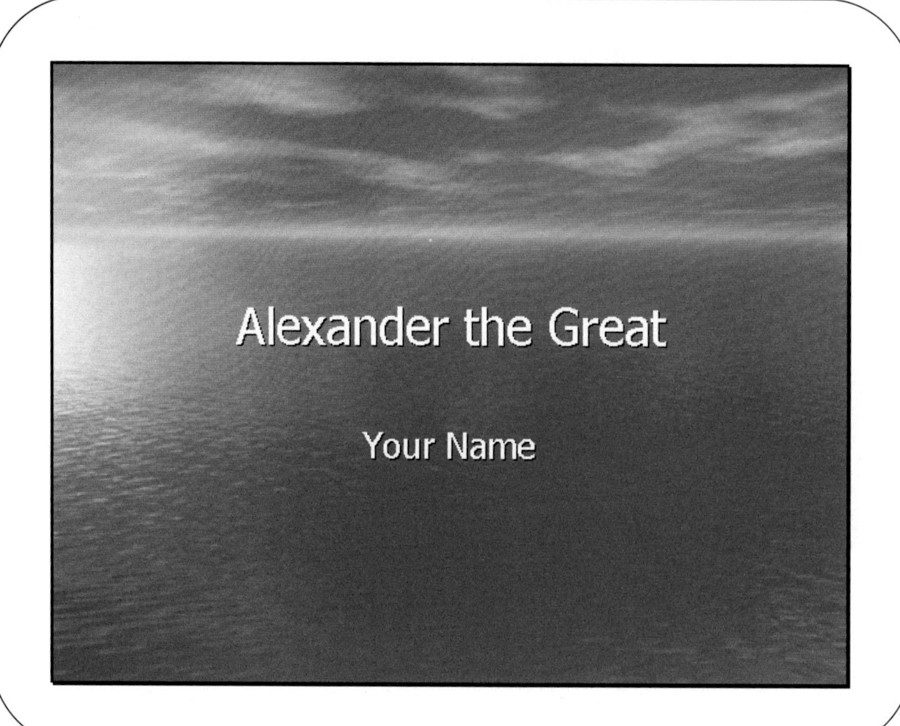
Alexander the Great
Your Name

PROJECT 1 **Practice**

Formatting Fonts

A **font** is the general shape and style of the characters in your document. After you select a font, you can change the font size and add emphasis by applying bold, italic, or underline formats.

When you have finished formatting the document, you will want to preview the document before you print it. When you preview your document, you have a chance to see what it will look like before you print. If necessary, you can make changes before you print your document.

Your Turn

1. Make the changes shown in the illustration at the left.

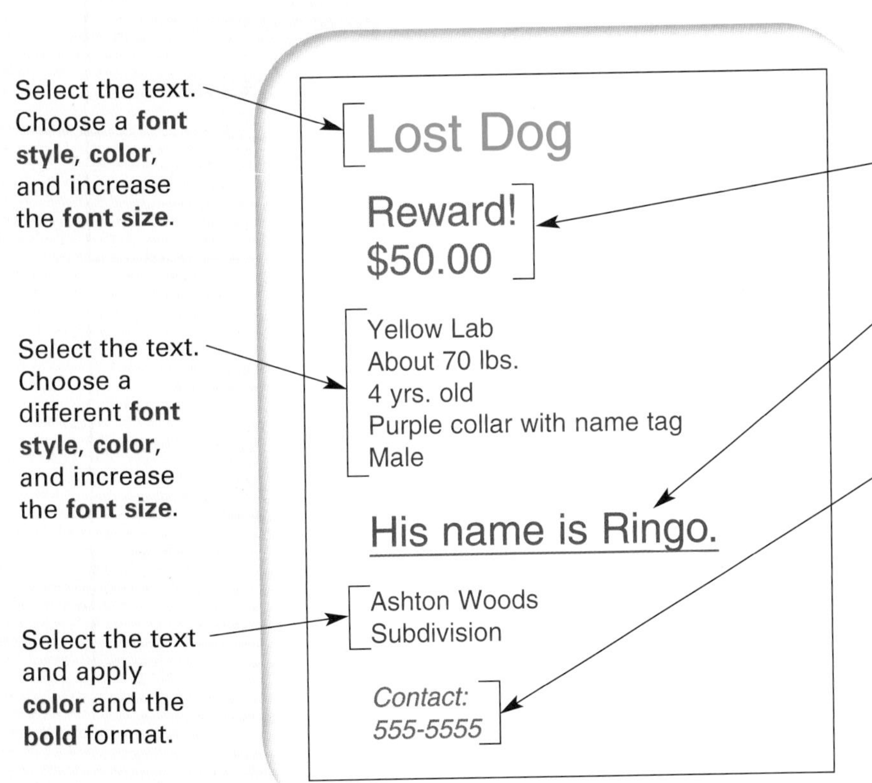

Select the text. Choose a **font style, color,** and increase the **font size.**
Lost Dog
Reward!
$50.00
Select the text. Choose a different **font style, color,** and increase the **font size.**
Yellow Lab
About 70 lbs.
4 yrs. old
Purple collar with name tag
Male
His name is Ringo.
Select the text and apply **color** and the **bold** format.
Ashton Woods
Subdivision
Contact:
555-5555

Select the text. Choose a **font style**, increase the **font size**, and change the **font color**.

Select the text. Choose a **font style, color**, increase the **font size**, and apply the **underline** format.

Select the text and apply **color** and the **italic** format.

2. Save the changes to the file.
3. Display the document in **Print Preview**. If necessary, make corrections and save the document again.
4. Keep the file open for Project 2.

PROJECT 4 Reinforce

Create a Basic Presentation

Reinforce what you have learned by creating a presentation.

Your Turn

1. Open a **new presentation**.
2. Create the slides shown using appropriate **slide layouts**.
3. Save the presentation as *urs*Rain Forest.

Protecting the Rain Forests

Your name

Slide 1

Rain Forest Facts

- Contain half of the world's species
- More than 4000 species destroyed every year
- Lose 22 million acres every year

Slide 2

Rain Forest Products

- Diesel fuel from trees
- Nutrients from trees
- Medicine from plants
- Medicine from snakes

Slide 3

Rain Forest Animals

- Spider Monkeys
- Sloths
- Jaguars
- Iguanas
- Scarlet Macaws
- Boas
- Ocelots
- Harpy eagles

Slide 4

4. **Apply** a **design template**.
5. Change to **Slide Show View** and preview the presentation.
6. Save the changes. Print and close the file.

PROJECT 2 Practice

Aligning Text and Printing Documents

You can also enhance the appearance of your document by changing the alignment of the text. **Alignment** is how text is positioned between the left and right margins. When you choose center alignment, your text is positioned at the center of the page between the left and right margins. Similarly, left alignment positions the text at the left margin, and right alignment positions the text at the right margin.

Your Turn

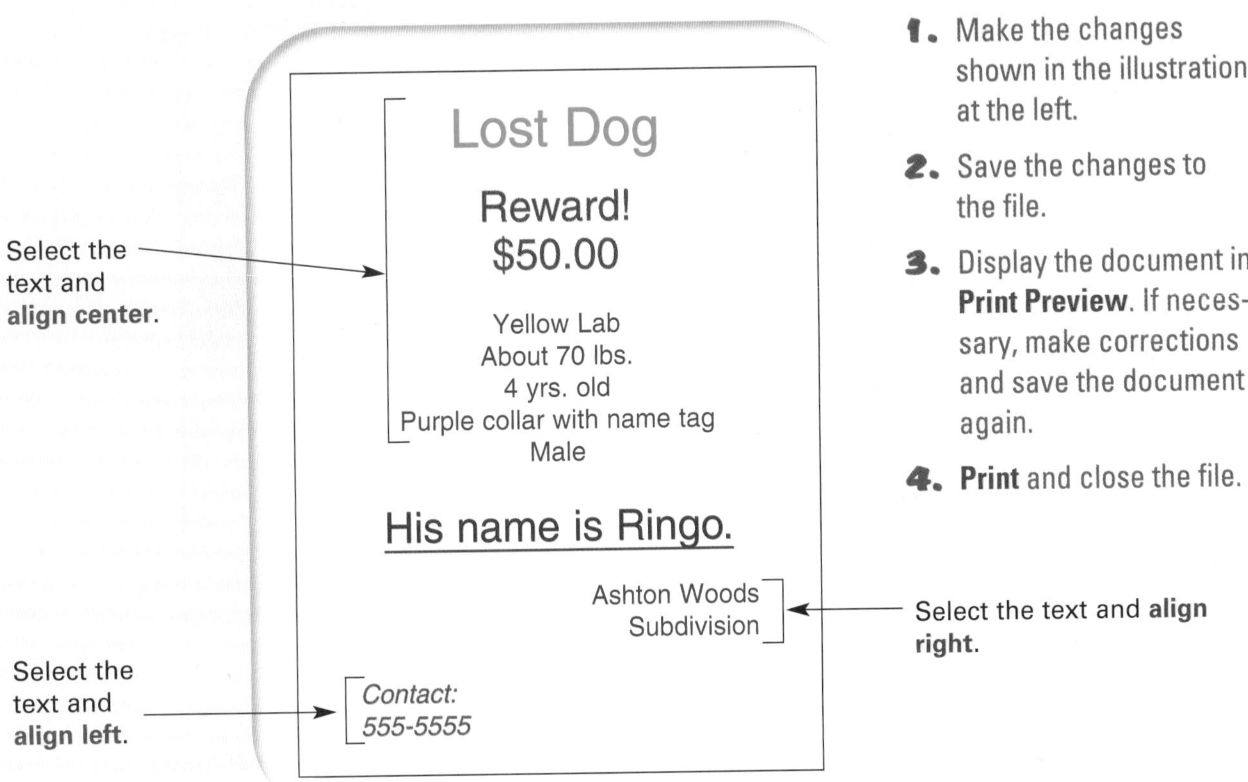

Lost Dog
Reward!
$50.00
Yellow Lab
About 70 lbs.
4 yrs. old
Purple collar with name tag
Male
His name is Ringo.
Ashton Woods
Subdivision
Contact:
555-5555
Select the text and **align center**.
Select the text and **align right**.
Select the text and **align left**.

1. Make the changes shown in the illustration at the left.
2. Save the changes to the file.
3. Display the document in **Print Preview**. If necessary, make corrections and save the document again.
4. **Print** and close the file.

PROJECT 3 Practice

Apply a Design Template

You can choose from many design templates to give the slides in your presentation a professional look.

Your Turn

1. Choose **Normal View**, and go to Slide 1.
2. Choose the **Apply Design Template** command.
3. Browse through the design templates, and apply an appropriate design.

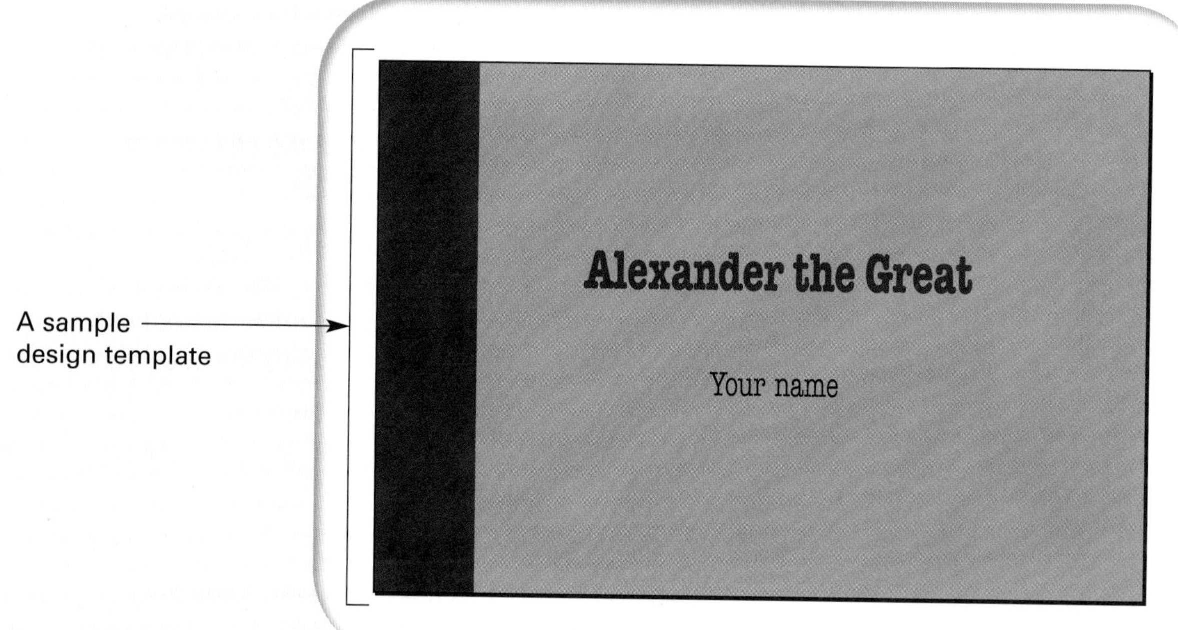
Alexander the Great
Your name

A sample design template

4. Change to **Slide Show View**, and preview the presentation.
5. Save the changes. Print and close the file.

PROJECT 3

Practice

Using Proofing Tools

The **Spelling** feature of your word processor can be used as an online dictionary to check your document for spelling errors. The **Grammar** feature will check for errors, such as punctuation and capitalization, in your writing.

Your Turn

1. Open the file **3-4 Project 3**, and save it as ***urs*Spelling**.
2. Check to see if errors have been flagged by the Spelling and Grammar checker. The errors are circled in the illustration.

1. frank, please move to to the end of the line.
2. The deed was takn to The bank deposit box.
3. my cousin's home in Lattasburg is on a farm.
4. john Coista received the london Service Award.
5. Susan, are you going with the team to Charlotte, north carolina next month?
6. Ms. Mar, did the romans have a large merchant flet?
7. The bus tripp began on July 5, 1996, and lasted three weks.
8. People travelled frm Buffalo, New York, to join with the tour.
9. carol Warren, M.D., studied the efects of motion sicknes.
10. Cassandra and and Mark enjoyd the comedy show.

3. Use the **Spelling and Grammar** feature to identify and correct the errors.
4. Save the changes, **print**, and close the file.

Create a New Presentation

Young Alexander
336–323 B.C.

- Macedonia
- Greece
- Bulgaria
- Russia
- Lebanon

- China
- Syria
- Israel
- Iran
- Afghanistan

4. Insert a new slide, and choose a Two-Column layout.

Click in the text box; then key each bulleted line.

Alexander's Contributions

- Helped bridge cultures
- Respected the arts and sciences
- Created strong governments

5. Insert a new slide, and choose a Bulleted List layout.

Click in the text box; then key each bulleted line.

6. Save the presentation as ***urs*Alexander**.

7. Keep the presentation open for Project 3.

PROJECT 4 **Reinforce**

Basic Editing Skills

Your Turn

1. Open the file **3-4 Project 4**, and save it as ***urs*Columbus**.
2. Use the **Spelling and Grammar** feature to identify and correct the errors.
3. Make the changes indicated in the illustration.

Select all the text. Choose a different **font style**, increase the **font size**, and **align center**.

Use **italic** for the names of the three ships.

Columbus's First Voyage

On August 3, 1492, Columbus set out from Palos, Spain. He had two smal ships, the Nina and the Pinta, and larger one, the Santa Maria, carrying a total of about 90 sailors. The smal fleet stopped at the canary islands for repairs and suplies, then it sailed westward into the unknown.

the ships had good winds, but after a month at sea the sailors began to wory. Provisions were runing low, and they had not sihgted any land. columbus wrote that he was "having trouble with the crew…I am told that if I persit in going onward, the best corse of action will be to throw me into the sea."

4. Save the changes.
5. **Print Preview** the file.
6. **Print** and close the file.

PROJECT 2 Practice

Create a New Presentation

When you create a slide, you can choose the type of layout to best match the information you want to put on the new slide. For example, a Title slide layout will guide you in creating the first slide in your presentation.

Your Turn

1. Open a **New Presentation** and choose a **Title Slide layout** similar to the one below.

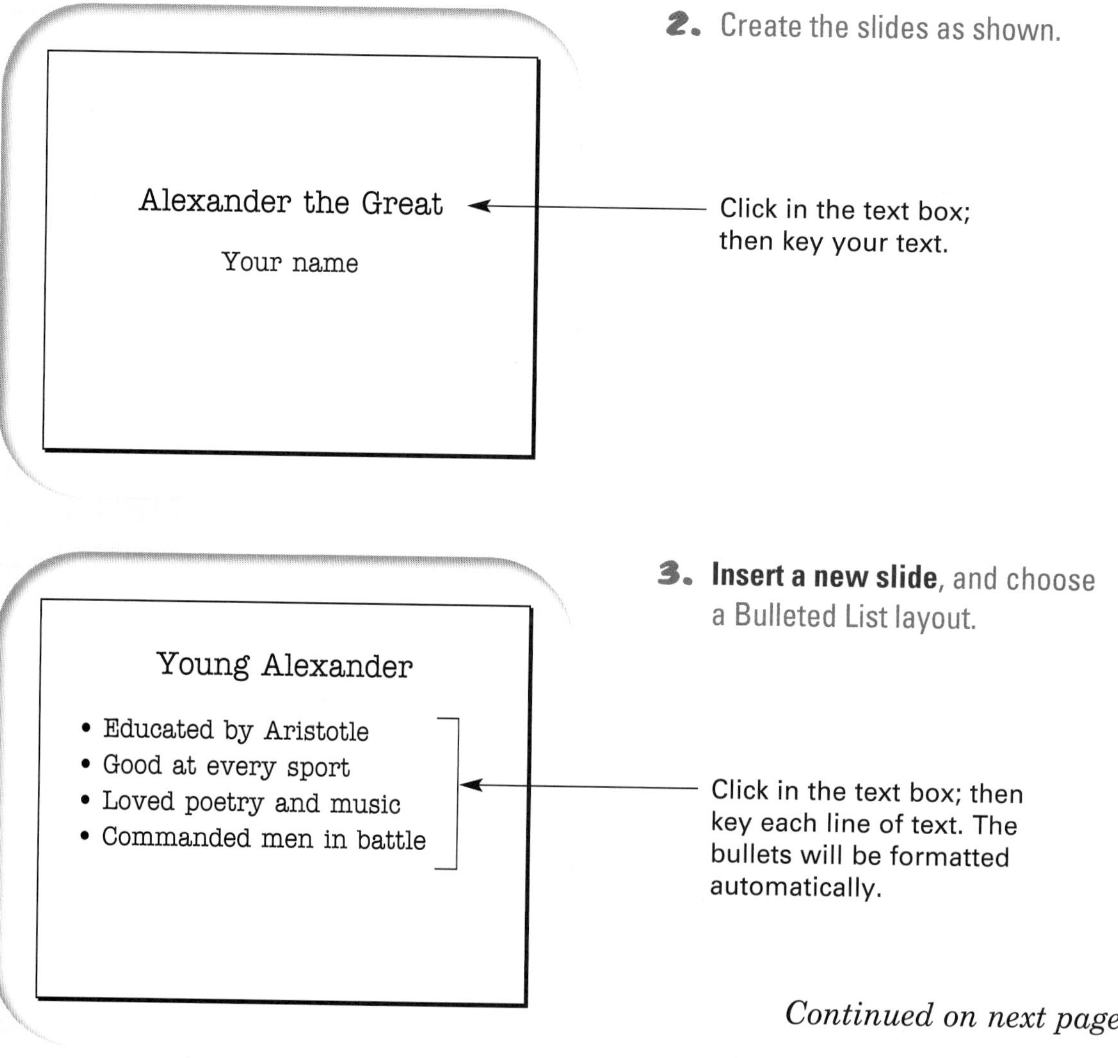

Alexander the Great
Your name
Click in the text box; then key your text.
Young Alexander
• Educated by Aristotle
• Good at every sport
• Loved poetry and music
• Commanded men in battle
Click in the text box; then key each line of text. The bullets will be formatted automatically.

2. Create the slides as shown.

3. **Insert a new slide**, and choose a Bulleted List layout.

Continued on next page

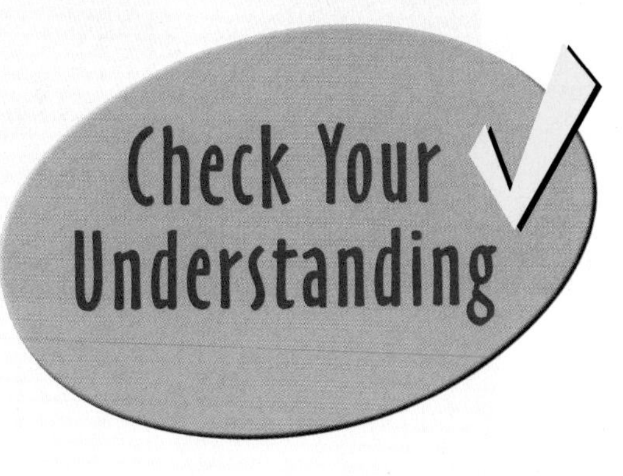

1. Did you make the following corrections in the Spelling document?
   - Sentence 1: Frank, delete the "to"
   - Sentence 2: taken, the
   - Sentence 3: My, no correction necessary for Lattasburg
   - Sentence 4: John, no correction necessary for Coista, London
   - Sentence 5: North Carolina
   - Sentence 6: Romans, fleet
   - Sentence 7: trip, weeks
   - Sentence 8: traveled, from
   - Sentence 9: Carol, effects, sickness
   - Sentence 10: delete "and," enjoyed
2. Did you make the following corrections in the Columbus document?
   - a. small
   - b. *Nina, Pinta, Santa Maria*
   - c. small, Canary Islands, supplies
   - d. The, worry
   - e. running, sighted, Columbus
   - f. persist
   - g. course

In this section, you learned how to review and edit a document about Columbus. That document contained information about the explorer's voyages. You can use the Internet to learn about other explorers.

1. Open your Web browser.
2. Locate the Yahoo.com directory.
3. Open the Arts link and open these categories in order: **Humanities, History, By Subject, Exploration** and **Explorers.**
4. Choose an explorer from the list, and click on his or her name.
5. Open one of these sites listed in the Yahoo Search Directory to read about this explorer's travels.
6. In a paragraph, identify the following: what made this person famous, where and when the exploration took place, and any unusual features of the trip(s).

PROJECT 1 Continued

Practice

Change Views and Navigate Through a Presentation

3. Change to **Slide Sorter View**, and click on slide 5.

Slide Sorter View lets you see miniatures of all the slides in the presentation.

My Favorite Poet
By
Andrew Bonner
1
Shel Silverstein
▪Born in 1932
▪Couldn't play ball
▪Couldn't dance
▪Liked to draw
▪Liked to dance
2
Background
▪Served in the Army
▪Wrote for the Army newspaper
▪Drew cartoons for the Army newspaper
3
Career Highlights
▪Cartoonist ▪Playwright
▪Songwriter ▪Poet
▪Singer ▪Children's author
4
Famous Poetry Books
▪*A Light in the Attic*
▪*Falling Up*
▪*Where the Sidewalk Ends*
5

4. Change to **Slide View**, and go to the first slide.

Slide view lets you edit and work on each slide.

My Favorite Poet
By
Andrew Bonner

5. Change to **Outline View**.

Outline view lets you organize all the text in your presentation.

Outline Slides
1 My Favorite Poet
By
Andrew Bonner
2 Shel Silverstein
• Born in 1932
• Couldn't play ball
• Couldn't dance
• Liked to draw
• Liked to dance
3 Background
• Served in the Army
• Wrote for the Army newspaper
• Drew cartoons for the Army newspaper
4 Career Highlights
• Cartoonist
• Songwriter
• Singer

6. Close the presentation without saving.

SECTION 3.5 Internet Basics

GOALS: Demonstrate the ability to:

- Use Boolean search operators for the Internet.
- Use hyperlinks.
- Add bookmarks.

WARMUP

Select Warmup from the Skillbuilding menu. Key each Warmup line 2 times.

Speed	1	I am quite sure that we have had rain every day this month.
Accuracy	2	Zanzibar, a part of Tanzania, exports cassava and coconuts.
Language Link	3	Except for one, all students wanted to take a French class.
Numbers/Symbols	4	Pets & Paws will groom my dog for $45 (that's a lot) today.

Making the Connection

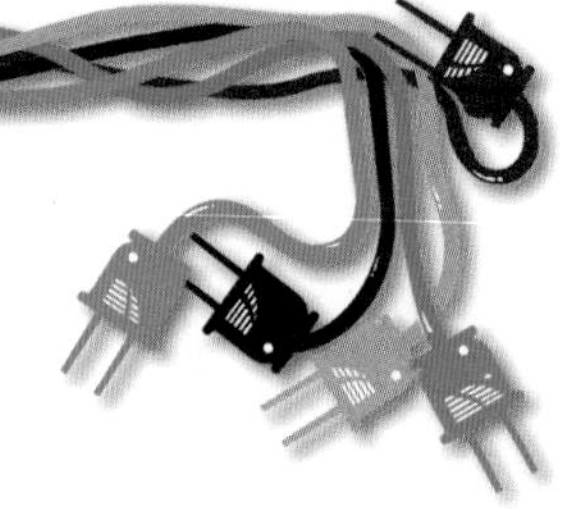

What's the difference between surfing the Internet and searching the Web? There is no difference. Where do you start? To find your way through the mass of information on the Internet, you can use search tools and more effective search techniques.

Your Turn

1. Open your Internet browser. Key Leonardo da Vinci in your browser. Are your results similar to the illustration below?

Results 1 - 10 of about 2,550,000

2. On a piece of paper, record the number of results from this search. You will need to refer to this information for Projects 1 and 2.
3. Keep your browser open for Project 1.

PROJECT 1 Practice

Change Views and Navigate Through a Presentation

In a presentation, each display is called a **slide**. You use **views** to look at the presentation and to work on your presentation.

Normal view lets you work on the presentation slides, outline, and notes.

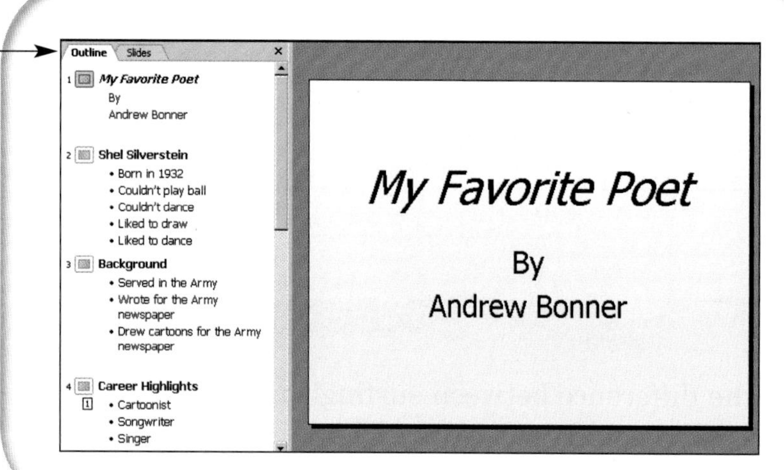
Outline
Slides
My Favorite Poet
By
Andrew Bonner
Shel Silverstein
• Born in 1932
• Couldn't play ball
• Couldn't dance
• Liked to draw
• Liked to dance
Background
• Served in the Army
• Wrote for the Army newspaper
• Drew cartoons for the Army newspaper
Career Highlights
• Cartoonist
• Songwriter
• Singer
My Favorite Poet
By
Andrew Bonner

Your Turn

1. Change to **Normal View**, and use the scroll bar to move to each slide.

Slide show view lets you preview your presentation.

My Favorite Poet

By

Andrew Bonner

2. Change to **Slide Show View**. Click the mouse, or use the right or left arrow keys to view each slide.

Continued on next page

PROJECT 1 Practice

Using Search Engines

Your Internet browser uses keywords to search for information. **Keywords** can be one or more words that help the search engine find the most appropriate matches. **Boolean operators** are keywords or symbols that refine your search.

Your Turn

1. Enter one of the keywords and operators in the search box of your search engine.

BOOLEAN OPERATORS AND OTHER RESTRICTIONS

Operator	Keywords	Results
AND	Leonardo da Vinci **AND** science	Finds Web pages with both words.
OR	Leonardo da Vinci **OR** science	Finds Web pages with either word.
NOT	Leonardo da Vinci **NOT** science	Finds Web pages about Leonardo da Vinci and not science.
Quotes " "	"Leonardo da Vinci"	Finds Web pages with only the exact phrase.
Title:	**Title:** Leonardo da Vinci	Finds Web pages with the keywords in the title.

2. Record the number of results of your new searches.
3. Compare the number of results using Boolean operators with your original search. Did using the Boolean operator technique reduce the number?

Presentation Basics

GOALS: Demonstrate the ability to:

- Change slide view of a presentation.
- Navigate through a presentation.
- Create a new presentation.
- Apply a design template.

WARMUP

Select Warmup from the Skillbuilding menu. Key each Warmup line 2 times.

Speed	1	The little black puppy ran to the door to greet his master.
Accuracy	2	Jeff amazed the audience by quickly giving six new reports.
Numbers/Symbols	3	Can't they find Check #953 for $840, which is dated May 16?
Language Link	4	Terry is taking English Literature 215 on Tuesday mornings.

Making the Connection

When you give an oral report, what speaking and visual aids do you use? Do you use index cards or a poster? Do you keep everyone's attention?

Using presentation software, you can easily create a professional-looking presentation that will keep your audience's attention.

My Favorite Poet

By

Andrew Bonner

Your Turn

1. Launch your presentation software and open the file **9-1 Project 1**.
2. Save the presentation as ***urs*****Favorite Poet**.
3. Keep the presentation open for Project 1.

PROJECT 2 Practice

Effective Searches

In this project, you will refine your Web searches.

Your Turn

1. Read steps 1–3 in "Steps for Effective Searches" shown below.

STEPS FOR EFFECTIVE SEARCHES

1. **Identify a topic.**
   Example: Leonardo da Vinci
2. **State your topic as a problem or question.**
   Example: How did Leonardo da Vinci influence the field of science?
3. **Make a list of keywords that might help you find more information.**
   Example: Leonardo da Vinci, science, invention, engineering, experiment

2. Conduct a search by following the steps in the figure below.

4. **Enter your keywords in the search box in a form a search engine will understand.**
   Example 1: "Leonardo da Vinci" AND science
   Example 2: "da Vinci" AND science NOT painting
5. **Press ENTER to begin the search.**

3. Record and compare your search results. Did you reduce the number of results?

   When a Web page interests you, you can create an electronic bookmark by clicking the **Bookmark** or **Favorite** command. The **bookmark** makes it easy to quickly return to a Web page in the future.

4. Keep your Web browser open.

1 - 20 of 11,300,000 | Next 20

You can click on a **hyperlink** to jump or link to information on another page.

Focus On

Good Keyboarding Habits

Focus on your wrists.
To avoid wrist strain:

- **Make sure your wrists do not rest on anything.**
- **Keep your wrists straight, not bent.**
- **Never curve your wrists right or left.**

PROJECT 3

Reinforce

Internet Search Results

Your Turn

1. Open **3-5 Project 3**, and print one copy. This file contains a form that will help you prepare for an effective Internet search.
2. Complete the form as indicated below.

This column identifies the topic.

State your topic as a problem or question.

Identify the keywords you will use in your search.

Use Boolean operators and other restrictions.

Record the number of results from your search.

Topic	Problem or Question	Keywords	Keyword Combinations	Results
Compare the populations of Boston, Chicago, Houston, and San Francisco.				
Compare length of time to travel to each planet in the solar system.				
Compare men's and women's world track records.				
Compare the height of geysers found in Yellowstone National Park.				

3. Keep your Web browser open.

UNIT 6 Presentations

GOALS:

- Demonstrate the ability to create and navigate through a new presentation.
- Demonstrate correct use of presentation editing and proofing tools.
- Demonstrate how to enhance a presentation with clip art and photos.
- Demonstrate how to enhance a presentation with animation and sounds.

1. Open a new word processing document.
2. Key your responses to the following questions:
   a. If you key Mohs Mineral Scale in the search box, what results would you expect to get?
   b. If you key Mohs NOT Scale, how would the Boolean operator affect the results?
   c. If you key "Mohs Mineral Scale" in quotations, how would the results be affected?
3. Save the document as *urs*Mohs.
4. Print the document.
5. Close the file.
6. Go to your Web browser and locate and use the bookmark you created for the Leonardo da Vinci Web page. Did the bookmark take you back to the correct page?

*inter*NET CONNECTION

In this section, you learned how to perform effective Web searches. Search engines also provide more information about how to define your search criteria in very specific ways.

1. **Open your Web browser.**
2. **Locate the Help feature related to a search engine of your choice.**
3. **Look for information and/or tips for using that particular search engine. Note two ways to refine your search.**
4. **Use what you have learned from this section plus information contained in the Help section to create a list of five "rules" for conducting effective Web searches.**
5. **On your own: compare two or three different search engines to determine whether the "rules" you created in Step 4 work in these search engines.**

COMPLETING UNIT 5

ENRICH

Curriculum Portfolio

Choose one of the following topics or one assigned by your teacher:

MATH:

Create a math facts Web page game.

Create a math game Web page for your peers. The purpose of the site is to review math concepts and to have fun. Organize the information on the Web page by topics, such as fractions, geometry, percentages, and so forth. Write a brief introduction to each topic and then provide links to other Web pages that offer math games, math quizzes, and homework helpers.

SOCIAL STUDIES:

Create and format a historical newsletter.

Create a historical newsletter about the Roman Empire. Format the newsletter in columns, create a masthead, and format headlines. Enhance the newsletter with pictures and objects and a divider. Consider the following suggestions for determining the content: facts and details about events, an editorial about an event, advertisements, and classified ads.

SCIENCE:

Create a science Web page game.

Create a science trivia quiz. Research fascinating facts about the world of science and then write 10–20 questions about the trivia. Your Web pages should provide links to other pages with the answers to the questions.

LANGUAGE ARTS:

Create and format a biographical newsletter.

Create a biographical newsletter about an author and the author's notable works. Format the newsletter in columns, create a masthead, and format headlines. Enhance the newsletter with pictures and objects and a divider.

SECTION 3.6 Data Collection

GOALS: Demonstrate the ability to:

- Switch windows between applications.
- Copy and paste information, an image, and a URL from a Web page to a document.
- Develop a basic understanding of citing Web sources.

WARMUP

Select Warmup from the Skillbuilding menu. Key each Warmup line 2 times.

Speed	1	Richard can ask what size tent he should take for the trip.
Accuracy	2	Jena quickly seized the wax buffer and removed a big patch.
Language Link	3	Publisher's Clearing House gave away three million dollars.
Numbers/Symbols	4	The booklets are AB-GN, catalog item XH479/162CLW @ $13.50.

Making the Connection

If you have ever searched the Web to find information for a report, copy a picture, download music, or gather any type of data, you have used information that was owned by someone.

When you gather information from the Web, give credit to the owner of the material and cite the source.

Your Turn

1. Open a new word processing document.
2. Key the title Citing Internet Sources; then center the title. Press ENTER 2 times. Save the document as *urs*Citing. Keep the document open for Project 1.

Review Project

7. Group the objects as a single unit.
8. Save the changes.
9. Complete the flyer by adding the graphics shown in the illustration below. Resize and position the graphics to fill the page.

Extreme Waves

The Ultimate Skateboard Park!

This park is for all ages and all skill levels. It is very family oriented, and it is the local skaters' pride and joy.

An enormous effort was put into constructing this park. There are both metal ramps and wood ramps. The entire park has great coping and clean-finished edges. You'll really enjoy the ramps and courses. You can also practice your technical tricks in the 15,000-square-foot concrete area.

This park has it all, and you can ride year round. Catch all the action at Extreme Waves! Helmets are required. Sorry, no bikes or scooters.

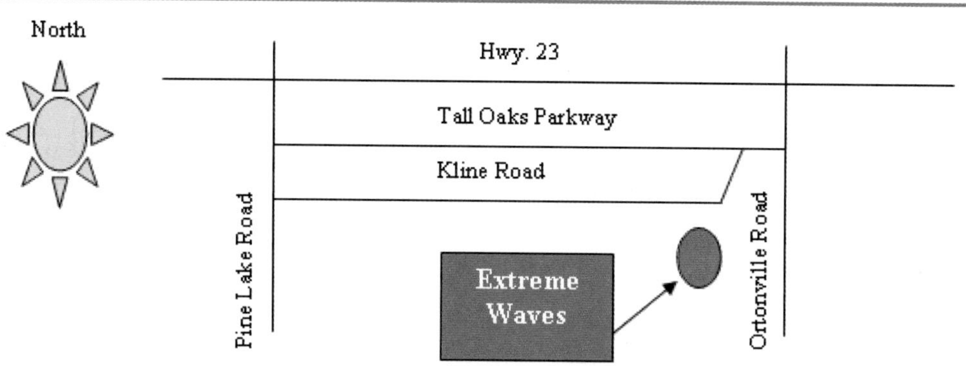

10. Save the changes. Print and close the file.

PROJECT 1 Practice

Collect Data From the Internet

Citing where you found information from the Web is very similar to citing information from a book, journal, or periodical. Cite the author or owner of the information to describe where you got the material.

Your Turn

1. Open your Web browser. Go to <**www.whitehouse.gov**> to find the home page of the White House. Find the history of U.S. presidents and the biography of George Washington. Refer to the illustration.

Biography of George Washington

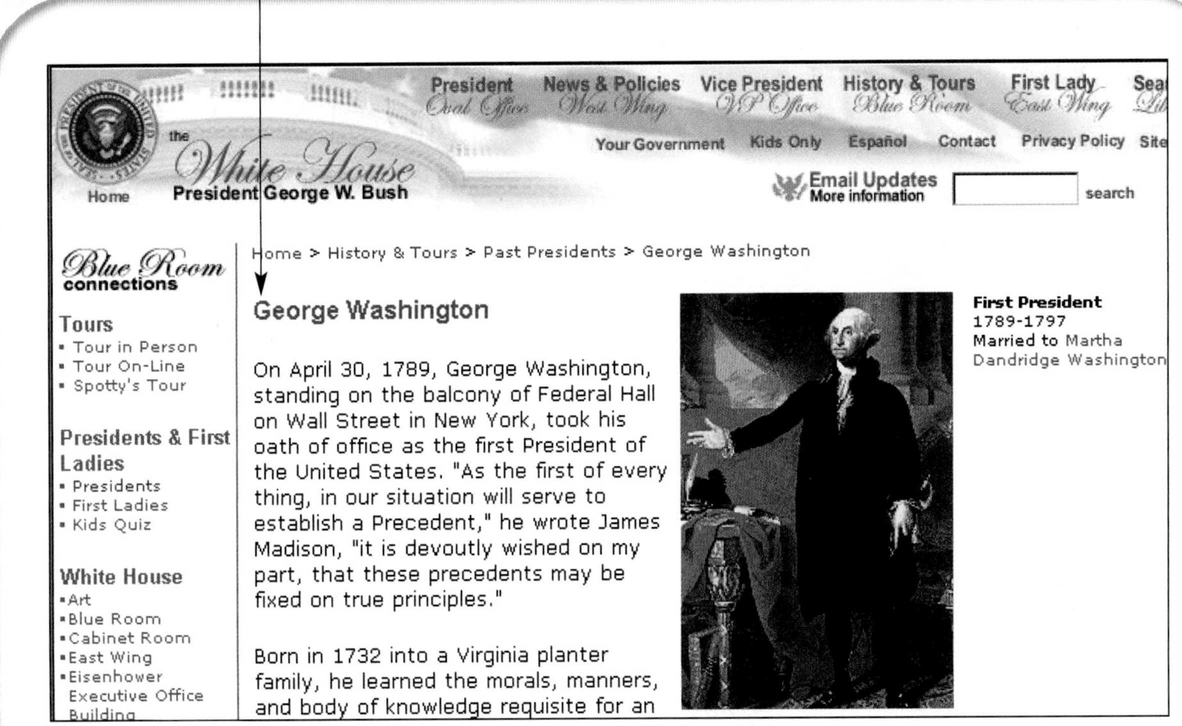

Continued on next page

Review Project

In this project, you will apply the desktop publishing skills you have learned to create and format a flyer. Refer to previous projects as needed.

Your Turn

1. Open a new document. Change to landscape orientation, and change all the margins to 1 inch.

> This park is for all ages and all skill levels. It is very family oriented, and it is the local skaters' pride and joy.
>
> An enormous effort was put into constructing this park. There are both metal ramps and wood ramps. The entire park has great coping and clean-finished edges. You'll really enjoy the ramps and courses. You can also practice your technical tricks in the 15,000-square-foot concrete area.
>
> This park has it all, and you can ride year round. Catch all the action at Extreme Waves! Helmets are required. Sorry, no bikes or scooters.

2. Key the text shown.
3. Format the text in 2 columns.
4. Save the document as *urs*Extreme Waves.
5. Spell-check, proofread, and correct errors.

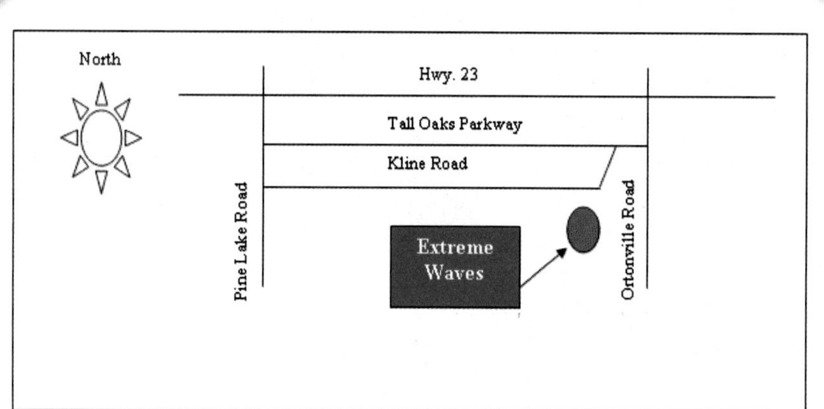

6. Below the columns of text, use drawing tools to create the map shown.

Continued on next page

PROJECT 1 Continued

Practice

Collect Data From the Internet

George Washington

On April 30, 1789, George Washington, standing on the balcony of Federal Hall on Wall Street in New York, took his oath of office as the first President of the United States. "As the first of every

2. Select and copy a few sentences of text about George Washington as shown at the left.
3. **Switch** to your word processing document, and paste the text as shown below.

Citing Internet Sources

Paste the text. → On April 30, 1789, George Washington, standing on the balcony of Federal Hall on Wall Street in New York, took his oath of office as the first President of the United States.

4. **Switch** to the Web page, and copy the Web site URL as shown.

Address http://www.whitehouse.gov/history/presidents/gw1.html

5. **Switch** to the word processing document, and paste the URL as shown.

Citing Internet Sources

On April 30, 1789, George Washington, standing on the balcony of Federal Hall on Wall Street in New York, took his oath of office as the first President of the United States.

Copy and paste the URL. → http://www.whitehouse.gov/history/presidents/gw1.html

6. Save the changes to the document. Keep the file and Web page open for Project 2.

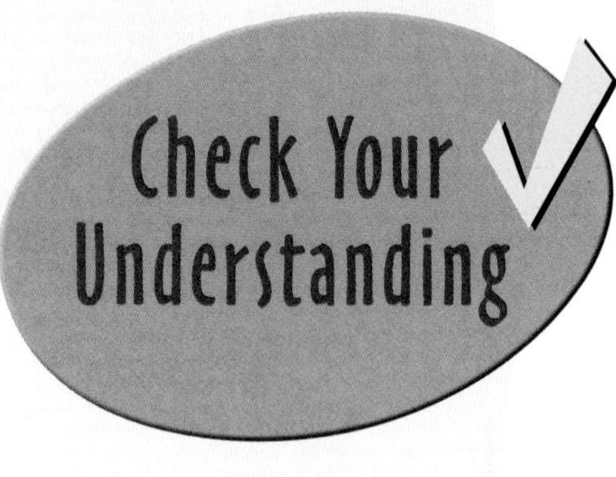

1. Open a new word processing document.
2. Key the answer to each question below using a complete sentence.
   a. What is the purpose of a hyperlink?
   b. Explain why you would create a link to another location on the same page.
   c. How can you tell that text has been formatted to link to another location?
   d. How can you tell that a graphic has been formatted to link to another location?
   e. Why should you preview a Web page in your Web browser?
3. Save the document as *urs***Hyperlinks**. Print and close the file.

8th Grade American History

On April 27, the 8th Grade American History students went on their annual field trip. They traveled by charter bus to Washington, D.C. The field trip was fantastic. Every one had fun and learned a lot.

Click on the link below to see pictures from the interesting sites we visited.

Photos of Landmarks

Top of the Document

Copyright 20--
Pleasant Valley Middle School Tech Team

Compare the illustration with urs*Field Trips.*

PROJECT 2 Practice

Complete the Source Citation

Now you will complete the citation for the information about George Washington that you copied from the Web.

Your Turn

1. Use the Internet text citation illustration below to help you complete your citation. Pay attention to each part of the citation. If the author is known, key the last name, a comma, then the first name. If necessary, remove the underline from the URL.

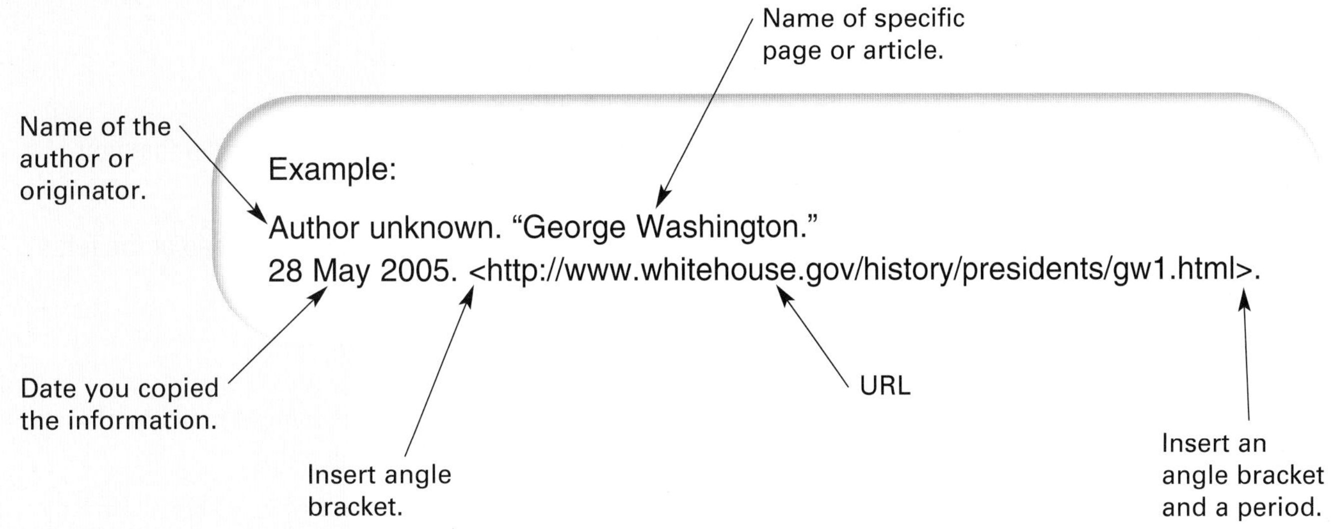

Continued on next page

PROJECT 4 Continued

Reinforce

Create Hyperlinks

8th Grade American History

On April 27, the 8th Grade American History students went on their annual field trip. They traveled by charter bus to Washington, D.C. The field trip was fantastic. Everyone had fun and learned a lot.

Click on the link below to see pictures from the interesting sites we visited.

Photos of Landmarks

Top of Document

Insert this new line of **text** and **create a hyperlink** to the Web page **Landmarks**.

Create a hyperlink to go to the top of the document.

Did you know?

* The White House was built between 1792 and 1800.
* John Adams was the first president to move in.
* Although it has been called the President's House and the President's Palace, it was officially designated the White House when Theodore Roosevelt put the name on his stationery in 1901.

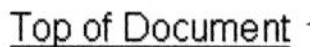

Top of Document

Create a hyperlink to go to the top of the document.

Insert an appropriate **clip art** image representing the home page, and then **create a hyperlink** from the graphic to the Web page **Field Trips**.

5. Open the Web page **Landmarks** that you created in Section 8.2.
6. Create the hyperlinks described at the left.
7. Add the following copyright notice at the bottom of each Web page.

Copyright 20-- Pleasant Valley Middle School Tech Team

8. Save the changes to each document.
9. Preview the Web page in your browser and test all the hyperlinks. Make any necessary corrections.
10. Save any changes. Print and close both files.

Complete the Source Citation

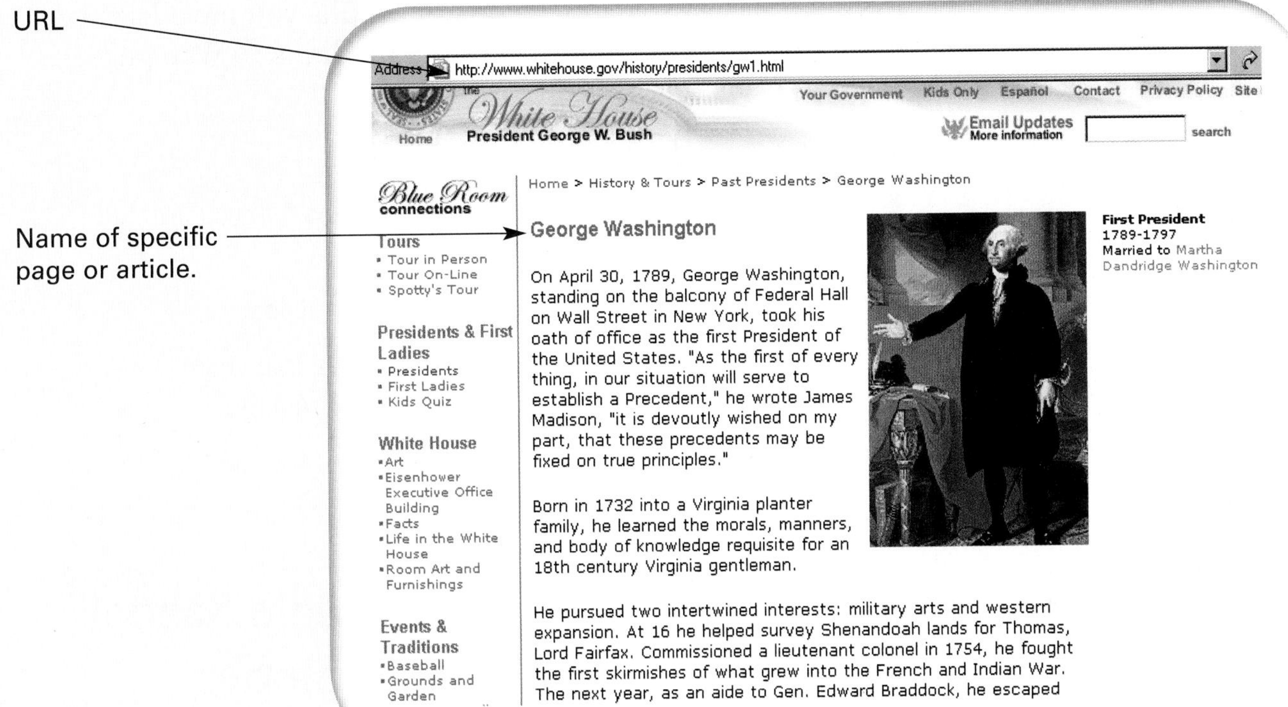

Citing Internet Sources

On April 30, 1789, George Washington, standing on the balcony of Federal Hall on Wall Street in New York, took his oath of office as the first President of the United States.

Author unknown. "George Washington." 28 May 2005. <http://www.whitehouse.gov/history/presidents/gw1.html>.

2. Find the necessary information on the Web page. Then **switch** to the word processing document, and key the rest of the citation. You will probably need to switch between the document and the Web page several times to complete the process.

3. Save the changes to the document. Keep the file and Web page open for Project 3.

PROJECT 4 **Reinforce**

Create Hyperlinks

In this project you will reinforce the skills you have learned by creating internal and external hyperlinks to Web pages from Sections 8.1 and 8.2.

Your Turn

1. Open the Web page document ***urs*Field Trips** that you created and saved in Section 8.1, Project 4.
2. Format the two side headings with heading styles.
3. Create the hyperlinks described below. Note that your Web page theme will probably be different from the pages illustrated.

Insert these new lines of **text** to create a list of contents.

Select each topic, and **create a hyperlink** to the heading with the same name.

Pleasant Valley Middle School
Field Trip Memories

7th Grade World History
8th Grade World History

7th Grade World History

On September 28, 7th Grade World History students took a journey back with wizards, peasants, nobles, and the royal court. They watched a play watching knights compete in a jousting event, and visited shopkeepers. T shopkeepers demonstrate glass blowing, armor making, and calligraphy.

4. Save the changes. Keep the file open.

Continued on next page

PROJECT 3 Practice

Copy Images From the Web and Cite the Source

Your Turn

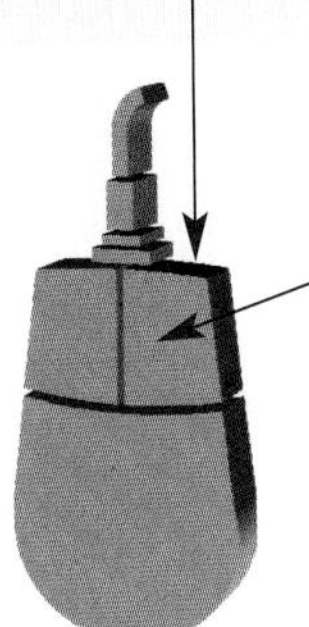

Press and choose Copy with the right mouse button.
Right-click to view the word processing options.

1. Return to the Web page on which you found the photo, or image, of George Washington. Position the mouse pointer over the photo of George Washington and click the right button of your mouse to copy the image.

2. **Switch** to your word processing document, and paste the image below the text citation as shown.

Citing Internet Sources

On April 30, 1789, George Washington, standing on the balcony of Federal Hall on Wall Street in New York, took his oath of office as the first President of the United States.

Author unknown. "George Washington." 28 May 2005. <http://www.whitehouse.gov/history/presidents/gw1.html>.

Paste image.

Continued on next page

PROJECT 3 Practice

Test Hyperlinks

As you create your Web pages, you can open them in your Web browser to see what they will look like on the World Wide Web. Text and graphics sometimes align differently when displayed in a Web browser, so you should always preview your Web pages. When you preview the pages in a Web browser, you can also test your hyperlinks.

Your Turn

1. **Preview** the **Web page** in your browser. If necessary, change the text and graphic formats so that the information is displayed correctly in your Web browser.
2. Test all the hyperlinks. When you click the link for the Venus Fun Facts page, the page should open—even though you just closed the document. Make any necessary changes so all the hyperlinks work correctly.
3. Save the changes. Print and close each file.

PROJECT 3 Continued

Practice

Copy Images From the Web and Cite the Source

3. Follow the illustration below to help you cite the source for the photo/image you copied.

Description or title of the photo/image.

Name of the author or originator.

Example:

Author unknown. "Photo: George Washington."
28 May 2005. <http://www.whitehouse.gov/history/presidents/gw1.html>.

The date you copied the information.

Insert angle bracket.

URL Remove the underline, if necessary.

Insert an angle bracket and a period.

4. Create the citation below the photo.

Copy and paste the URL to include in the citation. Add any necessary information.

Author unknown. "Photo: George Washington."
28 May 2005. <http://www.whitehouse.gov/history/presidents/gw1.html>.

Add angle brackets after you copy your citation < >.

5. Save the changes to the document. Print and close the file.

PROJECT 2 Continued

Practice

Create a Hyperlink to Another Web Page

4. If necessary, open the Web page **Venus** that you created in Section 8.1.

5. Create the hyperlink shown below.

It is very difficult to explore Venus because thick white clouds block the view of its surface. We cannot get close because the sulfuric acid clouds and the extremely high temperatures damage the spacecraft. Between 1990 and 1994, the American Magellan spaceship provided much data and many images of Venus.

Click here for Venus Fun Facts.

Insert this new line of text and **create a hyperlink** to the Web page **Venus Fun Facts**.

6. Save the changes. Keep the file open for Project 3.

PROJECT 4 **Reinforce**

Citing Internet Data

Your Turn

1. Open a new word processing document, and save it as *urs***Internet Data**.
2. Search for text and photos/images about one of the following topics:
   a. Your favorite athlete.
   b. Your favorite pet.
   c. A president of the United States.
3. Copy the text and images from the Web, and paste them into the word processing document.
4. Create the proper citations for each item you copy and paste into your document.
5. Save the changes. Print and close the file.

Being able to properly cite sources in reports for class is very important. Practice locating and citing information for a science report.

1. Open your Web browser and navigate to a search engine or directory.
2. Key in the word **"inventions."**
3. Select three articles that look interesting, making sure that at least one of them features photos of an invention.
4. Create a word processing document. Like a reporter who must answer "Who, what, where, why, and when?, "paste into this document the name and description of the invention, the year it was invented, and the name of its inventor. Paste in a photo to illustrate your description.
5. Create the proper citations for each item you copy and paste into your document.

PROJECT 2 Practice

Create a Hyperlink to Another Web Page

A **Web site** is two or more related Web pages. When you click on a hyperlink to another Web page, the second page is opened. Create a hyperlink for a graphic the same way you create a hyperlink for text—select the graphic and apply the hyperlink format.

Your Turn

1. Create the hyperlinks described below.

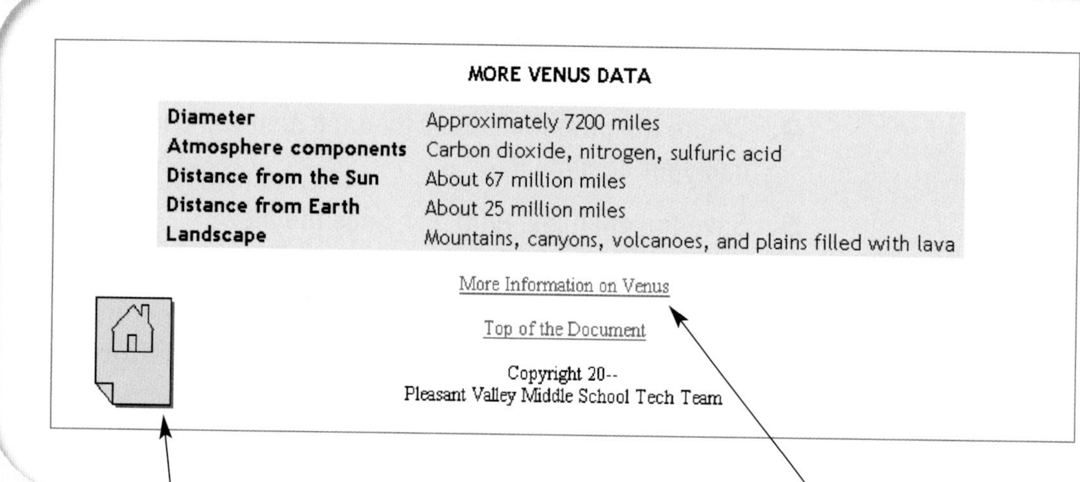

MORE VENUS DATA
Diameter
Approximately 7200 miles
Atmosphere components
Carbon dioxide, nitrogen, sulfuric acid
Distance from the Sun
About 67 million miles
Distance from Earth
About 25 million miles
Landscape
Mountains, canyons, volcanoes, and plains filled with lava
More Information on Venus
Top of the Document
Copyright 20--
Pleasant Valley Middle School Tech Team

Insert an appropriate **clip art** image representing the home page, and then **create a hyperlink** from the graphic to the Web page **Venus**.

Create a hyperlink to this Web address: http://www.nasa.gov

2. Apply a theme, add graphics, and change fonts to enhance the appearance of the Web page.
3. Save the changes to the file.

Continued on next page

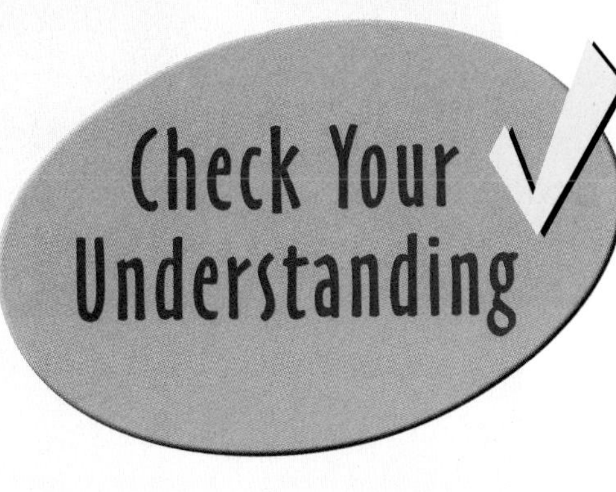

1. Open a new word processing document.
2. Describe where you usually find the author of the information you found at the Web site.
3. Describe where you usually find the name of the article at the Web site.
4. Describe how you switch between the Web page and the word processing document.
5. Describe how you copy a photo or image from a Web page.
6. Describe the differences between a text citation and a photo or image citation.
7. Save the document as ***urs*Citing Questions**. Print and close the file.

*inter*NET CONNECTION

In this section you learned how to cite Internet sources for text and photos/images. How would you cite sources for video clips or sound clips?

1. **Open your Web browser, and search for sites that provide examples for citing Internet sources.**
2. **Open a new word processing document. Provide an example of a citation for a video clip and a citation for a sound clip.**
3. **Now that you know how to cite video and sound clips, access the historic files available at the Library of Congress American Memory site http://memory.loc.gov/ammem/.**
4. **Locate a sound file of a song popular between 50 and 100 years ago. Add its citation and a brief description to your word processing document.**
5. **Locate a video file of a film made when your parents or grandparents were young. Add its citation and a brief description to your word processing document.**

PROJECT 1 Continued

Practice

Create a Hyperlink

4. Edit the bottom of the page as shown below.

MORE VENUS DATA

Diameter	Approximately 7200 miles
Atmosphere components	Carbon dioxide, nitrogen, sulfuric acid
Distance from the Sun	About 67 million miles
Distance from Earth	About 25 million miles
Landscape	Mountains, canyons, volcanoes, and plains filled with lava

Top of the Document

Copyright 20--
Pleasant Valley Middle School Tech Team

Create a hyperlink to go to the top of the document.

Insert this copyright notice at the end of the Web page.

5. Save the changes. Keep the document open for Project 2.

REVIEW SECTION 3 **APPLY**

Computer Basics

In this project, you will apply the basic editing skills you have learned to format a poem. You will also use your Internet search skills to find and collect information.

Your Turn

1. Open the file **3-Review**, and save it as *urs***Colossus**.
2. Edit the poem as shown in the illustration.

THE NEW COLOSSUS
By Emma Lazarus
Written in 1883

"keep, ancient lands, your storied pomp!" cries she
With silent lips. "give me your tired, your poor,
Your huddled masses yearning to breathe free,
The wretched will refuse of your teeming shore
Send these, the homeless, tempest-tossed to me,
I lift my lamp beside the golden door."

Not like the brazen giant of greek fame,
With conquering limbs astride from land to land;
Here at our sea-washed, sunset gates shall stand
A woman mighty with a torch, whose flame
Is the imprisoned lightning and her name
mother of exiles. From her beacon-hand
Glows world-wide welcome; her mild eyes command
The air-bridged harbor that Twin Cities frame.

Align center all three lines.

Format the title with an appropriate **font style**, **font color**, and **font size**.

move

3. Save the changes. Print and close the file.

Continued on next page

PROJECT 1 Continued

Practice

Create a Hyperlink

2. **Create a hyperlink** to a place in the current document.

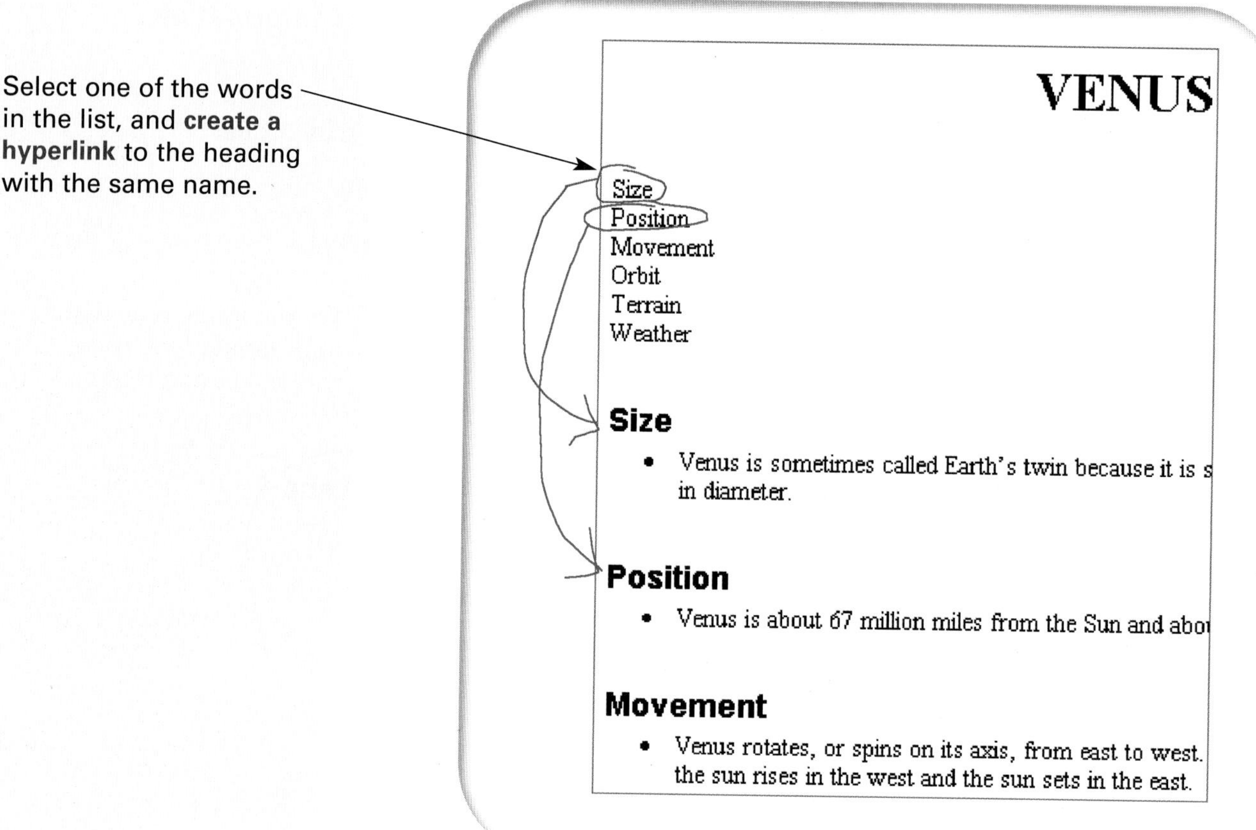

Select one of the words in the list, and **create a hyperlink** to the heading with the same name.
VENUS
Size
Position
Movement
Orbit
Terrain
Weather
Size
• Venus is sometimes called Earth's twin because it is s in diameter.
Position
• Venus is about 67 million miles from the Sun and abo
Movement
• Venus rotates, or spins on its axis, from east to west. the sun rises in the west and the sun sets in the east.

3. Create hyperlinks for each of the remaining words in the list of contents.

Continued on next page

REVIEW Continued

APPLY

Computer Basics

4. Open a new document, and save it as ***urs*History**.
5. Key the copy shown in the illustration below. Make the changes indicated.

Apply **italic** format to the name of the poem.

Align center, apply **bold** format, and increase the **font size**.

Finish the paragraph with your Internet research.

The History of The New Colossus

The poem "The New Colossus" was written in 1883 by Emma Lazarus to express what the Statue of Liberty meant to her.

Sources

6. Use a search engine to find information to answer the following questions. Then summarize your findings by adding the information to the last paragraph in the document. Be sure to cite your source(s).
   a. What is a colossus?
   b. Who is the "mighty woman with a torch"?
   c. What do you think the author is trying to say in the second paragraph that begins, "Keep, ancient lands, . . ."?
7. Use a search engine to find a photo or clip art image related to the poem. Copy and paste the image to the document; then position it appropriately on the page. Be sure to cite the URL of your source at the end of the document.
8. Check your spelling and grammar.
9. Save the changes. Print and close the file.

PROJECT 1 Practice

Create a Hyperlink

To help viewers quickly and easily navigate through the information on your Web page, you can create hyperlinks. A **hyperlink** is text or a graphic that you click to go to a file, to a location on the same Web page, or to a different Web page. Text with a formatted hyperlink is usually displayed in a different color and underlined.

In this section, you will learn to create shortcuts that will save you time navigating your Web pages by creating hyperlinks.

Your Turn

1. Edit the document as shown below.

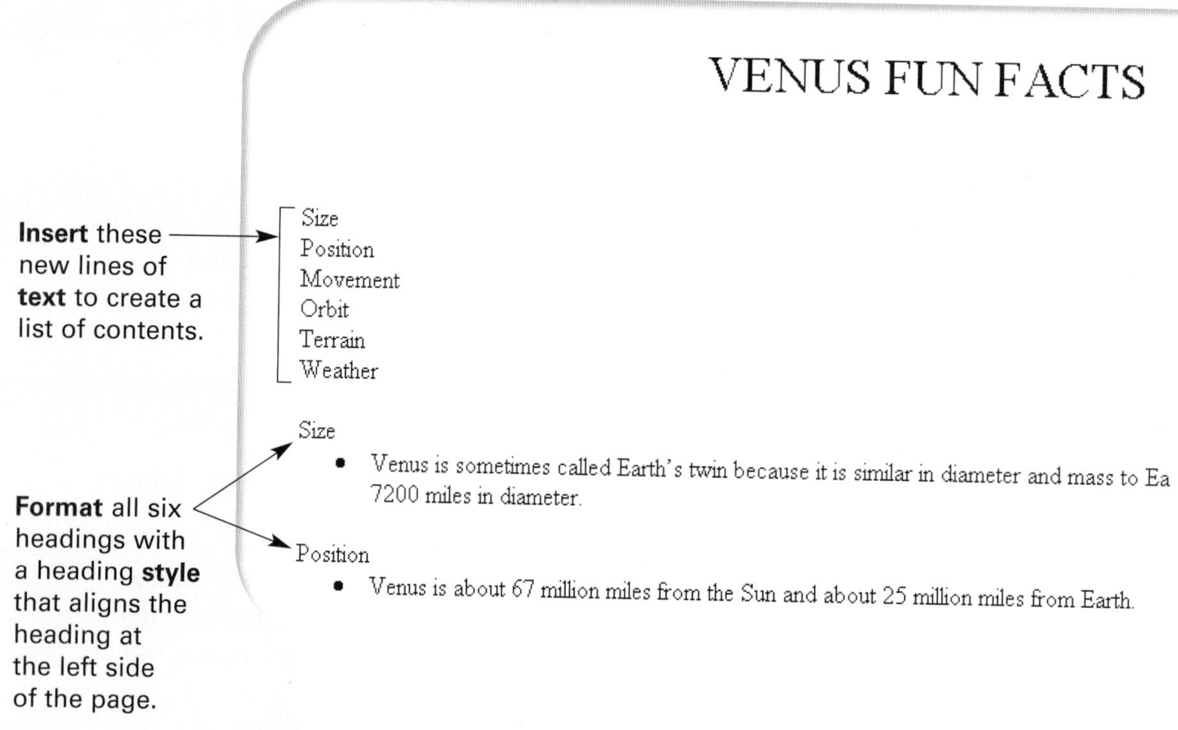

VENUS FUN FACTS
Insert these new lines of **text** to create a list of contents.
Size
Position
Movement
Orbit
Terrain
Weather
Format all six headings with a heading **style** that aligns the heading at the left side of the page.
Size
Venus is sometimes called Earth's twin because it is similar in diameter and mass to Ea
7200 miles in diameter.
Position
Venus is about 67 million miles from the Sun and about 25 million miles from Earth.

Continued on next page

COMPLETING UNIT 3

ENRICH

Curriculum Portfolio

Use the word processing skills you have learned to help you create your curriculum portfolio project. Choose from one of the following topics.

SCIENCE:

Compose a paragraph describing fossils.

What are living fossils? Use the Internet to find at least two examples. Compose a paragraph describing the fossils. Add a title. Be sure to cite your sources at the end of the paragraph.

SOCIAL STUDIES:

Compose two paragraphs about citizenship.

Persons born in the United States are citizens. Others, through naturalization, can become citizens and enjoy the same privileges and responsibilities. Use the Internet to find facts about the steps a person must take to successfully emigrate to the United States. Be sure to answer the following questions.

1. Who is a citizen?
2. If a person is not born in the United States, how can he or she become a citizen?
3. How does a person become a citizen?
4. What are the rights and duties of a citizen?
5. How can a citizen lose his or her citizenship?

Add a title. Be sure to cite your sources at the end of the paragraphs.

Continued on next page

SECTION 8.3

Create Hyperlinks for Web Pages

GOALS: Demonstrate the ability to:

- Create hyperlinks.
- Preview a Web page.

WARMUP

Select Warmup from the Skillbuilding menu. Key each Warmup line 2 times.

Speed	1	These short, easy words help you when you build your speed.
Accuracy	2	Even Jacques may gaze up to find six crows in the blue sky.
Numbers/Symbols	3	If we need 56 points, then 47, 29, 38, or 10 will not help.
Language Link	4	James and I grew up in Montana; we always go home in March.

Making the Connection

Navigating to different parts of a Web page or to other Web pages can be time consuming. See how long it takes you to find some information about Venus.

Your Turn

1. Open the Web page ***urs*Venus Fun Facts** that you saved in Section 8.2, Project 1.
2. Look at a clock, and write on a sheet of paper what time it is.
3. Now complete the steps to the right:
4. Look at the clock, and record the time. Calculate how much time you spent navigating the Web pages.
5. Keep the Venus Web page and the Venus Fun Facts Web page open for Project 1.

1. Scroll down to the bottom of the Web page and go to the facts on weather.
2. Go back to the top of the Web page.
3. Go to the facts on Terrain.
4. Go to the facts on Size.
5. Open the Web page document Venus that you saved in Section 8.1.
6. Go back to the Venus Fun Facts page and go to the facts on Movement.
7. Open your Web browser and go to this URL: http://www.nasa.gov.

COMPLETING UNIT 3 Continued

ENRICH

Curriculum Portfolio

LANGUAGE ARTS:

Compose two paragraphs about family traditions.

Does your family have a special celebration? Talk to your parents, grandparents, and other family members about a celebration that has become a tradition in your family. Add a title.

MATH:

Compose two paragraphs about George Boole.

George Boole was a self-taught mathematician. Use the Internet to research how Boole contributed to the creation of the Internet and the Information Age. Add a title. Be sure to cite your sources at the end of the paragraphs.

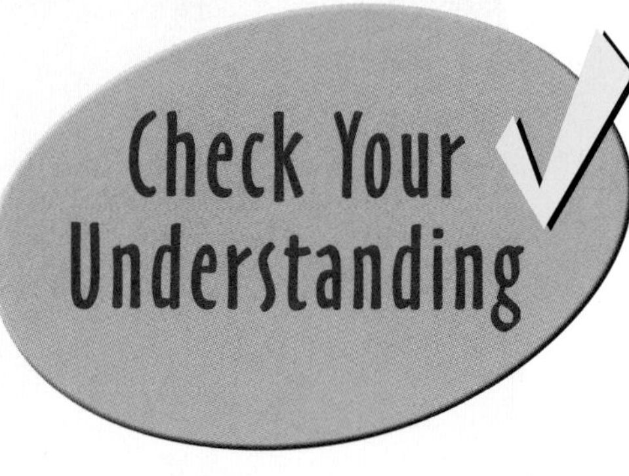

1. Open a new word processing document.
2. Compose complete sentences to respond to the following:
   a. Describe how you can position a table in the middle of a page.
   b. Describe the steps for removing table borders.
   c. Describe the steps for automatically adjusting the widths of the table columns.
3. Write a paragraph explaining how formatting a table is similar to formatting a graphic.
4. Save the document as ***urs*Table Formats**. Print and close the file.

Weather

- The temperature on the surface of Venus is about 900 degrees. That is hot enough to melt lead.
- The atmospheric pressure on Venus is about 90 times greater than on Earth. You would have to dive down nearly a half mile in the ocean to experience this pressure.
- Winds are very strong, and sometimes the winds are over 200 mph. On Earth, weather with 74 mph wind is classified as a hurricane.

MORE VENUS DATA

Diameter	Approximately 7200 miles
Atmosphere components	Carbon dioxide, nitrogen, sulfuric acid
Distance from the Sun	About 67 million miles
Distance from Earth	About 25 million miles
Landscape	Mountains, canyons, volcanoes, and plains filled with lava

Compare the illustration with urs*Venus Fun Facts.*

UNIT 4 Word Processing

GOALS:

- Demonstrate how to format and edit text.
- Demonstrate how to proofread and correct errors.
- Demonstrate how to create tables.
- Demonstrate how to format personal and business letters and envelopes.
- Demonstrate how to format reports, outlines, and title pages.
- Demonstrate how to format bibliography, reference, and works cited pages.

Create a Table

The Lincoln Memorial

Insert the file photo **Lincoln**, and resize as needed.

We had many stairs to climb to reach the Lincoln Memorial.

Key this caption below the photo.

Did you know?

* The Lincoln Memorial is a tribute to Abraham Lincoln.
* There are 36 columns - each column represents a state in the union at the time of Lincoln's death.
* It took about eight years to build the monument, and it cost about three million dollars.
* The memorial was dedicated in 1922 on Lincoln's birthday, February 12.

The White House

Insert the file photo **White House**. Resize the photo as needed.

The President was not at the White House when we visited.

Key this caption below the photo.

Did you know?

* The White House was built between 1792 and 1800.
* John Adams was the first president to move in.
* Although it has been called the President's House and the President's Palace, it was officially designated the White House when Theodore Roosevelt put the name on his stationery in 1901.

5. Save the changes. Print and close the file.

Focus On

Good Keyboarding Habits

Focus on your head and neck. To prevent neck strain:

- **Never lean your head back to view the monitor.**

- **Center your head and neck in the middle of your shoulders.**

- **Make sure the line of reading on the monitor is not above eye level.**

- **Relax your shoulders—never slump your shoulders.**

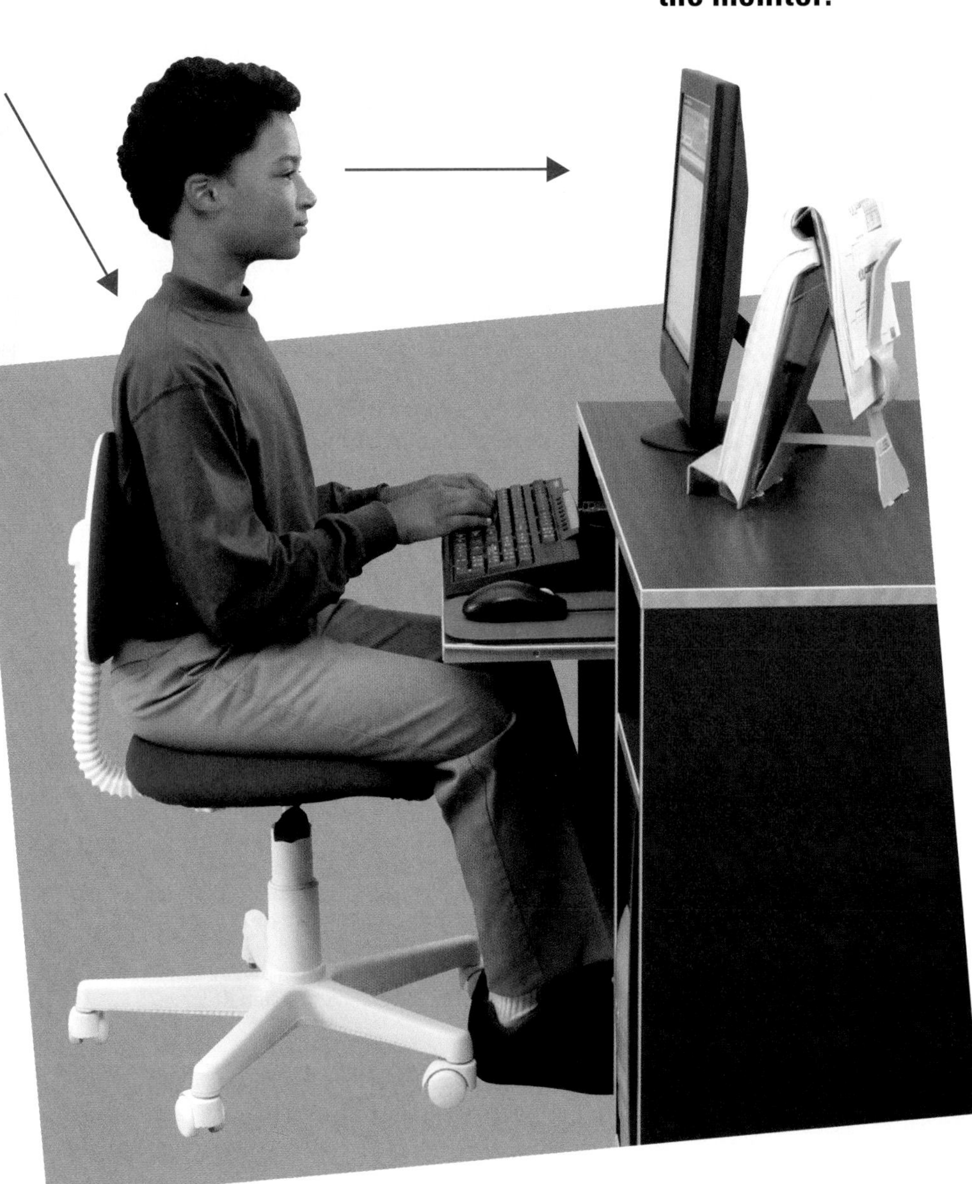

PROJECT 2 Continued

Reinforce

Create a Table

4. Enhance the Web page by adding the photos and captions identified in the illustrations below.

The Capitol Building

Insert the file photo **Capitol**, and resize as needed.

Key this caption below the photo.

We were lucky to visit the Capitol Building when the Senate was in session.

Did you know?

* President Washington selected the site for the building of the Capitol building.
* The cornerstone was laid in September 1793, and the construction began. The building was completed in 1807, but there have been many additions and renovations since then.
* The building has five levels and more than 500 rooms. The Senate and the House of Representatives are on the second floor.

History of Construction

1791	Construction begins
1793	Cornerstone laid
1800	Building not complete, but Congress occupies building
1812	British troops set Capitol on fire
1815	Restoration begins
1818	Construction of the Rotunda begins
1824	Original dome completed
1826	Original structure completed
1851	Library of Congress burned by fire
1856	Old dome removed
1859	New House and Senate chambers completed
1863	New dome completed

Continued on next page

Edit and Format Short Stories

GOALS: Demonstrate the ability to:

- Format line spacing.
- Work from rough-draft material.
- Proofread, use proofreaders' marks, and correct errors.
- Use command and function keys.

WARMUP

Select Warmup from the Skillbuilding menu. Key each Warmup line 2 times.

Speed	1	`The true beauty of that diamond was brought out by its cut.`
Accuracy	2	`Aquilla told Bix the difference in a xylophone and marimba.`
Language Link	3	`A number of fields of cotton and milo haven't been planted.`
Technique	4	`Paul Quan Rand Stan Trev Ulan Vern Ward Xerxes Yohann Zared`

Making the Connection

Practice reading a short story and correcting the errors in the story by using the proofreaders' marks.

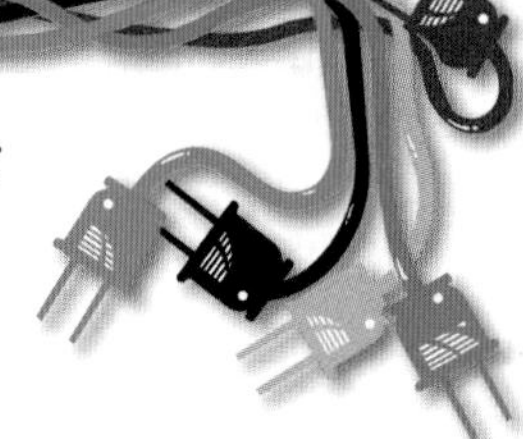

Your Turn

1. Open the file **4-1 Project 1**, and then save the document as ***urs*****Admire**.
2. Keep the file open for Project 1.

The Person I Most Admire

The person I most admire is Shawn. He is 19 years old, and I admire him because

PROJECT 2 **Reinforce**

Create a Table

In this project you will reinforce the skills you have learned and create and format a table on a Web page.

Your Turn

1. Open the file **8-2 Project 2**, and save the document as a Web page. Name the document ***urs*Landmarks**.
2. Apply a theme of your choice.
3. In the section about the Capitol Building, under the bulleted list, create and format the table shown below.

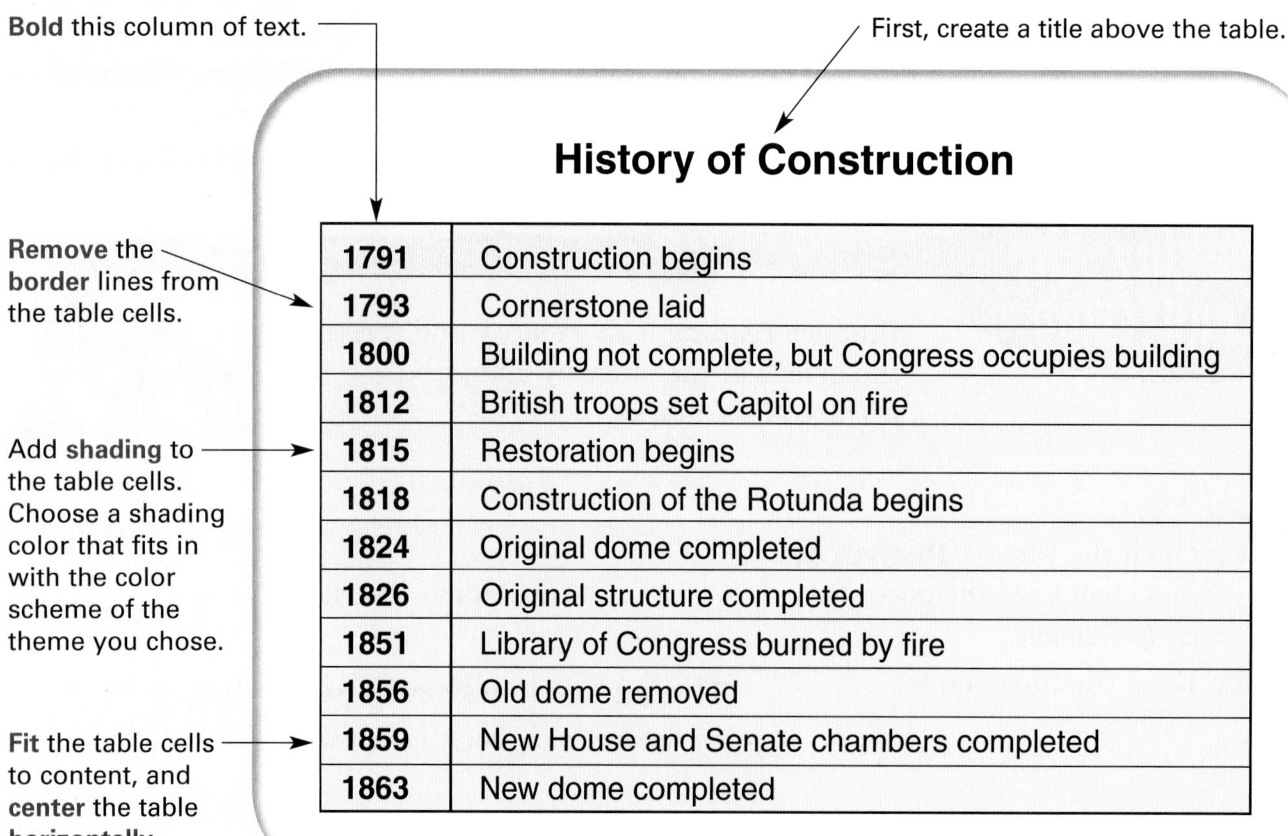

Bold this column of text.
First, create a title above the table.
Remove the **border** lines from the table cells.
Add **shading** to the table cells. Choose a shading color that fits in with the color scheme of the theme you chose.
Fit the table cells to content, and **center** the table **horizontally.**

History of Construction

1791	Construction begins
1793	Cornerstone laid
1800	Building not complete, but Congress occupies building
1812	British troops set Capitol on fire
1815	Restoration begins
1818	Construction of the Rotunda begins
1824	Original dome completed
1826	Original structure completed
1851	Library of Congress burned by fire
1856	Old dome removed
1859	New House and Senate chambers completed
1863	New dome completed

Continued on next page

Edit Short Stories

Notice the **proofreaders' marks** below. You will want to learn what each mark means. Use proofreaders' marks and a red ink pen or pencil to proofread and correct errors.

Proofreading includes checking for formatting and line spacing. Double-space means that there is 1 blank line between each line of text. **Line spacing** is the amount of space between lines of text.

Symbols			
≡	capital letter	⊙	add period
^	insert	^,	insert comma
℘	delete	/	lowercase
∽	transpose	#	add space
¶	new paragraph	DS	double-space

To use keyboard commands (CTRL + B).

Your Turn

1. To bold the title: select the title.
2. Press and hold down the CTRL key.
3. Then press the B key.
4. Then release both keys at the same time.

Continued on next page

PROJECT 1 Practice

Create and Format a Table on a Web Page

You can position a table anywhere on a Web page. You can also add fill colors (called **shading**), and you can even add or remove table cell borders.

You will save a document as a Web page, and then you will create and format a table on the Web page.

Your Turn

1. Position the insertion point at the bottom of the Web page.
2. Create and format the table shown below.

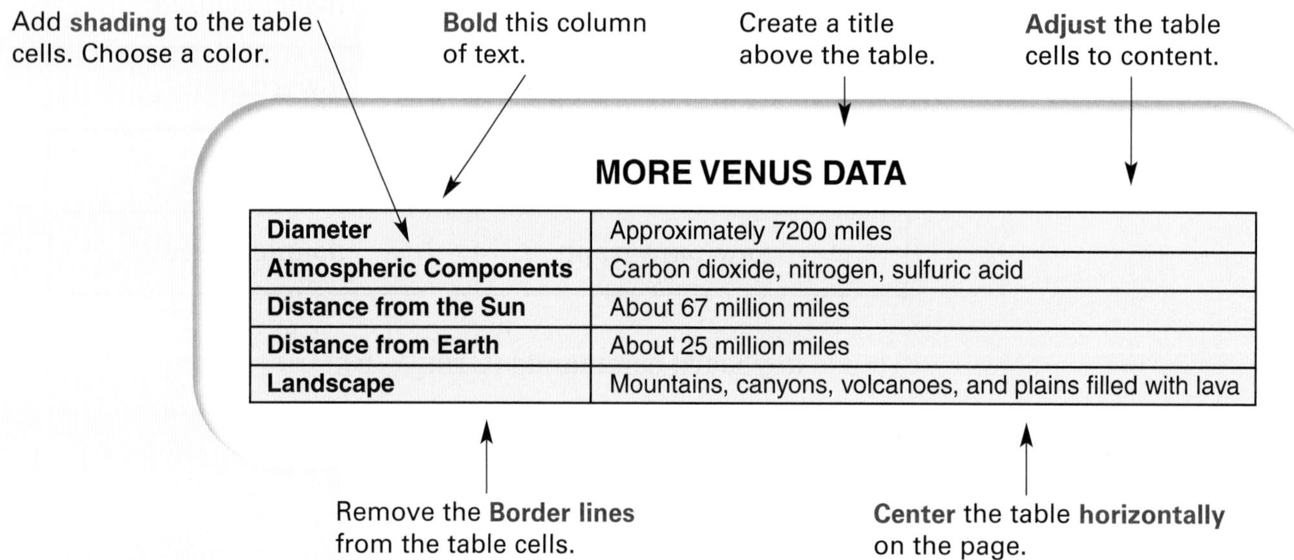

Add shading to the table cells. Choose a color.
Bold this column of text.
Create a title above the table.
Adjust the table cells to content.
MORE VENUS DATA
Diameter
Approximately 7200 miles
Atmospheric Components
Carbon dioxide, nitrogen, sulfuric acid
Distance from the Sun
About 67 million miles
Distance from Earth
About 25 million miles
Landscape
Mountains, canyons, volcanoes, and plains filled with lava
Remove the Border lines from the table cells.
Center the table horizontally on the page.

3. Save the changes. Print and close the file.

PROJECT 1 Continued

Practice

Edit Short Stories

Select the title, press the CAPS LOCK key, then rekey the text.

5. Make the corrections shown in the illustration below.

The Person I Most Admire

DS

The person I most admire is Shawn. He is 19 years old, and I admire him because he is like a brother to me. He makes me feel good when I don't. He takes me to get an ice cream cone when I wash his car. He taught me how to do a flip on a wakeboard. When I finally made a flip, this summer he was so happy for me.

Then one day Shawn was in a really bad car accident. They took him to the hospital. He had a spinal concussion, and he couldn't move from the waist down. I was scared that Shawn would never walk again. I did not know what to do if he was always going to be in a wheelchair. We wouldn't be able to go get ice cream. We wouldn't be able to go wakeboarding. ¶The next day Shawn was able to move. I was so happy. For two weeks he could not move very much, but he got better every day. Now Shawn is able to walk again, and he is living a good life. He is going to College and has many new friends. He still takes me for icecream, and he is teaching me more wakeboarding tricks.

Change the **line spacing** to **double** by selecting all the text and using CTRL + 2. The default line spacing is single.

6. Save the changes. Print and close the file.

Create a Table in a Web Page

GOALS: Demonstrate the ability to:

- Create a table in a Web page.
- Add shading to the table cells.
- Remove table border lines.
- Center a table horizontally on the page.

WARMUP

Select Warmup from the Skillbuilding menu. Key each Warmup line 2 times.

Speed	1	`The temperature last night dropped below the freezing mark.`
Accuracy	2	`Jack typed four dozen requisitions for hollow moving boxes.`
Numbers/Symbols	3	`The citation for the case is 795 F.2D 1423 (9th Cir. 1996).`
Language Link	4	`Then Coach said the prize went to whoever ran the farthest.`

Making the Connection

Tables are useful for organizing information on Web pages. When you add a table to a Web page, you can enhance the table with various formats.

Your Turn

1. Open the file **8-2 Project 1** and Save As a Web page. Name the document ***urs*Venus Fun Facts**.
2. Keep the file open for Project 1.

VENUS FUN FACTS

Size

- Venus is sometimes called Earth's twin because it is similar in diameter and mass to Earth.

PROJECT 2 Reinforce

Proofread and Edit Documents

Your Turn

1. Open a new word processing document.
2. Key the story shown below. Make the corrections shown by the proofreaders' marks as you enter the text.

How Did Salt Get in the Ocean Water?

Have you ever wondered why ocean water is salty? Well then I shall tell you. The story I'm about to tell you has been told for thousands of years. Once long ago, there was an Old Man named Hazard. He was no ordinary old man because he was over well sixty feet tall. Hazard said to the men and women in the village, I shall fill all the oceans with salt. Hazard found a mountain full of salt. He picked up the mountain and carried it to the ocean. He turned the mountain upsidedown and shook it like a salt shaker. The salt from the mountain poured into the ocean and that is why ocean water is salty.

3. Save the document as ***urs*Salt Water** by using the F12 key.
4. Spell-check, proofread, and correct errors.
5. Print and close the file.

Check Your Understanding

1. Open a new word processing document.
2. Key the answer to each question below using a complete sentence.
   a. List three or more examples of visuals that are common to Web pages.
   b. What is the purpose of a theme?
   c. How is it different inserting photos and clip art images on a Web page?
3. Save the document as *urs*Web Pages. Print and close the file.

interNET CONNECTION

After you create a Web page you may decide to publish it on the Web. That means that persons who have access to the Internet will be able to view your Web page.

1. **Use the Yahoo Search directory to locate five school Web sites.**
   http://dir.yahoo.com/Education/K_12/Schools/
2. **Describe the contents of each site in a word processing document. Indicate the following:**
   a. The name and location of the school.
   b. Whether students or staff created the site.
   c. What kind of student work is displayed, if any.
   d. If teachers put assignments on the site.
   e. Other items of interest.
3. **Which of the five sites was most effective? Describe the reasons for your selections in your word processing document.**
4. **On your own: Find out what the policy is at your school for publishing student Web pages. If no policy exists, find a few sample policies online and work with other students to share the best with the technology coordinator.**

Check Your Understanding

1. Open the file *urs*SaltWater.
2. Did you double-space the entire document?
3. Is the title of the story keyed in all-caps?
4. In the second sentence, did you insert a comma after the word "then"?
5. Did you make a new paragraph that begins with "Once long ago"?
6. Did you transpose the words "over" and "well"?
7. Check the third sentence in the second paragraph. It should read as follows:

   Hazard said to the people in the village,
   "I shall fill all the oceans with salt."

8. Did you insert a hyphen between "upside" and "down"?
9. Check the last sentence in the story. It should read as follows:

   That is why ocean water is salty.

10. Save any changes. Close the file.

inter NET CONNECTION

1. **Open your Internet browser.**
2. **Key in the words proofreaders' marks in the Internet search box.**
3. **Locate a site that provides examples of proofreaders' marks.**
4. **Bookmark the site so you can easily return to this site in the future.**
5. **Practice using these proofreaders' marks. Open a search engine, and key in the words "original student stories" or "student writing" to find examples of original writing.**
   1. **Print out a draft version of a story written by someone close to you in age.**
   2. **Use the proofreaders' marks to indicate what edits should be made in the story.**

PROJECT 4 Continued

Reinforce

Create a Web Page

4. Add clip art as shown below.

Pleasant Valley Middle School
Field Trip Memories

- **7th Grade World History**
  On September 28, 7th Grade World History students took a journey back in time. They spent the day with peasants, nobles, and the royal court. They watched a play by Shakespeare, enjoyed watching knights compete in a jousting event, and visited shopkeepers. They also watched shopkeepers demonstrate glass blowing, armor making, and calligraphy. This happened just 33 miles away at the annual Renaissance Festival. What a great experience it was to go back to the medieval times and experience life as it was in the 16th century.

Insert a clip art image.

- **8th Grade American History**
  On April 27, the 8th Grade American History students went on their annual field trip. They traveled by charter bus to Washington, D.C. The field trip was fantastic. Everyone had fun and learned a lot.

Insert an appropriate clip art image.

5. Save the changes. Print and close the file.

SECTION 4.2

Format and Edit Poems

GOALS: Demonstrate the ability to:

- Format paragraph alignment and fonts.
- Work from handwritten material.
- Use the thesaurus feature.

WARMUP

Select Warmup from the Skillbuilding menu. Key each Warmup line 2 times.

Speed	1	It will help to put away worry and doubt about your skills.
Accuracy	2	The dozen extra blue jugs were quickly moved from the pool.
Language Link	3	The number of items to remember to pick up is overwhelming.
Numbers/Symbols	4	(it is) [to the] {of a} 5 < 9 (in at) [by a] {be on} 7 > 1.

Making the Connection

Practice formatting poetry by keying in the poem at right.

Your Turn

1. Open a new word processing document.
2. Key the poem *Dust of Snow* by Robert Frost.
3. Save the document as ***urs*DustofSnow**. Keep the file open for Project 1.

Dust of Snow
by Robert Frost

The way a crow
Shook down on me
The dust of snow
From a hemlock tree

Has given my heart
A change of mood
And saved some part
Of a day I had rued.

Single space

Double space

PROJECT 4 Reinforce

Create a Web Page

In this project you will reinforce the skills you have learned by creating and formatting a Web page for Pleasant Valley Middle School. The purpose of the Web page is to communicate information about class field trips.

Your Turn

1. Open the file **8-1 Project 4** and save the document as a Web page. Name the document ***urs*****Field Trips**.
2. Format the Web page as shown below.

Format a horizontal line border.

Insert bullets.

Pleasant Valley Middle School
Field Trip Memories

7th Grade World History
On September 28, 7th Grade World History students took a journey back in time. They spent the day with peasants, nobles, and the royal court. They watched a play by Shakespeare, enjoyed watching knights compete in a jousting event, and visited shopkeepers. They also watched shopkeepers demonstrate glass blowing, armor making, and calligraphy. This happened just 33 miles away at the annual Renaissance Festival. What a great experience it was to go back to the medieval times and experience life as it was in the 16th century.

8th Grade American History
On April 27, the 8th Grade American History students went on their annual field trip. They traveled by charter bus to Washington, D.C. The field trip was fantastic. Everyone had fun and learned a lot.

3. Choose and apply a theme.

Continued on next page

PROJECT 1 Practice

Format Poems

You can change the font and alignment to make the poem more attractive. If you need additional help, use Function Key F1, the Help feature.

Your Turn

1. Format the poem as indicated.

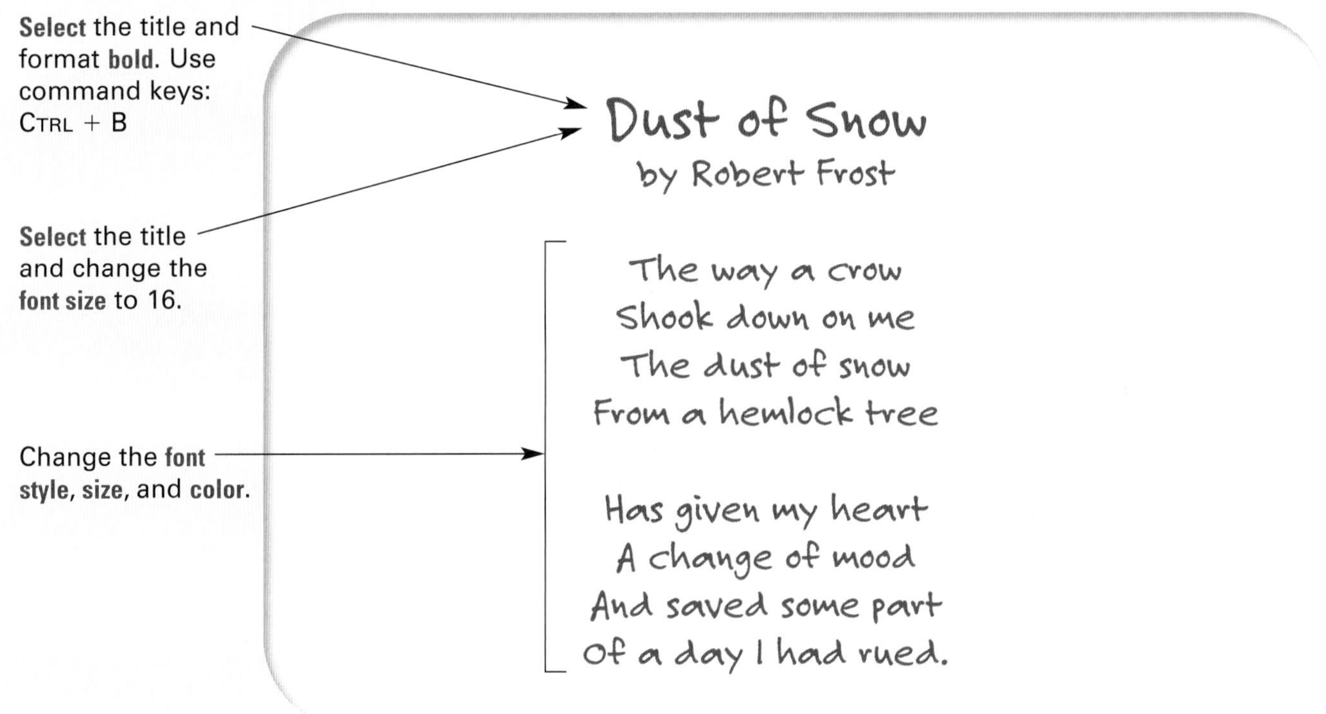

Select the title and format **bold**. Use command keys: CTRL + B
Select the title and change the **font size** to 16.
Change the **font style, size,** and **color.**
Dust of Snow
by Robert Frost
The way a crow
Shook down on me
The dust of snow
From a hemlock tree
Has given my heart
A change of mood
And saved some part
Of a day I had rued.

2. **Select** all the paragraphs. Apply **center alignment**.
3. Save the changes. Print and close the file.

PROJECT 3 Practice

Insert Photos and Graphics on a Web Page

You can insert photos and clip art images on a Web page just as you do in the documents you create.

Your Turn

1. Insert clip art as indicated below.

VENUS

Viewing Venus

Venus, the sixth largest planet, was named for the Roman goddess of love and beauty. Venus is Earth's closest neighbor. It is visible with the naked eye during daytime and nighttime. Only two objects are brighter than Venus—the sun and the moon.

Insert clip art about Venus. Resize as necessary.

2. Save the changes. Print and close the file.

PROJECT 2

Practice

Use the Thesaurus

The thesaurus can be very helpful when writing poetry. The **thesaurus** is a word list stored in the software. You can use the thesaurus to find suggestions for synonyms.

Your Turn

1. Open a new word processing document.
2. Key the cinquain poem shown below.

Puppy
Frisky, cuddly
Barking, running, sleeping
She likes to chew my dad's slippers.
Heidi

3. Apply **center alignment**. Select all lines and use command keys: CTRL + E.
4. Save the document as ***urs*Puppy**.
5. Use SHIFT + F7 to access the **thesaurus** feature to replace the word "frisky" with a synonym.
6. Save the changes. Print and close the file.

PROJECT 2 Practice

Apply a Visual Theme to a Web Page

Web pages are often displayed with many visual elements. You can apply a theme to give your Web page a decorative look. A **theme** is a set of unified design elements and color schemes that include a background design, customized bullets, and borders. When you apply a theme to your Web page, the bullet symbols and the borders are formatted to the theme you have chosen.

Your Turn

1. Choose and apply a **theme** to your Web page.
2. Notice that the text, bullets, and borders are now formatted for the theme you chose. The illustration below is provided as an example. Your Web page may look much different.

The **theme** includes a background image.

VENUS

Viewing Venus
Venus, the sixth largest planet, was named for the Roman goddess of love and beauty. Venus is Earth's closest neighbor. It is visible with the naked eye during daytime and nighttime. Only two objects are brighter than Venus—the sun and the moon.

Exploring Venus
It is very difficult to explore Venus because thick white clouds block the view of its surface. We cannot get close because the sulfuric acid clouds and the extremely high temperatures damage the spacecraft. Between 1990 and 1994, the American Magellan spaceship provided much data and many images of Venus.

The bullets and border line are automatically formatted when you apply a theme.

3. Save the changes. Keep the file open for Project 3.

PROJECT 3 Reinforce

Format Poems

Reinforce what you have learned about formatting poems and using the thesaurus feature.

Your Turn

1. Open the file **4-2 Project 3**, and format the poem as indicated.

What a Day! What a Day!

My cat Felix ran away,
And my dog Spot wouldn't obey.
And then much to my dismay,
My wave runner sunk in the bay.
What a Day! What a Day!

It seemed like things were not going my way.
So I decided to go to the park to play.
When I got to the park, the sky turned gray,
A tornado blew in and I ran home that day.
What a Day! What a Day!

Then just when I thought things were okay,
I talked to my best friend José.
We went to buy candy and he said I should pay.
What else could I say?
What a Day! What a Day!

By Maria

Format all paragraphs with **center alignment**.

Copy and **Paste** the title below each verse. To copy use CTRL + C. To paste use CTRL + V.

Replace the words "tornado" and "friend" with synonyms.

Right align the author's name.

2. Save the document as ***urs*What a Day**.
3. If desired, change the font style, font size, and/or font color.
4. Save the changes. Print and close the file.

PROJECT 1 Practice

Save a Document as a Web Page

Most documents you create on the computer can be displayed on Web pages. Web pages can contain text, graphics, photos, sound, and video. You will learn to insert **bullets** and save a document as a Web page.

Your Turn

1. Open a new word processing document, and key and format the paragraphs shown below.

Format a horizontal **border**.

Insert bullets.

Venus

- **Viewing Venus**

Venus, the sixth largest planet, was named for the Roman goddess of love and beauty. Venus is Earth's closest neighbor. It is visible with the naked eye during daytime and nighttime. Only two objects are brighter than Venus—the sun and the moon.

- **Exploring Venus**

It is very difficult to explore Venus because thick white clouds block the view of its surface. We cannot get close because the sulfuric acid clouds and the extremely high temperatures damage the spacecraft. Between 1990 and 1994, the American Magellan spaceship provided much data and many images of Venus.

2. **Save** the document **as a Web page**. Name the Web page ***urs*Venus**.

3. Keep the file open for Project 2.

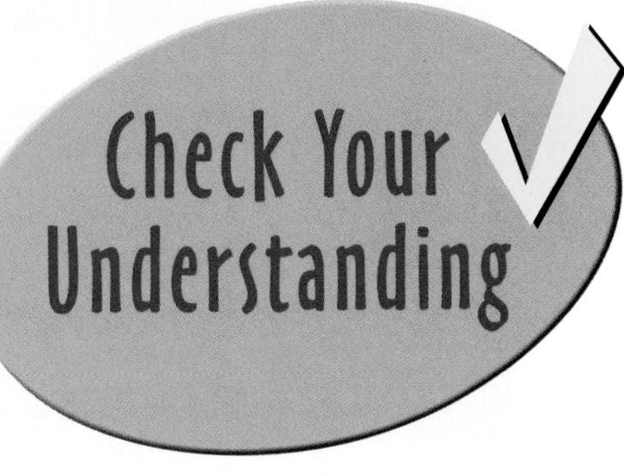

1. Open a new word processing document.
2. Key the following sentence: Alex was thankful that I helped format the poem.
3. Use the thesaurus feature to replace the word "poem."
4. Use the thesaurus feature to replace the word "thankful."
5. Describe how you would center all the paragraphs in a document at the same time.
6. Save the document as *urs*Poemcheck. Print and close the file.

*inter*NET CONNECTION

1. **Open your Web browser.**
2. **Open a search engine such as Google and key "cinquain" into the search field to locate a site that explains cinquain poems and provides examples.**
3. **In a word processing document, define "cinquain" and paste a copy of the poem. Add a proper citation noting where you found the poem. Be sure to name its author.**
4. **Follow the same procedure to add an example of Haiku and a Ballad.**
5. **At the end of the word processing document note how the three types are similar and how they are different.**
6. **On your own: create an original poem in each of the styles surveyed.**

SECTION 8.1 Create a Web Page

GOALS: Demonstrate the ability to:

- Save a document as a Web page.
- Apply a theme and bullets.
- Format a horizontal line border.
- Insert photos and graphics.

WARMUP

Select Warmup from the Skillbuilding menu. Key each Warmup line 2 times.

Speed	1	We are planning to have a cookout when we meet at the lake.
Accuracy	2	All four mixtures in the deep brown jug froze very quickly.
Language Link	3	We usually vacation at a place that is south of the border.
Numbers/Symbols	4	Invoice #70-2 read: 653$ "Extra" @ $4.89 per lb., less 10%.

Making the Connection

When you are proud of your work, you post it where others can see it. Web pages are a good way to share your work with others. Have you ever thought about publishing your work on the Web? To do this, you need to create a Web page.

Your Turn

1. Open your Web browser and go to your school's home page.
2. Look for things you enjoy seeing on a Web page, and make a list.
3. Share your list with a partner to see if you found similar visual elements.
4. Close your Web browser.

Colors
Bullets
Borders
Background Designs

SECTION 4.3

Format a Journal Entry and Proof Text

GOALS: Demonstrate the ability to:

- Format a journal entry.
- Use the grammar check feature.
- Proofread text and correct errors.
- Compose at the keyboard.

WARMUP

Select Warmup from the Skillbuilding menu. Key each Warmup line 2 times.

Speed	1	If you want to be the best typist, then practice correctly.
Accuracy	2	Xavier is amazed by the two jazz artists' expert qualities.
Language Link	3	The number of students involved in intramural sports is up.
Numbers	4	We are scheduled for April 29, May 14, June 30, and July 7.

Making the Connection

A journal is a record of day-to-day activities. People write journal entries about their experiences, their ideas, and their feelings. You may have a special book where you write journal entries. Have you ever thought about using your word processor to create an electronic journal?

Your Turn

1. Open a new word processing document.
2. Key today's date at the top of the document. Press ENTER 2 times.
3. Key the paragraph to the right exactly as shown. Be sure to press TAB to indent the first line of text.
4. Save the document as ***urs*Camp**. Keep the file open for Project 1.

(Today's Date)

Tomorrow I leave for camp. I am so excited, I had so much fun last year. I met a new friend Jesse. I hope Jesse will be their again this year.

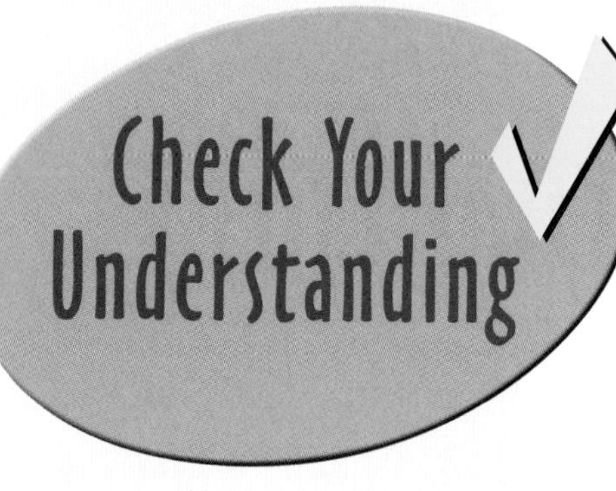

1. Open a new word processing document.
2. Key the answer to each question below using a complete sentence.
   a. What is the purpose of a template?
   b. What are the advantages of using a template?
   c. List three or more examples of templates that you can use.
3. Save the document as *urs*Templates. Print and close the file.

*inter*NET CONNECTION

Generally, the manufacturer of your software will provide additional document templates at its Web site. You can often download these templates at no additional cost.

1. **Open your Web browser and locate the site for the manufacturer of your desktop publishing software.**
2. **Explore the templates that are available. Create a table in a word processing document. Enter the name of the template in the left column. In the other columns, add notes about the template features, how it would be used, and its Web address. Identify at least three templates that you would likely use in the future in your own projects.**
3. **Choose one of the templates identified in Step 2, and use it to create a draft document. Below the table created in Step 2, describe whether the template was easy to use and faster than starting a similar document from scratch.**

PROJECT 1 Practice

Format a Journal Entry and Proof Text

Typical errors in grammar include the following:

- Punctuation errors
- Misused words
- Sentence fragments
- Subject and verb agreement
- Capitalization errors

The journal entry you just keyed for document ***urs*Camp** contains three grammatical errors. Can you find the errors?

If your software has a **grammar check feature**, possible errors may be identified with a wavy line as shown in the illustration below. However, you should always proofread your work carefully. The grammar check feature isn't always correct.

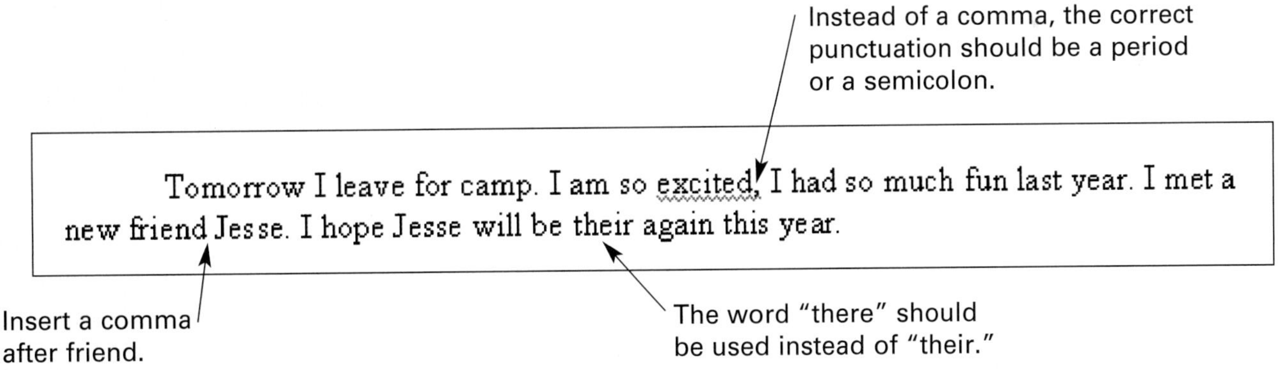

Instead of a comma, the correct punctuation should be a period or a semicolon.

> Tomorrow I leave for camp. I am so excited, I had so much fun last year. I met a new friend Jesse. I hope Jesse will be their again this year.

Insert a comma after friend.

The word "there" should be used instead of "their."

Your Turn

1. Make the corrections identified in the illustration above. If you see a wavy line, right-click the text and choose a suggested correction from the shortcut menu.
2. Save the changes. Print and close the file.

PROJECT 2 Reinforce

Create a New Document From a Template

Your Turn

1. Create a **new** document from a **template**. Choose a template for a calendar with photos or graphics. Be sure the calendar you choose is for the current year.
2. Locate the month when your birthday occurs.
3. Customize the calendar as indicated at left.

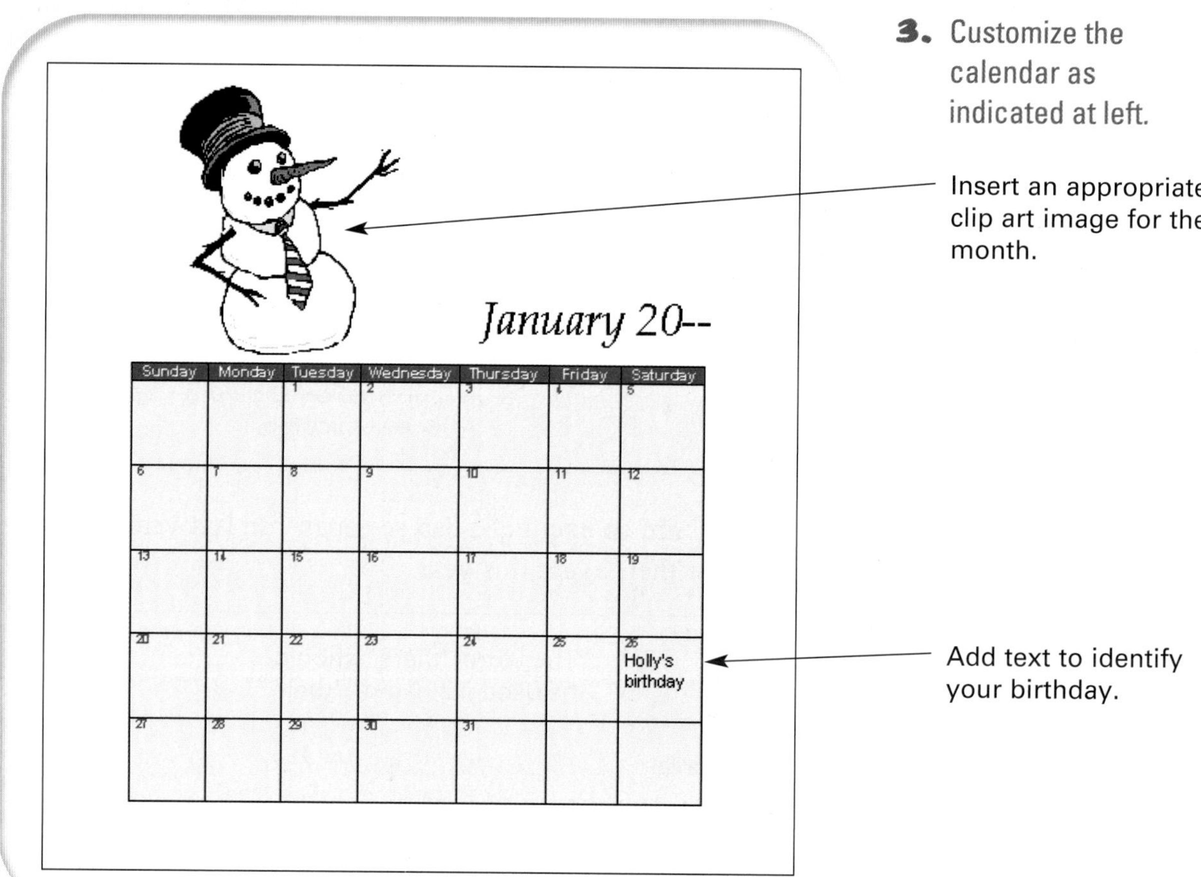

4. Save the document as *urs*Calendar.
5. Print the calendar page with your birthday and then close the document.

PROJECT 2

Reinforce

Format a Journal Entry

Reinforce what you have learned about formatting journal entries and proofreading text.

Your Turn

1. Open a new word processing document.
2. Key the journal entry exactly as shown below.

Today's Date

We one our basball game today. The score was 6 to 1. I struck out in the first inning. I was so embarrassed! I did better in the third inning. I got an hit and scored a run. I was happy because Coach Ruez told me I did a good job.

3. The journal entry contains two grammatical errors. Proofread carefully and correct the errors. Use F7 to quickly access the spelling and grammar feature.
4. Save the document as ***urs*Baseball**. Print and close the file.

PROJECT 1 Continued

Practice

Use a Template to Create a Business Card

3. Customize the first business card in the template by replacing the sample information with the personal information shown below.

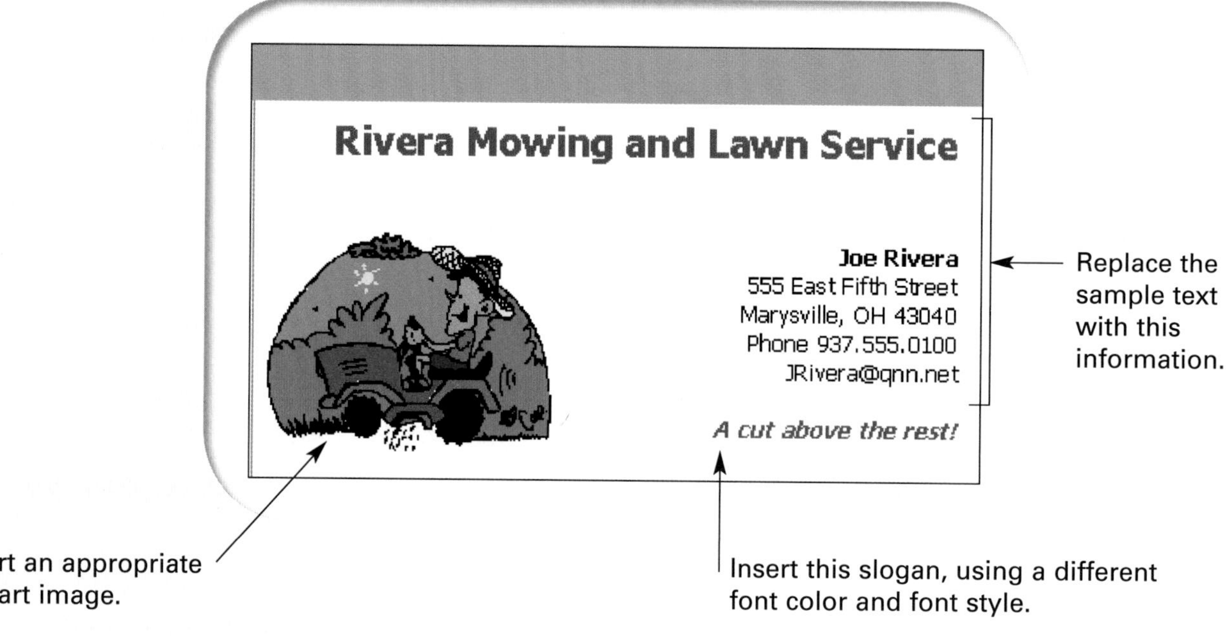

Rivera Mowing and Lawn Service
Joe Rivera
555 East Fifth Street
Marysville, OH 43040
Phone 937.555.0100
JRivera@qnn.net
A cut above the rest!
Replace the sample text with this information.
Insert an appropriate clip art image.
Insert this slogan, using a different font color and font style.

4. Copy all the content of the customized card to the Clipboard. Select the content on one of the sample cards and paste the contents from the Clipboard. Continue to select and paste until all the sample cards are replaced with the customized card contents.

5. Save the changes. Print one page of cards and close the file.

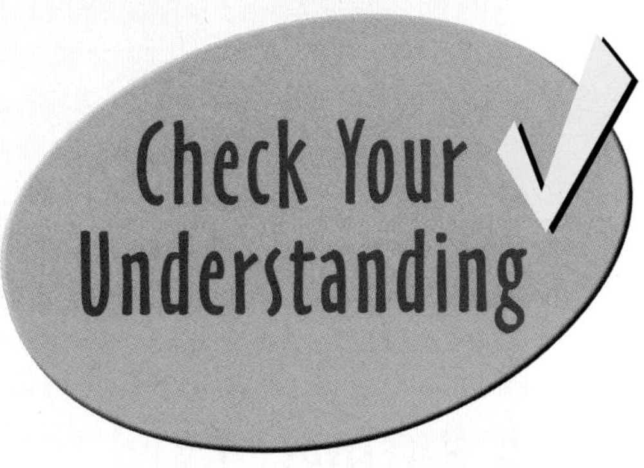

1. Open a new word processing document.
2. Describe some of the errors that the grammar checker can find. Provide at least one example. Then describe some of the errors the grammar checker may not find. Provide at least one example.
3. Save your document as *urs*Grammar Check. Print and close the file.

Write On!

You will write some electronic journal entries as a part of your projects. Remember to proofread your journal entries for content, and make sure the sentences make sense. If available, use the grammar check feature to help you correct possible errors.

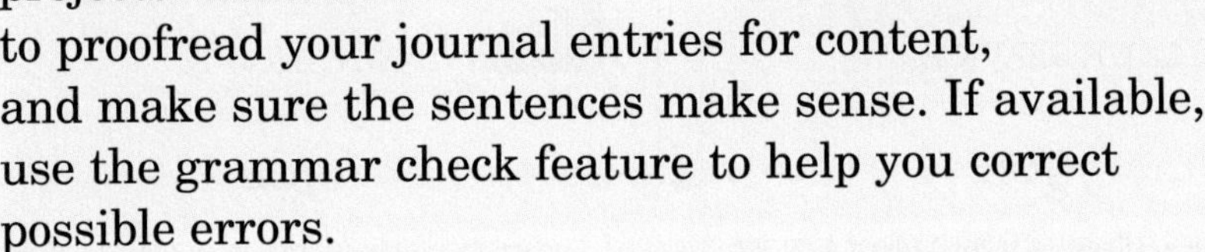

1. Open a new word processing document.
2. Key today's date.
3. Write a journal entry about your favorite movie. Explain why you like the movie. Provide some details.
4. Save the document as *urs*Journal.
5. Close the file.

PROJECT 1 Practice

Use a Template to Create a Business Card

You can create business cards by using a business card **template** that has preformatted margins and borders for you to fill in the information you want. You can even decorate your template.

Your Turn

1. Open a new word processing document. From the New Document section, choose a **template** for business cards. Find a template that provides a framework for multiple cards on the same page.

Generally, templates for business cards provide a framework to create 6–10 cards on a page.

You can replace the sample text with your own personal information.

You can replace the graphic with one that you choose.

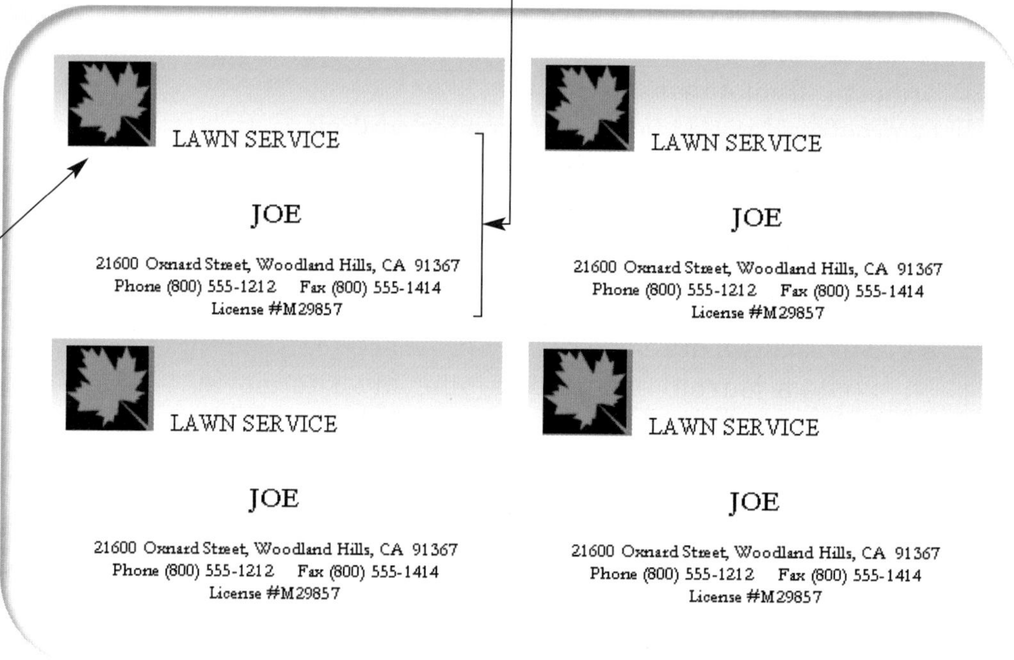

LAWN SERVICE

JOE

21600 Oxnard Street, Woodland Hills, CA 91367
Phone (800) 555-1212 Fax (800) 555-1414
License #M29857

LAWN SERVICE

JOE

21600 Oxnard Street, Woodland Hills, CA 91367
Phone (800) 555-1212 Fax (800) 555-1414
License #M29857

LAWN SERVICE

JOE

21600 Oxnard Street, Woodland Hills, CA 91367
Phone (800) 555-1212 Fax (800) 555-1414
License #M29857

LAWN SERVICE

JOE

21600 Oxnard Street, Woodland Hills, CA 91367
Phone (800) 555-1212 Fax (800) 555-1414
License #M29857

2. Save the document as *urs*Business Card.

Continued on next page

Create and Format Tables

GOALS: Demonstrate the ability to:

- Create a new table.
- Add a new row at the end of a table.
- Format cell contents.
- Align cell contents.
- Work from handwritten material.
- Proofread and make corrections to documents.

WARMUP

Select Warmup from the Skillbuilding menu. Key each Warmup line 2 times.

Speed	1	`You can learn to type at a fast speed if you will practice.`
Accuracy	2	`Olmec, Zapotec, Mixtec, and Aztec were early civilizations.`
Language Link	3	`The homework for math class was problems 45-49 on page 549.`
Numbers/Symbols	4	`Our company will buy 1/3 of their stock @ 22 7/8 per share.`

Making the Connection

An effective way to organize data is to use a table. You will learn how to create and format a table.

Your Turn

1. Open a new word processing document.
2. Key and center the title Effects on Litmus Paper.
3. Press ENTER 2 times. Press CTRL + L to left align.
4. Save the document as ***urs*Acid or Base**.
5. Keep the file open for Project 1.

Effects on Litmus Paper

Create Documents From Templates

GOALS: Demonstrate the ability to:

- Use a template to create a business card.
- Use a template to create a calendar.

WARMUP

Select Warmup from the Skillbuilding menu. Key each Warmup line 2 times.

Speed	1	`We have to learn to make introductions with poise and ease.`
Accuracy	2	`Mo brought back five or six dozen pieces of quaint jewelry.`
Numbers/Symbols	3	`She will visit our top offices (#1 & #2): DALLAS & EL PASO.`
Language Link	4	`The trip to Grandma's house was farther than they expected.`

Making the Connection

Joe Rivera gets paid to mow some of his neighbors' lawns and to rake leaves in the fall. Joe believes he can increase his business by using business cards. Joe will give business cards to his current customers and also to potential new customers in his neighborhood.

In this section, you will learn how to create your own business cards.

Your Turn

1. Open a new word processing document, and create a list of information that should be included on a business card.
2. In Project 1 you will learn an easy way to create a business card.
3. Close the document without saving the changes.

Name
Telephone
Hours available for work

PROJECT 1 Practice

Create a Table

The table feature makes creating a table quick and easy. A **table** contains rows and columns. The intersection of each column and row creates a **cell**. You enter data within the cells.

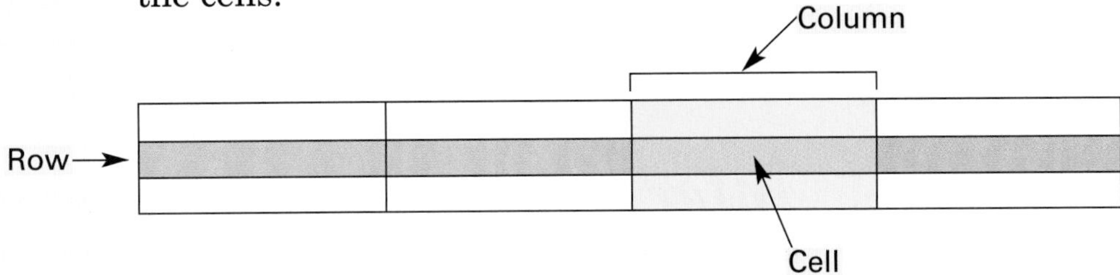

Your Turn

1. Make sure your document is open from Making the Connection. Position the insertion point below the title.
2. **Create a table** with 4 columns and 6 rows.
3. The insertion point should be positioned in the first cell. Key the data shown below. Press TAB to move from cell to cell.

Substance Tested	Blue	Red	No Change
Lemon juice		X	
Ammonia	X		
Baking soda	X		
Vinegar		X	
Table salt			X

Press TAB to create a new row.

4. You need to add one more row of data. Position the insertion point in the last cell in the last row and press TAB. Key **Cola** in the first cell and then key an **X** in the Red column.
5. Save the changes. Print and close the file.

Check Your Understanding

1. Open a new word processing document.
2. Key the answer to each question below using a complete sentence.
   a. What is a newsletter-style column format?
   b. What is the purpose of a column break?
   c. What information is contained in a masthead?
3. Save the document as *urs*Newsletters.
4. Print and close the file.

*inter*NET CONNECTION

School newsletters are a great way to share information about what is going on at school. Students, teachers, parents, and community residents enjoy reading school newsletters. To make the newsletters easily accessible, many schools are now publishing their newsletters on the Web.

1. **Open your Web browser and search for school newsletters.**
2. **Find a school newsletter that you like. For example, you might like a newsletter because of the information it contains or because of its attractive format.**
3. **Open a word processing document, and copy and paste the URL for the newsletter Web site. Then give the name of the newsletter, and write a paragraph describing why you think it is good.**
4. **Save the document as *urs*Online Newsletter. Print and close the file.**
5. **On your own: Plan out what you would include in a newsletter for your sports team, club, or family. Using the skills you have learned in this section, create a draft of your newsletter. Then ask classmates to review the draft before you finalize your newsletter.**

PROJECT 2

Practice

Format a Table

You can format text in a table just as you would format any other text in your document. Your word processor may have a feature that enables you to automatically adjust the column widths. If you do not want the table cell borders to show, you can remove them.

Your Turn

1. Open a new word processing document.
2. Key the title OCEAN DATA. (Leave the title formatted for left alignment.)
3. Press ENTER 2 times.
4. Create the table with 3 columns and 6 rows. Apply the formats indicated.

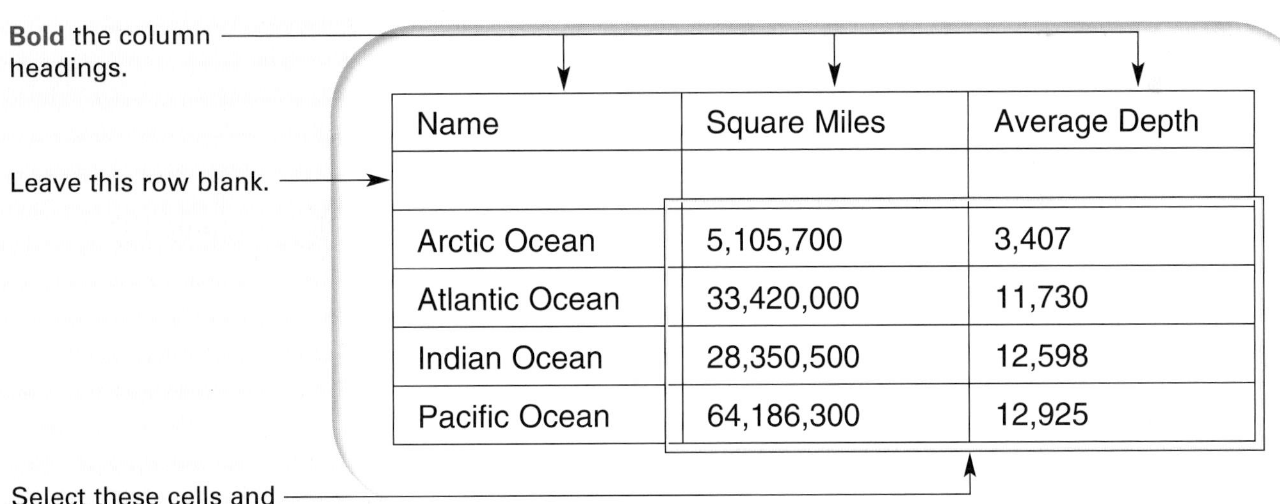
Bold the column headings.
Leave this row blank.
Select these cells and format **right alignment** by using CTRL + R.

Name	Square Miles	Average Depth
Arctic Ocean	5,105,700	3,407
Atlantic Ocean	33,420,000	11,730
Indian Ocean	28,350,500	12,598
Pacific Ocean	64,186,300	12,925

5. Save the document as ***urs*Ocean Data**.
6. **Fit** the table to adjust for the contents in the table.
7. **Remove** the **table borders** so that the borders do not show.
8. Save the changes. Print and close the file.

Create a Newsletter

2. Spell-check, proofread, and correct any errors.
3. Save the document as *urs***The Great Globe**. Keep the file open for the next step.
4. Format the newsletter similar to the one illustrated below.

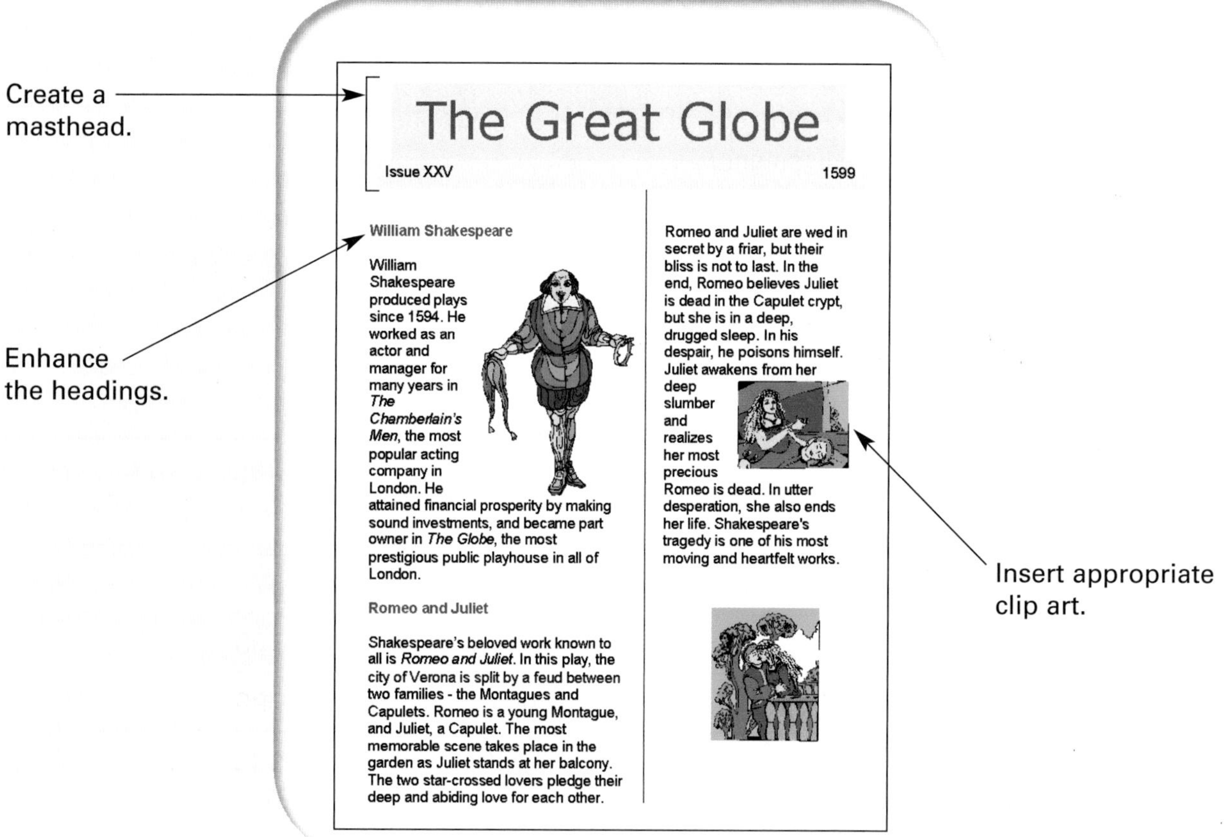
Create a masthead.
Enhance the headings.
Insert appropriate clip art.

The Great Globe

Issue XXV 1599

William Shakespeare

William Shakespeare produced plays since 1594. He worked as an actor and manager for many years in *The Chamberlain's Men*, the most popular acting company in London. He attained financial prosperity by making sound investments, and became part owner in *The Globe*, the most prestigious public playhouse in all of London.

Romeo and Juliet

Shakespeare's beloved work known to all is *Romeo and Juliet*. In this play, the city of Verona is split by a feud between two families - the Montagues and Capulets. Romeo is a young Montague, and Juliet, a Capulet. The most memorable scene takes place in the garden as Juliet stands at her balcony. The two star-crossed lovers pledge their deep and abiding love for each other.

Romeo and Juliet are wed in secret by a friar, but their bliss is not to last. In the end, Romeo believes Juliet is dead in the Capulet crypt, but she is in a deep, drugged sleep. In his despair, he poisons himself. Juliet awakens from her deep slumber and realizes her most precious Romeo is dead. In utter desperation, she also ends her life. Shakespeare's tragedy is one of his most moving and heartfelt works.

5. Save the changes. Print and close the file.

PROJECT 3 **Reinforce**

Create Tables

Reinforce what you have learned about creating and formatting tables. Suppose your club is selling concessions at the game tonight and you have volunteered to create a price list for the items you will sell.

Your Turn

1. Open a new word processing document.
2. Create and format the table shown below.

Select all the table cells. Change the **font style** and **font size** to make the text as large as possible—and still fit all the text on one page.

Format **bold** and **center align** the column headings. To center align select column headings and press CTRL + E.

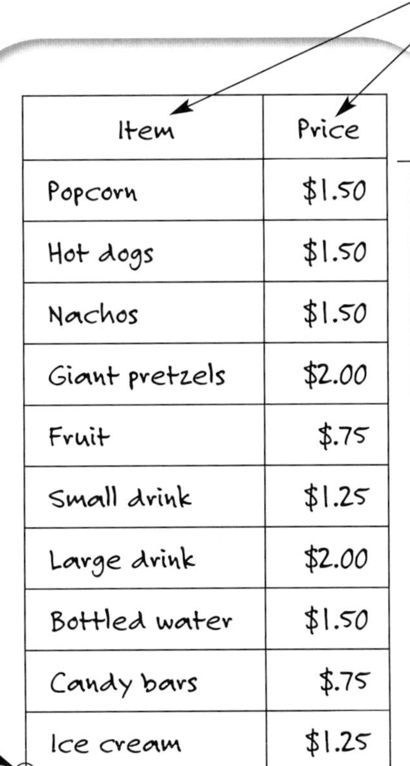

Item	Price
Popcorn	$1.50
Hot dogs	$1.50
Nachos	$1.50
Giant pretzels	$2.00
Fruit	$.75
Small drink	$1.25
Large drink	$2.00
Bottled water	$1.50
Candy bars	$.75
Ice cream	$1.25

Right align the *Price* column.

Remove the **table borders.**

3. Save the document as ***urs*Concessions**.
4. Print and close the file.

PROJECT 3 **Reinforce**

Create a Newsletter

Reinforce the desktop publishing features you have learned by creating another newsletter.

Your Turn

1. Key the newsletter article shown below.

William Shakespeare

William Shakespeare produced plays since 1594. He worked as an actor and manager for many years in *The Chamberlain's Men*, the most popular acting company in London. He attained financial prosperity by making sound investments and became part owner in *The Globe*, the most prestigious public playhouse in all of London.

Romeo and Juliet

Shakespeare's beloved work known to all is *Romeo and Juliet*. In this play, the city of Verona is split by a feud between two families—the Montagues and Capulets. Romeo is a young Montague, and Juliet, a Capulet. The most memorable scene takes place in the garden as Juliet stands at her balcony. The two star-crossed lovers pledge their deep and abiding love for each other.

Romeo and Juliet are wed in secret by a friar, but their bliss is not to last. In the end, Romeo believes Juliet is dead in the Capulet crypt, but she is in a deep, drugged sleep. In his despair, he poisons himself. Juliet awakens from her deep slumber and realizes her most precious Romeo is dead. In utter desperation, she also ends her life. Shakespeare's tragedy is one of his most moving and heartfelt works.

Continued on next page

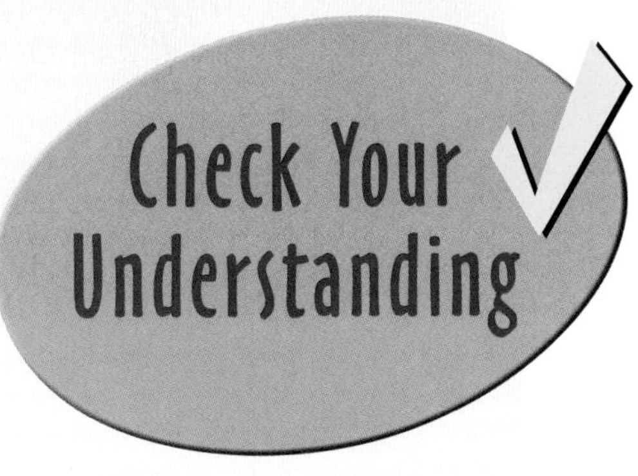

1. In Project 1, did you key each X in the correct column? Each X indicates the results of your lab activity. Compare your word processing document with the notes page shown in Project 1 to check for accuracy. If necessary, open Project 1 to make corrections. Save the changes.
2. In Project 2, did you key the values for square miles and average depth? It is easy to make mistakes when keying numbers. Have a partner help you check for accuracy. One partner reads the number while the other partner checks the document. If necessary, open Project 2 to make any corrections. Save the changes.
3. In Project 3, did you enter the correct price for each item? Use a ruler or something with a straight edge to help guide your eyes; then compare each line in the document with the handwritten copy. If necessary, open Project 3 to make any corrections. Save the changes.

*inter*NET CONNECTION

You will find the table feature useful when you are researching and gathering data from the Internet. You can create a table quickly, and the table format will help you organize the information.

1. **Open a new word processing document and create the table shown below.**

Which time zone is:	Name the time zone
Boston, MA	
Pittsburgh, PA	
Atlanta, GA	
Cincinnati, OH	
San Diego, CA	

2. **Save the document as *urs*TimeZone.**
3. **Open your Web browser and log onto http://www.timeanddate.com where you can obtain information about times for cities all over the world. Select North America and key in each city. Click on the city name from the list that is returned to find its time zone.**
4. **Enter the data in the table.**
5. **In which time zone is the city in which you live? Insert a row into the table for your city.**
6. **On your own: Add a column to the table you created for cities in Canada, Central America or South America that are in the same time zone as U.S. cities already listed and put them in the correct locations.**
7. **Save changes. Print and close the word processing file.**

Continued on next page

PROJECT 2 Practice

Format a Newsletter

You can make the newsletter more appealing by adding a **masthead**. The masthead displays the title of the newsletter and the issue number and date. You can make the newsletter appealing by formatting the headings and inserting clip art images.

Your Turn

1. Edit the document as shown in the illustration below.

Create a masthead by formatting the title, using clip art, and using text boxes. The issue number is 39 and the date is May 30, 20--.

Enhance the heading formats by changing the font, font size, and font color.

Insert clip art images, and format the text to wrap around the image.

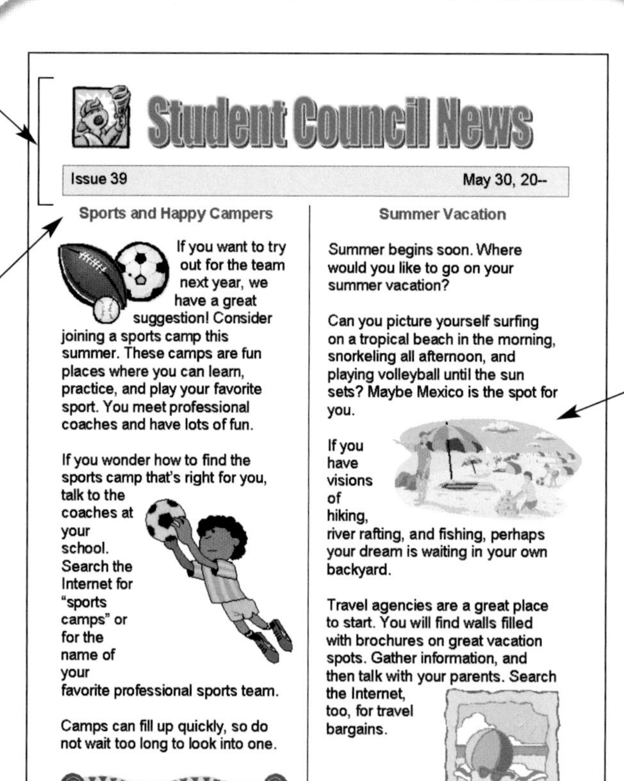

Student Council News

Issue 39 May 30, 20--

Sports and Happy Campers

If you want to try out for the team next year, we have a great suggestion! Consider joining a sports camp this summer. These camps are fun places where you can learn, practice, and play your favorite sport. You meet professional coaches and have lots of fun.

If you wonder how to find the sports camp that's right for you, talk to the coaches at your school. Search the Internet for "sports camps" or for the name of your favorite professional sports team.

Camps can fill up quickly, so do not wait too long to look into one.

Summer Vacation

Summer begins soon. Where would you like to go on your summer vacation?

Can you picture yourself surfing on a tropical beach in the morning, snorkeling all afternoon, and playing volleyball until the sun sets? Maybe Mexico is the spot for you.

If you have visions of hiking, river rafting, and fishing, perhaps your dream is waiting in your own backyard.

Travel agencies are a great place to start. You will find walls filled with brochures on great vacation spots. Gather information, and then talk with your parents. Search the Internet, too, for travel bargains.

2. Save the changes. Print and close the file.

Check Your Understanding Continued

4. Check Projects 2 and 3 to make sure you applied the text formats and alignments that are indicated in the directions. Save the changes. Reprint, if necessary. Close all files.

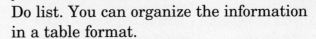

Write On!

The table feature can be useful for recording your journal entries. For example, suppose you want to create a To Do list. You can organize the information in a table format.

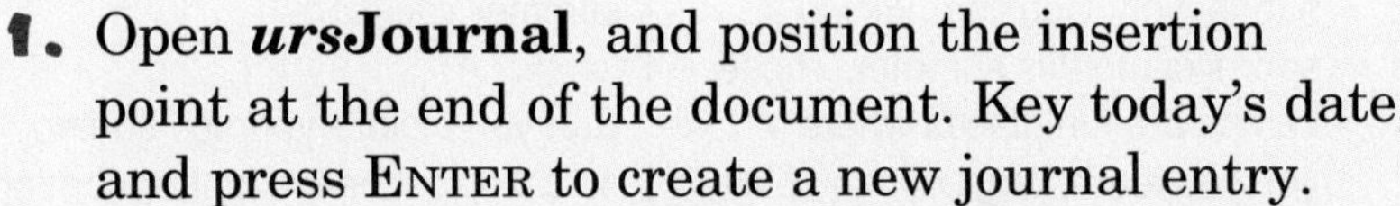

1. Open ***urs*Journal**, and position the insertion point at the end of the document. Key today's date, and press ENTER to create a new journal entry.
2. Write an opening sentence about things you need to get done.
3. Create a two-column table. In the first column, list the things you need to do, such as homework or study for a test.
4. In the second column of the table, list the due dates for each item.
5. Save the changes to your journal. Close the file.

PROJECT 1 Practice

Format Text in Columns

Text in newspaper-style **columns** flows from one column to the next. To format text in newspaper-style columns, you simply select the text and apply the column format.

Your Turn

Sports and Happy Campers

If you want to try out for the team next year, we have a great suggestion! Consider joining a sports camp this summer. These camps are fun places where you can learn, practice, and play your favorite sport. You meet professional coaches and have lots of fun.

If you wonder how to find the sports camp that's right for you, talk to the coaches at your school. Search the Internet for "sports camps" or for the name of your favorite professional sports team.

Camps can fill up quickly, so do not wait too long to look into one.

Summer Vacation

Summer begins soon. Where would you like to go on your summer vacation?

Can you picture yourself surfing on a tropical beach in the morning, snorkeling all afternoon, and playing volleyball until the sun sets? Maybe Mexico is the spot for you.

If you have visions of hiking, river rafting, and fishing, perhaps your dream is waiting in your own backyard.

Travel agencies are a great place to start. You will find walls filled with brochures on great vacation spots. Gather information, and then talk with your parents. Search the Internet, too, for travel bargains.

1. Change the top **margin** to 2 inches, and change all other margins to 1 inch.
2. Select the entire document, and **format** the text in 2 **columns** with a line between the columns.
3. **Insert a column break** before the heading Summer Vacation to force the start of a new column.
4. When you've made the changes the document should look similar to the illustration on the left. Save the changes. Keep the file open for Project 2.

SECTION 4.5 Format Outlines

GOALS: Demonstrate the ability to:

- Identify the parts of an outline.
- Key an outline from handwritten, unarranged copy.
- Use the alignment and outline features.
- Create an outline.

WARMUP

Select Warmup from the Skillbuilding menu. Key each Warmup line 2 times.

Speed	1	We will be happy to see the sun after so many days of rain.
Accuracy	2	Janita and six friends quickly zipped by the two villagers.
Language Link	3	The number of farmers helping their sick neighbor was huge.
Numbers/Symbols	4	Our 9 cakes, 45 pies, 60 doughnuts, and 72 cookies arrived.

Making the Connection

An outline is a list of main topics (major points) and subtopics (minor points) for a given subject. Indenting the points that are less important makes an outline clear and easy to follow.

Your Turn

1. Open a new word processing document.
2. Key the title (first line) and the list of topics exactly as shown on the right, including capitalization.
3. Save the Document as *urs*Ocean Water. Keep the file open for Project 1.

OCEAN WATER AND LIFE

WAVES AND TIDES
Waves
How waves move
How waves form
Tides
The gravitational pull of the moon
Spring and neap tides
Life in the intertidal zone
OCEAN CURRENTS
Definition of currents
Upwellings

SECTION 7.3 Create Newsletters

GOALS: Demonstrate the ability to:

- Format text in newspaper-style columns.
- Insert a column break.
- Format a newsletter with multiple columns and objects.
- Work from printed material.

WARMUP

Select Warmup from the Skillbuilding menu. Key each Warmup line 2 times.

Speed	1	You should always be honest with yourself about your goals.
Accuracy	2	David quickly put the frozen jars away in small gray boxes.
Numbers/Symbols	3	Two items (#20 & #21) were sold for $33 each--a great loss!
Language Link	4	Although Bill said it wasn't, Jason thought it was farther.

Making the Connection

Have you noticed that most newspapers are formatted into columns? Using columns allows you to display the text in a more interesting way. You will learn to design a new layout and to format the next publication of a student-council newsletter.

Your Turn

1. Open the file **7-3 Project 1**, and save the document as ***urs*Student Council Newsletter**.
2. Keep the file open for Project 1.

Sports and Happy Campers

If you want to try out for the team next year, we have a great suggestion! Consider joining a sports camp this summer. These camps are fun places where you can learn, practice, and play your favorite sport. You meet professional coaches and have lots of fun.

If you wonder how to find the sports camp that's right for you, talk to the coaches at your school. Search

PROJECT 1 Practice

Format Outlines

An **outline** begins with a title describing the subject of the outline. The main topics are the major points of the outline, and the subtopics are the minor points. You will continue creating the outline you began in Making the Connection, using the file ***urs*Ocean Water**.

Center the title, change the **font size** to 20 pt. and apply the **bold** format.

Level One Heading

Level Two Heading To indent, position the insertion point at the beginning of the line of text and press TAB 1 time.

Level Three Heading To indent, position the insertion point at the beginning of the line of text and press TAB 2 times.

Your Turn

1. Indent and edit the list of topics as shown below.

OCEAN WATER AND LIFE

WAVES AND TIDES
- Waves
  - How waves move
  - How waves form
- Tides
  - The gravitational pull of the moon
  - Spring and neap tides
- Life in the intertidal zone

OCEAN CURRENTS
- Definition of currents
- Upwellings

Continued on next page

Check Your Understanding

1. Open a new word processing document.
2. Key the answer to each question below using a complete sentence.
   a. List the drawing tools you used in this lesson.
   b. Describe some shapes you can create.
   c. What is the difference between a callout and a text box?
   d. What is the advantage of grouping objects?
3. Save the document as *urs*Shapes. Print and close the file.

interNET CONNECTION

In this lesson you created a visual timeline. There are many visual timelines published on the Web. The advantage to accessing an online timeline is that when you click on an image in the timeline, you may have access to a hyperlink. This provides details about what the image represents.

1. **Open your Web browser and search on the terms "image timelines" to find sites with visual timelines.**
2. **Find some sites where the images provide hyperlinks to more detailed information about the content of the timeline.**
3. **Conduct a focused search for timelines on any three of the following topics: inventions, transportation, climate, immigration, technology, fashion, music.**
4. **Create a word processing document, and list the best locations for the best timelines you found in your searches. Cite each source properly. Describe each site in one or two sentences. Conclude with a staement about when you would want to search for timelines in general and when to search for a specific kind of timeline.**

PROJECT 1 Continued

Practice

Format Outlines

2. Apply the **outline numbered list** feature. Choose an appropriate outline style. Your document should look similar to the one shown below, but your outline number style may differ.

OCEAN WATER AND LIFE

I. WAVES AND TIDES
    A. *Waves*
        1. How waves move
        2. How waves form
    B. *Tides*
        1. The gravitational pull of the moon
        2. Spring and neap tides
    C. *Life in the intertidal zone*
II. OCEAN CURRENTS
    A. *Definition of currents*
    B. *Surface currents*
    C. *Density currents*
    D. *Upwellings*

3. Add new topics to the outline:
    a. Position the insertion point at the end of the level two heading "Definition of currents."
    b. Press ENTER. A new paragraph formatted for a level two heading is inserted.
    c. Key Surface currents and press ENTER.
    d. Key Density currents.
4. Save the changes. Print and close the file.

PROJECT 4 **Reinforce**

Create a Timeline

Reinforce the desktop publishing features you learned by creating a timeline.

Your Turn

1. Open a new document. Change the margins to 1 inch.
2. Change the **page orientation** to landscape.
3. Create a timeline similar to the one shown below.

Order and group objects. Create the images with clip art, shapes, and callouts.

Insert a text box and use the Arrow tool to point to the timeline. **Fill** the text box with a **color**.

Create a table with 1 row and 5 columns. **Add shading** to the table cells.

Use the Line tool to draw lines above and below the table.

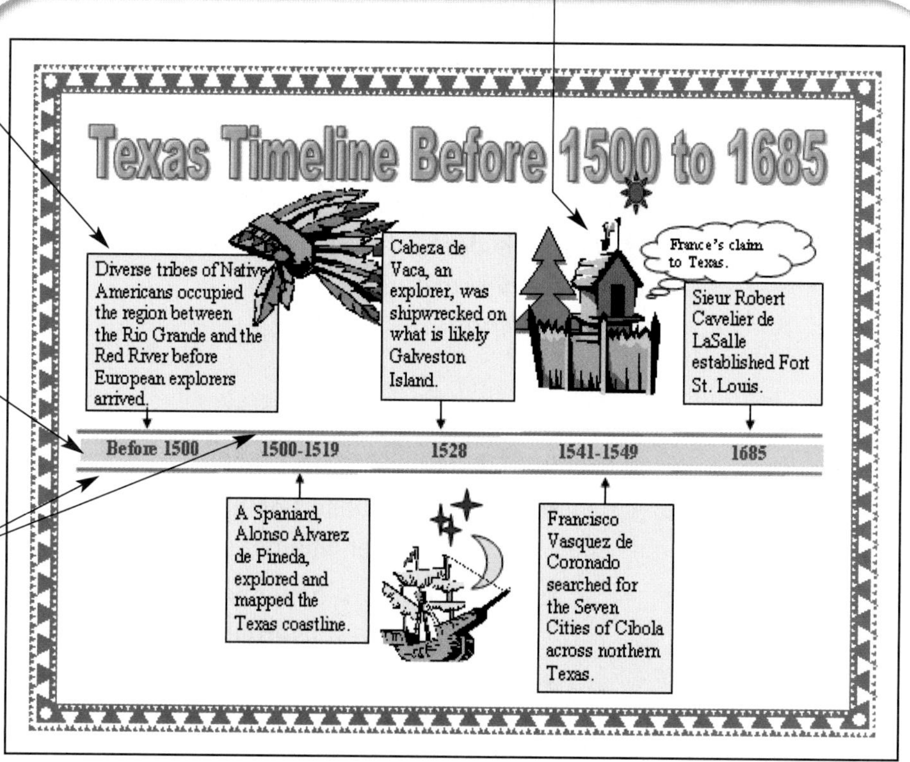

Texas Timeline Before 1500 to 1685
Diverse tribes of Native Americans occupied the region between the Rio Grande and the Red River before European explorers arrived.
Cabeza de Vaca, an explorer, was shipwrecked on what is likely Galveston Island.
France's claim to Texas.
Sieur Robert Cavelier de LaSalle established Fort St. Louis.
Before 1500
1500-1519
1528
1541-1549
1685
A Spaniard, Alonso Alvarez de Pineda, explored and mapped the Texas coastline.
Francisco Vasquez de Coronado searched for the Seven Cities of Cibola across northern Texas.

4. Save the document as *urs*Texas Timeline. Print and close the file.

PROJECT 2 **Reinforce**

Create an Outline

Your Turn

1. Open a new word processing document.
2. Key the outline illustrated below.

THE HUMAN BODY

BLOOD: THE TRANSPORTER OF LIFE
- Blood
  - Blood composition
  - Movement of blood
  - Plasma
- The Functions of Blood
- Plasma
- Constant Flow
  - Red blood cells

BLOOD: THE BODY'S DEFENSE
- Sealing the Leaks
- Natural Defense
- Specific Defenses
  - Active immunity
  - Vaccines
  - Passive immunity
- Communicable Diseases

3. Apply the outline numbered list feature. Choose an appropriate outline style.
4. Save the document as ***urs*Human Body**.
5. Position the insertion point after the level three heading "Red blood cells." Press ENTER and key the level three headings:

   Hemoglobin
   White blood cells
   Platelets

6. Save the changes. Print and close the file.

PROJECT 3 Practice

Group Objects

If you are working with multiple objects, you may find that it is often helpful to **group** objects. When you **group** objects, you create a single unit, making it easier to resize and position the objects.

A **callout**, which is similar to a text box, includes text as well as a leader that points to something on the page.

Your Turn

1. Add the objects illustrated and described below.

Create a callout. Key the text as indicated.

Insert an appropriate **clip art** image.

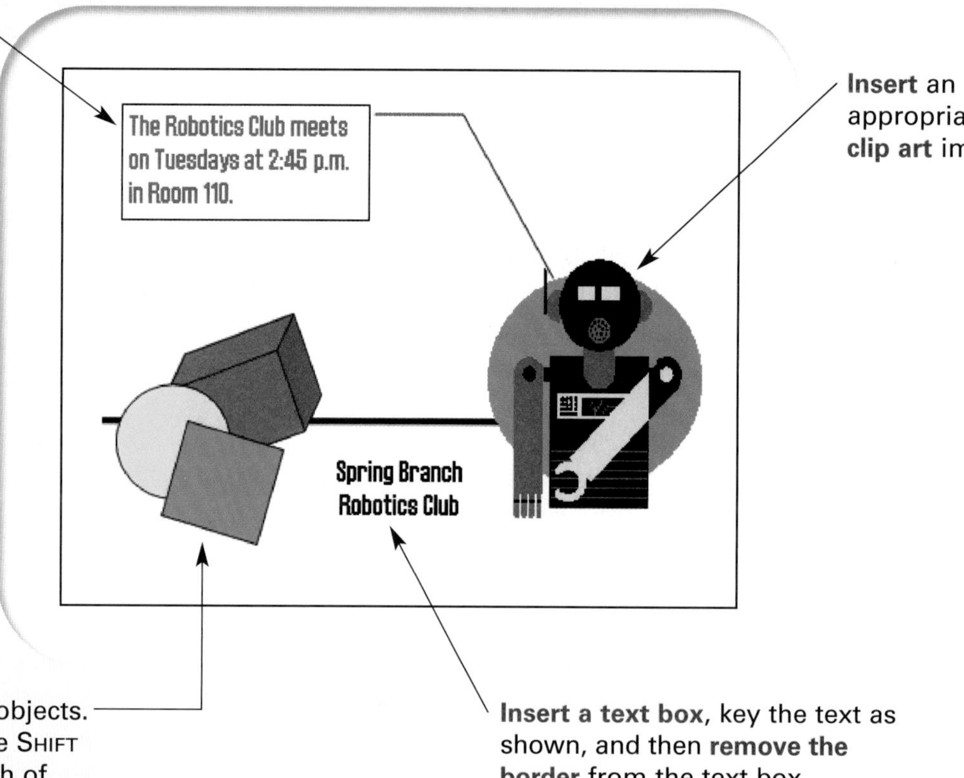
The Robotics Club meets on Tuesdays at 2:45 p.m. in Room 110.
Spring Branch Robotics Club

Resize the drawing objects. Then, hold down the SHIFT key and click on each of the remaining objects. When all of the objects are selected, **group the objects**.

Insert a text box, key the text as shown, and then **remove the border** from the text box.

2. Save the changes. Print and close the file.

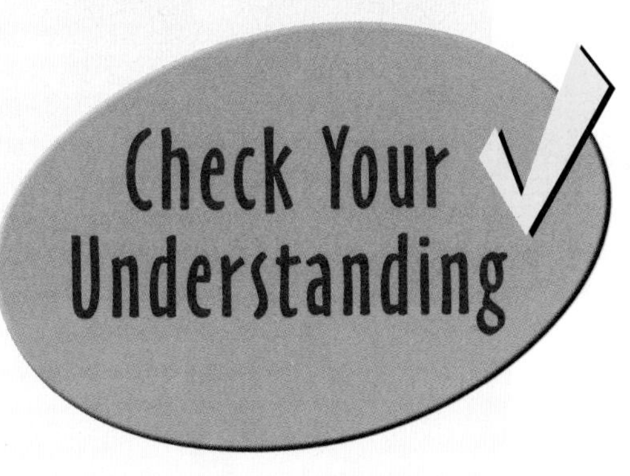

1. Open a new word processing document.
2. In your own words, describe the steps for creating an outline numbered list. Be sure to include directions on how to distinguish the heading levels in the outline.
3. Save the document as *urs*Outlinecheck. Print and close the file.

- Contact Us!
- Home Page
- Products
  - Orders
  - Samples
- Service
  - Customer Support
  - Technical Support
  - Downloads
  - Frequently Asked Questions
- Awards

*inter*NET CONNECTION

Many Web sites include a link to a site map.

1. **In your Internet browser's address box, key the URL address: http://www.usatoday.com.**
2. **Open a word processing document, and list the categories and features linked in the left navigation bar.**
3. **Scroll down to the bottom of the *USA Today* page to find a link to the site map. Click on this link to open the site map.**
4. **Notice the topics listed in the site map, and compare them to the topics listed in the navigation bar on the home page. Are the Web site topics displayed in an outline format? Add your observations to the word processing document. Save your changes. Print and close the file.**
5. **On your own: Create an outline numbered list to describe one of the categories for a search directory like http://www.yahooligans.yahoo.com.**

PROJECT 2 Practice

Position Objects

In this project you will use the drawing objects you created in Project 1 to complete a flyer.

You can change the arrangement or layer the objects by changing the order of the objects. For example, you can position an object in front of or behind another object. You can also rotate and flip objects.

Your Turn

1. Arrange the objects as shown.

Layer the objects.

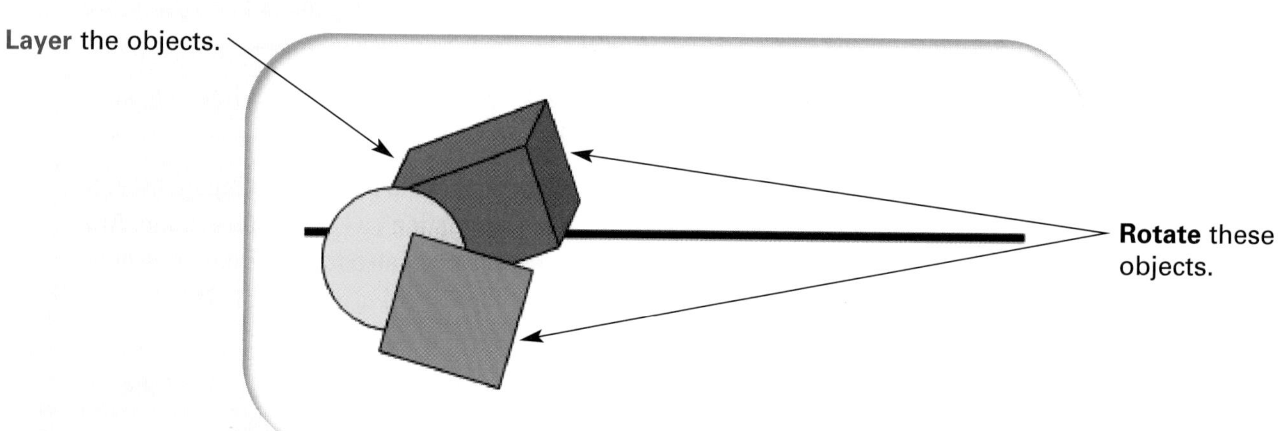

Rotate these objects.

Use the **nudge feature** to position the objects precisely.

2. Save the changes. Keep the file open for Project 3.

REVIEW SECTION 4

APPLY

Review Word Processing

You will apply the skills you have learned to create and format a document about bike trails.

Your Turn

1. Use CTRL + O to open the file **Sec4Review**, and save it as ***urs*Bike Trails**.
2. Edit and format the following document:

Bike Trails

We hope you enjoy the bike trails in our park ~~at any time~~. All trails are open from 5 A.M. to 10 P.M. No vehicles are permitted on the trails. For the safety of all, please obey the following rules.

Stay on the trail.
Keep to the right.
Wear protective head gear.

The park has bike trails for all ages and skill levels. The following information will help you choose a trail:

Create and format the table as shown. Remove the table borders.

Trail Name	Length of Trail	Trail Surface	Level of Difficulty
Cake Walk	6.2 miles	Paved	Easy
Mohican Trail	4.3 miles	Dirt	Easy
Tango	7.9 miles	Dirt	Moderate
Scorpion	12.8 miles	Paved	Moderate
Logger's Revenge	15.5 miles	Dirt	Challenging
Summit	7.6 miles	Dirt	Challenging

3. Spell-check, proofread, and correct errors.
4. Save the changes. Print and close the file.

PROJECT 1 Practice

Portrait Orientation

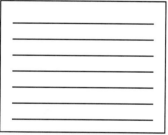

Landscape Orientation

Change Page Orientation and Create Objects Using Drawing Tools

Page orientation determines whether the page is displayed vertically or horizontally.

A variety of **drawing tools** is available for creating your own objects. You can customize the objects by changing the size and color. You can even change the way the objects display on the page by flipping and rotating them.

Your Turn

1. **Change the page orientation** to landscape.
2. Use the **drawing tools** to create the objects illustrated below. Use the Fill Color tool to change the color of the objects to the colors shown.

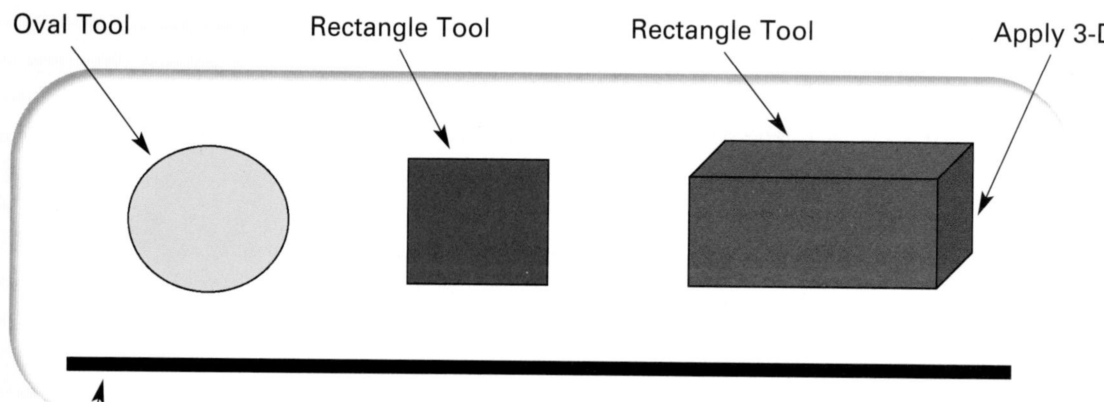

3. Save the document as ***urs*Robotics Flyer**. Keep the file open for Project 2.

COMPLETING SECTION 4

ENRICH

Curriculum Portfolio

Use the word processing skills you have learned to create your curriculum portfolio project. Choose from creating an outline, creating a table, or writing a descriptive paragraph.

If you choose to create an outline, each list contains three outline levels. The lists contain outline subtopics and supporting details. The headings are in the correct sequence for an outline.

Note: The outlines have three outline levels, and the subject for each outline is indicated above the list. Do not include the subject in the outline level headings.

SOCIAL STUDIES:

Create a table about state facts.

Pick five states you would like to know more about. Look up the information about the state flag, bird, motto, song, tree, and flower. Create a table to organize the data. Format the text in the table with appropriate headings and borders.

Continued on next page

SECTION 7.2 Design Pages With Drawing Tools

GOALS: Demonstrate the ability to:

- Change page orientation.
- Use drawing tools to create objects.
- Layer and group objects.
- Create callouts.

WARMUP

Select Warmup from the Skillbuilding menu. Key each Warmup line 2 times.

Speed	1	When the cat rests, it wants to lie down in the same place.
Accuracy	2	Jack was too lazy for the farm job; he proved quite vexing.
Numbers/Symbols	3	We will earn 12% more on #31 & #46 if they are sold @ $200.
Language Link	4	On Tuesday, it rained more than it did on Friday or Sunday.

Making the Connection

Sometimes content does not fit on the page. The page is simply not wide enough.

Instead of trying to reduce the content, think about how you can better utilize the space on the page. You might be able to solve the problem by changing the page layout.

The content is too wide for the page.

Your Turn

1. Open a new document, and change all the margins to 1 inch.
2. Keep the document open for Project 1.

ENRICH

Curriculum Portfolio

MATH:

Create an outline using the following title and list of topics:

COMMON WEIGHTS AND MEASURES
units of measure
weight and mass
pounds
ounces
grams
distance and length
miles
yards
feet
inches
time
days
hours
minutes
seconds
metric equivalents
meters
kilograms

LANGUAGE ARTS:

Write a descriptive paragraph.

You may have visited oceans, lakes, and rivers. Write a descriptive paragraph of your impressions of time spent by the water. Use a thesaurus to help you choose words that create a vivid picture.

SCIENCE:

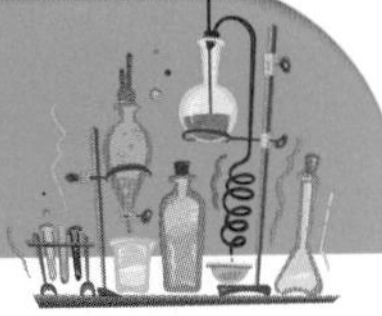

Create an outline using the following title and list of topics:

ENVIRONMENT
water
sources
lakes
streams
oceans
uses
keeps living creatures alive
helps plants grow
produces energy
air
global warming
the ozone layer
air quality

Check Your Understanding

1. Open a new word processing document.
2. Key the answer to each question below using complete sentences.
   a. What is the definition of an object in desktop publishing?
   b. List three or more examples of objects in desktop publishing.
   c. What is the purpose of a text box?
   d. What are the advantages to using a text box?
3. Save the document as **_urs_Objects**.
4. Print and close the file.

interNET CONNECTION

Oftentimes, you cannot find what you're looking for in your software's clip art gallery. As you know, you can find and download images from the Web. But how do you know you have permission to copy the image? Perhaps you have heard the term *public domain.* Items in the public domain can be used freely. This means anyone can copy and use the items as desired.

1. **Open your Web browser and search for sites that provide public domain images.**
2. **Bookmark the sites for future use.**
3. **In a word processing document, list four or five sites containing collections of public domain images that might prove useful in your schoolwork. Describe the contents of each site and tell how you would use them at school.**
4. **On your own: Use public domain images to create a set of greeting cards for friends or family. Create a birthday card, a get well card, and a congratulations card with the word processor.**

SECTION 5.1 Format a Personal Letter

GOALS: Demonstrate the ability to:

- Format a block-style letter.
- Format and print an envelope.
- Work from handwritten and printed material.
- Spell-check, proofread, and correct errors.

WARMUP

Select Warmup from the Skillbuilding menu. Key each Warmup line 2 times.

Speed	*1*	Janet works after school four hours a day at the town bank.
Accuracy	*2*	Buzz quickly designed five new projects for the wax museum.
Language Link	*3*	I waited for my best friend, and she was late getting here.
Numbers/Symbols	*4*	Interest charged on the $7,000 loan is 15% (down from 17%).

Making the Connection

You will learn how to key and format a personal letter. You have handwritten a letter to thank Mrs. Chavez for arranging a field trip for your class. Let's put your word processing skills to work.

Your Turn

1. Open a new word processing document.
2. Press ENTER 6 times and key the following:
3. 4112 Bay View Drive
   San Jose, CA 95192
   Today's Date
4. Save the document as *urs*Chavez Letter. Keep the file open for Project 1.

PROJECT 2 **Reinforce**

Create a Title Page

Reinforce the desktop publishing features you learned by creating another title page.

Your Turn

1. Open a new document, and change all the margins to 1 inch.
2. Create a title page similar to the one illustrated below.

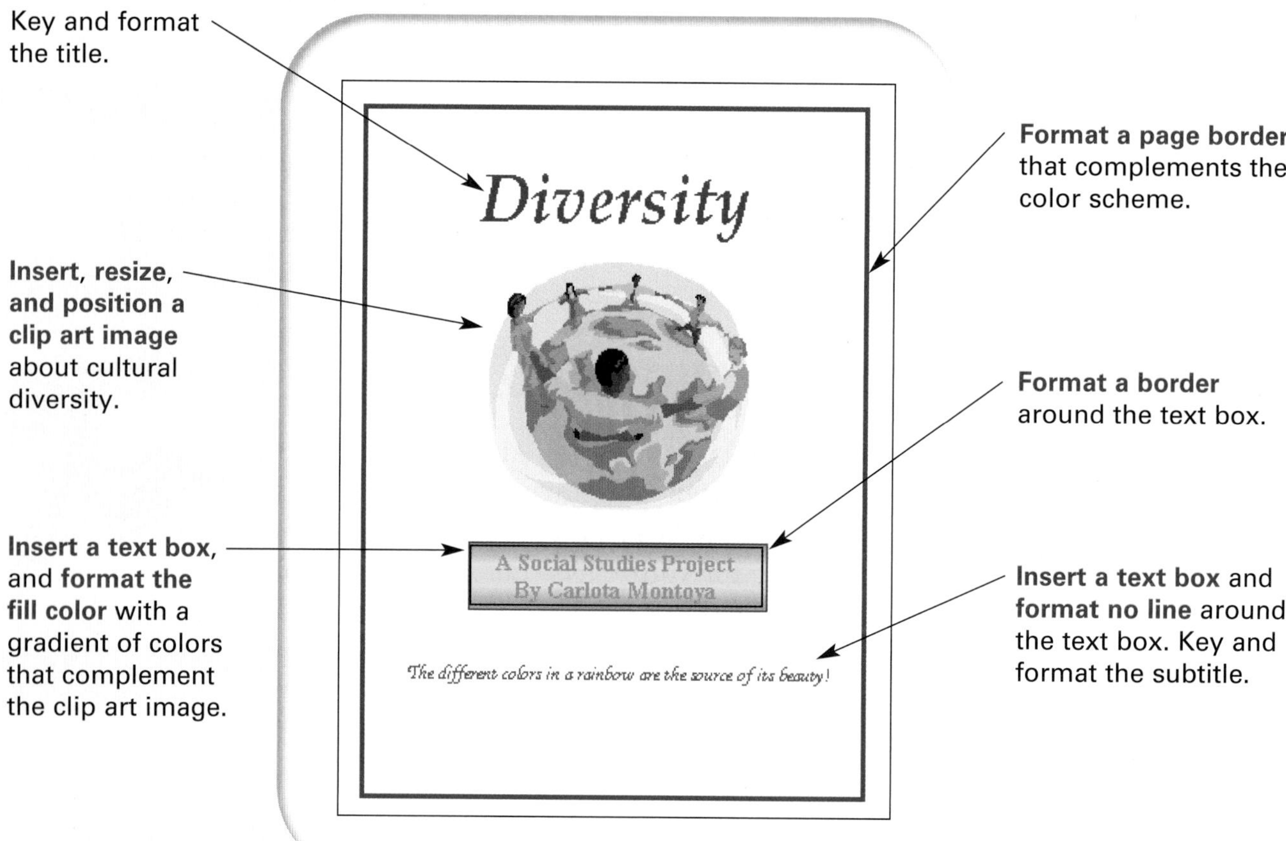

Key and format the title.
Insert, resize, and position a clip art image about cultural diversity.
Insert a text box, and format the fill color with a gradient of colors that complement the clip art image.
Format a page border that complements the color scheme.
Format a border around the text box.
Insert a text box and format no line around the text box. Key and format the subtitle.
Diversity
A Social Studies Project
By Carlota Montoya
The different colors in a rainbow are the source of its beauty!

3. Save the document as *urs*Diversity Title Page. Print and close the file.

PROJECT 1 Practice

Format a Block-Style Letter

A personal letter is a printed message addressed to a person or an organization. The parts of the letter are identified in the illustration below. In the **block-style** format, all paragraphs are positioned at the left margin.

Your Turn

1. Key and format the personal letter shown below using block style.

Return Address
Address of the writer.

4112 Bay View Drive
San Jose, CA 95192

Date
Date the letter was written.

Today's Date

Press ENTER 4 times.

Inside Address
Name and address of the person to whom you are writing.

Ms. Maria Chavez
1021 West Palm Blvd.
San Jose, CA 95192

Salutation
Usually the word *Dear* followed by the name of the person to whom you are writing.

Dear Mrs. Chavez:

Body
Text of the letter.

I wanted to thank you for taking our class on a field trip to the Mathematics, Engineering, and Science Achievement Program at San Jose State University. I know it is a lot of work to make all the arrangements for a trip like this, especially making sure that we are all safe, have enough to eat, and arrive everywhere on time.

Continued on next page

PROJECT 1 Practice

Create a Title Page With Enhanced Pictures and Objects

Clip art, pictures, and drawings are **objects**. You can move objects any place you choose on your page. A **textbox** is an object that holds text.

Your Turn

1. Change the margins to 1 inch, and create a title page similar to the one shown below.

Volcanoes

A Science Fair Project
By Amy O'Farrell

Format a page border. Choose a color and line style.

Format the report title with a font style, font size, and color.

Insert a clip art image for volcanoes. **Resize the graphic** as needed, and **position the graphic** on the page.

Create a text box to hold the text shown here.

Select the text box, and **add a fill color** and **shadow style**.

2. Save the changes. Print and close the file.

PROJECT 1 Continued

Practice

Format a Block-Style Letter

Body
Text of the letter.

I never thought about majoring in math and science in college, but now I think that is what I want to do. I really like the idea of being able to earn a scholarship to a MESA summer camp. I love spending time on my computer, and I want to try to compete for this scholarship.

The counselor said that part of the camp would be spent panning for gold in the American River! Maybe next year we can go to another great spot! Thank you again for opening up a whole new world to me.

Closing
Final words of the letter, followed by a comma.

Sincerely,

Press ENTER 4 times.

Your Name

2. Identify the parts of a personal letter to be sure you have included each part.

3. Save the changes. Keep the file open for Project 2.

Design Pages With Pictures and Objects

GOALS: Demonstrate the ability to:

- Format and add borders.
- Create text boxes.
- Add fill colors to text boxes.
- Create and format art objects.

WARMUP

Select Warmup from the Skillbuilding menu. Key each Warmup line 2 times.

Speed	1	We know that a good thing to do is to rest and read a book.
Accuracy	2	The lazy judge was very quick to pay tax money for the box.
Numbers/Symbols	3	Lee & Lou and Nate & Nat paid for 534# of #80 tape @ $1.28.
Language Link	4	Kia understands that the classroom rules apply to everyone.

Making the Connection

After you work hard to compose and format a report, you want to make sure your report is read. Let's explore what you can do to enhance the appearance of the report and create some memorable images that will attract interest.

Your Turn

1. Open a new word processing document.
2. Key the title Volcanoes.
3. Save the document as *urs*Volcanoes Title Page. Keep the file open for Project 1.

Volcanoes

PROJECT 2 Practice

Format an Envelope

Your word processing software will help you create an envelope. Format a return address unless your envelope has a preprinted return address.

Your Turn

1. **Create** a size $6\frac{3}{4}$ **envelope** for the letter you completed in Project 1.

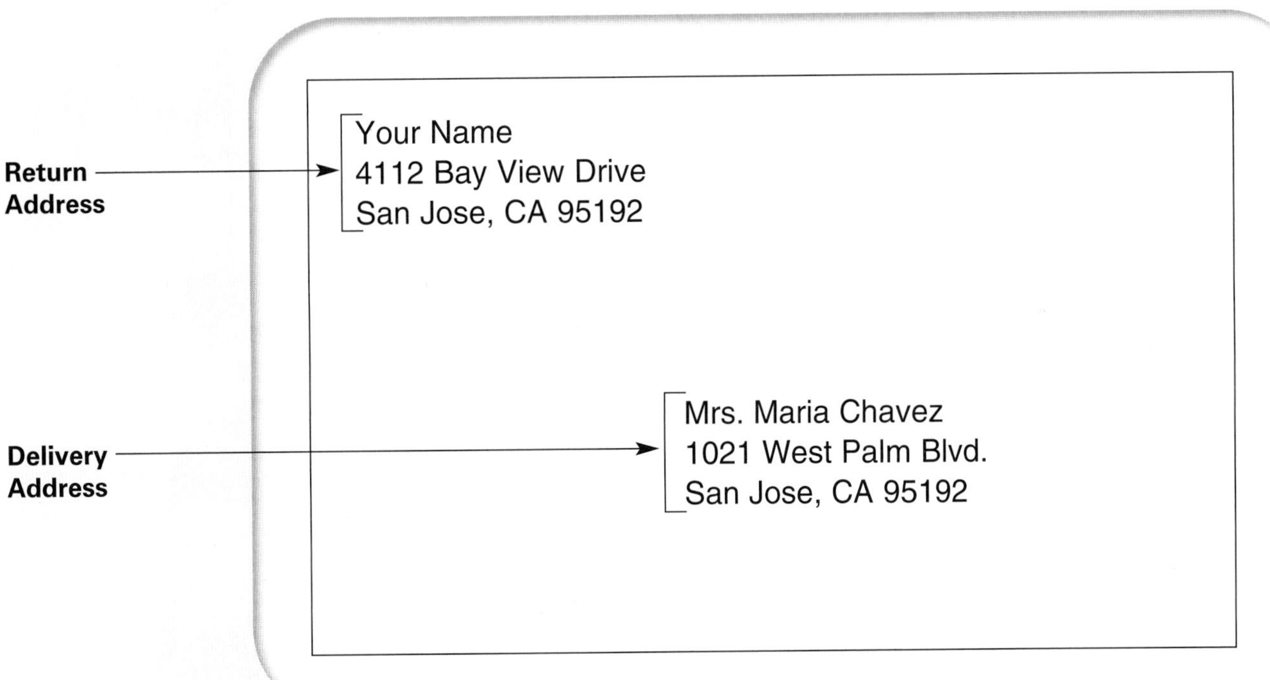

Return Address
Your Name
4112 Bay View Drive
San Jose, CA 95192
Delivery Address
Mrs. Maria Chavez
1021 West Palm Blvd.
San Jose, CA 95192

2. Print the envelope. Close the file.

Focus On

Good Keyboarding Habits

Focus on your arms and elbows.
Keep your arms and elbows:

- **So that your arms move your hands.**

- **At a 90-degree angle.**

- **Close to your sides.**

PROJECT 3 Reinforce

Format a Personal Letter With Envelope

Your Turn

1. Key and format the letter below in block-style as shown.

4112 Bay View Drive
San Jose, CA 95192
Today's Date

Mr. Ron Ashton
321 Park Avenue
San Jose, CA 95192

Dear Ron:

It was great meeting you during our class field trip to the Mathematics, Engineering, and Science Achievement Program at San Jose State University.

I am very interested in competing for the scholarship to the summer camp. Since the counselor said that we could have several people on the team, I was wondering if you would be interested in being on a team that I am organizing. There will be a total of four of us, and I think we would have a great chance at winning the scholarship.

Continued on next page

UNIT 5 Desktop Publishing

GOALS:

- Use draw tools to create text boxes, lines, and shapes.
- Use draw tools to layer and group objects.
- Format text into columns.
- Create a Web page from a template.
- Create hyper-links to navigate in a Web page.
- Apply a theme to a Web page.

PROJECT 3 Continued

Reinforce

Format a Personal Letter With Envelope

If you are interested, please call me at 805-555-3496.
I am looking forward to hearing from you.

Your friend,

Your Name

2. Change the font style to give your letter a personal touch.
3. Save the document as ***urs*Ron's Letter**.
4. Spell-check, proofread, and correct errors. Save the changes.
5. Print the letter and envelope. Close the file.

ENRICH

Curriculum Portfolio

MATH:

Research and report on metrics.

In the United States, we use the English system of measurement. However, most other countries of the world use the metric system.

Research the history and important dates in the chronology of the metric system. Write a report about your findings. Provide examples of why people must understand both systems, regardless of where they live. Include in your report if and when you think the United States will convert to the metric system of measurement.

LANGUAGE ARTS:

Compose a report about school dress codes.

Do you think your school should have a dress code? Now is your chance to voice your opinions to the school administration and the parent/teacher organization. Research the topic to find at least three credible sources that support your position on the issue.

Write a persuasive report that explains your views and your personal concerns. Provide facts to support your reasoning. Remember to keep your audience in mind as you write your report.

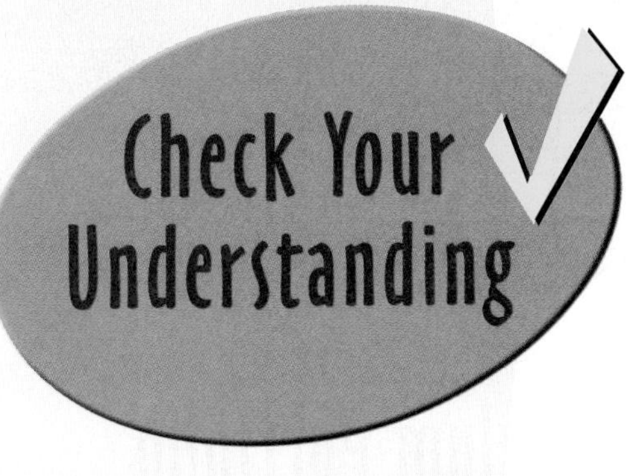

1. Open a new word processing document.
2. List the parts of a personal letter.
3. What information is included in the salutation of a personal letter?
4. What information is included in the closing of a personal letter?
5. Describe the formatting for a block-style letter.
6. Save the document as *urs*Letter Parts. Print and close the file.

interNET CONNECTION

1. **Open your Web browser and search for information on "spoken and written forms of address." Find the appropriate salutation you would use if you were to write a personal letter to the following individuals:**
   - **Governor of your state**
   - **President of the United States**
   - **Foreign ambassador**
   - **Judge**
   - **King or queen**
2. **Open a word processing document and create a two-column table. In the first column, key the names of the individuals listed above. In the second column, key the appropriate salutation for each.**
3. **Save the document as *urs*Salutation. Print and close the file.**
4. **On your own: Search for examples of letters available online to compare their salutations to the ones you found in Step 1. Search for letters from the Civil War or other soldiers, letters to newspaper or magazine editors, letters from presidents, from scientists, or from children to Eleanor Roosevelt during the Great Depression. Create a time line and show when each letter was written. Indicate whether the greeting was formal or informal. See if there is a relationship between when it was written and the degree of formality. Write a short paragraph describing what you learned in the research.**

COMPLETING UNIT 4

ENRICH

Curriculum Portfolio

Compose and format a multi-page report on one of the following topics. You can choose to format the report in MLA style or in another style. Be sure to cite your sources and provide a list of your sources at the end of the document. Use side headings to identify the main topics in your report. Your report should include a table of contents. Proofread your work carefully, and save the document with an appropriate filename. Print the documents.

SCIENCE:

Compose a report.

Earthquakes and volcanoes are among the most powerful and frightening types of change on Earth. They can cause massive damage. Still, we are often fascinated by them. Research the causes and effects of earthquakes and volcanoes.

Write a report on your findings. Explain what happens during an earthquake, and identify the locations of major earthquake and volcanic zones. Identify the three types of volcanoes, and explain what conditions might cause an eruption. Discuss the role geologists play in measuring earthquakes, collecting data, and predicting future earthquakes. You may also want to discuss some of the major earthquakes and volcanoes during the last few decades.

SOCIAL STUDIES:

Write a biographical report.

Choose an important person from the twentieth century who is no longer living. The person can be a hero or a famous person. Research and gather information about the person's childhood, education, career, and significant influences and/or contributions.

Write a biographical report about the person. Include in your report why you would have liked to meet that person.

Continued on next page

Format a Business Letter With Envelope

GOALS: Demonstrate the ability to:

- Format a business letter with letterhead.
- Format a return address and an enclosure notation.
- Key from printed copy.
- Spell-check, proofread, and correct errors.
- Compose at the keyboard.

WARMUP

Select Warmup from the Skillbuilding menu. Key each Warmup line 2 times.

Speed	1	I feel sure he will be here in time to drive the boys home.
Accuracy	2	Six jumped from the quarry blaze, right into Lake Cragview.
Language Link	3	Club dues must be paid now; however, you can pay next week.
Numbers/Symbols	4	Ryan saw Jack's dog's leash on Tim's brother's front porch.

Making the Connection

A business letter should have a formal rather than a casual tone. You will learn to format a business letter. To dress up the letter and to make it more formal, you format it in a standard business-letter style.

Your Turn

1. Open the file **5-2 Project 1**. This file contains a formatted letterhead.
2. Save the file as *urs***Computer Donation Letter**.
3. Keep the file open for Project 1.

6021 Brobeck Street • Flint, MI 48532
Phone: 810-555-9001 • Fax: 810-555-9004

REVIEW Continued

APPLY

Review Project

c. Create an appropriate header for all pages.

4. Position the insertion point at the end of the document and copy and paste the contents of the file **Sec6Review**.
5. Find the word "snow" and replace it with the word "hail."
6. Spell-check, proofread, and correct errors. Save the changes.
7. Insert a new page at the end of the document, and create a Works Cited page using the information provided below.

Works Cited

Brain, Marshall and Freudenrich, Craig C., Ph.D. *HowStuffWorks*. "How Hurricanes Work." 29 April 2002. <http://www.howstuffworks.com/hurricane2.htm>.

Moran, Joseph M. "Weather." *The World Book Encyclopedia 2002.* Chicago: World Book, Inc., Vol. 21, p. 156.

Palmer, Chad. *USA TODAY*. "More About Thunderstorms." 29 April 2002. <http://www.usatoday.com/weather/tg/wtsmwhat/wtsmwha1.htm>.

Williams, Jack. *USA TODAY Latest News*. "Ground, Upper-Air Combine for Tornadoes." 29 April 2002. <http://www.usatoday.com/weather/wtwist1.htm>.

WW2010 University of Illinois. "Air Masses: Uniform Bodies of Air." 29 April 2002. <http://ww2010.atmos.uiuc.edu/(Gh)/guides/mtr/af/arms/home.rxml>.

8. Open your Web browser and search for information about the costliest hurricanes in the United States. Add some information about the hurricane costs to the report under the heading *Tropical Storms and Hurricanes*. Be sure to cite your source(s) appropriately. Don't forget to add the source(s) to the Works Cited page.
9. Save the changes. Print and close the file.

PROJECT 1 Practice

Format a Business Letter in Block Style With Enclosure Notation

As you can see in the illustration below, a business letter has more parts than a personal letter.

Your Turn

1. The document you opened contains a preformatted letterhead.
2. Key and format the letter shown below.

Letterhead
The name, address, and other information about the sender.

6021 Brobeck Street • Flint, MI 48532
Phone: 810-555-9001 • Fax: 810-555-9004

Press ENTER 2–4 times.

Date
Date the letter was written.

Today's Date

Press ENTER 4 times.

Inside Address
Name and address of the person to whom you are writing.

Mr. Anthony Martinez
Cyber Foundation
4092 Barnes Avenue
Burton, MI 48529

Salutation
Usually the word *Dear* followed by the name of the person to whom you are writing and a colon.

Dear Mr. Martinez:

Body
Text of the letter.

My friends and I at Lincoln School want to help your organization.

Our district is replacing our computers with new ones. Our computer technology teacher Mrs. Jones explained that your

Continued on next page

APPLY

Review Project

Thunderstorms

Thunderstorms are formed by the rapid upward movement of warm, humid air. As the warm, moist air is forced upward, it cools and its water vapor condenses, forming cumulus clouds. Water droplets form in the clouds and begin falling. As the droplets fall through the clouds, they collide with other droplets and become larger. Sometimes, though, the raindrops evaporate and never reach the ground.

As the thunderstorm grows, electrical charges build up in the clouds. They connect with charged particles on the ground below and complete an electrical circuit. That's when we see a bright flash of lightning. The rapid heating of the air around a lightning bolt generates shockwaves. These shockwaves become soundwaves as they travel through the air. This is how thunder is produced.

Heavy rains from thunderstorms sometimes cause flooding and mudslides. Lightning can strike trees and other objects, setting them on fire, and lightning can electrocute people and animals. Strong winds can also cause damage.

These storms often contain large hailstones that can dent cars or destroy crops in a matter of minutes. Hail forms when strong currents rise up and carry water droplets above the freezing level into the thunderstorms. The water freezes into ice. Often the hail melts before it reaches the ground, but sometimes chunks of ice the size of softballs come to the ground (Palmer).

2. Save the document as ***urs*Wild Weather**.
3. Format the report.
   a. Use your name and today's date in the heading on the first page. The teacher's name is Mr. Tiemann, and the class name is Science.
   b. Adjust the margins for a bound report.

Continued on next page

PROJECT 1 Continued

Practice

Format a Business Letter in Block Style With Enclosure Notation

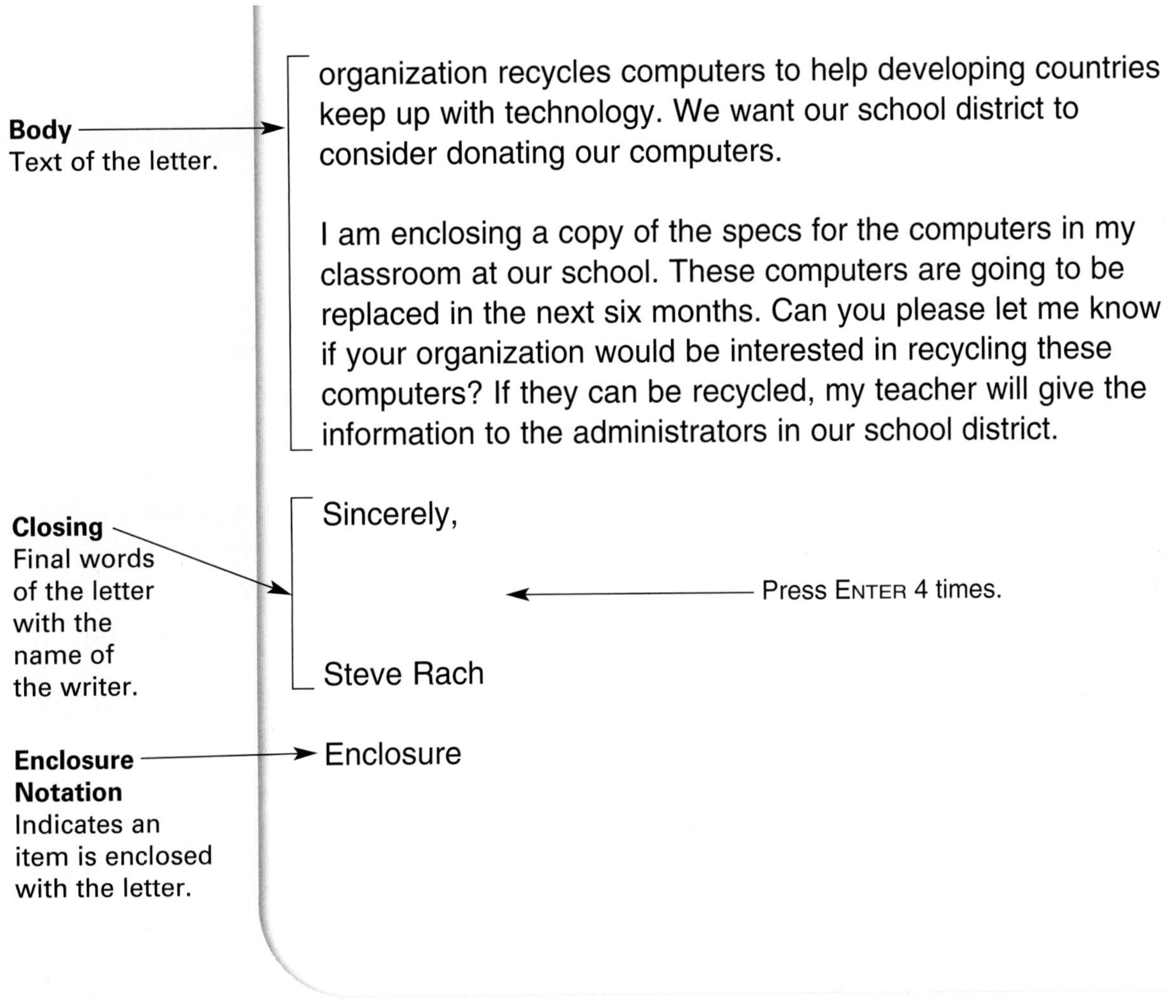
Body Text of the letter.

organization recycles computers to help developing countries keep up with technology. We want our school district to consider donating our computers.

I am enclosing a copy of the specs for the computers in my classroom at our school. These computers are going to be replaced in the next six months. Can you please let me know if your organization would be interested in recycling these computers? If they can be recycled, my teacher will give the information to the administrators in our school district.

Closing Final words of the letter with the name of the writer.

Sincerely,

Press ENTER 4 times.

Steve Rach

Enclosure Notation Indicates an item is enclosed with the letter.

Enclosure

3. Spell-check, proofread, and correct errors.
4. Save the changes to the file.
5. Print the file. Keep the file open for Project 2.

REVIEW SECTION 6

Apply

Review Project

In this project, you will apply the word processing skills you have learned to create and format a multipage report. Refer to previous projects as needed.

Your Turn

1. Open a new word processing document. Key the report shown below and on the next page.

Wild Weather

"Weather is the state of the atmosphere at some place and time." (Moran 156). Weather is important to us, each and every one of us every day. For example, we decide what clothes to wear based on the weather, and our outdoor activities are planned around the seasons and the daily forecasts. Even during warm-weather seasons, however, the weather conditions can be severe. Sometimes temperatures reach record highs, and utility companies must supply more power for air conditioning. Or high winds and storms damage trees and power lines. So I was wondering what causes the weather to go wild. Here's what I learned.

Air Masses

An air mass is a large body of air where all the air has about the same temperature and humidity. Air masses can be very cold, very hot, very dry, or very wet. An air mass that develops over land is dry compared with one that develops over water. An air mass that develops near the equator is warmer than one that develops at a higher latitude.

Air masses move and swirl over the surface of Earth. As the air mass moves, its temperature and humidity can change because of the ground conditions below. Because they move in different directions and at different speeds, they often bump into each other. Rain, thunderstorms, snow, tornadoes--all of these weather-related events can result when air masses meet (WW2010 University of Illinois).

Continued on next page

PROJECT 2 Practice

Format a Business Envelope

Your word processing software will help you create a business envelope. If your envelope has a preprinted return address, or if you plan to apply a preprinted return address label, you don't need to format a return address on the envelope.

Your Turn

1. **Create** a size 10 **envelope** for the letter you completed in Project 1.

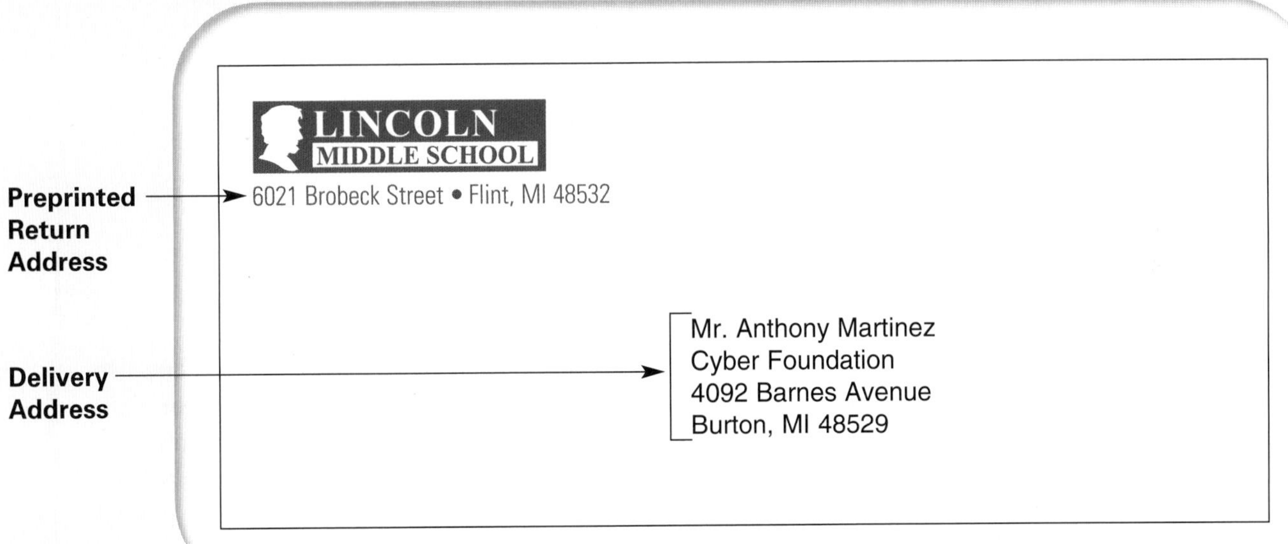

LINCOLN
MIDDLE SCHOOL
6021 Brobeck Street • Flint, MI 48532
Preprinted Return Address
Mr. Anthony Martinez
Cyber Foundation
4092 Barnes Avenue
Burton, MI 48529
Delivery Address

2. Print the envelope. Close the file.

Check Your Understanding

1. Open a new word processing document.
2. Key the answer to each question, using a complete sentence.
3. What is the purpose of a table of contents? What type of information is contained in a table of contents?
4. What are dot leaders, and what is their purpose?
5. Save the file as *urs*Table of Contents. Print and close the file.

*inter*NET CONNECTION

Visitors to Web sites can also find tools to help them find information within the site. Many times, the home page of a Web site provides links to the site's main topics. When you click on the hyperlink for a main topic, a list of subtopics is displayed. The list serves the same purpose as a table of contents, but hyperlinks eliminate the need for page numbers.

1. **Open your Web browser. Visit four of the sites listed below.**
   a. **Library of Congress** http://www.loc.gov/
   b. **NASA** http://www.nasa.gov/
   c. **National Geographic** http://www.nationalgeographic.com/
   d. **National Wildlife Federation** http://www.enature.com/
   e. **Ocean.com** http://www.ocean.com/
   f. **Rainforest Action Network** http://www.ran.org/
   g. **The Olympics** http://www.olympic.org/
2. **Create a table in a word processing document with 5 rows and 5 columns. Use the top row for headers and the others for information about the sites you visit. Make the column for the Web site name big, but the other columns small.**
3. **Make X's in the table to show how the contents of each site are presented. Is there a table of contents? A site map? Links to main topics? A site search tool?**
4. **Save the document as *urs*Web Contents. Print and close the file.**

PROJECT 3

Practice

Format a Business Letter With a Return Address

If you are not printing your letter on letterhead stationery, you will want to include your mailing address at the top of the letter, just above the dateline. That way the person who receives the letter will know how to contact you.

Your Turn

1. Key and format the letter shown below using block style.

← Press ENTER 6 times.

Route 14, Denman Road
Lexington, OH 44904
Today's Date

← Press ENTER 4 times.

Mrs. Celia Wingler, Principal
East Elementary School
123 Yorkshire Road
Lexington, OH 44904

Dear Mrs. Wingler:

Hi, Mrs. Wingler. Maybe you remember me. I used to attend East Elementary.

Continued on next page

PROJECT 2 Continued

Reinforce

Creating a Table of Contents

2. Open the file **6-6 Project 2.** Locate each heading, and enter the appropriate page numbers in the table of contents. Align the page numbers at the right side of the page with dot leaders. Close the report document without saving any changes.
3. Save the table of contents as ***urs*Rockets TOC**.
4. Spell-check, proofread, and correct errors. Print and close the file.

PROJECT 3 Continued

Practice

Format a Business Letter With a Return Address

I really enjoy working with small children, and I would like to volunteer at your school to work with kindergarten and first grade students. I can read to them and listen to them read. I can also help the teacher with activities in the classroom. I would also like to assist Mrs. Karnes in the media center if I can be of some help there.

I am available to help on Mondays and Wednesdays. My school day ends at 2:30 and I can be at your school by 2:45 p.m. That means I could be there for the last hour of your school day.

Please call me at 555-8807 and let me know if I may volunteer in one of your classrooms or in the media center.

Sincerely,

← Press ENTER 4 times.

Caitie O'Neil

2. Identify the parts of a business letter to be sure you have included each part.
3. Save the document as *urs***Volunteer Letter**.
4. Spell-check, proofread, and correct errors. Save the changes.
5. Print the letter and an envelope. Close the file.

PROJECT 2 Reinforce

Create a Table of Contents

Reinforce the word processing features you learned by creating another table of contents.

Your Turn

1. Open a new word processing document and create a table of contents using the information illustrated below.

Change the left and right **margins** to 1 inch.

CONTENTS

INTRODUCTION
HISTORY OF ROCKETING
RESEARCH
Newton's Laws
Kinetic and Potential Energy
Mass and Velocity
THE ROCKET MODEL
Building the Rocket
Testing the Rocket
Rebuilding the Rocket
Safety Tips
APPLICATION
BIBLIOGRAPHY

Continued on next page

PROJECT 4 **Reinforce**

Format a Business Letter With a Return Address

Reinforce the word processing features you learned by keying and formatting another business letter with a return address, an enclosure notation, and an envelope.

Your Turn

1. Open the file **5-2 Project 4**, and save the document as ***urs*Complaint Letter**.
2. Edit the body of the letter using proofreaders' marks as shown.

Add the letter parts shown.

5419 Mirra Loma Drive
Reno, NV 89502
Today's Date

Mainstream Music, Inc.
270 Clara Street
San Francisco, CA 94107

Ladies and Gentlemen:

About ~~a month~~ four weeks ago, I mailed you an order for a DVD movie package. I ~~ordered~~ purchased DVD package #41-809 from page 5 of your catalog. The total cost of the DVD package with shipping and handling was $47.35.

Continued on next page

PROJECT 1 Practice

Create a Table of Contents

A **table of contents** is a listing of all the main topic headings and subtopic headings. A table of contents is generally used only for long reports. Sometimes, dot leaders (periods) are used to guide the reader's eyes from the section headings to the page numbers.

Your Turn

1. Complete the table of contents page by entering and formatting the information shown below.

Change the left and right **margins** to one inch.

Format a right-aligned **tab stop with leaders.** Set the tab stop at the right margin.

CONTENTS

2. Save the changes.
3. Spell-check, proofread, and correct errors. Print and close the file.

Reinforce

Format a Business Letter With a Return Address

Today, I saw a package at my door, I was so excited that my order package had finally arrived. But I was really disappointed when I opened it and saw that you sent me the wrong DVDs.

I am returning the DVD package with this letter and I am enclosing the order return form. I am asking for a full refund of $47.35. And I also want to be reimbursed for the $5.00 it cost me to ship the DVD package back to you. Please send the refund to me at the above address.

Sincerely,

Martine Pico

Enclosure

Add the closing letter parts shown.

3. Identify the parts of a business letter to be sure you have included each part.
4. Spell-check, proofread, and correct errors.
5. Save the changes. Print the file.
6. Create and print an envelope. Be sure to include the return address on the envelope. Close the file.

Table of Contents

GOALS: Demonstrate the ability to:

- Key and format a table of contents.
- Format a tab stop with dot leaders.
- Spell-check, proofread, and correct errors.

WARMUP

Select Warmup from the Skillbuilding menu. Key each Warmup line 2 times.

Speed	1	It was a good idea to start to write your report this week.
Accuracy	2	My ax just zipped through the fine black wood quite evenly.
Symbols	3	What a sight! Good luck! Watch out! At last! No way! Never!
Language Link	4	The accident was distressing; however, no one was impaired.

Making the Connection

Many newspapers provide a directory (often labeled *Index*) at the bottom of the front page of the newspaper. The directory provides an overview of the sections and topics covered in the newspaper, and it shows the page numbers for those sections and topics.

If you have a long report with several pages, you can provide a directory of the contents to help your readers identify the main ideas in your report and find information.

CONTENTS

INTRODUCTION	1
PROBLEM	1
HYPOTHESIS	1
RESEARCH	2
THE EXPERIMENT	5
Materials	5
Procedures	5
Results	7
CONCLUSION	8
BIBLIOGRAPHY	9

Your Turn

1. Open a new word processing document.
2. Key, center, and bold the title CONTENTS. Then press ENTER 2 times.
3. Save the document as *urs*Yogurt TOC.
4. Keep the file open for Project 1.

Check Your Understanding

1. Open a new word processing document.
2. Describe how a business letter differs from a personal letter.
3. Explain why your return address is included at the top of a business letter.
4. Explain the purpose of an enclosure notation.
5. Save the document as *urs*Letterinfo. Print and close the file.

interNET CONNECTION

In this lesson you learned to format a business letter to be mailed within the United States. What if your letter were to be mailed outside of the United States? What information would you need to include on the envelope? Would you need to format the envelope differently?

1. **Open your Web browser and search for information on how to address envelopes for international addresses properly. Choose an international location.**
2. **Open a new word processing document and key an example of the inside address you would create for the letter. Then add any additional information that should be included on the envelope.**
3. **Save the document as *urs*International Addresses. Print and close the file.**

Write On!

1. Open your journal and position the insertion point at the end of the document. Enter today's date to create a new journal entry.
2. Write at least one paragraph about a formal event that you have attended or wish you could attend (a wedding, an awards banquet, or a social event in your community). Describe how you would dress for the event and the proper etiquette that would be expected of you.
3. Save the changes to your journal. Close the file.

Check Your Understanding

1. Open a new word processing document.
2. What is the difference between a direct quotation and a paraphrase?
3. What is the difference between a footnote and an endnote?
4. Describe the process for converting footnotes to endnotes.
5. Save the file as *urs*Footnotes. Print and close the file.

Write On!

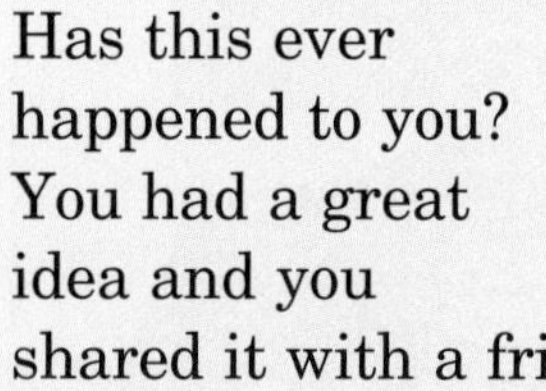

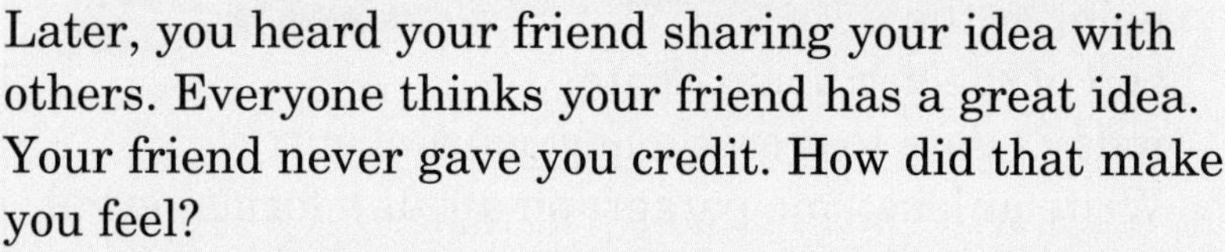

Has this ever happened to you? You had a great idea and you shared it with a friend. Later, you heard your friend sharing your idea with others. Everyone thinks your friend has a great idea. Your friend never gave you credit. How did that make you feel?

1. Open your journal and position the insertion point at the end of the document. Enter today's date to create a new journal entry.
2. Write at least one paragraph about how you did (or would) feel if someone used your ideas as his or her own and did not give you credit.
3. Save the changes to your journal. Close the file.

interNET CONNECTION

Most people realize that when they quote the work of another, they must cite the source. But did you realize that you must also cite the source if you paraphrase or summarize another person's work? If you don't cite your source, you are guilty of not giving people credit for their work.

1. **Open your Web browser and search for an online dictionary.**
2. **Find the definition for the term "plagiarism."**
3. **Open a word processing document. In your own words, define *plagiarism*. Then explain why it is important to give credit to others for their words and ideas.**
4. **Do a search on plagiarism to find recent examples of reporters or authors who have been accused of plagiarism. List the names of the people you located.**
5. **Save the document as *urs*Plagiarism. Print and close the file.**

SECTION 5.3 Format an E-Mail Message

GOALS: Demonstrate the ability to:

- Format an e-mail message.
- Attach a document to an e-mail message.
- Key from printed copy.
- Spell-check, proofread, and correct errors.
- Compose at the keyboard.

WARMUP

Select Warmup from the Skillbuilding menu. Key each Warmup line 2 times.

Speed	1	Building typing skill seems easier if you type short words.
Accuracy	2	Maxine will become eloquent over a zany gift like jodhpurs.
Language Link	3	Evi went to math, history, and art; but she missed English.
Numbers/Symbols	4	She decided that 1/3 of $36 = $12 and that 20% of $30 = $6.

Making the Connection

Keith and his classmates correspond with pen pals regularly about a variety of topics. Generally, the pen pals communicate via e-mail, so they like to call themselves key pals! This month Keith is contacting his key pal to collect data so the class can compare the prices of pizza.

Your Turn

1. Open **5-3 Project 1**. Notice that the document contains a table for collecting data about the prices of pizza.
2. Close the file without making any changes.

From:	
To:	J_Jaimeson@Hartland.k12.ak.us.edu

PROJECT 3 Continued

Reinforce

Format Footnotes and Endnotes

7. Locate the second paragraph on Mass and Velocity and add the endnote shown below.

The velocity is the speed and direction of motion. The speed is determined by the power of the engine. The direction will be the angle of the launch rod unless there is wind. The wind can change the direction of the rocket after it is launched. The velocity affects how stable the rocket is in the air.

Insert a footnote for paraphrased material:
Brain, Marshall. *Howstuffworks*. "How Rocket Engines Work." 17 May 2002. <http://www.howstuffworks.com/rocket1.htm>.

8. Save the changes. Proofread and make any necessary corrections.
9. Save a copy of the same document as *urs***Rockets2**.
10. Convert all the footnotes to endnotes. Adjust the page breaks if necessary.
11. Save the changes. Print and close the file.

PROJECT 1 **Practice**

Create an E-Mail Message With Attachment

Your e-mail format will vary depending on the e-mail software you are using. However, your e-mail header form will probably include all the parts illustrated below.

Your Turn

1. **Create** the **e-mail message** illustrated below. Note that you will probably not need to enter your e-mail address in the From: box.

Sender's e-mail address, filled in automatically.

Recipient's e-mail address. If message is to multiple recipients, separate by a semicolon or comma.

E-mail address of recipient(s) receiving a copy of message.

Descriptive name for the message.

Name of file sent with e-mail, filled in automatically when document is attached.

From:	
To:	J_Jaimeson@Hartland.k12.ak.us.edu
Copy:	
Subject:	Pizza Survey
Attach:	

Hi, Joel. How's it going? Is it cold there in Alaska?

This month our math class is doing a survey on the prices of pizza. We want to see if there is a difference in pizza prices across the nation. It would really help us a lot if you would participate in this survey.

Continued on next page

Format Footnotes and Endnotes

4. Locate the paragraph shown below and add another endnote.

It wasn't until 1942 that the first A4 rocket was launched. On the first try, the rocket flew only about one-half mile into the clouds and landed in the ocean. On the second try, the rocket flew about 7 miles high and then exploded. On the third try, though, the rocket flew about 120 miles and landed on target. This marked the beginning of the space age.

Insert a footnote for paraphrased material:
Benson, Tom. NASA Glenn Learning Technologies. "Brief History of Rockets." 15 May 2002. <http://www.grc.nasa.gov/WWW/K-12/TRC/Rockets/history_of_rockets.html>.

5. Locate the paragraph on Newton's Laws and add the endnote indicated below.

will depend on the thrust created by the engine. When the thrust stops, gravity takes over and the rocket falls to the ground.

Insert a footnote for paraphrased material: Genesis Search for Origins. "Newton's Laws of Motion and Rockets." 17 May 2002. <http://www.genesismission.org/educate/scimodule/LaunchPropulsion/L&P_PDFs/B8_STnewtonslaws.pdf>.

6. Keep the file open for the next step.

Continued on next page

PROJECT 1
Continued

Practice

Create an E-Mail Message With Attachment

All we need you to do is to tell us how much you have to pay for a large take-out pizza with one, two, and three toppings. I'm attaching a document that will help you provide the information we need. The document has a table that will make it easy for you. Please enter prices in the table and send the document back to me. I need this information by next Friday.

When we get all the data, our class will graph the information. We'll let you know the results.

E-mail shorthand. This means "Talk to you later." → TTYL

Keith :)

Emoticons help express your feelings. This key combination means "happy."

2. **Attach** the **file 5-3 Project 1**.
3. Spell-check, proofread, and correct errors.
4. Print the e-mail and close it without saving. Do not attempt to send this e-mail.

PROJECT 3 **Reinforce**

Format Footnotes and Endnotes

Reinforce the word processing features you learned by creating another multipage report with footnotes and endnotes.

Your Turn

1. Open the file **6-5 Project 3**. Save the file as ***urs*Rockets**.
2. Locate the first paragraph on the history of rocketing and edit the document as indicated below.

HISTORY OF ROCKETING

The Chinese were the first on record to launch a rocket in the thirteenth century. They used something called a "fire arrow" against the attack of the Mongols. Then as technology grew, the Chinese began experimenting with gun-powder rockets. They attached bamboo tubes to arrows and launched them with bows. Soon they figured out when they used gun-powder, the rockets could launch themselves. Then because of war, the use of rockets spread quickly across Asia and Europe. Italy designed a rocket-powered running surface torpedo to set other ships on fire. Many other uses of rockets were known because of war. For example, each side used rockets in the American Civil War.

Insert a footnote for paraphrased material:
Cliff, Eugene M. "Rocket." *The World Book Encyclopedia 2002.* Chicago: World Book, Inc., Vol. 16, p. 384.

3. Keep the file open for the next step.

Continued on next page

PROJECT 2 **Reinforce**

Create an E-Mail Message With Attachment

Practice what you have learned by creating a new e-mail message and attaching a document to be sent with the message.

Your Turn

1. **Create** the **e-mail message** illustrated below.

From:	
To:	CityCouncil@Fenton.gov
Copy:	
Subject:	River Relief Project
Attach:	

My neighbor told me about the annual River Relief project for the Shiawassee River. I am interested in helping clean up the streambank this year and so are some of my friends. However, we don't know any of the details. We need to know what days are scheduled, what time we should be there, and if we need to bring anything such as trash bags, rakes, etc.

Continued on next page

PROJECT 2 Continued

Practice

Convert Footnotes to Endnotes

6. Compare your endnotes page with the one shown below.

ENDNOTES

[1] Sullivan, James A. Bacterial Growth Cam. "Bacteria Cam: Growth of *Streptococcus pneumoniae*." 14 May 2002. <http://cellsalive.com/ecoli.htm>.
[2] Dairy Research and Information Center. "An Introduction to Bacteria." 12 May 2002. <http://drinc.ucdavis.edu/html/dairyb/index.shtml>.
[3] Dannon Yogurt Products. "The History of Cultures." 13 May 2002. <http://www.dannon.com/pages/dannon_browser.cfm/mode.article/jid.15/aid.182/>.
[4] Kendall, Pat. PENpages College of Agricultural Sciences. "Live, Active, and Probiotic: Yogurt Culture." 14 May 2002. <http://www.penpages.psu.edu/penpages_reference/12101/121012735.html>.
[5] pageWise, Inc. "Benefits of Yogurt." 13 May 2002. <http://mimi.essortment.com/yogurtbenefits_oex.htm>.
[6] Manning, Edna. *Natural Life Magazine #43.* "Yogurt—Food of Centenarians." 14 May 2002. <http://www.life.ca/nl/43/yogurt.html>.
[7] Author unknown. "Cheap-Quick_&-Easy Homemade Yogurt." <http://surfboard.surfside.net/prussell/Yogurt.htm#ingredients>.

7. Save the changes. You may need to manually insert some page breaks so that side headings are not separated from the first paragraph of text below the heading.
8. Create a title page for this report.
9. Print and close the file.

PROJECT 2
Continued

Reinforce

Create an E-Mail Message With Attachment

I am attaching a list of names, phone numbers, and e-mail addresses so someone can contact my friends and me.

Nik Klopf :)

2. **Attach** the **file 5-3 Project 2** so it will be sent with the e-mail message.
3. Spell-check, proofread, and correct errors.
4. Print the e-mail and close it without saving. Do not attempt to send this e-mail.

PROJECT 2 Practice

Convert Footnotes to Endnotes

Endnotes are another common type of reference page at the end of the document that provide references for text within the document. Endnotes are the same as footnotes—they just appear in a different location in the report. Sometimes the endnotes are inserted on a page by themselves as the last page in the document.

When you cite a source in a document, you choose between the footnote and the endnote format. However, if you change your mind, you can convert footnotes to endnotes and vice versa.

Your Turn

1. **Save** the document ***urs*Yogurt1 as** *urs*Yogurt2. Use F12 to save.
2. Position the insertion point at the end of the document and insert a new page break.
3. Key, **center**, and **bold** the title ENDNOTES. Then press ENTER.
4. **Convert** all **the footnotes to endnotes**.
5. Keep the file open for the next step.

Continued on next page

Check Your Understanding

1. Open a new word processing document. Save the file as **ursEmail**.
2. Describe the information that goes in each of the following e-mail header boxes.
   From:
   To:
   Copy:
   Subject:
   Attach:
3. Explain how to send an e-mail to more than one recipient.
4. Save the changes. Print and close the file.

Write On!

Imagine that you do not have access to telephone or e-mail. The only way you can keep in touch with your friends or relatives who live in a different neighborhood, city, state, or country is by writing letters.

1. Open your journal and position the insertion point at the end of the new document. Enter today's date to create a new journal entry.
2. Write a paragraph or two in your journal responding to the above scenario. How often do you think you would write a letter? Would you be able to communicate as well? Why or why not? Do you think your relationship with your friends and relatives would change? Why or why not?
3. Save the changes to the journal. Close the file.

interNET CONNECTION

When you communicate via e-mail, you cannot use facial expressions or your tone of voice to let your reader know how you feel. Therefore, you must follow some common courtesies (etiquette) when writing your messages.

1. **Open your Web browser and research information on "netiquette" for e-mail.**
2. **Research the Web for e-mail shorthand and emoticons.**
3. **Create a table in a word processing document. Enter 10–15 emoticons and their meanings.**
4. **Write a paragraph telling about an experience you had last week. Use emoticons wherever you want to describe how someone felt.**

PROJECT 1 Continued

Practice

Insert a Footnote

3. Locate the paragraph that begins "As Pat Kendall, . . ."
4. Edit the paragraph as indicated below.

Insert a footnote for a direct quotation:
Kendall, Pat. PENpages College of Agricultural Sciences. "Live, Active, and Probiotic: Yogurt Culture." 14 May 2002. <http://www.penpages.psu.edu/penpages_reference/12101/121012735.html>.

As Pat Kendall, a food science and human nutrition specialist, says, "Yogurt deserves its reputation as a healthful food." Yogurt contains protein, potassium, magnesium, vitamin B-12, riboflavin, and zinc. It is low in fat and it helps the immune system. The good bacteria in yogurt aid digestion. It can even help fight acne.

Insert a footnote for paraphrased material:
pageWise, Inc. "Benefits of Yogurt." 14 May 2002. <http://mimi.essortment.com/yogurtbenefits_oex.htm>.

5. Proofread and make any necessary corrections.
6. Save the changes. Keep the file open for Project 2.

REVIEW SECTION 5

Apply

Word Processing Review

You will apply the word processing skills you have learned to create and format a business letter. Refer to previous projects as needed.

The writer's return address is:
1113 Grand Avenue
Wausau, WI 54403

Use Today's Date.

Send the letter to:
Flagstaff Area National Monuments--WACA
6400 N. Hwy 89
Flagstaff, AZ 86004

For the salutation, key Gentlemen:.

For the closing, key Sincerely,.

The writer's name is Kevin Tolzmann.

Your Turn

1. Open a new word processing document.
2. Format a letter in block style.
3. Use the following information to key and format the letter.

This summer, I will be visiting my grandparents in Flagstaff. I am very interested in learning more about Native Americans. I was browsing the Web, and I learned that the ancestors of Native Americans lived in cliff dwellings in the Walnut Canyon. Then I learned that the Walnut Canyon is close to where my grandparents live in Flagstaff.

I want to ask my grandparents to take me to the Walnut Canyon National Monument. Please send me some information about the Walnut Canyon National Monument. I need to know how to get to the park, and I need to know the cost of admission. I also would like information about park activities and any special programs for the month of July.

Please send the information to me at the above address. Thank you.

4. Save the document as ***urs*Walnut Canyon** letter.
5. Spell-check, proofread, and correct errors.
6. Save the changes.
7. Create a No. 10 envelope for the letter. Print and close the file.

PROJECT 1 Continued

Practice

Insert a Footnote

Insert a footnote for paraphrased material:
Sullivan, James A. Bacterial Growth Cam. "Bacteria Cam: Growth of *Streptococcus pneumoniae.*" 14 May 2002. <http://cellsalive.com/ecoli.htm>.

RESEARCH

In my research I learned that bacteria grow, eat, and then reproduce. If the conditions are right (such as the right temperature and the right environment), each bacterium grows slightly in size or length. A new cell wall grows through the center of the bacterium, and then the bacterium splits into two identical daughter cells. I found a Web site that showed real E.coli bacteria growing and splitting. First there was one. After about 20 minutes there were two. Then after 20 more minutes there were four. Then there were eight, then sixteen, then thirty-two, and so on. Within just a few hours there was a colony of hundreds of bacteria.

I also learned that not all bacteria are bad. Some bacteria can cause disease, but others can cure. For example, antibiotics are made from bacteria. We also use bacteria to make several foods. We use bacteria to make cheese and buttermilk from milk. We use bacteria to make vinegar from alcohol.

Insert a footnote for paraphrased material:
Dairy Research and Information Center. "An Introduction to Bacteria." 14 May 2002. <http://drinc.ucdavis.edu/html/dairyb/index.shtml>.

Continued on next page

ENRICH

Curriculum Portfolio

Choose one of the following topics or use a topic assigned by your teacher. Research the topic and compose correspondence to communicate your thoughts on the issue. You can create a personal letter or you can create an e-mail message. Proofread your work carefully and save the document as *urs*Letter Portfolio. Print an envelope if you create a letter.

SCIENCE:

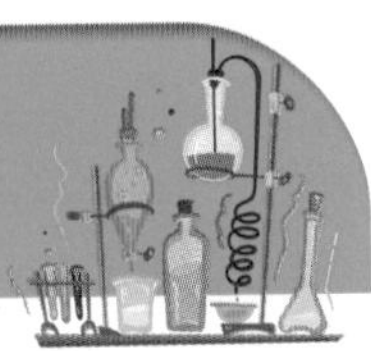

Compose a personal or business letter.

Select an endangered animal. Research what has caused the animal to become endangered, the status of the animal, and what can be done to save the animal from extinction.

Write a letter to a U.S. senator or representative. In your letter, express how you feel about the endangered species and why you feel it is important to protect it. You can find the names and addresses of senators and representatives on the Web or at your local library. Be sure to use the proper greeting in your letter.

SOCIAL STUDIES:

Compose a personal or business letter.

Think about a service project you can do for your community. For example, you could help to clean up the local park. You could organize a group of youths and adults to pick up the litter, improve the landscaping, and paint some of the equipment.

Once you have a plan, determine whom you should contact in your community to help plan and carry out your service project. For example, you may need to write the mayor, the city council, or the city parks and recreation department. Write a letter that defines your goals and explains why your plan is good for the community. Be sure to use the proper greeting in your letter. You can find the names and addresses of community officials and departments on the Web or at your local library.

Continued on next page

PROJECT 1 **Practice**

Insert a Footnote

Footnotes are notes at the bottom of a page that provide references for text on the same page. You can use a footnote to give credit to the source by telling the reader where you found the information. If you quote from a source word for word, you need to format the information as a direct quotation and cite the source. When you put someone else's ideas into your own words (paraphrase), you must also give credit by citing the source.

Your Turn

1. This report already contains three footnotes. Take some time to look through the report and locate the footnotes. The first footnote is on page 2. See the illustration below.

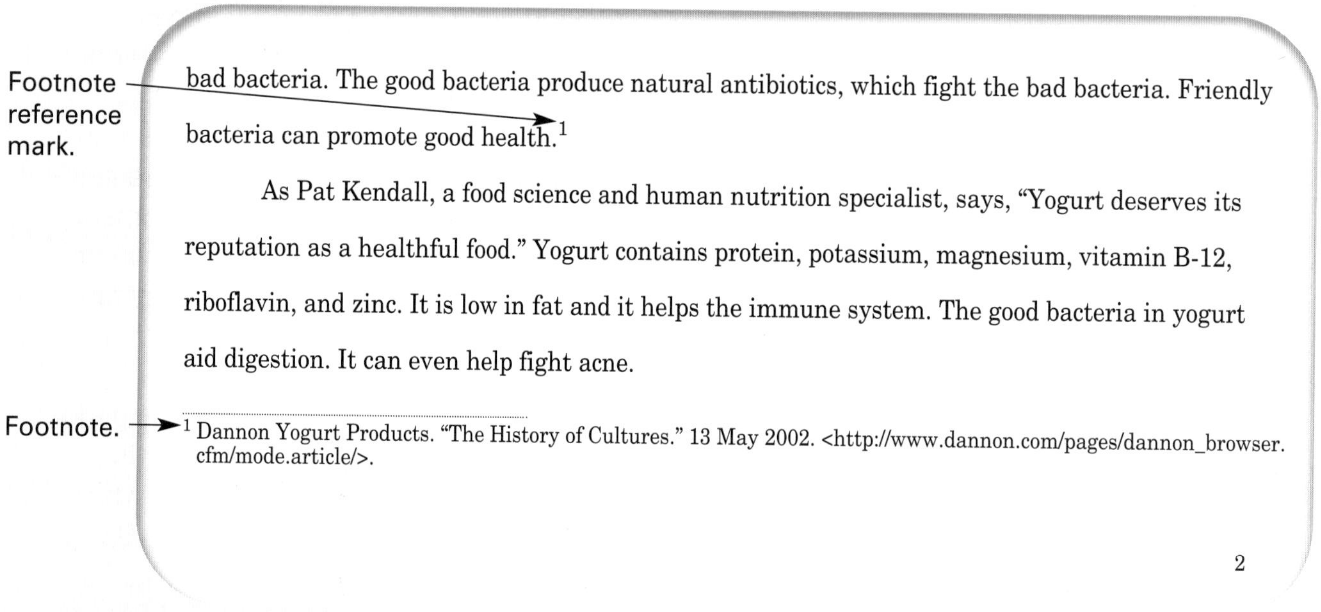

Footnote reference mark.

bad bacteria. The good bacteria produce natural antibiotics, which fight the bad bacteria. Friendly bacteria can promote good health.[1]

As Pat Kendall, a food science and human nutrition specialist, says, "Yogurt deserves its reputation as a healthful food." Yogurt contains protein, potassium, magnesium, vitamin B-12, riboflavin, and zinc. It is low in fat and it helps the immune system. The good bacteria in yogurt aid digestion. It can even help fight acne.

Footnote.

[1] Dannon Yogurt Products. "The History of Cultures." 13 May 2002. <http://www.dannon.com/pages/dannon_browser.cfm/mode.article/>.

2

2. Locate the main topic, RESEARCH, and edit the document as indicated on the following page.

Continued on next page

ENRICH

Curriculum Portfolio

MATH:

Compose a personal or business letter.

Suppose you belong to a service club at your school. The club has 88 members. Your club has decided to sponsor a fundraiser to raise money for a family that lost its home and all personal belongings in a recent fire.

The club has decided to sell community discount cards for $10 each, and the club will keep $5 for every card sold. You estimate that 65 percent of the members will participate in the project, and you think they can each sell 10 cards. Calculate the potential profit your club can make with this project.

Write a letter to your principal asking for approval of the fundraiser. Explain why the club wants to participate in this project and describe the details. Be sure to mention how much profit your club is anticipating.

LANGUAGE ARTS:

Compose a personal letter.

Do you have a favorite book or poem? Have you ever thought about the author who created the story or the poem? For example, you might be curious about how old the author was when he or she wrote the story or poem. You may wonder where the author was born and grew up, or you may want to know why the author wrote the story or poem. Gather information and learn as much as you can about the author.

Write a letter to the author expressing why you enjoy reading the author's work. If the author is no longer living, or if you are unable to find an address for the author, create a fictitious address to use in your letter.

SECTION 6.5

Format a Report With Footnotes or Endnotes

GOALS: Demonstrate the ability to:

- Key and format footnotes and endnotes.
- Convert footnotes to endnotes.
- Work from printed and unarranged material.
- Spell-check, proofread, and correct errors.

WARMUP

Select Warmup from the Skillbuilding menu. Key each Warmup line 2 times.

Speed	*1*	I could not read the small print on the map she sent to me.
Accuracy	*2*	A dozen jumpy zebras quickly zipped over the six big gates.
Symbols	*3*	it's hasn't we'll aren't they'll couldn't you've don't I've
Language Link	*4*	Because I had good grades, my scholarship has been renewed.

Making the Connection

When you work really hard on an assignment, you like to take credit for your time and efforts. Sometimes you even feel proud of your work, and you probably like it when people notice what you have done.

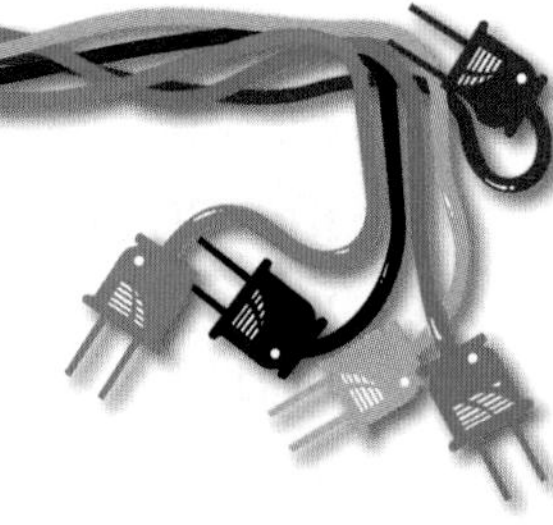

When you research a topic for a report, most likely you will gather your information from a magazine, a newspaper, an encyclopedia, or a Web site. Did you ever stop to think who organized and reported that information?

In this section you will learn about giving credit to the sources of information you use in your reports.

bad bacteria. The good bacteria produce natural antibiotics, which fight the bad bacteria. Friendly bacteria can promote good health.[1]

As Pat Kendall, a food science and human nutrition specialist, says, "Yogurt

Your Turn

1. Open the file **6-5 Project 1**, and save the document as *urs*Yogurt1.
2. Keep the file open for Project 1.

SECTION 6.1

Format a One-Page Report

GOALS: Demonstrate the ability to:

- Format a one-page report.
- Format margins, paragraph alignment, and line spacing.
- Copy and paste text between documents.
- Find and replace text.
- Proofread and correct errors.

WARMUP

Select Warmup from the Skillbuilding menu. Key each Warmup line 2 times.

Speed	1	Check our lists to be sure that we are ready for this trip.
Accuracy	2	Zachariah analyzed the situation and queried the witnesses.
Numbers/Symbols	3	Our seat assignments are 30-41, 56-72, 88-109, and 111-114.
Language Link	4	One box of staplers and tape dispensers was shipped Monday.

Making the Connection

You're probably familiar with the saying, "Work smarter, not harder." That's what word processing is all about. The more features you learn, the smarter you can work. In this section you will learn some features that will make your work easier.

Your Turn

1. Open a new word processing document.
2. Key the text as shown.
3. Save the document as *urs*Charlie.
4. Keep the file open for Project 1.

ALL THE CHOCOLATE YOU CAN EAT!

By Rachelle Cantin

I read the book Charlie and the Chocolate Factory. The author of the book is Roald Dahl. The book is 155 pages long, and it was published by Puffin.

Check Your Understanding

1. Open a new word processing document. Answer the following using complete sentences.
2. What is a citation?
3. Define a header and explain what information is included in the header.
4. What is a works cited page?
5. What is the difference, if any, in how a works cited page is formatted compared with a bibliography page?
6. Save the document as *urs*Citations. Print and close the file.

Write On!

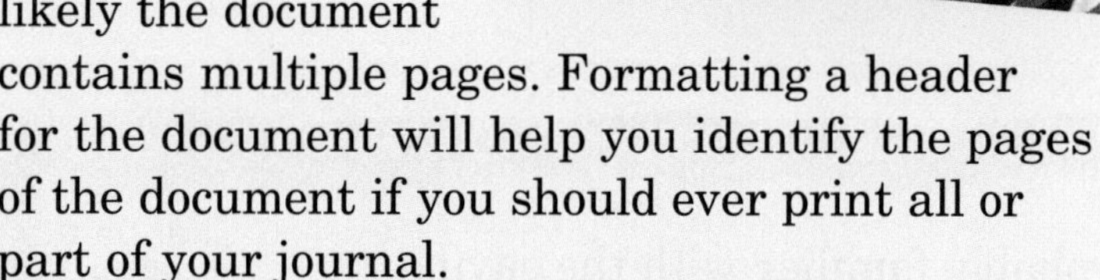

By now you have created several entries in your journal. Most likely the document contains multiple pages. Formatting a header for the document will help you identify the pages of the document if you should ever print all or part of your journal.

1. Open your journal and create a header with your name and the page number.
2. Position the insertion point at the end of the journal. Enter today's date to create a new journal entry.
3. Think of a situation when you (or maybe one of your classmates) did not receive credit for a classroom assignment because you forgot to put your name on your work or because some of the pages were misplaced or lost. What did you learn from that experience? Write about the experience in your journal.
4. Save the changes to your journal. Close the file.

*inter*NET CONNECTION

In this lesson, you formatted a report about Davy Crockett. An image would help the reader understand more about your report.

1. **Open your file *urs*Davy Crockett and save the document as *urs*Davy Crockett2.**
2. **Open your Web browser, and search the Internet for an image of Davy Crockett.**
3. **Copy the image into the document. Resize and position the image within the document. Include the proper citation for the image in the Works Cited page.**
4. **Save the changes. Print and close the file.**

PROJECT 1 Practice

Change the Margins and Format the Report

The blank space around the edges of the page is called the **margin**. When you create a new document, the default margins are already set. However, you can change those margins. Use 1-inch margins for full-page or multi-page reports.

Your Turn

1. Edit and key the remaining text in the document as shown.

Title Center, bold, and all-capital letters.

Byline Center.

ALL THE CHOCOLATE YOU CAN EAT!

By Rachelle Cantin

I read the book *Charlie and the Chocolate Factory*. The author of the book is Roald Dahl. The book is 155 pages long, and it was published by Puffin.

Charlie Bucket is a poor boy who lives in a tiny house with his parents. Both sets of grandparents also live with Charlie in that tiny house. Charlie didn't have any money, but he found a dollar bill in the street. He used the money to buy a Wonka candy bar. The Willy Wonka Chocolate Company held a contest. When Charlie opened the candy bar, he found a golden ticket. He was one of five winners.

Format Charlie and the Chocolate Factory in **italic**.

Change the line spacing to double.

Change the left and right **margins** to 1 inch.

Body Press TAB to indent the first line of each paragraph.

2. Spell-check and proofread the file. Make any necessary corrections and save the changes.
3. Keep the file open for Project 2.

PROJECT 4 Continued

Reinforce

Create a Multipage Report With Citations

6. **Insert a new page break** at the end of the document, and create a Works Cited page using the references shown below.

Works Cited

Author unknown. "Davy Crockett Biography." 6 April 2002. <http://www.infoporium.com/heritage/crockbio.shtml>.

"Davy Crockett." *Microsoft Encarta Online Encyclopedia 2002.* <http://encarta.msn.com>.

Davy Crockett Birthplace Association. "American West-Davy Crockett." 6 April 2002. <http://www.americanwest.com/pages/davycroc.htm>.

Lofaro, Michael A. "Davy Crockett." *The World Book Encyclopedia 2002*. Chicago: World Book, Inc., Vol. 14, pp. 1148d-1149.

The Texas State Historical Association. *The New Handbook of Texas-Online.* "Davy Crockett (1786-1836)-Biography." 6 April 2002. <http://www.alamo-de-parras.welkin.org/history/bios/crockett/crockett.html>.

7. Save the changes. Print and close the file.

PROJECT 2

Practice

Copy and Paste Text Between Documents

You already know how to copy and paste text within the same document. Did you know you can copy and paste text from one document to another? With both documents open, you simply copy the text in one of the documents, switch to the second document, and paste the text you copied.

Your Turn

1. Open the file **6-1 Project 2**. You now have two files open, but the file you see on the screen is the one you just opened. See the illustration below.

The other four winners were Augustus Gloop, Violet Beauregarde, Veruca Salt, and Mike Teavee. Charlie went on the tour of the chocolate factory with his Grandpa Joe. The other four winners were there with their parents. They saw lots of amazing things, and they met the Oompa-Loompas. The Oompa-Loompas were the tiny people who lived and worked in the factory.

The other four kids behaved very badly on the tour. When they didn't follow directions, Willy Wonka punished them and funny things happened to them that made them disappear. But Charlie was kind and polite. Willy Wonka liked Charlie and he knew he could trust Charlie. At the end of the tour, Charlie was

Continued on next page

PROJECT 4 Continued

Reinforce

Create a Multipage Report With Citations

Davy lived with his family in Tennessee until he was 13. He went to school, but he didn't like it. He skipped school a lot. He ran away from home because he knew his dad was going to punish him for playing hooky. He joined a cattle drive to make money. He drove the cattle to Virginia almost 300 miles away. He stayed in Virginia and worked a lot of jobs for over two years. He returned to his family in Tennessee when he was 16 ("Davy Crockett Biography").

Copy and paste the entire contents of file **6-4 Project 4**. →

3. Close the file 6-4 Project 4.
4. Proofread and make any necessary corrections.
5. Save the document as ***urs*Davy Crockett**. Keep the file open for the next step.

Continued on next page

PROJECT 2 Continued

Practice

Copy and Paste Text Between Documents

the only kid left and Willy Wonka gave him the chocolate factory. Charlie and his family could live at the factory and Charlie could have all the chocolate he could eat!

My favorite part about this book was that when the other four kids didn't follow directions, Willy Wonka punished them. Charlie followed directions and Willy Wonka rewarded him for that.

2. **Select** the entire file, and **copy** the selected text to the **Clipboard**.
3. Close the file **6-1 Project 2** without saving any changes. The file ***urs*Charlie** is still displayed.
4. Position the insertion point at the end of the file, and **paste** the contents from the **Clipboard**.
5. Save the changes. Keep the file open for Project 3.

PROJECT 4 **Reinforce**

Create a Multipage Report With Citations

Create another multipage report with citations.

Your Turn

1. Open a new word processing document.
2. Key the first part of the report as indicated.

Change the left and right **margins** to one inch.

Create a header with your name and the page number for all pages.

Your Last Name #

Your First and Last Name

Your Teacher's Name

Class

Today's Date

King of the Wild Frontier

"Be always sure you are right, then go ahead" (Lofaro 1148d). You're probably wondering what that means. Well, a guy named Davy Crockett used to say that. It is one of his best known quotes. Read on to find out more about this legendary person.

Actually, his name was David Crockett. He was born in a small cabin in Tennessee on August 17, 1786 ("Davy Crockett"). His family lived in a cabin on the banks of the Nolichucky River. Davy had eight brothers and sisters. Four were older and four were younger.

Continued on next page

PROJECT 3 **Practice**

Find and Replace Text

The Find feature enables you to quickly locate a word or a group of words. The Replace feature enables you to find and replace the word or group of words with a different word or group of words.

Your Turn

1. Use the file ***urs*Charlie**. Position the insertion point at the beginning of the third paragraph.
2. Edit the file as indicated in the illustration below.
3. **Find and replace** "Willy" with "Mr." in the last two paragraphs of the file.

The other four kids behaved very badly on the tour. When they didn't follow directions, Willy Wonka punished them and funny things happened to them that made them disappear. But Charlie was kind and polite. Willy Wonka liked Charlie and he knew he could trust Charlie. At the end of the tour, Charlie was the only kid left and Willy Wonka gave him the chocolate factory. Charlie and his family could live at the factory and Charlie could have all the chocolate he could eat!

My favorite part about this book was that when the other four kids didn't follow directions, Willy Wonka punished them. Charlie followed directions and Willy Wonka rewarded him for that.

4. Save the changes. Print and close the file.

PROJECT 3 Practice

Format a Works Cited Reference Page

A **Works Cited** page is a common type of reference page. This page is a list of all the sources you cited in the report.

Your Turn

1. **Insert** a **page break** at the end of the document.
2. Create the works cited page as shown in the illustration below.

Select the entire document and change the **line spacing** to **double**.

Format each source with a **hanging indent.**

Works Cited

"Augustus." *Microsoft Encarta Online*. 10 Dec. 2002. <http://encarta.msn.com>.

Cavazzi, Franco. "Emperor Augustus." *Illustrated History of the Roman Empire*. 10 Dec. 2002. <http://www.roman-empire.net/emperors/augustus-index.html>.

Cavazzi, Franco. "Roman Society." *Illustrated History of the Roman Empire*. 10 Dec. 2002. <http://www.roman-empire.net/society/society.html>.

Cavazzi, Franco. "The Late Roman Republic." *Illustrated History of the Roman Empire*. 10 Dec. 2002. <http://www.roman-empire.net/republic/laterep-index.html>.

3. Proofread and make any necessary corrections.
4. Save the changes. Print and close the file.

PROJECT 4 Reinforce

Format a One-Page Report

Reinforce the word processing features you learned by keying and formatting another one-page report.

Your Turn

1. Open the document **6-1 Project 4**, and save it as ***urs*Crabtree**.
2. Format the document as indicated.

Select the entire document and change the **line spacing** to double.

Center the title and subtitle. **Bold** the title.

LOTTA CRABTREE
By Alexa Aroyo

My report is about *Lotta Crabtree Gold Rush Girl.* The book was written by Marian T. Place, and it was illustrated by Gary Morrow. The Bobbs-Merrill Company, Inc., published the book in 1958 and in 1962, and the total number of pages is 200.

The story took place in the 1840s. The main character is Lotta Crabtree, a girl who likes to sing and dance. Lotta's mother is a very good mother, but she can't cook. Lotta's dad, who says he is going to strike it rich one day, owns a bookstore.

Change the left and right **margins** to 1 inch.

3. Open the file **6-1 Project 4b**. Select the entire document and copy the contents to the Clipboard.
4. Close the file **6-1 Project 4b**. Paste the contents in the Clipboard at the end of the document named ***urs*Crabtree**.
5. Save the changes. Keep the file open for the next step.

Continued on next page

PROJECT 2 Continued

Practice

Format a Header

2. Edit the document as indicated below.

setting up a fire brigade and a police force and encouraged learning by building Rome's first library (Cavazzi, "Roman Society").

Augustus ruled for 41 years and brought peace to Rome. He gave Romans a new sense of pride and reorganized the government of Rome so that it ran well for more than 200 years (Cavazzi, "The Late Roman Republic"). The peace that he brought to Rome was called the Pax Romana. For the most part, Rome and its people prospered, civilization spread, and cultures mixed.

In the early years of the empire, about 1 million people lived in Rome. It suffered from many of the same problems as cities today--too little housing, air pollution, crime, unemployment, and a high cost of living. Many Romans could not find jobs and had to pay taxes on almost everything.

3. Save the changes. Keep the file open for Project 3.

PROJECT 4 Continued

Reinforce

Format a One-Page Report

6. Complete the report by keying the final paragraphs shown in the illustration below.

When Lotta was sixteen, she returned to New York and became America's favorite comedienne. For twenty-two years, Lotta was the star actress in light comedy. She was often called "The California Diamond." Some of her friends had a statue made of her, and they put it in the center of Portsmouth Square in San Francisco. Then in 1891, Lotta retired and gave up acting.

The thing I liked about Lotta Crabtree was that she did a lot of things with very little money.

7. **Find and replace** all occurrences of "New York" with "New York City."
8. Spell-check and proofread the document. Make any necessary corrections.
9. Save the changes. Print and close the file.

PROJECT 2 Practice

Format a Header

A **header** is information that appears at the top of each page in a document. A **footer** is information that appears at the bottom of each page in a document. Include your name and the page number in a header.

Your Turn

1. Format a header as shown below.

Create a **header** with your last name at the right margin and the page number at the right.

Format the **header** to appear on all pages.

Your Last Name #

Augustus wanted boundaries that would be easy to defend. So he rounded out the empire to natural frontiers--the Rhine and Danube rivers in the north, the Atlantic Ocean in the west, and the Sahara in the south. Augustus also stationed soldiers there.

Augustus was not interested in gaining new territory for Rome. Instead, he worked on governing the existing empire. He paid provincial governors large salaries so that they would not feel the need to overtax the people or keep public money for themselves.

To make sure that people did not pay too much or too little tax, Augustus ordered a census, or population count, to be taken from time to time. He made Rome more beautiful. He wrote strict laws to govern the way people behaved in public. He protected the city by

Continued on next page

Write On!

In this lesson, you learned to locate specific text in a word processing document and replace it with new text. There are many more ways you can use the Find command to work smarter. For example, if you want to review journal entries that you have previously written about a particular subject or experience, you can use the Find command to locate quickly those entries.

1. Open your journal and use the Find command to locate all the entries that contain the word "letter." Your results should include entries about personal letters and business letters.
2. Position the insertion point at the end of the new document. Enter today's date to create a new journal entry.
3. Think about other ways you could use the Find command to work smarter, and describe them in your new journal entry. If you cannot think of other ways to use the Find command, write a paragraph describing how you used the Find command to work smarter in this lesson.
4. Save the changes to your journal. Close the file.

*inter*NET CONNECTION

Did you know that you can use the Find command to locate specific text in Web pages? Let's see how it works.

You want information about the best roller coasters in the world. You want to know how high they are and how fast they are.

1. **Open your Web browser, and search for the keywords "*roller coasters + amusement parks*."**
2. **When you locate a Web page that looks like it contains the information you are looking for, choose the Find command in your browser to search for the specific details. (The Find command is usually in the Edit menu.)**
3. **Search for keywords like "height" and "speed." These searches will highlight the best parts of a database or which links to explore in a collection.**
4. **Make a list of the three highest roller coasters and the three fastest roller coasters. Compare your results with those of a classmate.**
5. **On your own: Use the find command to locate the oldest (Hint: search for "year") roller coasters still running and add names, locations, and what they are made of to your list.**

Format a Report With Citations

(Cavazzi, "The Late Roman Republic")
Country". He took for himself the title of Augustus, or revered one. Octavian then became the first Roman emperor, or absolute ruler of an empire.

Augustus was a clever politician. He held the offices of consul, tribune, high priest, and senator all at the same time. However, he refused to be crowned emperor. Augustus knew that most Romans would not accept one-person rule unless it took the form of a republic.

Open the file **6-4 Project 1b**. **Copy and paste** the contents of the file.

3. Close the file **6-4 Project 1b.**
4. Save the changes. Keep the file open for Project 2.

SECTION 6.2

Format a Report With a Bibliography

GOALS: Demonstrate the ability to:

- Format a multipage report.
- Format margins, side headings, page numbers for a report.
- Insert a new page.
- Create and format a bibliography.
- Work from rough-draft copy material.
- Spell-check, proofread, and correct errors.

WARMUP

Select Warmup from the Skillbuilding menu. Key each Warmup line 2 times.

Speed	1	James was not here when all of us signed the card for Rita.
Accuracy	2	Jacqueline was glad her family took five or six big prizes.
Technique	3	Will students use the SHIFT LOCK to type in SOLID CAPITALS?
Language Link	4	The picnic is always Labor Day (first Monday in September).

Making the Connection

In this section you will learn how to create and format a multipage report. You will learn how to make an adjustment to the left margin so that the left and right margins look even when the report is bound on the left.

Your Turn

1. Open the file **6-2 Project 1**. Save the document as ***urs*Banner**.
2. Keep the file open for Project 1.

THE STAR-SPANGLED BANNER

By Hallie Thompson

During the War of 1812, Americans knew that the British would likely attack the city of Baltimore. In the summer of 1813, Major George Armistead was the commander at Fort McHenry at the Baltimore harbor. He asked Mary Young Pickersgill to make a flag for the fort. Armistead wanted the flag to be

PROJECT 1

Practice

Format a Report With Citations

When you format a report, your name, teacher, class, and the date appear on the first page at the beginning of the report.

When you format your report in MLA style, you cite briefly each source by giving the author's name and the page number in a **citation** in the body of the report. The reader can get more specific details about the source in a section at the end of the report called *Works Cited*.

Your Turn

1. Edit the document as indicated below.
2. **Change** left and right **margins** to one inch.

The MLA heading replaces the need for a title page in a report.

Enter this information, double-spaced and aligned at the left margin.

Your First and Last Name

Your Teacher's Name

Class

Today's Date

The Roman Empire Under Augustus

Roman power was crumbling and would likely have ended had it not been for two great statesmen: Gaius Julius Caesar and his great-nephew Augustus, also known as Octavian (Cavazzi, "Emperor Augustus"). In 27 B.C., Octavian told the Senate that he had restored the republic. When he offered to give up his job, the Senate gave him several offices ("Augustus"). It named him "first citizen" and "Father of the

Key the citations as shown.

Continued on next page

PROJECT 1 **Practice**

Format a Bound Report With Side Headings and Page Numbers

Side headings are the major subdivisions or major topics of a report. Side headings help to emphasize the main ideas in your report. Multipage reports are often bound or stapled on the left side of the page. You need to leave a larger left margin to allow room for the binding. Because your report has more than one page, use the page number feature to automatically number each page.

Your Turn

1. Edit the report as indicated in the illustration.

Center and **bold**.

Center.

Select the entire document and change the **line spacing** to double.

Add **side headings** and format **bold**.

Format 1.5-inch left **margin**.

Format 1-inch right **margin**.

THE STAR-SPANGLED BANNER

By Hallie Thompson

The Story Behind the Flag

During the War of 1812, Americans knew that the British would likely attack the city of Baltimore. In the summer of 1813, Major George Armistead was the commander at Fort McHenry at the Baltimore harbor. He asked Mary Young Pickersgill to make a flag for the fort. Armistead wanted the flag to be so big that the British would be sure to see it from a distance.

Mary's 13-year-old daughter Caroline helped her make the flag. They cut 15 stars. Each star was two feet long from point to point. They also cut eight red stripes and seven white stripes. Each stripe was two feet wide. It took them several weeks to make the flag. When they sewed everything together, the flag measured 30 feet by 42 feet. The flag weighed 200 pounds.

Francis Scott Key's Point of View

Francis Scott Key was 35 years old, and he was a well-known and successful lawyer in Georgetown, Maryland. He opposed the War of 1812, but in 1814 he had to get involved. His long-time friend Dr. William Beanes was being held prisoner on a British warship.

On September 3, 1814, Key and a government agent named John S. Skinner boarded a ship that flew a flag of truce. They went to the British warship and negotiated the release of Beanes. On September 7, the British agreed to let Beanes go, but by

Continued on next page

SECTION 6.4

Format a Report With a Reference Page

GOALS: Demonstrate the ability to:

- Key and format a multipage report in MLA style.
- Cite sources in a report.
- Format a header.
- Create a works cited reference page.
- Proofread and correct errors.

WARMUP

Select Warmup from the Skillbuilding menu. Key each Warmup line 2 times.

Speed	1	Emi would like to buy the dress if it comes in green denim.
Accuracy	2	Karl may sign up with five or six dozen clubs for jonquils.
Symbols	3	My brother-in-law gave Trev that you-know-what-I-mean look.
Language Link	4	When our orders arrived, a number of lightbulbs were taken.

Making the Connection

When you don't put your name on your assignments, your teacher does not know who did the work. Multipage reports that follow the MLA style have a header that contains the writer's name and the page number. Some teachers ask you to include the hour of your class and/or the date. That information makes the teacher's recordkeeping tasks easier.

In this section, you will learn to format your document so your name will automatically appear on every page of the document.

Your Name
Your Teacher's Name
Class
Today's Date

The Roman Empire Under Augustus

Roman power was crumbling and would likely have ended had it not been for two great statesmen: Gaius Julius Caesar and

Your Turn

1. Open the file **6-4 Project 1**, and save the document as ***urs*****Roman Empire**.
2. Keep the file open for Project 1.

PROJECT 1 Continued

Practice

Format a Bound Report With Side Headings and Page Numbers

then Key, Skinner, and Beanes knew too much about the planned attack on the city of Baltimore. So the British held all three Americans as prisoners on the warship while they attacked Baltimore.

On September 13, the three American prisoners watched from the warship as the British battleships fired upon Fort McHenry. They knew it would be difficult for the American soldiers to fight off the British. The battle continued through the night, and they feared the American soldiers would surrender.

Add **side headings** and format **bold**. →

The Story Behind the Song

When the sun rose the next morning, they saw a big American flag flying over the fort. It was the flag Pickersgill had made. The Americans had survived the battle.

Insert page number. →

Oh! Say, can you see, by the dawn's early light,

What so proudly we hailed at the twilight's last gleaming?

Whose broad stripes and bright stars, through the perilous fight.

O'er the ramparts we watched were so gallantly streaming?

And the rocket's red glare, the bombs bursting in air,

Gave proof through the night that our flag was still there.

Oh! Say, does that Star-Spangled Banner yet wave

O'er the land of the free and the home of the brave?

Format all the text **italic**.

Center each line of text.

2. Save the changes.
3. Position the insertion point at the end of the document, and key and format the first verse of the *Star-Spangled Banner* as shown at left.
4. Save the changes. Keep the file open for Project 2.

Check Your Understanding

1. Open a new word processing document.
2. List the information that you should include on a title page.
3. Describe how you can enhance the appearance of a title page.
4. Save the document as *urs***Title Page Notes**. Print and close the file.

*inter*NET CONNECTION

The World Wide Web is a source for lots of information. However, just because you read it at a Web site does not mean that it is true. Before you rely on information that you find on the Web, you should evaluate the source.

1. **Open your Web browser and search for a site that provides suggestions or student guidelines for evaluating Web pages.**
2. **Open a new word processing document. Create a list to identify the questions you should ask and the information you should look for to verify that you can trust the source. Save the document as *urs*Evaluation.**
3. **On your own: Do a search on the space shuttle. Choose three sites. Make sure two of them are not NASA sites. Use your evaluation document to review all three sites.**

Write On!

The student forum wants to sponsor Crazy Hat Day. If students donate 25 cents, they will be permitted to wear silly hats throughout the school day. The money collected will be used to purchase a new flag for the school. As president of the student forum, it is your job to persuade the principal to approve this event. How will you convince the principal that sponsoring Crazy Hat Day would be good for the school?

1. Open your journal and position the insertion point at the end of the new document. Enter today's date to create a new journal entry.
2. Write a paragraph or two describing the main points you will make to persuade the principal to approve Crazy Hat Day.
3. Save the changes to your journal. Close the file.

PROJECT 2 **Practice**

Format a Bibliography

A **bibliography** is an alphabetical list of the sources of information you used in writing a report. The sources are single-spaced and formatted with a hanging indent. In a **hanging indent**, the first line of the paragraph begins at the left margin and all other lines in the paragraph are indented.

Your Turn

1. Position the insertion point at the end of the document, and then **insert a new page break**.
2. Key and format the bibliography as illustrated.

Single-space the sources, and leave a blank line between the sources.

Internet reference.

Format with **hanging indent**.

Online encyclopedia reference.

BIBLIOGRAPHY

Armed Forces Collections. "Star-Spangled Banner and the War of 1812." 10 May 2002. <http://www.si.edu/resource.faq/nmah/starflag.htm>.

Author unknown. "Francis Scott Key." 10 May 2002. <http://www.usflag.org.francis.scott.key.html>.

Goertzen, Valerie Woodring. "Star-Spangled Banner." *The World Book Encyclopedia 2002.* Chicago: World Book, Inc., Vol. 18, pp. 853-854.

"Star-Spangled Banner." *Microsoft Encarta Online Encyclopedia 2002.* <http://encarta.msn.com/encnet/refpages/refarticle.aspx?refid=761575047>.

3. Save the changes. Print and close the file.

PROJECT 2 Reinforce

Format a Title Page

Your Turn

1. Create and format the title page illustrated below.

Change the **vertical alignment** of text to center.

ARGENTINA

Prepared by

Nathan Chin
Notre Dame Academy

Prepared for

Mr. Jorgensen
Social Studies—3rd Hour

Today's Date

2. Save the document as ***urs*Argentina Title Page**.
3. Print and close the file.

PROJECT 3 **Reinforce**

Format a Multipage Report With a Bibliography

Reinforce the word processing features you learned by keying and formatting another multipage report with a bibliography.

Change the left **margin** to allow for the space needed for binding on the left side.

Your Turn

1. Key and format the report as illustrated.

ARGENTINA

By Nathan Chin

Argentina is the world's eighth-largest country, and its land varies greatly. It has some of the world's tallest mountains, and it also has grassy plains and deserts.

Add the side heading **Borders** and format **bold**.

Argentina is bordered by Chile, Uruguay, Brazil, Paraguay, and Bolivia on its northern borders. Argentina is also bordered by the Pacific and Atlantic Oceans. Its southern tip reaches almost to the continent of Antarctica.

Continued on next page

PROJECT 1 Practice

Format a Title Page

A title page gives a formal, finished look to the report. It identifies what the report is about. You can enhance the appearance of the title page by adding graphics and borders and by changing the font style, size, and color.

Your Turn

1. Key and format the title page as indicated.

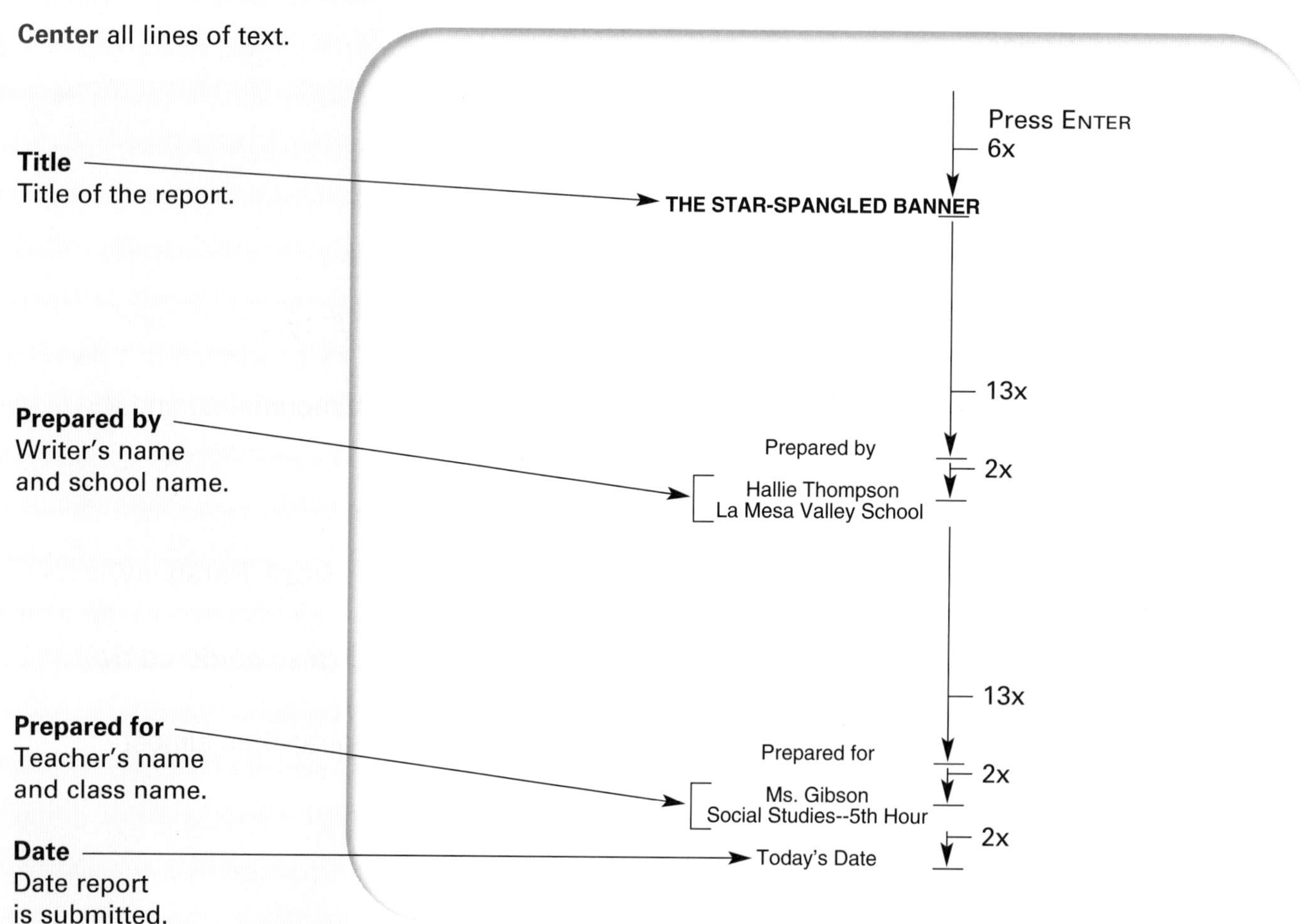

2. Change the **vertical alignment** of text to **center**.
3. Save the changes. Print and close the file.

PROJECT 3 Continued

Reinforce

Format a Multipage Report With a Bibliography

Add the side heading **Terrain** and format **bold**.

Argentina's varied geography includes the Perito Moreno glacier in the southern Andes. This is one of the few glaciers in the world still advancing.

Argentina has 1,056,640 square miles. It is South America's second-largest country, after Brazil. Argentina is about one-third the size of the United States.

Copy and paste all the content from the file **6-2 Project 3**.

Insert page number.

2. Save the document as ***urs*Argentina**.
3. Spell-check and proofread the file. Save any changes.
4. Position the insertion point at the end of the file, and insert a new page break.

Continued on next page

SECTION 6.3 Format a Title Page

GOALS: Demonstrate the ability to:

- Key and format a title page.
- Center text vertically on a page.
- Enhance appearance of a title page.

WARMUP

Select Warmup from the Skillbuilding menu. Key each Warmup line 2 times.

Speed	1	The Sun is the closest star in our very large solar system.
Accuracy	2	The Aztecs built Tenochtitlan on an island in Lake Texcoco.
Numbers/Symbols	3	Buy 2# of pears (#1 Bartlett*) @ $1.98 at the Fruit & More.
Language Link	4	A number of students were excused from their science class.

Making the Connection

The hard part is done. You have keyed your report, formatted it, proofread it, and corrected all errors. Now it's time for the finishing touch—creating a title page. Not only do you want the title page to include all the necessary information, but also you want it to make a good first impression!

Your Turn

1. Open a new word processing document.
2. Key the information for a title page.
3. Save the document as *urs*Title Page.
4. Keep the file open for Project 1.

Press ENTER 6x

THE STAR-SPANGLED BANNER

PROJECT 3 Continued

Reinforce

Formatting a Multipage Report With a Bibliography

5. Create and format the bibliography illustrated below.

BIBLIOGRAPHY

"Argentina." *Microsoft Encarta Online Encyclopedia 2002.* 3 May 2002. <http://encarta.msn.com/find/Concise>.

"CIA—The World Fact Book 2002—Argentina." 3 May 2002. <http://www.odci.gov/cia/publications/factbook/geos/ar.html>.

Wilkie, Richard W. "Argentina." *The World Book Encyclopedia 2002*. Chicago: World Book, Inc., Vol. 1, pp. 646-660.

6. Proofread the bibliography page, and make any necessary corrections.
7. Save the changes. Print and close the file.

Check Your Understanding

1. Open a new word processing document.
2. If you are binding multiple pages of a report on the left side, how much extra space should you add to the left margin?
3. Explain the benefit of adding side headings to a report.
4. What is the purpose of a bibliography?
5. What is a hanging indent?
6. Save the document as *urs*Report. Print and close the file.

Write On!

In this section you learned to add page numbers to your report. By now, you must have multiple pages in your journal.

Add page numbers to your journal document. That way, if you print your journal in the future, you can keep the pages organized. Save the changes to your journal. Close the file.

*inter*NET CONNECTION

Did you know that you can tell what country a Web site is from by looking at its URL? Domain names for sites within the United States usually include *.net, .com, .edu,* and *.org.* Domain names for sites outside the United States have two-letter extensions that identify the country. For example, the letters "*uk*" in a URL indicate that the Web site is from the United Kingdom.

1. **Open your Web browser and locate a site that will help you identify "Internet country abbreviations."**
2. **Identify the countries for the following two-letter abbreviations: *bz, ma,* and *aq.***
3. **Search for national parks in each of the countries listed in Step 2.**
4. **Open a word processing document. List the names, cities, and URL of one or two parks for each country.**